From Border
to Middle Shire
Northumberland
1586-1625

From Border to Middle Shire Northumberland 1586-1625

S. J. Watts with Susan J. Watts

Leicester University Press   1975

First published in 1975 by Leicester University Press

Distributed in North America by Humanities Press Inc., New Jersey

Designed by Arthur Lockwood

Set in 11 pt Granjon 1 pt leaded
Printed in Great Britain by Western Printing Services Ltd, Bristol
Bound by Redwood Burn Ltd, Esher

ISBN 0 7185 1127 1

Preface

This study had its origins in a University of Maryland dissertation which was approved in 1965. Since then it has been completely altered and rewritten in the light of further research. I was introduced to the history of northern England during the Tudor–Stuart period by the late David Harris Willson at the University of Minnesota. I was further encouraged in this field by Professor Donald C. Gordon at the University of Maryland and by Professor S. T. Bindoff at the Institute of Historical Research in London. I am particularly grateful to Dr Trevor Cliffe for the suggestions which he made after reading through various stages of the manuscript. I am also grateful for the encouragement offered by Dr Ramon Powers and by William H. Pickett at crucial stages in the process of revision. Research in record depositories in the summer of 1967 was facilitated by a grant from the National Endowment for the Humanities and in the summer of 1968 by a grant from the University of Missouri–Kansas City. I should like to thank the staffs of the Public Record Office, the British Museum, the Northumberland County Record Office, the Newcastle upon Tyne City Library, the Durham University Library, the Cumbria County Record Office in Carlisle, the Wilson Library in Minneapolis and the Folger Shakespeare Library in Washington, D.C., for their courteous help and assistance. I am grateful to His Grace the Duke of Northumberland for permission to consult manuscripts housed in Alnwick Castle.

My wife has closely co-operated with me in all stages of the recasting and revision of this manuscript. As a professional geographer, she has contributed most extensively to chapters one, two and eight. She has also drawn the maps. For all shortcomings and imperfections, I alone bear full responsibility.

New Haven, Connecticut   S.J.W.
1974

Contents

Maps

The maps fold out at the back of the book. They are based on quarter-inch Ordnance Survey maps.

1. Physical features and raiders' routes
2. Northumberland estates in 1603
3. Wards and frequently mentioned places

Abbreviations

Ag. H. R.	*Agricultural History Review*
Alnwick MSS.	Duke of Northumberland's MSS. at Alnwick Castle
Arch. Aeliana	*Archaeologia Aeliana*, the Society of Antiquaries of Newcastle upon Tyne
Arch. Cantiana	*Archaeologia Cantiana*
B. M.	British Museum
Belsay MSS.	N. R. O., Middleton, Belsay MSS.
C 2, 3	P. R. O., Chancery Proceedings, series I and II
C 66	P. R. O., Chancery, Patent Rolls
C 142	P. R. O., Chancery, Inquisitions Post Mortem
C 181	P. R. O., Chancery, Entry Books of Commissions (Crown Office)
C 193	P. R. O., Chancery, Miscellaneous Books (Crown Office)
C 4211, 4212	P. R. O., Chancery, Crown Office Docquet Books
Cal. B. P.	*Calendar of Letters and Papers relating to the Borders of England and Scotland*, ed. Joseph Bain, Edinburgh, 1894–6
Cal. Pat. Rolls	*Calendar of Patent Rolls*
Cal. S. P. Dom.	*Calendar of State Papers, Domestic*
Cal. S. P. For.	*Calendar of State Papers, Foreign*
Cecil MSS.	Microfilm, Folger Library, Washington, D. C., MSS. at Hatfield House belonging to the Marquis of Salisbury
Corbridge MSS.	at Cumbria County Record Office, Carlisle
D. N. B.	*Dictionary of National Biography*
Delaval Papers	N. R. O., from the Waterford MSS. at Ford Castle
Duke of Nd's MSS.	Microfilm, Library of Congress, Syon and Alnwick MSS. now at Alnwick Castle
E 112	P. R. O., Exchequer K. R. Bills and Answers
E 123, 124, 125	P. R. O., Exchequer K. R. Entry Books of Decrees and Orders, series I, II, III

E 134	P. R. O., Exchequer K. R. Depositions taken by Commission
E 163	P. R. O., Exchequer K. R. Miscellanea of the Exchequer
E 164	P. R. O., Exchequer K. R. Miscellaneous Books, series I
E 178	P. R. O., Exchequer K. R. Special Commissions of Enquiry
E 179	P. R. O., Subsidy Rolls
E 377	P. R. O., Exchequer Pipe Office Series, Recusant Rolls
E 401	P. R. O., Exchequer of Receipt Loans on Privy Seal
E 407	P. R. O., Exchequer of Receipt Miscellaneous Books and Papers
E. H. R.	*English Historical Review*
Ec. H.R.	*Economic History Review*
Hist. MSS. Com.	Historical Manuscripts Commission
Hodgson	John Hodgson, *A History of Northumberland* (3 pts in 7 vols, Newcastle, 1820–5)
Hunter MSS.	Durham Cathedral Library, Hunter MSS.
K. R.	King's Remembrancer
L. C.	Library of Congress, Washington, D. C.
L. & P. Hen. VIII	*Letters and Papers of Henry VIII*
L. R. 2	P. R. O., Land Revenue Office, Miscellaneous Books
List of Sheriffs	P. R. O., *List of Sheriffs for England and Wales*, P. R. O. Lists and Indexes No. IX (Kraus, New York, 1963)
Martin	Mary Martin (comp.), Newcastle Public Library, 'Index of the Northumberland Forfeitures in the Recusancy Rolls in the P. R. O.' (1909)
N. C. H.	Northumberland County History Committee (ed.), *History of Northumberland* (15 vols, 1905–40)
N. R. O.	Northumberland Record Office, Newcastle
Ornsby	George Ornsby (ed.), *Selections from the Household Books of the Lord William Howard of Naworth Castle* (Surtees Society, LXVIII: Durham, 1878)
P. C. 2	P. R. O., Privy Council Office, Registers
P. R. O.	Public Record Office
Pennington-Ramsden MS.	Cumbria County Record Office, Carlisle
Req. 2	P. R. O., Court of Requests, Proceedings
Rymer, *Foedera*	Thomas Rymer (ed.), *Foedera, Conventiones, Literae Et Cujuscunque Generis Acta Publica, inter Reges Angliae etc.* (20 vols, London, 1727–35)
S. P. 12, 13	P. R. O., State Papers Domestic, Elizabeth I
S. P. 14	P. R. O., State Papers Domestic, James I
S. P. 15	P. R. O., State Papers Domestic Addenda, 1547–1625
S. P. 16	P. R. O., State Papers Domestic, Charles I
S. P. 38	P. R. O., State Paper Office, Docquets
S. P. 46	P. R. O., State Papers Supplementary
S. P. 59	P. R. O., State Papers Borders
Sanderson	Roundell P. Sanderson (ed.), *A Survey of the Debateable and Borderlands adjoining the Realm of Scotland and belonging to the Crown of England 1604* (Alnwick, 1891)

Spec. Coll.2	P. R. O., Special Collections, Court Rolls
Syon MSS.	MSS. belonging to the Duke of Northumberland, formerly at Syon House, now at Alnwick Castle
Sta. Cha. 5	P. R. O., Star Chamber Proceedings, Elizabeth I
Sta. Cha. 8	P. R. O., Star Chamber Proceedings, James I
Talbot	Clare Talbot (ed.), *Recusant Records* (Catholic Record Society, LIII: London, 1960)
Tough	D. L. W. Tough, *The Last Years of a Frontier: a History of the Borders during the Reign of Elizabeth* (Oxford, 1928)
Trans. R. H. S.	*Transactions of the Royal Historical Society*
V. C. H.	*Victoria County History*
Vetera Indictamenta	N. R. O., 'Vetera Indictamenta: Criminal Records of the General Gaol Delivery and General Quarter Sessions of the Peace for Northumberland, 1594–1630', typescript by H. A. Taylor
Visitations, 1575	C. H. Hunter Blair (ed.), *Visitations of Yorkshire and Northumberland in A. D. 1575* (Surtees Society, CXLVI: Durham, 1932)
Visitations, 1615, 1666	Joseph Foster (ed.), *Pedigrees Recorded at the Heralds' Visitations of the County of Northumberland made by Richard St George . . . 1615 and William Dugdale . . . in 1666* (Newcastle, 1891)
Wards 5	P. R. O., Court of Wards and Liveries Foedaries' Surveys
Wards 7	P. R. O., Court of Wards and Liveries Inquisitions Post Mortem
Wills and Inventories	Surtees Society, *Wills and Inventories from the Registry at Durham* (Durham, 1835, 1900, 1906, 1929)
Y. A. J.	*Yorkshire Archaeological Journal*

Note In quoting from manuscript sources spelling, capitalization and punctuation have been modernized. However quotations from primary printed sources have been transcribed verbatim, except for very occasional changes necessary to clarify the sense. Spelling of place-names follows that of the Ordnance Survey maps. Days of the month are old style, but the year has been taken to begin on 1 January rather than on 25 March, as was the custom in England during the period covered.

The figures given in diamond brackets at the top of each recto page refer to the page on which the notes will be found.

Introduction

It is commonly accepted that the study of history concerns the study of change. For this reason historians and the wider public have long been interested in the period stretching roughly from 1530 to 1660 which saw the transformation of medieval England into a recognizably modern pre-industrial state. But because the process of modernization did not occur as rapidly in all parts of the realm as it did in and around London and the Home Counties, it is tempting to exaggerate the backwardness of some areas. Indeed until recently historians of the national scene could take it for granted that few changes of any significance took place in the remote county of Northumberland in the decades preceding the union of the Crowns of England and Scotland in 1603. They could assume that Northumbrians, like the inhabitants of the Tudor North as a whole, were feudal and tradition-bound, generally Catholic in sympathy and excessively prone to vicious feuding amongst themselves. M. E. James, B. W. Beckingsale and others have now shown that the North lost many of the distinctive characteristics attributed to it far earlier than previously supposed.[1] Yet it is important to realize that in the late sixteenth and early seventeenth centuries, the memory of these earlier regional differences still contributed to men's mental image or perception of Northumberland.

For historians of Northumberland or of the three other northernmost English counties, Cumberland, Westmorland and County Durham, the period extending from 1586 to 1625 is of critical importance, for it spans the last years of the frontier with its border reivers and perverse wardenry officials, the union of the Crowns and the relatively peaceful reign of King James I. A great amount of detailed and useful information concerning this period can be found in the standard multi-volumed histories of Northumberland;[2] yet in layout and general presentation these volumes tend to reflect the rather narrow genealogical, antiquarian and archaeological interests of leisured landed gentlemen. Several of the more recent popular studies of Northumberland and the border counties seem designed to cater for the interests of readers in search of the picturesque and the bizarre.[3] These studies make considerable use of spicy statements written by Elizabethan and Jacobean gentlemen and clerics which at first sight appear to confirm Northumberland's reputation as a barbarous, Catholic-dominated backwater. But closer investigation shows that many of the people who made these derogatory comments had ulterior, and sometimes sinister, motives for so doing. If the county really had any of the characteristics ascribed to it by unfriendly contemporary commentators, it might well have been due quite as much to the policies followed by great officers of state in London, York and Edinburgh, as to any qualities inherent in the people of Northumberland.

In our study we have attempted to come to terms with the complex of inter-related economic, social and political developments which together constitute the total environment of the county during the 40 years when it was transformed from a reputedly turbulent border shire into one of the tranquil Middle Shires of Great Britain. The four initial chapters deal with the economic and social situation on the eve of the union of the Crowns. The first chapter discusses some of the institutions peculiar to border society; the wardenries, the domestic and international laws of the marches, the surnames and patterns of thievery. It demonstrates that there was a long tradition of hostility between the inhabitants of the eastern and southern lowlands and the people of Redesdale and North Tynedale in the western highlands. The second chapter describes the agrarian régimes followed in the highlands, the lowlands and in the transitional zone lying between the two. It also shows that the county as a whole was not profiting from the mining of coal and other related industrial activities in and around Newcastle. In the third and fourth chapters we analyse Northumberland's social hierarchy and religious complexion and attempt to compare them with those in more prosperous counties further south; the results are sometimes surprising. We are now in a position to deal with the complex and often devious political history of Northumberland from 1586 to 1625. This is the central concern of four of the five remaining chapters. The penultimate chapter analyses the agricultural changes which gradually came about after 1603. This juxtaposition of political, economic and social history enables readers to judge for themselves how far the poverty and misery of the majority of Northumbrians was the result of Scottish raids, poor harvests and plagues, or of the political mismanagement and chicanery of private gentlemen and government officials.

The area under consideration encompasses the present county of Northumberland together with the district lying between it and the north bank of the Tyne but excluding the old chartered borough of Newcastle. It is bounded on the west by the northern portion of Cumbria (the former county of Cumberland), on the south by the River Tyne and the town of Newcastle, on the east by the North Sea and on the north by Scotland. During the Elizabethan period the area so described was divided into two marches or wardenries, each under the jurisdiction of a lord warden. The East March, much the smaller of the two, extended from the warden's headquarters at Berwick-upon-Tweed southward along the coast to the northern bank of the River Aln. From the coast the march extended westward to the Scottish border and the Cheviot. The remainder of Northumberland was co-terminous with the Middle March. The West March consisted of the counties of Cumberland and Westmorland and was centred upon the red-walled cathedral city of Carlisle. Across the international border, the English wardenries confronted the three Scottish marches, East, Middle and West, and the keepership of Liddesdale.[4]

For purposes of civil administration by justices of the peace and sheriffs, Northumberland was divided into six wards. However, during the period 1586–1625 part of the area which constituted the county until the spring of 1974 lay beyond the jurisdiction of the Northumberland sheriff. Aside from the town of Berwick-upon-Tweed (which was not incorporated into Northumberland until 1842) the three most important enclaves outside the sheriff's control were Norhamshire and Islandshire in the East March and Bedlingtonshire in the Middle March. Collectively these three enclaves were known as North Durham and were subject to the jurisdiction of the bishop of Durham as lord of the Palatine of Durham. Yet as gentlemen living in North Durham honourably served as Northumberland J. P.s and sheriffs, they must be counted "right Northumberland men". A small part of Northumberland was completely surrounded by the county and town of Newcastle. This was the area around the old Norman castle where assize judges and other commissioners of oyer and terminer held sessions of gaol delivery for Northumberland.

I

The Northumberland border and border institutions in 1586

Marauders from the southern counties of Scotland were still crossing the border to harry Northumberland nearly 300 years after Edward I's abortive invasion first aroused their countrymen's enmity towards England and more than a quarter of a century after treaties ended the last of the Anglo-Scottish wars. Successive governments in Edinburgh seemed either unable or unwilling to prevent their depredations. Then early in 1586 James VI, the young Scots sovereign, and Queen Elizabeth I of England agreed to send agents to Berwick-upon-Tweed to negotiate a treaty of alliance and "straiter friendship."[1]

These negotiations, so important to borderers on both sides, followed several years of tortuous diplomatic activity. Soon after her accession Elizabeth had reversed her predecessors' bellicose policy towards Scotland. By 1560 she had entered into friendly negotiations with the struggling Protestant party headed by the Lords of the Congregation. Urged on by her Principal Secretary, William Cecil, she had permitted English troops to assist the Lords to expel the French supporters of Mary of Guise, the Catholic Queen Mother.[2] Unfortunately this initial instance of Anglo-Scottish co-operation had been followed by a long period of governmental instability in Edinburgh and continued violence along the southern frontier. Queen Mary Stuart, Mary of Guise's daughter, returned from France to begin her personal rule in 1561 and gave birth to a son, the future King James VI, in 1566. Two years later she fled in disgrace to England. For several chaotic years thereafter Protestants of various hues struggled for control of the young king's person and, with it, control of the realm. But James was a precocious youth. By the time he was 19, he was beginning to assert his personal authority and to demonstrate that he was more than a match for most troublesome highland chiefs and border lairds. The members of the new government which he appointed not long before the treaty negotiations began in Berwick in June 1586 represented a coalition of diverse interests which he could play off against each other much as his kinswoman, Elizabeth Tudor, played off moderates and radicals, 'new men' and aristocrats in her Privy Council. Thus it could be argued that under King James and the talented man shortly to become his first minister, John Maitland of Thirlstane, Scotland at last had an effective central government which well deserved foreigners' respect and confidence.[3]

The middle-aged virgin queen of England thought otherwise. Her opinion of young James in no way improved when Thomas Randolph, William Lord Eure and the Earl of Rutland, her representatives at Berwick, informed her that the king had asked that she openly recognize his claims to be her successor. In response Elizabeth instructed her agents to reach an understanding with their Scots counterparts that the two nations would come to each other's assistance if either were attacked by a third power, presumably Philip II's Spain. This agreement was subsequently incorporated into the treaty which was concluded at Berwick in July. But on the succession question Elizabeth would only say that she would do nothing to derogate James's claim to be her heir. To make it clear that she was keeping all of her options open and that she regarded Scotland as a mere satellite she refused, ostensibly on the grounds of economy, to increase James's annual pension from £4,000 to £5,000. However, her government was spending an average of more than £15,000 each year to maintain garrisons at Berwick and Carlisle. Wages and allowances at Berwick alone amounted to £10,918 14s. 4d. in 1603. As this fortress was of little military significance the Scots could be forgiven for thinking that its main function under Elizabeth was "to offend her child Scotland".[4]

Thus the results of the international conference held in the summer of 1586 gave King James cause to be less than grateful to his powerful English cousin. Thereafter the proud but penurious young sovereign felt no compulsion to prevent his subjects from raiding into Northumberland and the other English border shires. Indeed until 1601, when Secretary Robert Cecil secretly assured him that he supported his claims to the English throne, a condition more closely resembling war than peace often existed along the frontier.

Northumbrians did not hesitate to make their plight known to Randolph and the other treaty commissioners at Berwick. Typical of many piteous complaints was the petition presented on behalf of the inhabitants of the lordship of Bewick in the Till valley. The Bewick tenants claimed that their district had been "so pillaged by open day forays and by night raids and hardships by the thieves of Esk and West Teviotdale" since 1560 that they were no longer able to pay their annual rents to the queen. The tenants reminded the commissioners that they had attempted to bring their distress to the government's attention some time earlier. Two of them had gone up to Court in February 1586 but had been curtly informed by Secretary Francis Walsingham that

Randolph, recently appointed English ambassador to Scotland, was the proper authority to consider their grievances. Despite the great expense one man from Bewick had then gone to Edinburgh and had sought out Randolph. But the ambassador had said that he and the other treaty commissioners would not consider local grievances until they were in Berwick-upon-Tweed.[5]

In addition to finally learning about conditions in the lordship of Bewick, the treaty commissioners heard from the villagers of Rochester in Redesdale. These people claimed that the Scots had permanently ruined their village. In the course of three terrible raids five years earlier they had taken 180 oxen and kine, 60 sheep and goats, and household gear worth £60.[6] And, according to a report from the parish of Embleton on the coast north of the River Aln, many of the queen's tenants there "were oppressed, spoyled, and greatlye impoverished by the Scottes and their goodes and cattel taken awaye, to diverse of theire utter undoinge, and sondrye of them by very extreame povertie were forsed to give upp their tenementes". Similar complaints could be made by the inhabitants of many other villages.[7]

Some measure of the impact which Scottish raiders made on various parts of Northumberland can be obtained from reports of the phenomenon known to contemporaries as 'decay'. In this context decay refers to the decline in the number of men who were able to serve effectively in defence of the borders. Men owed service under the command of a lord warden or keeper by virtue of their tenure of certain lands. It should be noted that border service was distinct from the obligation common to all men in England between the ages of 16 and 60 to serve in the county militia and to attend musters.[8]

Commissioners appointed by the Privy Council in accordance with the 1581 Act for fortifying the borders reported on the decay of the service in 1584.[9] The base line for this survey was the regnal year 27 Henry VIII (1535/6), just before the Pilgrimage of Grace. According to these returns men from at least 1,522 tenancies in the East and Middle Marches owed border service in 1535/6. Of these only 200, 13 per cent, still provided men in 1584. If the tantalizing gaps in the returns had been filled with figures instead of the words "all decayed", the total number of known decayed tenancies would have been much larger. As might be expected, there were marked local variations in the incidence of decay. For instance, the report for the Middle March shows that none of the 37 Redesdale men or the 103 men from North Tynedale who ought to have been furnished were still service-worthy in 1584. In the frequently raided lands of South Tynedale only eight of the 93 men originally furnished still stood. In contrast, 80 of the old quota of 271 remained ready for service in the relatively safe lowlands of eastern Coquetdale and in Morpeth and Castle wards. In the East March less than 7 per cent of the 1535/6 quota remained standing. But in Bamburgh ward, an area dominated by Sir John Forster, the aged warden of the neighbouring Middle March, 20 of the 61 men, almost a third of the old quota remained service-worthy. It may have been that Forster prevailed upon his fellow decay commissioners to round up as many furnished men as possible in that ward in order to refute rumours that he was personally responsible for the decay of the service.[10] It would appear that unfurnished men could be converted to furnished men at short notice. In 1587 Henry Lord Hunsdon, warden of the East March, noted that "I had word brought me this morning that Northumberland men have bought 100 horses at Saint Luke's fair at Newcastle, and do provide themselves of jacks and other furniture, whereof they were utterly unfurnished, only upon a speech that I used at Newcastle, that I would shortly see every man's furniture."[11]

A second commission surveyed the decay of the border service in 1596, after Forster had been dismissed as warden. In contrast to the earlier survey, the base-line for this report was 10 Elizabeth I (1567/8), just before the second of the great revolts which had shattered the peace of the Tudor North, the Rebellion of the Northern Earls. According to the 1596 report 540 tenements in the East March and 1,245 in the Middle March had decayed since 1567/8. The commissioners attributed 48 per cent of the decays in the East March and a quarter of those in the Middle March to Scottish raiders.[12]

Local political and personal considerations aside (for it was possible for an Englishman to come to a private agreement with his Scottish tormentors) the impact which the marauders were able to make upon a particular district in Northumberland was related to its position with regard to manned fortifications and natural access routes.[13] In itself proximity to the border was not always important. For instance, the lower Tweed valley across which ran the Great North Road, the principal north–south route for ordinary travellers in time of peace and for great armies in time of war, was adequately protected from casual Scottish marauders by the garrison at Berwick-upon-Tweed.[14] However raiders could easily outflank this fortress. Following the course of Bowmont Water they could enter the county near the village of Mindrum and ride to the valley of the Till. From thence they had easy access to the valley of the upper Aln and, further south, to upper Coquetdale. In 1550 Sir Robert Bowes recommended that a strong watch-tower be built at Mindrum, seeing that it "lyeth soe in the high streete and waye whereby the Scotts passe and repasse into those marches of England".[15] Between the Bowmont valley and the passes further south lay the Cheviot, a twenty-square-mile granitic outcrop which reaches an elevation of 2,676 feet. After viewing it in 1541 Sir Robert Bowes and Sir Ralph Ellerker reported that:

the most p'te thereof and esp'ially towarde the heighte ys a wete flowe mosse so depe that scarcely eyther horse or cattall may goo thereupon excepte yt be by the syde of certayne lytle broukes & waters that springeth forthe of the said mountaine by reason whereof the said forrest ys not Inhabytable nor serveth very lytle for the pasture of any cattalle excepte onely wylde bestes as redde dere & rooes.[16]

The English Middle March was accessible to raiders who followed Scottish river valleys to the west and south of the Cheviot and crossed the exposed watershed which "devydethe England and Scotland by the heighte of yt as the water descendeth & falleth."[17] Marauders could follow the Kale valley, cross the border at an elevation of about 1,450 feet and descend into the valleys of the upper Coquet and Aln. Alternatively, from the Roman camp at Coquet Head raiders could go south along Gammel's Path – the Roman Dere Street – to the valley of the Rede. Raiders could also cross the border into Redesdale from the Jed valley by way of Redeswire (el. 1,370 feet), a strategic site on the actual border which was often used as a meeting place for English and Scottish wardenry officials during international days of truce. From Liddesdale, a notoriously lawless area, thieves could follow any one of a number of tributaries of Liddel Water and cross the open watershed into the valley of the North Tyne or, riding across the desolate fells east of the head-waters of this stream, reach the upper Rede. Once in western Northumberland, thieves who did not wish to retrace their steps could return to Scotland by way of the valley of the South Tyne and eastern Cumberland.

The valleys of the Rede, North Tyne and Coquet gave thieves easy access to farms in the fertile lowlands of south-eastern Northumberland. Sir Robert Delaval, one of the leading gentlemen in that district, knew this well from personal experience. While in London on business in 1600 he wrote to his son Ralph:

> You say that on the second of September Archibald Elliott [of Liddesdale] and divers others with him came to Dissington and did take thirty cattle of my son John's but they were rescued by the good help of our friends at which time you say you and your brothers were both from home; but God be thanked it was no worse and I have no doubt but both you and he will be careful to cause watch and search nightly where our goods go.[18]

Autumn and winter were the best seasons for raiding. According to an experienced border official "then are the nights longest, their horse at hard meat and will ride best, cattle strong and will drive furthest; after Candlemas [2 February] the nights grow shorter, all cattle grow weaker and oats growing dearer, they feed their horses worst and quickly turn them to grass."[19]

As long as England's relations with Scotland were not on a secure footing, the condition of fortified places in Northumberland was a matter of some concern to the central authorities. In 1583, following precedents laid down in 1541, 1550 and 1561, the Crown appointed commissioners to inquire into the decay of border fortifications and to recommend which of them should be repaired or regarrisoned.[20] All of these reports attest to the differences between the fortified buildings in the coastal and southern lowlands when compared to those in the highlands. The former areas were characterized by castles and peels, the latter by rather humbler buildings.

Castles had been built soon after the Norman Conquest at Wark-on-Tweed and Norham to control the routes through the Tweed valley and the eastern coastal plain. Later, massive castles were constructed at Alnwick, Warkworth, Bamburgh and Morpeth and on the lower Tyne at Newcastle and Prudhoe. One of the last of the great castles to be built was the early-fourteenth-century fortress at Dunstanburgh. But in 1584 the royal commissioners noted that it was "decayed for want of repairing by long continuance."[21] Far less elaborate than Dunstanburgh or Norham were the free-standing stone keeps known as peels or peel towers. Peels provided living accommodation for lowland Northumbrians of local prominence together with their families and attendants. They were generally oblong in shape, two, three or four stories in height with an interior staircase. Many peels were associated with a barmkin. This was a stout wooden palisade or a stone wall enclosing a yard which could be used as a place of refuge by humble people and livestock from nearby farms and villages. Peels and barmkins continued to be built during the late fourteenth and fifteenth centuries. Indeed the peel at Doddington in the Till valley was built as late as 1584. Although this L-shaped, three-storied, gabled structure measuring 57 x 25 feet externally was slightly more convenient in plan than most earlier peels, its defensive function was clearly proclaimed by its thick stone walls and its small windows.[22] At some time between 1541 and 1596 the old peel at Downham, eight miles west of Doddington, was restored and a stone barmkin built to one side of the tower. This new structure proved its worth. In November 1596 William Selby wrote to his nephew William (later of Branxton)[23] that Scottish raiders equipped with great axes had recently hewed away at the wooden gates of the barmkin "which held them 'til cock-crow" when they retreated.[24]

The peels and castles which Christopher Dacre and the other royal commissioners were most interested in restoring and regarrisoning in 1583/4 lay in a great arc which cut through Northumberland rather than following the actual border with Scotland. South of Wark-on-Tweed this line followed the eastern fringe of the highlands south-east and then south to the castle at Harbottle on the upper Coquet. Potentially this castle was of great strategic importance. From it garrison soldiers could easily control access to the valleys of the Aln, the Rede and the North Tyne as well as the Coquet. Yet in 1584, as in 1541, commissioners reported that the fortress was in great disrepair.[25] From Harbottle the line delineating what Dacre called the "plenished ring of the border" followed the River Coquet east to the peel tower at Tossen, ran due south to the peels at Fallowlees and Kirkwhelpington and then south-west to the peel at Chollerton on the North Tyne.[26] In earlier surveys this line continued west from Chollerton to Naworth Castle in Cumberland.[27]

Until sometime after 1550 Northumbrians living in the quarter of the county lying north and west of the line delineated by Dacre, in the highland valleys of the North Tyne and Rede, had access to few forts built of stone. In 1541 commissioners appointed by Henry VIII reported that the only stone fortress in North Tynedale was the "little tower" at Hesleyside which belonged to the Charltons. Most of the other leaders of local society lived in strong wooden houses with turf roofs. The commissioners found that these habitations were so well hidden amongst the mosses and morasses that they were virtually inaccessible to strangers.[28]

Yet in the century or so after these Henrician officials made their report, some of the more substantial farmers in Redesdale and North Tynedale as well as in eastern Cumberland provided themselves with the distinctive fortified stone houses which scholars have recently termed 'bastles'.[29] Bastles were two-storied, steeply gabled structures about 35 feet long and 25 feet wide. Access to the ground floor, a defensible shelter for livestock which was often vaulted in stone, was through a narrow door in a gable end. Access to the family's living quarters on the first floor was probably by a movable exterior ladder. In their time bastles were the only buildings in the British Isles in which cattle were kept on the ground floor and people lived on the floor above. No comparable buildings were found in the marches of Wales or elsewhere in England. In contrast to peel towers, which were larger and generally located some miles apart, two or more bastles were often found in close proximity to each other. When attempting to date these structures, it may be significant that all surviving examples are located within 20 miles of the Scottish border. As R. W. McDowall and Eric Mercer have pointed out, this was the width of the statutory defensive zone established by Parliament in 1555 and 1581.[30] No bastle-like structures were mentioned in the 1541, 1550 or 1584 surveys. But in 1596 the warden, Ralph Lord Eure, reported that Scottish borderers had recently built "strong tower houses... even upon the front" near the head-waters of the Liddel, Rede and North Tyne. He recommended that his own government pay for the construction of a "bastle" or strong house at Tynehead and another at the head of the Rede. Troops stationed at the new forts could, Eure reasoned, force the busy Scots to keep to their own side of the border.[31]

With an entirely different purpose in mind Christopher Dacre recommended in 1584 that the Crown build four new castles, each costing £500 and capable of garrisoning 100 soldiers. Three of the castles were to be located between the River Tweed and Harbottle and the fourth between Harbottle and Cumberland. To explain why he thought that the line of fortifications cutting through Northumberland should thus be strengthened, Dacre wrote "lastly and chief of all that a good part of that which is to be so left out is inhabited by such as have always been as hurtful to the true subjects as the Scottish borderers, and at no time any hurt done by the said Scots but by some of their helps and furtherances, as hath always been reputed."[32]

As Dacre suggested, the highlanders had a most unenviable reputation amongst their countrymen to the south and east of the commissioners' line. In 1554 the Newcastle Merchant Adventurers, the most prestigious guild in that town, ruled that, as it was common knowledge that young Redesdalers and Tynedalers were by "education and nature" not of "honest conversation", none of them should be accepted as apprentices by members of the Company. The list of the Company's apprentices between 1554 and 1678, two years after this rule was repealed, shows that it was rigorously enforced.[33] It may well be that the Hostmen's Company of Newcastle had a similar rule. None of the 46 young men whom it accepted as apprentices between 1603 and 1700 hailed from Redesdale or North Tynedale.[34] Anti-highland prejudices are also reflected in the survey which Edmund Hall and William Humberston made in 1570 of the estates which the rebel earls of Northumberland and Westmorland had recently forfeit to the Crown for treason. After viewing the former Percy barony of Alnwick the surveyors reported that "more harm is done to the poor country-men by the raiders of Tynedale than by their open enemies, the Scots."[35] And in the former Neville baronies of Bywell and Bulbeck people "have very good farms and able to keep much cattle and yet plenty of corn and hay, were it not for the continual robberies and incursions of the thieves of Tynedale which so continually assault them in the night as they can keep in no more cattle than they are able to lodge either in house or like safety in the nights".[36]

Perhaps it was inevitable that lowland Northumbrians should distrust the inhabitants of the relatively isolated valleys of the Rede and the North Tyne in the 1580s. For it was only comparatively recently, well within the memory of men then living, that highlanders and lowlanders had come to share more or less the same forms of government and social organization. Before the Norman Conquest Redesdale and North and South Tynedale had been given the status of liberties. These were areas of special jurisdiction in which the king's writ did not run. Like other such areas they were used as sanctuaries by criminals fleeing from the sheriffs of surrounding counties.[37] After the Conquest Redesdale was granted to the Umfravilles and later to the Talbot family. In the 1540s, after Henry VIII had acquired the liberty from Elizabeth, sister of the last lord Talbot, Redesdale was incorporated into Northumberland and opened to the sheriff.[38] But as late as 1620 Redesdale freeholders claimed that, unlike felons on shired ground who forfeited their land when they were convicted, "their lands are not forfeited unless they do or commit murder, treason, manslaughter or robbery out of the said franchise or liberty."[39] The liberties of Tynedale, which included lands along the South Tyne as well as along the North Tyne, were in the hands of the kings of Scotland for nearly 200 years before they were seized by the English Crown in 1289.[40] The special status of North Tynedale, as well as South Tynedale, was terminated by Act of Parliament in 1495/6.[41] According to constitutional theory this statute enabled Northumberland sheriffs to serve their writs freely throughout Tynedale. But in 1550 Sir Robert Bowes reported that, in contrast to the people of South Tynedale, "the inhabitants of North Tynedall be more obedient to theire owne keeper or the Lord Warden of the middle Marchies then to the Shreiffs of Northumberland clay[m]inge and usinge alwayes the old Liberties of that countrey as it was before the makinge of that statute".[42]

During the first two-thirds of the sixteenth century the presence of surnames, a highly localized form of social organization, further distinguished North Tynedale and Redesdale from the rest of the county. Until their power was broken during the period 1560–86, Northumberland surnames provided mutual protection and security to near neighbours who were related by ties of blood. Like similar groups in Cumberland and on the Scottish side of the border, Northumberland surnames were probably organized in the fourteenth century in response to the uncertainties of endemic warfare between England and Scotland.[43] The word surname was first used with reference to kinship groups on the English side of the border in 1498.[44] Half a century later Sir Robert Bowes found that North Tynedale was inhabited by a "wild and mis-demeaned people" who were divided among four principal surnames. The Charltons were the chief surname, followed by the Robsons, Dodds and Milburns. The Halls were the principal surname in Redesdale followed by the Reads, Potts, Hedleys, Dunns and Fletchers.[45]

Each surname was headed by one or more headmen who protected and assisted their followers and dependants. It was with such headmen that war-denry officials negotiated when they wanted to take pledges for the good be-haviour of the surname. Thus in 1524, at a time when local surnames un-questionably were a serious menace to other Northumbrians, Lord Dacre, warden of the East and Middle Marches, apprehended the principal headmen of North Tynedale, the brothers William, Roger and Thomas Charlton, "by whom all the inhabitaunts were governed". Dacre reported that he had also "taken pledges of the reversion of all the other sirnames of Tynedale, and them have in sure warde for the good of the countrye".[46] During this same troubled period some heads of lowland Northumberland gentry families contracted agree-ments with surname leaders. For example in August 1536 Alexander Hall of Monkridge, near Elsdon in Redesdale, and two other Halls posted £100 bond and promised on behalf of their followers to "save and keep harmless" Sir John Delaval of Seaton Delaval, his heirs, tenants and servants.[47] As a few weeks later surname leaders played an important part in the Northumberland phase of the Pilgrimage of Grace, Sir John can be seen to have made a timely bargain. After the revolt loyalists asserted that the whole county "would faine be revenged on Tynedale and Redesdale which have spoiled them so sore that they are weary of their lives."[48]

Possibly the most effective weapon in a surname's armoury was the 'deadly feud'. If any outsider injured, insulted or killed a surname member, the whole of the surname would combine to seek revenge. It was said that lowland Northumbrians preferred to accept in compensation a token portion of the goods they had lost to Redesdale or North Tynedale surname members, rather than risk a deadly feud by having the thief lawfully seized, indicted, tried and executed. Once begun, a feud between a Northumberland surname and a low-land county family might drag on for years. One of the last of the old feuds outstanding between highlanders and lowlanders was finally settled in 1591. This feud had begun around 1555 when Edward Delaval, of the house of Seaton Delaval, and a member of the Hall surname had a "sodden falling out and particler quarrell".[49]

In the 1580s and 1590s the Scots appear to have been more zealous in their pursuit of deadly feuds than was anyone in Northumberland. In 1586 Sir John Forster noted that the Elliots, Armstrongs, Croziers and other Scottish surnames were still at feud with lowland Northumberland families such as the Ogles, Widdringtons and Fenwicks as well as with the highland Halls, Potts and Reads.[50] Referring to the way in which Scots surnames pursued their feuds, John Leslie, bishop of Ross between 1566 and 1592, wrote that once begun a feud was not "of one against one, or of a few against a few, but of them all, how numerous soever the tribe may be, against all of the opposite name, however innocent or ignorant of the alleged injury".[51] Walter Scott, the famed laird of Buccleuch and keeper of Liddesdale between 1594 and 1603, reminded the Charltons that the death of the generation of men who had become involved in the original incident did not end a feud. Intending to avenge an insult which his grandfather had allegedly suffered many years before, in June 1595 Buccleuch assembled 300 of his followers, rode into North Tynedale and killed four Charltons.[52]

In 1560 Sir Ralph Sadler, an English privy councillor who often visited the borders, mentioned the nefarious practice of demanding blackmail in goods or kind and noted that "the like precedent" was never heard of in this country before".[53] By the end of the century the Scots were apparently demanding blackmail with far more frequency than were the English borderers. Around 1600 an English official who was more familiar with conditions in Northumberland than in Cumberland went so far as to define blackmail as "a yearly rent paid by the Englishman to a Scot upon condition that the Scot shall either save his goods from stealing either generally from all men or especially from his friends, or being stolen shall promise speedy restitution without form of law."[54]

Borderers, more frequently Scottish than English, also demanded ransom for prisoners. In 1584 Scots took nearly 40 prisoners from Redesdale to Liddesdale.[55] Four years later Ralph Wallace of Knarsdale in South Tynedale was taken as a prisoner to Liddesdale by James Douglas and other Scots. While in Scotland Wallace sent a message back to Edward Charlton, the leader of what was left of the North Tynedale surname, asking him to pay 20 marks for his release. Charlton obligingly wrote to Martin Elliot, the leader of the flourishing Elliot surname and a friend of James Douglas, promising to deliver Wallace's horse as security for the ransom. However, once safely back in England, the ungrateful Wallace refused to repay Charlton the expenses the latter had incurred in obtaining his release. It should be noted that rather than settling with Wallace in the traditional bloody fashion, Charlton took the matter to the Court of Requests in London.[56]

In 1601 Parliament passed an Act prohibiting Englishmen from paying or receiving blackmail or ransom. This statute referred to those who extorted blackmail as "Men of Name, and friended and alied withe divers in those partes, whoe are co[m]monly knowen to be greate Robbers and Spoile takers within the said Counties" of Northumberland, Westmorland, Cumberland and County Durham.[57] These words nicely illustrate the time-lag between the thinking of officials at Court and in Parliament and conditions in the field. For by 1601 the Northumbrian surnames were of little significance. But as their decline had been masked by the continuing strength of surname groups in Cumberland and Scotland we must briefly turn our attention to conditions in those two areas.

The Scottish surnames owed their survival in large measure to local wardenry officials. For financial reasons King James VI (who in some years after 1586 received not a shilling of his English pension) found it convenient to employ as wardens and keepers lowland lairds who already possessed extensive estates and large personal followings along the borders. In lieu of the pay which the king could not afford to give them, the lairds of Cessford, Buccleuch and other wardenry officials received the satisfaction of becoming quasi-feudal leaders. They found that they could win and retain the loyal support of surname members if they demonstrated that they had all the manly virtues traditionally associated with a surname leader. By nurturing the surnames, they increased their own stature.[58]

For somewhat different reasons the Grahams and other surnames continued to flourish in western Cumberland until 1603. At least in part their continued survival was a consequence of Queen Elizabeth's refusal to decide whether the house of Howard or the uncles of young George Dacre (d. 1569) should be granted the vast Dacre inheritance in the county. As the gentry of Cumberland were sharply divided on this question, Graham headmen were generally able to find allies in one or other of the opposing camps.[59] In 1583 one of the Grahams' opponents, Thomas Musgrave, warned Lord Burghley that Cumberland surname members:

> are a people that will be Scottish when they will and English at their pleasure; they keep gentlemen of the country in fear . . . Hardly dare any gentleman of the country be of any jury of life and death if any of them be indicted . . . they are grown so to seek blood, for they will make a quarrel for the death of their grandfather and they will kill any of the name they are in feud with.[60]

In March 1603, after the death of Queen Elizabeth, the Grahams, Armstrongs, Elliots and other surnames caused the great disturbance in Cumberland known as the Busy Week. So at the end of 1604 George Earl of Cumberland, warden or guardian of the West March as well as the Northumberland Middle March, could not expect any privy councillor to fault him when he asserted that:

This people stand altogether upon clans and surnames; [it is] not therefore to be presumed that a poor constable or sheriff's bailiff can or dare attack one of those in the midst of his friends... Their kindred and alliances so great, matching commonly amongst themselves, and their consciences so small, that hardly any proof can be got according to the rule of the common law...as appeareth by certain articles exhibited by the gentlemen of Northumberland.[61]

The earl neglected to point out that Northumberland had remained quiet during the Busy Week. But as we will see when we discuss border politics, it was often in the interests of courtiers and aggressive Protestant gentlemen in Northumberland to exaggerate the extent of lawlessness in the county. This is the explanation for the use of such terms as "bangsters of the thievish surnames" by Protestant commissioners from Northumberland and their allies at Court as late as 1607.[62]

Less prejudiced sources indicate that even by 1586 the Northumberland surnames were in irreversible decline. This decline can probably be said to have begun soon after Queen Elizabeth dismissed the seventh earl of Northumberland from his post as warden of the Middle March in 1559. As befitted a traditional border magnate who had lands in Tynedale, Earl Percy had often worked in alliance with surname members. In 1560 the queen chose Sir John Forster, a lowland Northumbrian squire, as the earl's successor in the wardenship. Thereafter by retaining control of the Crown lands where the surnames lived and by other measures, the queen made certain that Forster could not follow the example of Scottish wardens and set himself up as a leader or patron of the upland surnames under his jurisdiction.[63] As the Crown probably intended, all of the new warden's actions were nicely calculated to weaken the surnames and to discredit their leaders. Rather than employing Earl Percy's assistant, surname leader John Hall of Otterburn, as keeper of Redesdale, Forster gave this sensitive post to his own brother-in-law, Sir George Heron.[64] Early in 1567 Forster alleged that one John Hall was an ally of the Liddesdale Armstrongs and Nixons who had recently carried off 480 of his sheep. The warden then reported that he had executed six leading Redesdale thieves, one of them the brother of John Hall.[65] Forster dealt the surnames a staggering blow just before the Rising of the Northern Earls. In March 1569 he rode into Redesdale, destroyed the houses of alleged evil-doers and took Michael Hall and other headmen hostage for the good behaviour of their followers.[66]

If one can credit complaints which were presented to Thomas Randolph and the other commissioners at Berwick in the summer of 1586, the surnames of Scotland were Forster's chief weapon against the surnames of Northumberland. The inhabitants of Elsdon, the largest village in Redesdale, informed the commissioners that in September 1584 Martin Elliot and 500 other Liddesdalers had burnt down their habitations, murdered 14 men, taken and held for ransom

400 prisoners, driven away 400 kine and oxen and 400 horses and taken household goods to the value of £500. John Hall of Otterburn, the displaced keeper, informed the commissioners that several of the prisoners had paid their ransoms to the Liddesdalers in Sir John Forster's garden at Alnwick. Strangely enough the Scots appeared to have free access to Forster, though Redesdalers and North Tynedalers found it virtually impossible to persuade him to force the Scots to redress their losses. Hall noted that on one occasion he had managed to secure a licence from the warden to recapture large numbers of sheep and cattle stolen by Martin and Robin Elliot of Liddesdale. But after he had ridden into Scotland and returned with the lost cattle, he was captured by Forster's men and delivered to the Elliots. Hall suspected that Forster had covertly given the Scots permission to demand £1,000 for his ransom.[67]

In March 1587 a spy known only by his alias John Fortescue informed his employer, Secretary Walsingham, that Redesdalers and North Tynedalers were "sore oppressed and much mated by Sir John Forster, whom in truth they hate – yea they say plainly he has always more esteemed a Scot than his own nation". Although Fortescue had no apparent reason to sympathize with the highlanders, he told Walsingham that he had found them "no less forward than perfect English" in resisting recent Scottish raids and in defending Queen Elizabeth's honour. "Believe me, sir, this tale made my heart leap to hear the good minds of my northern country men."[68]

By 1586 the military potential of Redesdale and North Tynedale had been seriously weakened by Scottish demands for exorbitant ransoms, and the countless murders, farmstead burnings and other unredressed grievances which had been accumulating since 1560. John Hall of Otterburn informed the commissioners at Berwick that while he was keeper of Redesdale under the Earl of Northumberland he had commanded 50 light horsemen all of whom had belonged to his own kinship group. Surnames in other parts of Redesdale who owed service to Harbottle Castle had maintained an additional 300 able-bodied horsemen, making a total of 350 men. Hall claimed that in all of Redesdale there were now less than 20 horsemen fit for border service.[69] But Redesdale may have been even weaker than Hall admitted. As we have seen, the commissioners who surveyed the decay of the service in 1584 did not find a single man in either Redesdale or North Tynedale who was adequately furnished to ride in the service of the borders.[70] In contrast, according to a rough estimate made in 1592, the Graham surname in Cumberland was able to turn out five hundred able-bodied men.[71]

All this leads us to conclude that, within the context of late-sixteenth-century border politics, a surname could only survive as a meaningful social unit if it were given encouragement by a powerful local magnate, a party of gentry or a lord warden. So it was that the Northumberland surnames disintegrated within 20 or 30 years after they were denied patronage in 1560. It follows that the concept of loyalty to a headman also fell into abeyance. Indeed at the time

29

of his death in February 1595 the status of John Hall of Otterburn, the former keeper of Redesdale, was apparently no more than that of a patriarchal head of a large family of small farmers.[72] For his part Edward Charlton actively sought to be accepted as a respectable gentleman and an equal of the lowland gentry rather than as a mere North Tynedale surname leader. At times his methods were a shade dubious. For instance, in 1585 Forster informed Walsingham that Charlton had somehow gained access to information which would explain why Sir Francis Russell had recently been murdered by the Scots at a day of truce.[73] Charlton very likely invented this information. Notwithstanding, he did attain 'respectability' eventually. He was joined to the commission of oyer and terminer for Northumberland in 1607 and was appointed a J. P. in the following year.[74]

For Charlton and many of his name in the late 1580s and 1590s the disadvantages of surname membership must have far outweighed the advantages. As we have seen, Buccleuch and his fierce Scottish companions, perhaps with the connivance of their sovereign, were reviving long-forgotten feuds with Northumberland men of name. Many died as a result. By this time the sole apparent advantage of surname membership was that it gave a Northumbrian highlander a claim to a share in the upland summer pasture held collectively by his surname. Whether it was worth while defending these pastures from Scottish raiders was another matter; some Redesdalers decided that it was not.[75] For like their fellow countrymen, Redesdalers and North Tynedalers fully realized that they owed chief obedience and loyalty not to a surname leader, but to the gentlemen who represented the authority of the queen locally; the sheriff and justices of the peace. They also owed obedience to the lord wardens, keepers and other special officers. It is to these offices, institutions and customs peculiar to Northumberland and the border that we now turn.

In return for their obligation to perform service on the border under the command of a warden and to bear the first brunt of Scottish attacks, the inhabitants of Northumberland, Cumberland, Westmorland and County Durham were exempted from paying any of the subsidies voted by Elizabethan Parliaments.[76] In 1581 the basis of this privilege was reiterated in the preamble to the Act for fortifying the borders, 23 Elizabeth I, c. 4.

During the remainder of the reign it was this Act which regulated men's obligations to serve on the border. As we have already mentioned, this statute required people who held tenements which had owed border service in 1535/6 to contribute actively to that service. Moreover it empowered the Crown to appoint special commissioners to assess as well as to redress the decay of the service. When commissioners found a tenant who was willing to serve but too poor to equip himself with weapons, they could compel his landlord to provide the necessary gear. On the other hand, the commissioners could compel tenants who were unwilling to serve to find arms at their own expense. Similarly, if the commissioners found tenements had been subdivided since 1550/1 they were to require the various tenants to contribute money or material to the principal tenant to enable him to perform border service. If tenants wilfully neglected their obligations, the Act reminded landlords that they could expel defaulting tenants and replace them with men willing to fulfill the obligations owing from the tenements. The Act stated that if landlords refused to expel defaulting tenants, the Crown could give the decay commissioners or the wardens authority to do the task for them.[77]

But to a considerable extent the way in which the Crown chose to enforce this statute was determined by the circumstances which surrounded its passage through Parliament.[78] In its early stages the bill was bitterly opposed by conservative northern landlords. These gentlemen were concerned about the rights of property – their property. Their spokesmen claimed that the queen's councillors had based the measure upon faulty information provided either by people who knew nothing about the intricacies of border society and customs or worse, "by the under-sort and tenants". They complained that the bill "abridges the subject of the right they have both by the law of God, nature and man to dispose of their land and goods as they think fit." The landlords argued that if they were personally and publicly rebuked by inquisitive decay commissioners, their surly tenants and under-tenants would grow bold and rebel. They warned that, once begun, this peasant rebellion would spread to other parts of the realm.[79] Queen Elizabeth's ministers could not be persuaded that the common people of England would welcome a northern version of Wat Tyler or Jack Cade. However, they were concerned about the loyalty of the gentlemen who so reviled their scheme for defending the borders. They did not need to be reminded that twice in the last half-century conservative northern landlords such as these had revolted against the domination of the central government and the South.[80] Thus warned, the privy councillors deemed it prudent not to offend property holders unnecessarily. Although the bill for fortifying the borders passed into statute law, the councillors expressly forbad the decay commissioners whom they subsequently appointed to fine or in any way coerce landlords who did not provide tenantry for border service. They were merely to survey the existing state of the service, to determine why it had decayed and to recommend how it could be strengthened.[81]

The 1581 Act in no way detracted from the authority of the two most powerful royal officials in Northumberland, the lord wardens of the East and Middle Marches. As we have seen, the wardens had command over men performing border service. They were also supposed to maintain the fortifications within their wardenry in a state of military preparedness. They conducted negotiations with Scottish wardenry officials and enforced the customary laws peculiar to the borders in their courts of wardenry. Elizabethan wardens received commissions out of Chancery which gave them essentially the same prerogatives as their predecessors had enjoyed since the fourteenth century.[82] Wardens appointed their own deputies, warden clerks and other under-officers. The two principal under-officers in the Middle March were generally the keepers of Redesdale and Tynedale. Until 1596 the warden of the East March was also lord governor of Berwick. In this capacity he was assisted by a special council which, in addition to himself, consisted of a marshal, treasurer, chamberlain, gentleman porter and three other officials.[83]

The international aspects of border administration were governed by March Laws. Many of these laws were written into treaties contracted by English and Scottish sovereigns between 1237, when the present Anglo-Scottish border was first established, and 1597.[84] March Law may be divided into two categories. The first dealt with offences for which wronged Englishmen and Scots could seek redress from wardenry officials in the opposite march. Such crimes included cattle theft, murder, wounding, maiming or capturing men from the opposite nation in time of peace, and the burning of forts, farmsteads and crops. The second category of March Law concerned procedures used at international days of truce and at the trial of men suspected of offending against March Law.

The frequency with which days of truce were held depended upon the current state of Anglo-Scottish relations and the personal links between English and Scottish wardenry officials. In the best of times they were held at monthly or two monthly intervals; in the worst, not at all. In preparation for a day of truce the two wardens' clerks collected bills. These were written accusations directed against named suspects in the opposite march. It follows that the clerk could only collect detailed information of this sort if he was served by an efficient network of spies and informers on the other side of the border. After the clerk had enrolled the bills, they were sent to the opposite warden so that he could ensure that the accused would be present for trial at the day of truce. Men could be tried by several methods. Common to them all was the precept that an accused person could only be found guilty by his own countrymen, be they regular jurors or men who avowed to his guilt. Scots found guilty by one means or another were handed over to the English warden for execution in exchange for the guilty Englishmen who were delivered to the Scottish warden.[85]

In addition to this business, English and Scottish wardens or deputy wardens meeting at days of truce settled outstanding accounts between those of their borderers who had lost sheep, cattle and other goods to raiders from the nation opposite. Both sides generally assessed their losses at an inordinately high level so that they would not have a deficit when restitution was finally made.[86] Until a new treaty regulating border affairs was negotiated at Carlisle in 1597, wardens had the right to ride unheralded over the border in hot pursuit of a thief carrying stolen goods. If a warden could catch a man red-handed, the goods were returned directly to their owner without reference to the clumsy procedures used at a day of truce.[87]

After the appointment of Thomas Randolph as a fully accredited English ambassador to the Scottish Court early in 1586, wardens lost much of their earlier importance as sources of information about affairs in Scotland. They also lost much of their power to influence the course of international relations. If privy councillors learned that a warden and his counterpart had not held regular days of truce because of personal animosities, they might well appoint special border commissioners to settle outstanding differences without reference to the wardens. In 1586 and 1597 officials holding special commissions exchanged bills and performed all the international functions formerly monopolized by the lord wardens.[88]

Queen Elizabeth's privy councillors thus clearly recognized that wardens were no longer essential to the administration of the international frontier. However, they did not appreciably curtail the authority of the wardens over the people within their marches. After 1586, as before, commissioned wardens might still convene courts of wardenry which had criminal jurisdiction over men accused of infringing the customary domestic laws of the marches by committing what was known as March Treason. March Treason might include such crimes as the unlicensed sale of arms or munitions other than swords and daggers to Scots, betraying the persons or goods of Englishmen to Scots, or wilfully suffering thieves or invaders to escape back into Scotland. Men accused of March Treason were tried before a jury of border freeholders under the presidency of the lord warden. After the jurors had reached their verdict the warden pronounced sentence. Men found guilty were liable to summary execution and the forfeiture of their goods and lands.[89]

These procedures seem fair enough until one realizes that as English domestic border law was never written down or codified, borderers could not know for certain just what constituted a March Treason. Each warden was at liberty to define the term as he saw fit. In theory, after his appointment a warden met with a jury of experienced borderers within his wardenry to establish and delimit March Treasons.[90] According to a commentator writing in the late 1590s, if the jurors thought the new warden was "covetous through greedy desire of confiscations" and he was on good terms with them personally, they would term many crimes March Treason, and thus have "all the laws written with blood". But if the jurors feared that they could not trust or control the new warden, they would recommend that grievous crimes worthy to be March Treasons only be considered mean trespasses, "foreseeing that otherwise themselves or their near family should daily fall within compass of law and danger of death through their wicked demerits."[91] In 1580/1 another commentator noted that because of the ambiguity and uncertainty of domestic march law, borderers stood in constant danger of being sentenced to death under laws "not always nor in all the wardenries at one time taken for laws and therefore such as . . . subjects can not reasonably take notice of."[92]

Wardens might apply march justice as they saw fit. It was rumoured that Sir John Forster and his successor Ralph Eure convened secret wardenry courts in their private chambers on short notice.[93] The more common practice

33

was to announce sessions well in advance so that men could arrange to attend in decent order. Custom allowed a warden to empanel jurors from amongst his own household servants or from a faction known to be unfriendly to the accused. In sharp contrast to the procedures used when men were on trial for their lives before common law courts,[94] suspected march traitors were not allowed pre-emptory challenge or challenge for cause against any of the jurors. It was also alleged that unscrupulous wardens commonly usurped the Crown's prerogatives and pardoned convicted march traitors if they were offered adequate bribes.[95] In other instances wardens threatened men of doubtful repute with punishment for March Treason although they had no intention of ever bringing them to trial. And according to a custom which Sir John Forster took care to maintain, a warden was entitled to seize for his own use the goods of a man suspected of March Treason before he was convicted. In 1586 men from Rochester claimed that Forster had kept them in prison for a year before they were arraigned and found to be innocent. Notwithstanding, he "took their whole goods, and kept it to his own use."[96] At this time the warden of the Middle March was paid about £300 a year. Forfeitures and the proceeds of his wardenry court made the office worth about £1,000 a year.[97] The salaries of each of his two assistants, the keepers, were less than £20 a year. However, these officers had the right to the proceeds of justice in cases in any way related to the enforcement of the customary laws within their keepership. In 1594 the keepership of Tynedale was said to be worth £300 a year and that of Redesdale £333.[98]

Tudor privy councillors could not convincingly plead ignorance of the use which unscrupulous wardens and keepers might make of unwritten domestic March Law. In 1537, after putting down the Pilgrimage of Grace, Thomas Howard, third duke of Norfolk, had cogently argued that March Law should be codified so that it would be consistent throughout the English wardenries.[99] Forty years later the Earl of Huntingdon, Lord President of the Council of the North, suggested that the Crown appoint a commission to study the laws of the marches.[100] Perhaps as a result of Huntingdon's professed concern, a rough draft of a bill for March Treasons was circulated among the privy councillors while Parliament was in session in 1581.[101] This project came to nothing. It is likely that the northern landlords who opposed the Act for fortifying the borders believed that it would be easier to keep the lower orders in line if March Treason remained vague and ill-defined.

Thereafter, Queen Elizabeth's government made no serious attempt to reform or abolish domestic border law. Neither did they make any effort to counterbalance the influence and authority of the wardens. The most obvious way to have done this would have been to create in each county a strong, independent commission of the peace headed by a competent *custos rotulorum*. Properly used, this office could serve as the linchpin of an efficient local administration. For it was the duty of the *custos rotulorum* to see that other J. P.s kept their sessions regularly and that sheriffs, coroners and other civil officials performed their allotted tasks. However in late Elizabethan Northumberland the *custos rotulorum* was generally one and the same person as the lord warden of the Middle March.[102]

The lord wardens, Northumberland J. P.s and other county officials were subordinate to the Council of the North in York as well as to the Privy Council in London. As it was reconstituted in 1537, the Council of the North had jurisdiction over the three Yorkshire ridings, Northumberland and the three other border counties. Among its *ex officio* members were the lord wardens and the governor, marshal and treasurer of Berwick. The bishop and the dean of Durham, the ecclesiastics responsible for the spiritual welfare of the inhabitants of the archdeaconry of Northumberland, were also members by virtue of office. Yet with the exception of Cuthbert, seventh and last lord Ogle (*d.* 1597), no non-office-holding Northumbrians were admitted to the Council. In contrast, Yorkshire was represented by a substantial number of private gentlemen.[103]

The authority of the Council of the North was based on special commissions of oyer and terminer and commissions of the peace issued by Chancery as well as instructions given to lord presidents by the Privy Council.[104] The northern council's work fell into two broad areas; judicial and administrative. As a court of law it was equipped to hear both criminal and civil cases. It combined the functions of the Court of Star Chamber and the Court of Requests. One of the Council's most useful functions as far as Northumbrians were concerned was to provide them with a court more accessible than those in London before which to settle land tenure cases. A few examples show that men even from remote parts of the shire had recourse to the Court at York. Around 1586 it issued a decree confirming Geoffrey Robson in a tenement in Charlton in North Tynedale and another confirming George Hymer in a tenement in Kirkwhelpington. In 1589 the Privy Council asked the northern councillors to determine whether some time before 1559 the deputy captain of Norham Castle had illegally deseized two messuages in Buckton, Norhamshire, formerly held by Ralph Wade.[105]

The judicial aspects of the Council's work were conducted by the lord president, or in his absence by the vice-president, together with a secretary, various clerks and lawyers of the quorum who, in contrast to the non-legal councillors, were bound to constant attendance. As a court of law the Council held four month-long sessions each year. In the 1560s the Privy Council prevailed upon the northern councillors to hold one of their annual sessions in either Newcastle or Carlisle. But during the presidency of the Earl of Huntingdon (1572–95), the councillors met only once in Newcastle. After 1572 they held virtually all of their sessions in the King's Manor in York.[106]

In its administrative capacity the Council of the North had considerably less impact upon Northumberland than it had as a court of law. Working at all times under the direction of the Privy Council, the northern council was supposed to supervise local justices of the peace. But it appears that the Council found it difficult even to obtain the co-operation of Yorkshire J. P.s, let alone those in distant Northumberland.[107] However, in 1583 and 1593 some of the northern councillors did work in conjunction with the special commissioners appointed to survey the decay of the border service.[108]

The last mentioned task was closely related to the Earl of Huntingdon's novel peacetime role as lord lieutenant of the northern shires. Before 1580 the Crown had only employed lord lieutenants as its deputies in the field in time of war with Scotland or during periods of acute civil disorder. In peacetime control of the military affairs of most counties had generally been given to special commissioners of array. But this arrangement no longer seemed adequate in view of the deterioration of Anglo-Scottish relations in 1579. Young King James had fallen under the influence of his dashing French cousin, Esmé Stuart d'Aubigné, who was reputed to be an agent of the Duke of Guise, the leader of the pro-Spanish and militant Catholic faction in France. Fearing the worst, Elizabeth's councillors decided to organize the northern military command on a more permanent basis. In addition to drawing up the Act for fortifying the borders, they appointed Huntingdon lord lieutenant of several northern counties. When his commission of lieutenancy was renewed in 1586, Huntingdon was specifically given command of the shire levies in Northumberland and the border counties as well as those in Yorkshire.[109]

However, command over the Northumberland county militia did not give the lord lieutenant control over men performing border service under their lord warden. For as Edward Aglionby wrote in 1592, the wardens still had "charge as General in all affairs of the marches under her Majesty".[110] It was this unhealthy concentration of power in the hands of wardens who often were not even capable of protecting Northumberland from Scottish terrorists which led one late-sixteenth-century commentator to assert that "the state of honest men of all degrees on the borders of England is more miserable in this time of peace than in any war that hath been in some ages past."[111]

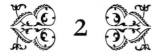

2

The economic background
in the late sixteenth century

Infinitely remote, rough and ill-cultivated, afflicted alike by a harsh climate and by harsh and violent men; these were the characteristics which William Camden, the late Elizabethan antiquarian, and other educated southern Englishmen commonly associated with Northumberland.[1] Perhaps such attributes were self-evident. On the other hand, they may only have reflected southerners' intolerance for landscapes, peoples and life styles which differed from those to which they were accustomed. One may ask whether Northumberland's reputation was justified. This question can be partially answered on an impressionistic level by referring to contemporary comments and witticisms about such things as extreme weather conditions, transportation difficulties and poverty. However, on a more objective level, detailed contemporary surveys, inventories and similar sources should be used to gain an understanding of the manner in which lowlanders and highlanders actually made their living. These sources reveal that, like most people in the British Isles, the vast majority of Northumbrians were agriculturalists. Yet a survey of economic conditions in the late sixteenth century cannot neglect the burgeoning Tyneside coal industry centred on Newcastle.

Even in comparison with Sussex and other counties which, when seen from the Court and capital, might appear inconveniently far off,[2] Elizabethan Northumberland was remote and isolated. Newcastle was approximately 275 miles from Charing Cross. Berwick, on the Scottish border, was 50 miles further north. Postal arrangements between these northern towns and London, as well as within Northumberland itself, were notoriously inefficient. In 1589 Sir Henry Widdrington, the marshal of Berwick, discovered that it had taken 25 hours for an urgent message he had sent to his superior in London to be carried to Newcastle and an additional 16 hours for it to reach Durham only 14 miles further south.[3] In November 1605 Sir William Selby of Branxton, a special law-enforcement officer, did not learn that the government had discovered a gunpowder plot in which some Northumbrians seemed to be implicated until five days after this news was public knowledge in London.[4]

Such was the condition of Northumberland roads and bridges that officials found it most convenient to travel about the countryside on horseback. In 1625 Bishop Neile of Durham thought it worthy of comment that those few coaches which were used along major Northumbrian routes were laid up after the first snows fell.[5] A short time earlier the bishop would have found that the main route between Newcastle and Carlisle could not readily be travelled by coach in any season because of the ruinous condition of the bridge over the Tyne at Corbridge. The closure and collapse of this bridge greatly inconvenienced Newcastle merchants. As their spokesmen pointed out when complaining of the matter to Parliament, every week corn, iron, pitch, tar, flax, hemp, fruits and wines were transported along this route by carriage or on horseback. Carriers could ford the River Tyne when it was low, but when it was in flood it could only be crossed by ferry. Northumberland's ferries were apparently in no better condition than its bridges. According to those spokesmen "above three score persons at a time drowned in ferrying over at Hexham."[6] Not long after the central authorities persuaded Northumberland J. P.s to levy a rate for the repair of the bridge at Corbridge, the bridge ten miles further up the Tyne, at Haydon Bridge, collapsed.[7]

Unseasonable weather might make travel exceedingly unpleasant. Late in September 1597 Sir William Bowes, a member of the well known County Durham family, rode on official business north from Newburn-upon-Tyne to Norham Castle and then forded the Tweed to Scotland. He later reported "this journey has been painful and dangerous to us that travelled by reason of exceeding storms of snow, wind and rain and thereby the waters so great that most of us that passed over them rode wet in our saddles".[8] Another gentleman who experienced difficulties with the weather was Sir William Selby. In May 1606 he arranged a 'hunting party' with a number of other officials hoping to capture some fugitives from Cumberland whom they suspected were hiding in the highlands of Tynedale. Selby later informed Sir Robert Cecil that he and his Tynedale guides arrived at the appointed meeting place at 10 p.m. but found nobody else about. Then:

> after five hours' travel, by reason of great rains and a thick mist which covered the mountains, the guides lost all knowledge of the country as well in the day light as night, so that Sir William Selby and his company wandered on the mosses with great difficulty drawing their horses after them by the space of ten hours before they could fall on any habitable place . . .[9]

Such was the climate and location of Berwick that it was widely thought to be the most undesirable post to which a southern official could be assigned.

Weather conditions were reportedly so severe in January 1595 that soldiers were blown off the town walls and hurled to their deaths.[10] That December Lord Willoughby, the lord governor, vowed that "If I were further from the tempestuousness of Cheviot Hills and were once retired from this accursed country, whence the sun is so removed, I would not change my homliest hermitage for the highest palace there."[11] Doubtless poor Willoughby had Queen Elizabeth's shining countenance in mind quite as much as the cloud-concealed heavenly body. Six months later he was dead of a great cold and fever.[12]

The inhabitants of remote Northumberland were generally considered to be relatively poorer than their countrymen further south. This was an unenviable reputation at a time when it was estimated that between a third and a quarter of England's population lived below the poverty line.[13] Northumberland's poverty is born out by E. J. Buckatzsch's general study of the distribution of wealth in England. Buckatzsch prepared a comparative index of the wealth of all the English counties based on the relationship between the area of a county and the total amount it was assessed for various land taxes. He calculated that in 1503, when King Henry VII was collecting feudal dues for knighting his deceased son Arthur, Northumberland ranked thirty-sixth in wealth among 37 counties; only Cumberland was poorer. The next Northumberland figures date from 1641, after the county had suffered a Scottish invasion. At that time it ranked thirty-eighth among 39 counties, again followed only by Cumberland. However, as Buckatzsch's figures represent the average land tax per acre, the poverty of counties like Northumberland which contain large acreages of upland of limited agricultural use, would be somewhat exaggerated.[14]

Northumberland was one of the least densely populated of the English counties. In the absence of detailed diocesan reports and reliable sets of parish registers for this period, the best sources for estimating the total population of the county are the muster returns. These reports list the total number of able-bodied men between the ages of 16 and 60 whom local military commanders could call upon to defend the county. It may be supposed that in an area notorious for its lawlessness, many men had no desire to attract attention to themselves by appearing at musters. It is also uncertain how many recent Scottish immigrants saw fit to attend musters. Many such people were, it was said, brought in under suspicious circumstances by profit-minded landlords. In June 1586 John Aneill of Ilderton in Glendale accused his landlady, Mrs Robert Roddam of Little Houghton, of forcibly displacing him and four other loyal English householders in favour of Scottish settlers. Randolph, the English ambassador to Scotland to whom Aneill addressed his complaint, noted that: "This thing is so common among all men of any wealth that have land near unto the borders . . . It is commonly reported that every third man within ten miles of the borders is either a Scot, tenant or servant to an Englishman, both in Middle and East Marches."[15] In addition to the men, English as well as

Scottish, who avoided musters for personal reasons, there were many households which were not represented at musters because their menfolk had been killed by Scottish terrorists.[16]

It would thus appear that in comparison with other counties in England, a fairly high multiplier should be used to obtain from the musters an estimate of the total population of Northumberland. In 1950 E. E. Rich contended that muster returns from southern counties could reasonably be multiplied by four.[17] Writing a quarter of a century earlier, D. L. W. Tough used a multiplier of five in estimating the population of the border counties.[18] More recently, W. G. Hoskins suggested that figures obtained from muster rolls should be multiplied by six or even seven.[19] Roger Howell has followed Hoskins' lead and used six as a "conservative multiplier" when estimating the population of Newcastle upon Tyne in the early seventeenth century.[20] Population estimates for Tudor Cumberland and Westmorland based on the 1563 diocesan returns certainly support the use of a multiplier higher than that used by either Tough or Rich. C. M. L. Bouch and G. P. Jones estimated that the combined population of these two border counties was slightly more than 73,000 in 1563.[21] If this figure is then divided by the number of men in the West March who attended musters in 1584, the result is 7.7.[22] Taking everything into account, it seems reasonable to apply the multiplier 6.5 to muster figures for Northumberland.

But not all the muster reports are equally useful. The musters held in 1580, 1593, 1595 and 1596 all appear to have been poorly attended.[23] Of the Elizabethan musters, that of 1584 appears to be most complete. Returns list 10,589 footmen and horsemen in the East and Middle Marches, that is to say all of the county including North Durham, but excluding the chartered towns of Alnwick, Morpeth and Berwick.[24] The population in the mid-1620s can be estimated from the 1627 muster returns which give totals from each of the six wards in the county. In 1627 the total number of men who mustered in Northumberland, excluding North Durham, Berwick, Morpeth and Alnwick, was 11,679.[25] This figure bears a reasonable relationship to the number mustered in 1584.

The 10,589 men who mustered in 1584 would represent a population of 68,828 if the multiplier 6.5 was used. To this total must be added the approximately 5,500 people who lived in Alnwick, Berwick and Morpeth.[26] This results in an estimated total population of 74,300 in 1584. Applying the same multiplier to the number of men mustered in 1627 gives us 75,813. Adding the population of North Durham[27] and the chartered towns we arrive at an estimated total population of 85,000 for early Caroline Northumberland. But the population increase between 1584 and 1627 may be more apparent than real since the 1627 returns were probably more complete than those of 1584.

The 1584 estimate suggests that there were about 35 people per square mile in Northumberland. This figure is the same as that which Bouch and

Jones give for Westmorland and slightly higher than that for Cumberland, 30 per square mile.[28] The Northumberland average is below the 40 per square mile which is derived from J. T. Cliffe's figure for late-sixteenth-century Yorkshire.[29] The average density for the whole of England in 1600 was probably about 74 per square mile, given a total population of about 3.75 million.[30]

The least densely populated parts of Northumberland were the western highlands which covered about a quarter of the total area of the county. In 1541 Sir Robert Bowes and Sir Ralph Ellerker estimated that there were no fewer than 1,500 able horsemen and footmen in North Tynedale and Redesdale.[31] These figures would suggest a population of approximately 10,000; a density half that of the county as a whole forty years later. Within the highlands the population was concentrated in the narrow valleys of the North Tyne, the Rede and their tributary streams. In 1584 decay commissioners found no permanent settlement further up the North Tyne than the hamlets of Yarrow and Emmethaugh, ten miles beyond the confluence of the Rede and the North Tyne. Permanent settlement on the Rede ended five miles south of the border at Burdhope and the Sills, just north of Rochester. The commissioners noted that all these settlements had been "spoiled by the Scots".[32]

Considering the constant danger of Scottish attack and the small amount of cultivable land, it is not surprising that Bowes and Ellerker were convinced that North Tynedale and, more especially, Redesdale were "overcharged" with inhabitants "Whereby the yonge and actyve people for lacke of lyvynge be constrayned to steall or spoyle contynually ether in England or Scotland for the mayntenu[n]ce of their lyvynge."[33] William Camden assured the readers of his *Britannia* that late Elizabethan Redesdale and North Tynedale, "their hilles hard by, so boggy and standing with water in the top, that no horsemen are able to ride through them", still produced an abundant supply of thieves.[34] But in Camden's day, as earlier, opportunities for honest employment within the highlands were extremely limited. The only town in North Tynedale where bread, ale and other victuals were sold for money was Bellingham. A market was kept there every Sunday in the year and a fair was held on the twentieth of March, St Cuthbert's day. No regular market was held anywhere in Redesdale.[35] In the absence of opportunities in trade, most young people who elected to stay in the highlands became farmers.

The best source of information about the agrarian régime in Redesdale and North Tynedale is the 1604 survey of the royal manors of Harbottle (in Redesdale) and Wark.[36] In the river valleys the surveyors found small hamlets or isolated farms surrounded by enclosed arable and meadow. The closes around each farmstead were held individually and were planted in spring with oats and a low grade of barley known locally as 'bigg'. The growing season was too short and the soil too poor for the cultivation of wheat. Hay was grown on meadows in the valleys to provide winter fodder for the cattle which were grazed on upland summer pasture.[37] As we shall see, this type of agricultural system was entirely different from that found in common field villages in the Northumberland lowlands.

The size of the average North Tynedale farmer's closes suggests that few people lived above bare subsistence. Most of the customary tenants had only six or seven acres of arable and four to six acres of meadow in individually-held closes. In addition each tenant had anything up to 20 acres of rougher grazing land. In the manor of Harbottle the average acreage in enclosed fields was even less than in Wark. Most of the 202 customary tenants on royal land in Redesdale held between four and five acres of arable; only eight of them held more than ten acres. The majority of farmers held one to six acres of meadow. Small groups of farmers shared a winter pasture. In the parishes of Elsdon and Corsensides there was also a large common pasture with an average share of 80 acres for each household. Temporary additional pasture was available when the meadow and arable closes were thrown open for common grazing after the last crops of the year had been harvested.

In addition to the winter farms in the valleys, highlanders used upland pastures known as summerings or shieldings. In Harbottle both customary tenants and freeholders claimed collective rights to these pastures as descendants of a surname "or race of men to whom such a summering belongeth".[38] In April or May, as soon as the barley had been planted in the winter farm, the whole family drove their sheep and cattle to the shielding. They left early in August when the hay in the enclosed meadows was ready for harvesting. The bailiff set the date when everyone was to go to and from the summerings. In 1620 Roger Widdrington, a local estate agent, explained that the reason for this custom "in the time of the late borders" was that "people were not permitted to go straggling one before another or remain straggling one after another, in respect of the dangerous and deadly feuds abroad and in respect of ill-neighbourhood and wronging one another in their husbandry and at home."[39] Everyone paid the same rent for the summering and returned each summer to the same summer house or shieling.[40] As the summerings were unstinted there was no limit to the number of sheep and cattle which a family could pasture. In practice, however, the number was limited by the availability of hay from the lower meadows and pastures. Tenants in North Tynedale practised transhumance in much the same manner as did their neighbours in Harbottle.[41]

Between the highlands proper and the lowlands to the east and south was what might be described as a transitional zone. Within this zone livestock predominated and summer shieldings were sometimes used in association with meadows and pastures in the valleys. Shieldings were recorded in the Forest of Cheviot. In 1603 tenants-at-will of Sir Ralph Gray of Chillingham living in villages west of the River Till claimed that they had recently had summer houses on the Cheviot. But because of a quarrel among the Grays, Selbys and Forsters, the tenants had been deprived of the use of their summer pasture and thus "of the benefit of the milk of their kine (being the greatest part of their livelihood)".[42] Today the place name 'shield' is still commonly found in the transitional zone, for example, at Linn Shield near Featherstone in South Tynedale, and at Harwoodshield and Spital Shield on Hexham Common, at elevations of over 900 feet. Although shielding was not recorded at these places in the sixteenth century, it was probably practised there before that time. In 1608 tenants in the regality of Hexham and the neighbouring baronies of Langley and Bulbeck claimed rights to unstinted moorland pastures.[43] The use of unrestricted pasture distinguished their pastoral economy from that found in most parts of the lowlands.

The inventories of gentlemen and yeomen living in this transitional zone illustrate the central importance of livestock. The value of the goods of Richard Wallace, a yeoman of Kirkhaugh in South Tynedale who died in 1586, totalled only £24 13s. 4d. His "insight geir and fire vessell" and apparel were worth only £4; his livestock was worth £20 13s. 4d.[44] Nearly 70 per cent of the value of the goods of Lancelot Thirlwall, of Thirlwall in South Tynedale, consisted of cattle, sheep and horses. As the inventory was taken in January (1583) it attests to the survival of large numbers of cattle and sheep through the winter. Its mention of "corne berryed and unberyed", worth £10, shows that some grain crops, probably rye and wheat, were sown in the autumn.[45] William Blenkinsopp of Blenkinsopp, a mile north of Thirlwall, also planted winter corn on his lands. On his death in 1581 he left 12 acres of corn, 13 acres of haver (a poor variety of oats) and a large number of livestock. The livestock included sheep and cattle of various ages and oxen used for ploughing. Altogether his livestock was worth £46 19s., over 60 per cent of the value of the inventory. Although Blenkinsopp was the head of a well-established gentry family his household goods and apparel were worth only £13 3s. 2d.[46] Two years later his nearest gentle neighbour, Lancelot Thirlwall, left household goods of a similar value, £13 6s. 2d.[47] These amounts were only slightly more than the average value, £10 to £12, of household goods belonging to farmers of yeoman status in Wigston Magna, Leicestershire, in 1600.[48] But as we shall see, many lowland Northumberland gentry were only marginally more prosperous than Blenkinsopp or Thirlwall.[49]

Taken in their entirety, the coastal lowlands of Northumberland were the richest part of the county. But in the 1590s a traveller riding south from Berwick along the rutted Great North Road might not see much evidence of prosperity about him for many a mile, thanks to the Scots. At the beginning of his journey he would cross the neglected but potentially rich rolling limestone plain of Norhamshire which extended for more than ten miles inland from the coast.[50] Further south the plain narrowed to a width of little more than three miles. As the traveller rode past Holy Isle towards Bamburgh, the rocky stronghold of the sixth-century Bernician kings who had raised ancient Northumbria to a position of pre-eminence among the rude Anglo-Saxons, he passed through lands which were still frequently ravaged by Scottish raiders.

Further south, the fertile coastal plain widened towards the Earl of Northumberland's populous barony of Alnwick, centred around the mighty castle on the south bank of the River Aln. It was only after the traveller crossed the turbulent River Coquet into Morpeth ward that he began to observe fields and farmsteads which were only occasionally visited by thievish marauders.[51]

Much of the land which a traveller might view in the coastal lowlands or in the lower Tyne valley in the late sixteenth century was associated with a nucleated village and its common field system. This agrarian régime was considerably more reliant upon livestock than were common field systems elsewhere in England. Yet it is hazardous to generalize about the procedures which these Northumbrian communities employed to regulate the use of arable, meadow, pasture and waste or about the size and number of the fields which the customary tenants used in common. Detailed recent research[52] has shown that significant variations might occur between villages or townships within the same manor no less than between manors. The use to which land was put and the way in which its use was controlled were all part of an on-going, evolving process which reflected current attitudes towards subsistence or market economies, current technology, population pressures, climatic cycles, physiographic features and so on. Thus there were a variety of reasons why some lowland farmers elected to live on isolated farmsteads and hamlets[53] rather than in the more typical sort of lowland community, the common field village.

Under a common field régime each customary tenant held a farm or husbandland which was sufficient to support him and his family. At least in theory, each husbandland was of approximately the same acreage as other husbandlands in the same township. It consisted of a number of strips or riggs scattered amongst the various fields pertaining to the village and was associated with the right to graze cattle on the common pasture and the use of other communal facilities.

Possibly because of the 'Ancient Duetie of Service' upon the borders which was attached to many tenancies in Northumberland[54] husbandlands more commonly survived there as roughly equal, identifiable units of cultivation and privilege than in counties south of the Tees.[55] Thus a survey made in 1608 of Crown lands in the royal manor of Bewick in the Till valley listed 11 tenants in East Lilburn. Eight of these tenants had what appears to be a full husbandland. Each held 26 acres of arable land scattered in three fields, three acres of meadow together with rights to pasture on Bewick Moor. Two tenants each held what was described as "half a tenement" and one tenant held two tenements. In Old Bewick, in the same manor, 11 farmers each had 33 acres of arable in the "cornfields", four acres of meadow and the right to pasture in Whitecross Field and on Bewick Moor; one tenant had two husbandlands.[56] In Tynemouthshire proper, husbandlands and the associated standard customary rents could still be easily identified in six villages in 1608. Indeed in five of the villages all of the 38 customary tenants listed in the survey still held a single husbandland and in the sixth village, five of the nine tenants held one.[57] The survival of the husbandland as a meaningful unit in the common field system in the early seventeenth century can also be traced, though less clearly, in the Percy barony of Alnwick and in the lordship of Warkworth.[58]

In favoured lowland townships the possibility of expanding the common fields was facilitated by the abundance of nearby waste. This land might be brought under cultivation in order to replace a field suffering from soil exhaustion or to accommodate population increase. Butlin suggests that the inequality in the size of the common fields at Rennington and Ingoe in the early seventeenth century was due to continuing enclosure from neighbouring wastes. A survey of Acklington in 1616 stated that 98 acres, known as Moor Lands, had recently been taken in from the waste and that seven acres in the North Field had been deliberately left as unploughed common, possibly because of soil exhaustion.[59] Though an effort might well be made to maintain an equal division of land amongst all customary tenants in the village, the manner in which new land was distributed might differ from the system used earlier.[60] For example, it was reported in 1622 that the tenants of Prudhoe, on the lower Tyne, had three fields "for corn, lying in common, everie man his rigg as it falleth", but in the fourth field all the tenants held individual closes of equal size.[61] This suggests than an extra field had been added to the three existing fields by enclosing a part of the neighbouring waste.

An analysis of 25 inventories dating from the 1580s shows that in addition to keeping cattle and sheep, most lowland farmers grew a wide range of grains. These included rye and wheat, collectively known as hard corn, as well as oats and barley. Oats were the most widely grown grain for they could be raised profitably on lands too infertile for wheat. Although they were a low-value crop their yield per acre was higher than other cereals. Oats sown at Togston, on the coastal plain south of the Coquet, were expected to yield five times the amount of seed sown; hard corn and barley only three times.[62] Oats were the most versatile of the cereals for they could be used for bread, for flat cakes, for porridge or for malting. In lowland Northumberland they were also widely used as fodder for cattle. In contrast, farmers in Wigston Magna, Leicestershire, grew virtually no oats and used peas and beans for fodder; almost half of the acreage of their common fields was devoted to these two crops.[63] Conversely, peas and beans were rarely grown in Northumberland. Only two of the 25 inventories mentioned these crops; one from the Gray estate at Elwick and the other from the Forster estate at Beadnell, both on the narrow coastal plain near Bamburgh.[64] In all but one inventory, that of the Radcliffe estate at Dilston, the value of wheat was higher than that of any other grain.[65] Since wheaten bread was preferred to bread or cakes made with oats, the market price of wheat was anything up to three times that of oats. But, as we have seen, wheat yields were generally lower than oats and less reliable. Even in comparatively fertile and agriculturally advanced Kent, wheat yields might vary from three to six times the seed sown.[66]

Much of the eastern lowlands was covered with heavy glacial clay which was difficult to plough even with oxen. In 1567 the surveyor George Clarkson found that the village of Shilbottle, four miles south of Alnwick, was "a very poore towne" largely because the arable consisted of "a baire clay grounde and will take moche soile or donge before yt be brought to any good perfeccon or fertylytye."[67] This soil was doubtless better suited for pasture than arable. Yet in some villages nearby, pasture was in relatively short supply. At Birling there were only 300 acres of common pasture for 450 acres of arable. Because of the shortage of pasture, the Birling tenants put their cattle on pasture belonging to the adjacent village of Low Buston and in Shilbottle woods. Apparently there was no shortage of pasture when the crops had been harvested and the fields thrown open for grazing.[68]

In some lowland common field villages the right to pasture cattle in the stubble after the harvest was insecure. In 1580 customary tenants in the royal manor of Elswick accused local freeholders of enclosing meadow, planting grain where it had never been before and ploughing within a month after the first crops had been harvested. This last action was "contrary to custom" and worked great hardship on the customary tenants.[69] Another indication of pressure on pasture was the use of stints or beastgates proportional to a man's holding in the common fields. In 1608 each copyholder in Backworth, Tyne-mouthshire, had a 24-acre husbandland, six beastgates on enclosed meadow and the right to pasture six cattle, two horses and 30 sheep on the common fields. Each copyholder in Whitley had pasture in the common fields for 12 cattle, 30 sheep and two horses.[70] In Corbridge and Dilston, on the middle Tyne, poorer pasture was left unstinted and the better quality stinted. In order to preserve the grass during the winter months, the period of least growth, tenants were only allowed to use half a stint; during the summer they might use their full allotment.[71]

Villagers using unfenced common pasture frequently found themselves in conflict with the inhabitants of an adjacent village whose unfenced common abutted on theirs. Sometime before 1603 a Percy tenant at High Buston, near Warkworth, wrote of the difficulties which he and his fellow tenants encountered with people from neighbouring Wooden and Bilton, whereby "divers quarrells and variances have hapned and daylie like to ensue betweene the tenants of bothe townes by chasinge, rechasinge and impoundinge of theire catle, damage fezant which cannot be kept out but by contynuall staffeheardinge, to the greate charge of your lordship's poor tenants."[72] In 1586 George Clarkson reported that the greatest cause of the poverty of the Percy tenants at Newham, near Bamburgh, was the trespass of cattle from nearby villages, not only on to Newham's common pasture, but also on to the arable.[73] The best solution to a problem such as this was enclosure.

In discussions of the enclosure of common field villages in Northumberland the term 'division' was often used. This term may refer to a type of enclosure in which each of the tenants received a field or a group of fields to be held individually and separated from neighbours' fields by fences or hedges. This is invariably what happened when divisions were made after 1603, but before the union of the Crowns a rather different form of division took place. In larger villages, those with approximately 20 tenants or more, the area of the common fields was divided into two parts. Some tenants were assigned strips in one part and some in the other. R. A. Butlin has suggested that this form of division was a half-way stage in the creation of individually-held farms.[74] At a time when men were still urgently needed to defend the border, it preserved the same number of men for border service that the village had furnished before it was divided. By requiring men to continue to co-operate with each other in the cultivation of their scattered strips, this arrangement possibly encouraged them to co-operate with each other in pursuit of stolen goods and in border service. From a purely agricultural point of view, a two-fold division obviated the greatest practical difficulty of common field cultivation, the great distance between homesteads and outlying strips. After division had taken place, strips in the two fields could more easily be manured with household refuse and protected from the incursions of neighbours' cattle.[75]

One of George Clarkson's purposes in surveying the Percy lands in Northumberland in 1566 and 1567 was to decide whether some of the larger villages should be divided. After considerable disputation, the tenants of Chatton, a village containing 21 husbandlands, agreed to a division of the village into two parts and to the consolidation of the demesne which had been scattered throughout the common fields. Within each half, the tenants were to continue their former strip cultivation.[76] Long Houghton, like Chatton, was a large village, having 27 tenants. As the houses were strung out for half a mile along the village street the distance from the homesteads to the peripheral fields might be considerable. Sometime before 1567 Long Houghton had been divided into a northern and southern part and the villagers assigned land in their respective half of the village. But Clarkson found that some of the villagers believed that they had not received their fair share. To end such disagreements Clarkson made a new survey which confirmed the division. Within the two parts of the village cultivation in long narrow strips continued as before. But mindful of the villagers' earlier disagreements, Clarkson recommended that the two parts of the village be divided by a quickset hedge. Surveys of Long Houghton in 1614 and 1619 show that strip cultivation in the two divisions persisted even after leases began to replace customary tenures. It was only in the later years of the seventeenth century that this layout was gradually modified.[77]

In 1567 Clarkson also recommended that Shilbottle, a village with 20 tenants, be divided.[78] But in other cases, as at Acklington, where there were

18 tenants, Clarkson did not think that division would be beneficial. As he noted, "This towne ys not to be devyded otherwayes than yt ys nowe presentlie, for that ye inequalitie of ye goodnes of the grounde as also ye scyte of the towne, which ys yn all respectes scytuated for ye most comodetie to all the said inhabitaunts."[79] Clarkson also advised against the division of the common field village of Lesbury, "a very trime lordship" with 20 tenants. Although Lesbury was a street village and some of the houses were far from outlying strips, the difficulties of obtaining a fair division, given the great variations in the quality of the soil, led Clarkson to recommend that the present layout be maintained.[80]

A few Northumberland common field villages were fully enclosed and divided into separate farms even before the need to perform border service came to an end with the union of the Crowns in 1603. In 1567 Clarkson referred to the recent enclosure at Tughall, near Bamburgh. The tenants had "ther groundes severallie enclosed by themselves, wherfor they dyd lye in common".[81] An enterprising tenant at High Buston, one William Bednell, attempted (apparently without success) to persuade the Earl of Northumberland to license the division of that small township among the tenants and freeholders. Bednell ingeniously argued that division in severalty "would greatlie strengthen the said village, and aide your lordship's tenants against th'incursions of Scotts and forren ryders, which otherwise, lyeing open, cannot be defended by the nomber there, whoe are forced to watche generallie together everie night, to theire great charge and indurable toyle."[82]

Elizabethans who accepted the premise that able-bodied local men should always be on hand to defend the borders against Scottish invaders roundly condemned any form of enclosure which might lead to depopulation. In August 1583 Sir Valentine Brown, the treasurer of Berwick, warned Secretary Walsingham that the eastern part of the English border "is now laid waste for sheep and husbandry, and the people clean driven away that should have been succours to such as might have been placed there. I do not mention the towns and villages by the west from the sea...likewise laid waste for profit of cattle."[83]

A number of oft-quoted examples of depopulating enclosure in the East March at first sight seem to support Brown's contention. Sometime before 1584, 12 tenements at Outchester and 14 at Hetton were converted from arable to pasture.[84] Eight tenements on royal land in East Newbiggin and Howtel were converted after the Rising of the Northern Earls when at least two of the under-tenants found themselves on the losing side. But it should be noted that before the end of the sixteenth century some of the land at Howtel had been returned to arable.[85] Sometime before 1593 Ralph Gray of Chillingham converted Elwick and the 15 tenements at Ross to pasture.[86] And according to "the reporte of the inhabitants thereabouts" tempo James I, Sir Thomas Gray of Chillingham (d. 1590) expelled "seaventene score men, women, and children, all upon one day" from Newham, near Bamburgh.[87] Another well-known example of depopulating enclosure occurred, this time in the Middle March, when Sir Robert Delaval displaced customary tenants from the common field villages of Hartley and Seaton Delaval, near Newcastle. But when an historian recently used this example to demonstrate the "way in which the family farmers here were rudely swept into great industrial centres" he neglected to mention that of the 15 tenants at Hartley, six were given new holdings in Seaton Delaval and five got cottages in Hartley.[88] Moreover it was well known locally that Joshua Delaval of Rivers Green, the man who brought these enclosures to the attention of the central authorities around 1596, was at odds with Sir Robert Delaval, his wealthy kinsman.[89] This would suggest that Joshua's report should be regarded with caution.

In 1596 royal commissioners presented the Privy Council with the results of a detailed survey of the causes of the decay of the border service since 1567/8. This report should have laid to rest the myth that depopulating enclosure *per se* had seriously weakened northern defences. Only 7 per cent of the decays in the East March and 8 per cent of those in the Middle March could be attributed to the conversion of arable land to pasture. However the commissioners did find that some landlords had so impoverished their tenants by increasing fines, rents and services that they could no longer perform border service. This was the cause of 45 per cent of the decays in the East March and 65 per cent of those in the Middle March. As we have already seen, Scottish raids were responsible for the remaining decayed tenancies.[90]

The socially disruptive consequences of depopulating enclosure were discussed at great length in Parliament in 1597. Following several bad harvests, there were serious food shortages in many parts of England. Local stores were exhausted in the inland parts of Northumberland and Cumberland and people were compelled to travel to Newcastle to buy grain shipped in from southern England and the Continent. Early in July Henry Sanderson, keeper of the prison for recusants at Brancepeth, County Durham, warned Sir Robert Cecil that many of the people flocking into plague-stricken Newcastle had not eaten bread for 20 days and that the town's grain supplies were running dangerously low. Rye was selling for 96s. a quarter; in 1591 it had sold for 16s. and in 1596 for 24s. a quarter. This crisis was temporarily relieved on 8 July when three Dutch grain ships braved the plague and came into Newcastle harbour.[91]

William James, the recently appointed dean of Durham Cathedral and former dean of Christ Church Oxford, believed that the appalling food shortage had been caused by depopulating enclosures which he assumed were as widespread in Northumberland as they were in Oxfordshire.[92] Early in 1597, in a frequently-quoted diatribe, the dean argued that:

the decay of fallow and dispeopling of villages offends almighty God...
dishonours the prince...weakens the commonwealth...oppresses the
poor, burdens the neighbours adjoining, hazarded and endangered often
times for want of good neighbours...and is even against the laws of nature
as heathen philosophers have taught...what waste and want is hereby crept
into Northumberland, Westmorland and Cumberland, many of them coming
this last year from Carlisle to Durham, three-score long miles to buy bread,
where through this canker and ill-neighbourhood in sundry places for
twenty miles' space there is no inhabitant.[93]

Such testimonials were welcomed and possibly solicited by Sir Robert Cecil
and Sir Francis Bacon at a time when they were attempting to persuade
Parliament to include Northumberland within the provision of an anti-
enclosure bill. On this occasion they prevailed.[94]

But in 1601, after Parliament reviewed the anti-enclosure statutes, it decided
not to include Northumberland in a new bill directed against enclosures.[95]
This decision was fully in accord with progressive ideas about the economic
benefits of specialization for the market. As Sir Walter Ralegh reminded the
House during debates on the bill, the Dutch grew no corn at all, yet by
producing a great surplus of goods for export they could afford to buy foreign
grain on advantageous terms: "And therefore I think the best course is to set
it [the market in grain] at liberty, and leave every man free, which is the
desire of a true English man." Ralegh noted that, at a time when the law
compelled people to cultivate arable land, "many poor men are not able to
find seed to sow so much as they are bound to plough, which they must do, or
incur the penalty of the law."[96] William Selby, Member of Parliament for
Northumberland and the son of one of the wealthiest coal merchants in
Newcastle, enlarged upon Ralegh's arguments. He contended that it was
senseless to prevent landlords from enclosing their land if they wished.
Northumberland "was so nigh Scotland, and their Country was so infected
with the Plague, that not only whole Families, but even whole Villages, have
been swept away with that calamity". Selby reasoned that it was better that
land in Northumberland be used for sheep than be left utterly deserted.[97]
Parliament agreed.

The inventories of large farmers who had estates in several parts of
Northumberland show that some specialization had begun to take place. In
1581 Lady Isabel Gray's estates at Fenton and Doddington, east of the River
Till, were used primarily for arable cultivation; the cereals grown on the two
estates were valued at £90. Livestock was clearly of most importance on the
Gray lands at Ogle in the upper Blyth valley. On this estate there were 47
milch cows, 28 calves, 40 young heifers and oxen as well as 450 sheep. The
Gray lands at Yeavering, near the buried ruins of the old Saxon palace, were
used primarily for fattening sheep and cattle.[98] Similarly Robert Widdrington

of Plessey, the absentee sheriff of Northumberland in 1595, used his lands at Plessey and Cowpen mainly for fattening cattle for the market.[99]

Many Northumberland farmers produced considerable quantities of wool, although they did not necessarily specialize in sheep to the exclusion of other livestock. But the London-based Company of Merchant Adventurers, which had a monopoly of the sale and export of all wools, considered Northumberland wool to be of too inferior a quality for them to include within their monopoly.[100] In consequence, Northumberland sheep farmers were free to sell their wool to whomever they could persuade to buy it. Not infrequently the customer was a Scottish trader.[101]

In addition to wool, merchants from Scotland purchased considerable quantities of grain from Northumberland. In 1593, a year when that commodity was in critically short supply in the county, the aldermen and mayor of Berwick complained to Lord Burghley that some profit-minded local gentlemen, including Forster the lord warden, were busily selling grain to Scottish traders.[102] Yet even in normal years, local farmers in the East March apparently did not produce enough surplus to provision the families of the 2,000 soldiers garrisoned in Berwick. Grain, peas and beans were brought into the town by government contractors from ports in Norfolk and further south.[103]

Berwick was one of only seven regular markets in Northumberland. The others were held at Alnwick, Morpeth, Wooler, Bellingham, Haltwhistle and Hexham.[104] Until 1603 Bywell, a town on the middle Tyne half-way between Hexham and Newcastle, "built in length all in one street", was also something of a trading centre. In 1570 surveyors described its inhabitants as "craftsmen whose trade is all in iron work for the horsemen and borderers of that country as in making bits, stirrups, buckles and such other wherein they are very expert and cunning".[105]

A centre of far greater commercial importance than any in Northumberland proper was Newcastle upon Tyne. The third or fourth largest town in England, Newcastle owed its great wealth to its position as the trading capital of the North, as an international port and as the centre of the flourishing coal trade. The fortunes of the coal trade became closely linked with those of the Newcastle Hostmen's Company after Alderman William Selby (d. 1613) and Henry Anderson (1545–1605) negotiated the purchase of the Grand Lease on behalf of the Company in the 1580s. The Lease gave the Hostmen access to a great supply of easily-won coal in the manors of Whickham and Gateshead in County Durham. In 1600, after acquiring control over several mines on the Northumberland side of the Tyne as well as additional mines in County Durham, the Hostmen achieved a second notable success: the Crown granted them a monopoly of the sale of all coals shipped from Tyneside port facilities.[106]

Several small operators attempted to circumvent the Hostmen's monopoly by shipping coals from the little ports of Amble, Blyth and Whitley on the

Northumberland coast. When this trade was at its peak in the early seventeenth century, almost 2,000 tons of coal were shipped from these ports annually. Though this was only about 1 per cent of the tonnage which the Hostmen shipped from Newcastle,[107] some people thought that fortunes could be made from coal mines which were not controlled by the Hostmen. In 1604 surveyors of the royal manors of Harbottle and Wark scornfully noted that the locals were so well supplied with turf and peat that they made no effort to mine the coal in their areas; yet if Redesdale and North Tynedale "were inhabited by industrious men of Trade, the mynes would bee of great value".[108] During this period some owners of mines in Ord, Kyloe, Unthank and Murton in North Durham strove to increase their production so that they could accumulate sufficient capital to develop the harbour facilities at Berwick. However, the Berwick coal trade collapsed during the troubled 1620s when even the Newcastle Hostmen sometimes found it difficult to vend their coals as profitably as before.[109]

The Hostmen had several advantages over their small competitors in addition to their all-important monopoly. Because they operated more than 20 mines, some of very considerable size, they could use the profits from all of them to defray the costs of docks and other facilities along the Tyne. Most small operators did not have sufficient capital or credit to withstand delays in return on investment in mining or trade. The coals were shipped during the summer months and sold to London householders in the winter. Thus it might be six months or more before financial returns reached the coal producer.[110] Neither could small producers afford to outbid the Company in the hiring of mining experts or raise the money to buy the pumps and other equipment necessary to win coals from deep pits. Then too, many of the small mines run by Northumberland gentlemen were too far from the coast or any navigable river to be exploited profitably. As Lawrence Stone has shown, the movement of coal three miles by land might increase its cost by 60 per cent.[111] The same point was made in 1622 when it was noted that "The mannor of Hexam lyith so far in the land from all vent by sea, or water, or in anie other kinde, saving to a small companie of poore villages, that coales being gotten, theare can be no great proffit expected."[112]

Even the ninth earl of Northumberland, the largest and wealthiest private owner of coal fields in the county, recognized the futility of trying to compete with the Hostmen. Potentially one of the most productive coal-producing areas under the earl's control was the manor of Newburn, located a few miles west of Newcastle. From 1589 to 1616 the earl had leased his Newburn mines to various members of the Hostmen's Company. Then, after falling out with a lessee, the earl decided to run his mines without reference to the Company. He entrusted several of those in Newburn to two of his principal estate agents, George Whitehead and Thomas Fotherley. The Hostmen promptly retaliated. In 1617 Whitehead wrote "I fynd all the Newcastle men very loathe that your

Lo: should come in amonge them, and therefore noe trust to be reposed in anie of them."[113] The earl was also encountering problems with flooded mines. As a result of all this, in 1617 he lost more than £620 in the Newburn enterprise. Two years later he capitulated and agreed that two Hostmen should sell his coal on his behalf. Later the earl leased the mines outright to members of the Company.[114] Comparable experience with mines in Tynemouthshire strengthened Earl Percy's conviction that coal mining and related industrial pursuits were "not the road to great riches" for any aristocrat.[115] Neither were they for the country squire who lived at Seaton Delaval.

In order to avoid difficulties with the Hostmen, in the 1590s Sir Robert Delaval used the coal he mined at Hartley, on the coast four miles north of Tynemouth, for the production of crude salt. At best this was a precarious business. Six tons of coal were required to extract one ton of salt from sea water as it was necessary to keep the salt pans at white-heat for three and a half days.[116] Subjected to such harsh usage, salt pans – and the value of Delaval's capital investment – rapidly deteriorated. In 1592 he complained to Lord Treasurer Burghley: "I have to pay a great rent [for the pans leased from the Crown] for so it is my good lord I have found out it is a dead rent, and repairs within three or four years last past cost four hundred pounds more and by reason of the said privileges I cannot vent my salt but at ten shillings in every wey loss."[117] The privilege to which Sir Robert referred was the monopoly in salt which Queen Elizabeth had granted to Sir Thomas Wilkes, founder of the lucrative salt industry at South Shields in County Durham.[118] Within the limits set by Wilkes's monopoly a private operator like Delaval had to try to sell his salt as best he could.

In this he was not altogether unsuccessful. While he was in London in 1600 Sir Robert sent his son Ralph instructions to dispose of the salt stored at Blyth. Apparently the Delavals chartered two small trading vessels to bring their supply to Yarmouth where it would be used for curing herring. A later letter suggests that Sir Robert worried lest the master of the ships cheat him of the profits: "They have both the salt and the money, yet I hope well of them." Eventually the master paid the Delavals for the cargoes he had carried, at least in part. Sir Robert reported that the master had sent him a hogshead of claret worth £30 but only £17 in hard cash. Yet Sir Robert remained optimistic that in time he would receive the full value of the cargoes and suggested to Ralph that they might profitably hire another ship to bring the salt to London where it was selling for 50s. a wey.[119] But a short time later Sir Robert's right to use the port at Blyth was effectively challenged by Thomas Cramlington. By 1605 the Delavals had almost given up attempting to produce or market salt. Soon after Sir Robert's death in 1607, Ralph found that the coal mines at Hartley, so necessary for the continued production of salt, were "drowned and no hope of recovery".[120]

Sir Robert's cousin, Peter Delaval of London and Tynemouth, a man who dabbled in trading ventures of all kinds, was no more successful in his attempts to profit from trade in salt and coal. Together with Ambrose Dudley, a member of a prominent Newcastle family, Peter obtained a royal lease to salt pans and coal mines at Bebside and Cowpen in 1595. But within two years Delaval, by then in partnership with his brothers Ralph and Clement, was in conflict with the freeholders of Cowpen about rights to mine coal in the common fields. Exhausted by pursuing his claims in the courts, in 1602 Peter Delaval retired from the Cowpen enterprise and for £360 handed over his lease to Sir Robert Delaval. Sir Robert in turn assigned it to Sir John Ashburnham, the Sussex ironmaster, and Huntingdon Beaumont of Nottingham. In time these men ran into serious difficulties with the monopolistic Hostmen. Although there were said to be 54 small coal pits in Cowpen in 1599, reports made in 1607 and 1621 show that the works were entirely deserted.[121]

The only Northumberland gentleman who managed to profit from coal mining, despite or perhaps because of the Newcastle Hostmen's Company, was Anthony Errington. In 1602 Anthony and his cousin Roger leased the mines at Denton for 21 years, paying £10 annually for any new pit they dug. In 1610 the Erringtons were engaged in a dispute with the ninth earl of Northumberland about rights to dig coal in Sugley Common. The Erringtons claimed that this land was part of Denton, whereas the earl claimed it as part of his manor of Newburn; the suit apparently went in favour of the Erringtons.[122] By 1622 Anthony was deriving most of his income from coal. In that year he built a new mansion-house overlooking his mines at Denton.[123] But in his building activities, as in his mining enterprises, Errington was quite untypical of the Northumberland gentry as a whole.

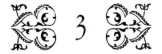

The social hierarchy

By 1586, if not by 1569 or even earlier, the resident landed gentry of Northumberland had become the acknowledged leaders of local society. As was the case in other northern counties, the emergence of the gentry was a consequence of the Crown's deliberate policy of curtailing and in some cases destroying the territorial influence of the old aristocracy. As echoes of this long-drawn-out contest might still be heard in the period with which we are most directly concerned, it would be well for us to examine it briefly.

Until the middle years of the reign of Henry VIII, the Percy earls of Northumberland had dominated the affairs of their titular county. Elsewhere in the North, the Percy influence had only been matched by the Neville earls of Westmorland and by a combination of lesser aristocratic families such as the Cliffords and the Dacres. In the fourteenth century the position of the leaders of northern aristocratic families had been considerably strengthened when the Crown began to indenture them as wardens to defend the Marches against Scotland. A Percy was warden of a march in Northumberland for almost 60 of the years between 1377 and 1485. In the West March this record was nearly equalled by the Nevilles.[1] Such conditions favoured the development of what might be called regional communities.

According to this medieval concept, of which faint traces remained in the late sixteenth century, the Percy earls and their tenants in Yorkshire, Cumberland and in the baronies of Alnwick, Prudhoe, Langley and elsewhere in Northumberland were tied to each other by bonds of mutual obligation and responsibility. Leading tenants might serve as deputy military commanders, hold their estates from the Percys in fee by knight's service and attend the annual knight's court at Alnwick Castle. Such tenants, also known as mesne tenants, might serve the Percys as estate or household agents. Like that of earlier kings, the household maintained by the peripatetic earls was the centre of a vast administrative network. Through it the earls exercised their obligations of good-lordship, sheltering their tenants and followers from adversity and protecting them from their enemies. Percy tenants willingly accepted the paternalism of successive earls and looked upon them as the natural and accustomed rulers of the North.[2]

Such ideas came into conflict with those held by King Edward IV and his grandson Henry VIII. These sovereigns believed that the Crown should assert its influence in border and wardenry affairs directly rather than working through intermediaries. To this end Henry's great minister, Cardinal Wolsey, built up a substantial following for the Crown among Northumbrian squires who had formerly served the house of Percy. One of the first gentlemen to take advantage of Wolsey's overtures was Thomas Forster of Adderstone (d. 1526) who was rewarded with the marshalship of Berwick. Another was Reynold Carnaby of Halton (d. 1543), the treacherous squire who persuaded the weak-willed sixth earl of Northumberland (d. 1537) to surrender his estates to the Crown; the Percy inheritance remained in royal hands until the late 1540s.[3] Other Percy families who joined Wolsey's Court party were the Widdringtons of Widdrington and the Grays of Chillingham. After the cardinal's fall in 1530, Thomas Cromwell, Sir Ralph Sadler, William Cecil and other privy councillors continued to nurture Court parties in Northumberland and elsewhere in the North.[4]

In 1544, two years after English forces led by Thomas Wharton, a Westmorland squire, had decisively defeated King James V of Scotland at the Battle of Solway Moss, Henry VIII decided that it was now appropriate to give the wardenships, so long a prerogative of the old aristocracy and princes of the blood, to leading members of these northern Court parties. Accordingly, Wharton was ennobled and given the West March. Another of the new men, Sir William Eure, a Yorkshireman who held only a few small estates in Northumberland, was made a baron and given the East March.[5]

Henry VIII's policies were carried to their logical conclusion by his daughter, Queen Elizabeth. In part because she deliberately excluded them from positions of trust along the border, the earls of Northumberland and Westmorland broke out in open revolt late in 1569. Almost immediately Lord Hunsdon, a near relation of the queen who had recently been appointed warden of the East March, warned the central authorities that the situation could become extremely serious; northerners knew no prince but a Percy.[6] But the course of events proved Hunsdon wrong. For in Northumberland at any rate, the old cry 'A Percy, a Percy' no longer evoked what Lawrence Stone has termed "a Pavlovian response of unthinking loyalty among the gentry and peasantry".[7]

Only ten Northumberland gentlemen were later indicted for rebellion and conspiracy. Seven of them were either younger sons or members of cadet gentry families. Such men probably had little hope of ever exercising political power in their own right. The three remaining rebel squires were only slightly more prominent. They were Tristram Fenwick of Brinkburn (whose lands were subsequently sold for £760), Thomas Bates of Morpeth and John Carnaby of Langley. Bates had been a Member of Parliament for Morpeth in 1554 and 1559. At the time of the Rebellion he was chief steward for the Percys in the barony of Alnwick. After three years' imprisonment in the Tower he served as the eighth earl's feodary and died in 1587 at the Percy castle at Prudhoe. John Carnaby, ironically, was a nephew of Sir Reynold Carnaby, the leader of the Court party in the 1530s and early 1540s. John was still living at Langley when heralds visited the county in 1615.[8]

The common people were no more eager to join the rebellious earls than were most of the local gentry. Lord President Huntingdon (who was less given to rash generalizations than was Lord Hunsdon) later estimated that only 80 or 100 horsemen had followed the Percy banner out of Northumberland to join the main rebel force in County Durham. Huntingdon thought that only about 60 horsemen from the Neville baronies of Bywell and Bulbeck had come out in support of the Earl of Westmorland.[9]

The chief result of the Rebellion was to diminish the already weakened influence of the old aristocracy in the North. The rebel earls had sought refuge with Mary Stuart's supporters in Scotland after they had realized that their forces were no match for the government's. The Earl of Westmorland later fled to the Continent. He was tried *in absentia* and his lands were forfeit to the Crown.[10] The Earl of Northumberland was betrayed into the hands of the Scottish government by Hector Armstrong of Harelaw on Christmas Eve 1569, attainted *in absentia* in 1571, sold to the English and brought down to York for execution in 1572.[11]

The seventh earl's fall weakened but did not destroy the house of Percy for his brother and eventual heir, Sir Henry Percy (1532–85), had carefully nurtured the friendship of Sir William Cecil and the Protestant connection at Court.[12] Sir Henry remained loyal to the ruling dynasty in 1569 even though Sir Ralph Sadler suspected him of double dealing. Then in 1571 Sadler convinced his fellow privy councillors that Percy was connected with the Ridolfi plotters. As this could not be proved, Sir Henry was imprisoned in the Tower on the pretext that he had neglected to perform his proper duties as captain of Tynemouth Castle. After his release in 1573 he was given the livery of the Percy lands in Northumberland and in 1576 he took his seat in the House of Lords as the eighth earl of Northumberland. But as a precaution against further treachery, the earl was warned never to return to his northern estates. Henceforth he lived at Petworth in Sussex. In 1584 Earl Percy was accused of complicity in the Throckmorton Plot and was again imprisoned in the Tower. He died on the night of 20–21 July 1585. Some men thought that he had committed suicide; others that he had been murdered.[13]

The eighth earl was succeeded in his titles and estates by his son Henry (d. 1632). The ninth earl was an urbane but rather naive man who never resided in Northumberland after he came into his inheritance. As he had virtually no interest in the county's political affairs, he allowed the Earl's Council, which had consisted of all the Northumberland gentry associated with the Percys, to fall into abeyance. By the late 1580s the Percy interest in Northumberland consisted of little more than estate agents and bailiffs.[14]

The disposition of another northern aristocratic inheritance which, like the Percy lands, fell to the Crown in 1569/70, was bitterly disputed by rival claimants for many years. The lands in question were those formerly held by the Dacres of the North: the barony of Morpeth in Northumberland, the lordships of Greystokes and Gilsland in Cumberland as well as lands in County Durham and Yorkshire. In May 1569 young George, the last Lord Dacre, had fallen to his death from his wooden rocking-horse. Shortly thereafter Leonard Dacre, the boy's hunchback uncle, claimed the Dacre inheritance. This claim was disputed by Thomas, fourth duke of Norfolk, the head of one of the greatest aristocratic families in the realm. Norfolk had married as his third wife George Dacre's widowed mother. He was also the guardian of the boy's three sisters and possible co-heiresses. By arranging marriage alliances between the three Dacre sisters and his own sons, Philip, Thomas and William, Norfolk thought to establish the Howards as a major territorial influence in the North.[15] This goal had also been pursued, but with no success, by the second and third dukes of Norfolk, the fourth duke's great-grandfather and grandfather.[16]

Even though the fourth duke had recently been involved in a wild scheme to free the imprisoned queen, Mary Stuart, and to make her his fourth wife, Leonard Dacre feared that Queen Elizabeth might grant Howard the Dacre lands. Throwing caution to the winds, Dacre decided to defend his own claims by force of arms. He defiantly established himself at the Dacres' old seat at Naworth Castle just west of the Northumberland border. But as Thomas Wharton had asserted more than 30 years earlier, the day was past when a Dacre could successfully defy the central authorities.[17] After Leonard Dacre was defeated by a force led by Lord Hunsdon on 20 February 1570, he fled to Scotland and later to Flanders. After his death in 1573, his claims were pressed by his brother Francis.

Subsequently there were several potentially dangerous confrontations between Francis Dacre and Howard partisans in Northumberland. For instance, in April 1587 when the burgesses of Morpeth were preparing to pay suit to a court held by Dacre, they learned that Lord William Howard's constable, Edward Gray, had entered the town accompanied by Sir John Forster, the lord warden, and a large troop of armed gentlemen and borderers. Rather than be the cause of bloodshed, Dacre and his little party slipped quietly away.[18] Several more years would elapse before Queen Elizabeth finally decided upon the disposition of these disputed lands.

As a result of the dramatic changes which had taken place since 1569, there was only one resident aristocrat in all of Northumberland in 1586: Cuthbert, seventh lord Ogle of Bothal. After Ogle died without male heirs in 1597, his son-in-law Edward Talbot, the third son of the sixth earl of Shrewsbury, took up residence in Bothal Castle. Talbot was the *custos rotulorum* of Northumberland from 1603 until his death in 1618. But during most of his long career he was not a peer of the realm for he did not succeed to the earldom until 1616.[19] All of the other aristocrats who held land in Northumberland between the years 1586 and 1625 maintained their principal seats elsewhere in England and only fleetingly visited their Northumbrian estates when they happened to be there on other business. Three of these aristocrats were Crown servants; Henry Lord Hunsdon, warden of the East March and governor of Berwick, Ralph Lord Eure, son and heir of one of the English treaty commissioners at Berwick in 1586, and George Home, Earl of Dunbar, after 1603 one of King James's principal advisers on border affairs. Other absentee aristocratic landowners were Dunbar's son-in-law, Theophilus Lord Walden and Lord Walden's uncle, Lord William Howard.

In the absence of a resident aristocracy, men of gentry status were of necessity the leaders of local society. It thus behoves us to examine in some detail the composition of the gentry class and the wealth, marriage and office-holding patterns of its members. Our first concern is to determine which Northumbrians should be classified as gentry. In 1587 William Harrison, an acknowledged expert on such matters, asserted that a gentleman was one who lived without manual labour, bore the "port, charge and countenance of a gentleman" and, most important of all, had had arms bestowed upon him by heralds.[20] In 1575 and again in 1615 heralds from the College of Arms visited Northumberland. Unfortunately the returns from the earlier visitation are so incomplete – only 11 families are listed – that the 1615 visitation must form the basis for our analysis.[21] However, the ranks of the gentry appear to have remained relatively stable during this 40-year period.[22]

The list of gentlemen visited in 1615 by Richard St George, Norroy King of Arms, has been supplemented by information derived from lists of sheriffs, commissions of the peace and similar sources.[23] These additions have been necessary because a number of substantial resident landholders, such as Thomas Carr of Ford, were not recorded in this visitation. We must also take into account the fact that this visitation did not extend to North Durham and thus excluded four armigerous families which lived within the geographical area of our study. These families were the Ordes of Ord, the Haggarstons of Haggarston, the Swinhoes of Goswick and the Selbys of Twizel.[24] In all, the list of armigerous families compiled by the herald has been supplemented by four families from North Durham and five from Northumberland. It should also be noted that we have counted as separate units the younger brothers of the heads of prominent armigerous families when such men had adult sons in 1615.[25] For this reason Sir Ralph Gray of Chillingham and his brother, Edward of Morpeth (Lord William Howard's constable in 1587), are listed as heads of separate families. So too are the three sons of Sir John Selby of Twizel (*d.* 1595). In three instances we have included brothers with younger families as both brothers played a prominent part in county affairs and had separate residences. These gentlemen were Sir Henry Widdrington and Roger of Cartington, Sir Ralph Delaval of Seaton Delaval and Sir John of Dissington and the half-brothers, Sir John Fenwick of Wallington and Sir William of Meldon. This gives us a grand total of 89 gentry families in 1615. This was a remarkably small class; one gentle family for approximately 900 inhabitants. In Yorkshire the ratio was about 1 to 400.

For several reasons we have not included in our total the 23 armigerous Newcastle families which the Norroy King of Arms recorded in 1615. This was in line with contemporary practice. In 1607, for instance, officials surveying the religious sympathies of the principal families of Northumberland confined their attention to the county gentry.[26] William Gray made a similar distinction between county and town gentry in 1649 when writing his history of Newcastle.[27] Members of the Newcastle oligarchy were very conscious of their separateness and successfully prevented any Northumberland family or group of families from exercising any considerable influence in the affairs of the town[28] or, as we have seen, from winning any substantial profits from the coal trade between Newcastle and the capital. Indeed, compared to the situation in York and in other great provincial towns, leading Newcastle merchants had very few social contacts with the county gentry. Only two of the 19 wives of the armigerous Newcastle gentlemen about whom information is available (including two second wives) came from Northumberland. Similarly, only three heads of Northumberland gentry families took their wives from Newcastle and of these only one, John Clavering of Callaly, married the daughter of a Newcastle gentleman of any great prominence, Thomas Riddell. In a few instances sisters of the heads of Northumberland families did marry into prominent Newcastle families. The most noteworthy example was Margaret Selby, daughter of Sir John of Twizel in Norhamshire. Margaret married Sir George Selby, a gentleman who does not appear to have been related to her. Sir George was the eldest son of William Selby, one of the two Hostmen who had contracted the Grand Lease on behalf of the Company. It might be noted that the other lessee, Henry Anderson, had taken as his second wife Fortuna, daughter of Sir Cuthbert Collingwood. Their son, Henry Anderson, played a prominent role in Northumberland politics during the Jacobean period but as there is no record that he held lands of any consequence in Northumberland or resided in the county, he is not counted as a Northumbrian gentleman. Nor was he so accounted by his contemporaries.[29]

In the late 1590s wardenry officials sometimes complained that gentlemen who ought to maintain sizeable households and full stables for the defence of the border were deserting Northumberland.[30] However, surviving evidence suggests that between the years 1586 and 1615 only one gentle family permanently left the county. This was the Raymes family of Aydon and Shortflatt headed in 1586 by Robert Raymes esquire (*d.* 1600). Robert had been entrusted with the shrievalty of Northumberland during the final months of 1569 when the earls were in rebellion. In 1604 his grandson, Henry of Witton-le-Wear, County Durham, sold his share of Aydon. Seven years later Henry sold his manors of Shortflatt and Bolam to Sir William Selby.[31]

This Sir William Selby, a vocal member of the Parliament of 1601, was the head of one of the three families which according to the criteria of landownership, residence, office-holding and social status, entered the ranks of the Northumberland gentry between 1586 and 1615. Selby, the second son of the Newcastle Hostman, Sir William Selby, was knighted in 1613 and served on the local commission of the peace after 1 July 1615.[32] The second recent arrival among the Northumberland gentry was Robert Brandling (1574–1636) of the family of that name from Newcastle and Felling, County Durham. Brandling purchased Newminster Abbey, near Morpeth, in 1609 and before 1615, when his second son was recorded as being admitted to Middle Temple, he purchased Alnwick Abbey. Brandling was sheriff in 1617–18 and in 1630–1, having refused to serve in 1628. This turbulent squire was M. P. for Morpeth in 1620.[33] The Charltons, descendants of the North Tynedale surname leaders, were the third family to achieve gentry status during this period. On his death in 1613 Edward Charlton J. P. was succeeded by his nephew, the recusant William.[34]

Until 1611, when King James I began to sell baronetcies to men with incomes of over £1,000 a year, there were three recognizable social gradations within the Northumberland gentry, knights, esquires and gentlemen. Eleven heads of families who were flourishing in 1586 were knights or would become knights when James, who was less sparing of honours than was Queen Elizabeth, passed through the county on his triumphant passage south in 1603. Fifteen of the 89 heads of families flourishing in 1615 were knighted. Two of their number, Sir John Fenwick of Wallington and Sir Claudius Forster of Bamburgh, later purchased baronetcies. Two gentlemen not of knightly status also purchased baronetcies; Francis Radcliffe of Dilston in 1620, and Henry Haggarston in 1643.[35] Some solid country gentlemen were much offended with this buying of honours. In 1621 Sir Henry Widdrington, Member of Parliament for Northumberland, told the House that "it grieved him to see skipjacks prank before men whose ancestors have gained a place in the commonwealth and by blood, and that not only before me but before all my posterity. And their patents recite the sums they give."[36] Widdrington's fellow knight of the shire was Sir Willam Gray, baronet, eldest son of Widdrington's long-time rival, Sir Ralph Gray of Chillingham.

Heirs male of knights and baronets were termed esquire. This style was also used by armigerous non-knightly heads of ancient families who had appreciably more wealth than most of their fellow gentry. By courtesy it was also given to gentlemen of more modest means as long as they continued in office as a sheriff or justice of the peace. The rank of esquire was the highest ever achieved by the heads of 32 Northumberland families flourishing in 1615. The 40 remaining men were simply termed gentlemen.

There was a close relationship between the rank of a Northumberland gentleman and his annual income. Some impression of a landed proprietor's wealth might be gained from his will and the inventory of his possessions which was drawn up after his death. A more reliable source would be his estate and household accounts and his personal papers. Unfortunately few papers of this sort survive for gentlemen heading families either in 1586 or in 1615.[37] However, official sources, which became increasingly prolific after the turn of the century, can be used. These include recusancy rolls, inquisitions post mortem and, if the deceased landowner held lands from the Crown by knight's service, surveys taken by feodaries from the Court of Wards and Liveries. After Sir Robert Cecil became master of this court in 1599, the appraised values set down by the feodaries more closely resembled market values than they had under his immediate predecessors.[38] For North Durham, another important set of sources are the distraint of knighthood records. These purport to give the annual value of the lands of those substantial gentlemen who failed to take up knighthood at the coronation of Charles I in 1625. From them we learn, for instance, that Thomas Haggarston of Haggarston had lands in North Durham worth £450 a year and that Henry Gray of Kyloe, the brother of the Thomas Gray flourishing in 1615, had lands worth £120.[39] Generally the amount which a gentleman was assessed for his distraint of knighthood payment was directly related to his subsidy payment.

The subsidy rolls kept among the records of the Exchequer contain no entries for Northumberland earlier than 1610, when landowners in the northern counties finally lost their exemption from payment.[40] Unfortunately the book of rates which laid down the amount which landholders in Northumberland proper would be assessed for a parliamentary subsidy or distraint of knighthood payment, was compiled long before the union of the Crowns and took no account of inflation or of changes in the value of land.[41] In 1637 Sheriff Sir William Widdrington asserted that fertile lands near the border which had been of little worth while they were threatened by Scottish marauders in the years before 1603, were now extremely profitable, yet they were still rated at the old value. Widdrington also reported that demesne lands were generally rated very low, while townships held by customary tenants or leaseholders were rated high.[42]

Inequalities similar to those about which Sir William complained were reflected in Northumberland subsidy assessments dating from the middle years of James's reign. In the first surviving subsidy list, the average amount, £2 17s. 1d., paid by men in Tynedale ward who were not of gentry status was more than the average of £2 13s. paid by the armigerous gentlemen. The same situation prevailed in Coquetdale ward where Sir William Widdrington's prosperous uncle, Roger of Cartington, and his great-uncle, Sir Ephraim Widdrington, were both assessed only £1 1s. 4d.[43] Such figures obviously reflect a lack of correlation between the status of a gentleman and his financial resources, and suggest favouritism on the part of tax assessors. But despite these irregularities, subsidy assessments do provide at least a rough guide to the landed income of many of the 89 heads of gentry households flourishing in 1615.

In his study of the Yorkshire gentry J. T. Cliffe considers that men assessed £20 at a subsidy generally had an annual landed income of £1,000 or more Those assessed at £10 had an income of around £500 while few gentlemen who were assessed at £1 or £2 had an income of over £100 a year.[44] Thomas Wilson had some instructive things to say about the relationship between wealth and social status. In his *State of England Anno Domini 1600* he concluded that knights generally had landed incomes of between £1,000 and £2,000 a year and that esquires had incomes of between £500 and £1,000. Wilson went on to say that: "Especially about London and the Countyes adoiyning, where their landes are sett to the highest, he is not counted of any great reckning unless he be betwixt 1,000 marks or £1,000, but Northward and farr off a gentleman of good reputacion may be content with 300 and 400 yerly".[45]

Northward and far off Northumberland certainly was. Using Wilson as our guide, but taking into account inflation between 1600 and 1615, we may perhaps use his last mentioned figure, £400, as a rough dividing line between men of good reputation and those of lesser worth. For purposes of further analysis it is convenient to divide the gentry into four categories; those with landed incomes of less than £100 a year, those with incomes of between £100 and £400, those with incomes of between £400 and £1,000 and those with over £1,000 a year. The 89 families can thus be classified as follows:

income over £1,000 (principal gentry)	7 families	8%
income £400–£1,000 (middling gentry)	18 families	20%
income £100–£400	28 families	32%
income under £100	36 families	40%

Unless they happened to be convicted recusants who were barred from exercising public office by the terms of the statute of 3 & 4 James I, c. 5, gentlemen with annual incomes in excess of £1,000 could expect to be members of their county's commission of the peace and to serve at least one year's term as high sheriff. This was the case with the heads of the seven principal families in Northumberland. Except for the recusant Francis Radcliffe of Dilston, they all held local office and one of them, Sir Ralph Delaval of Seaton Delaval, was almost constantly engaged in county business. He was three times sheriff of Northumberland, an active member of the commission of the peace and *custos rotulorum*, a border commissioner and a commissioner of oyer and terminer, one of the ecclesiastical commissioners for the diocese of Durham and a deputy lieutenant.[46]

Gentry of middling status, those with annual incomes of between £400 and £1,000, were also normally expected to accept responsible positions in local government. But as it happened, seven of the 18 heads of middling gentry families in 1615 served neither as sheriffs nor as justices of the peace. Three of these gentlemen were clearly excluded because they were recusants. Another of the non-office holders, William Ridley of Willimontswick in South Tyne- dale, headed an ancient and honourable family which was apparently in financial difficulties. In 1587 Warden Hunsdon charged William's father (*d.* 1599) with the heinous March Treason of bringing Scottish raiders into the town of Haydon Bridge.[47] In 1607 it was noted that Mr Ridley was "not yet out of his wardship" and that the rest of the Ridleys were "men of meane estate".[48] In 1614 the Crown required Ridley to surrender his lease to the manor and castle of Wark so that these properties could be regranted to the Waldens.[49] The Ridley family was not represented on the county's commission of the peace until 1620. In April of that year William's first cousin, Cuthbert Ridley M.A., since 1604 rector of Simonburn in North Tynedale, was joined to the commission.[50]

Three of the middling gentry who were never granted commissions of the peace were made to serve as high sheriffs of Northumberland: Matthew Forster of Adderstone, Edward Gray and Robert Brandling. In the best of times gentlemen shunned this office for it was costly and time consuming. Sheriffs were expected to entertain judges of assize and other visiting digni- taries virtually at their own expense, serve writs from the common law courts in London, collect monies owing the Crown and see that they were paid into the Exchequer. Although under-sheriffs might perform some of these duties, the sheriffs were financially liable for any shortages.[51] However, northern gentlemen were not ruled solely by financial considerations. Sir Henry Widdrington, sheriff in 1606, Sir Henry Anderson of Newcastle, sheriff in 1615–16, and one or two others were well aware that the sheriff was in a particularly good position either to protect his own followers or to destroy those of his rivals. The sheriff had considerable influence in choosing the petty jurors who served at sessions of gaol delivery when men were on trial for their lives. He also chose the time to serve writs and to distrain property for debt. In other matters which might be of vital concern to recusants or to the harried inhabitants of Redesdale and North Tynedale, the sheriff could use his own discretion.

Until the dissolution of the wardenries in 1603, Northumberland sheriffs were required to accept search warrants for persons wanted by a warden and to bring them to the latter's residence. As the warden of the Middle March was often the same person as the *custos rotulorum*, the shrievalty must have been a most unattractive position for any gentleman who was not on good terms with the warden.[52] Thus it may not have been coincidental that several of the sheriffs whom the Crown appointed in the 1580s were near relations to Sir John Forster. William Fenwick, sheriff in 1589–90, was the mighty warden's son-in-law. Anthony Radcliffe, sheriff in 1588 before he was summarily dismissed and indicted for recusancy, was the father-in-law of Forster's bastard son Nicholas. The Nicholas Ridley who was married to Forster's niece became sheriff in November 1585.[53] Two months later he died because, as Forster alleged, of "certain witchcraft and other devilish practices".[54]

After it became apparent that Forster would be forced to resign the wardenship and during the years when the office was held by non-Northumbrians, it would appear that prosperous Protestant gentlemen of good reputation successfully persuaded the Crown and their influential friends at Court not to burden them with the shrievalty. In consequence in five of the seven years between 1594 and 1600 the sheriffs were gentlemen of small means and influence. All three of these hearty squires were still living in 1615. They were George Muschamp of Barmoor, sheriff in 1597 and again in 1600–1, Lancelot Carnaby of Halton, sheriff in 1598–9, and Thomas Bradford, sheriff in 1594–5. As Bradford's two successors, Robert Widdrington of Plessey and Sir Cuthbert Collingwood of Eslington, refused to leave their estates in County Durham to accept the shrievalty, he was made to serve a second term and part of a third.[55] It is not altogether surprising that in 1602 one "J. S.", possibly John Savile, at that time a judge of assize for the northern circuit and a baron of the Exchequer, complained that Northumberland sheriffs had performed their duties improperly, if at all. In recent years they had often neither served the king's writs nor levied the fines imposed by judges and justices at quarter sessions. More important, as far as "J. S." was concerned, they had not accounted to the Exchequer. Exchequer records show that the sheriffs who held office between 1594 and 1602 finally got together and rendered their accounts in a lump sum.[56] King James avoided some of these difficulties by always choosing substantial and middling gentry as his sheriffs of Northumberland.

Even when the state of county politics was less turbulent than it was in the 1590s, there were still not enough middling or prime gentry in Northumberland to fill all the higher positions in local government. Both Elizabeth's and James's advisers felt that, in addition to the sheriff, there should be approximately 20 working members on the Northumberland commission of the peace. This was rather more than the number of prosperous, well-reputed Protestant families in the whole of the county. To make up this deficiency, the Crown could either employ gentlemen whose seats and influence lay outside the county or those Northumbrian squires whose annual incomes at 1615 values were between £100 and £400. As a general rule Queen Elizabeth preferred to give office to suitably qualified non-Northumbrians – often members of the Council of the North at York – while King James made a special effort to employ local gentlemen. In 1621 there were 21 Northumbrians on the local commission of the peace with 12 of them of the quorum, compared to only 12, six of the quorum, around 1586.[57]

All told, the representatives of 24 Northumbrian landed families served as justices of the peace between the years 1586 and 1625. Seven of the 28 heads of lesser gentry families in the £100 to £400 income bracket in 1615 served in this capacity. Two of them were particularly colourful characters: Richard Fenwick of Stanton and Sir John Selby. In 1600 Selby was a rash young man serving as one of the captains at Berwick. He grew disillusioned with the autocratic lord governor, deserted his command and joined the Earl of Essex in his rebellion against the queen. John was later pardoned thanks to the timely intercession of his eldest brother, William Selby of Branxton, and Secretary Robert Cecil. He was knighted by King James in 1604 and was a Member of Parliament for Berwick in 1621 and 1625.[58] Had Richard Fenwick of Stanton been as fortunate in his friends as was John Selby, he too might have flourished. In 1597, after his lands had been ravaged by Scottish raiders for 30 years, Fenwick plaintively reminded Lord Burghley that his father had been a knight (which in fact he had not) and that his great-great-grandfather, Sir Roger Fenwick, and his great-grandfather, Sir Ralph Fenwick, had served King Henry VIII as keeper of Tynedale and warden of the Middle March respectively. Hoping to obtain office in that wardenry by showing his eagerness to dash the Scots, Richard Fenwick ran afoul of Sir John Forster. After the warden had him removed from the commission of the peace, the maverick squire never again held office. However in 1620, his son and heir, William Fenwick, was appointed a justice of the peace.[59]

Among the 36 heads of gentry families making do with annual incomes of less than £100 the only office-holder was Oliver Ogle of Burradon. Ogle was the Crown's receiver for Northumberland in 1596. Between 1605 and 1617, 17 of the gentlemen in this income category, including Ogle, occasionally served as grand jurors at the assizes or at extra-ordinary sessions of gaol delivery. Many of their fellow jurors were yeomen like Richard and Anthony Gofton of Ponteland and Nicholas Crane of Crow Hall.[60]

For almost three-quarters of the Northumberland gentry – those with annual incomes of less than £400 a year – thrift was a necessary virtue. Indeed, even gentlemen with incomes of over £400 a year might not have found it an easy matter to maintain the port and dignity of a gentleman. In 1630 Sir John Fenwick of Wallington stated that many of his fellow gentry were so impoverished that "a good part of their means will hardly pay their debts."[61] Of course this may have been an oblique way of saying that Northumberland gentlemen were not eager to contribute to forced loans.

Whatever their financial status, landed gentlemen were acutely conscious of the need to marry so that they might have legitimate children to succeed them in their estates. As far as can be ascertained all 89 heads of gentry families flourishing in 1615 did marry, including Sir Matthew Forster who was himself illegitimate.[62] Irrespective of their religious sympathies, there was a significant difference in the marriage patterns of the lesser gentry and those with incomes of over £400 a year. Of the 60 lesser gentlemen about whom we have the necessary information, only 12 found wives from beyond the confines of the county. Five of these wives came from County Durham (excluding North Durham), two from Cumberland, three from Newcastle, one from Yorkshire and one from Lancashire. In contrast, almost half of the gentlemen with incomes of over £400 a year, 12 of the 25, found wives from outside Northumberland or North Durham. The greater range of their social contacts, when compared to lesser gentlemen, is reflected in their wives' county of origin. Three of their wives came from south of the Trent. Lady Dorothy Selby of Branxton was from Kent; Lady Dorothy Gray, the second wife of Sir Ralph of Chillingham, was from Somerset and Lady Catherine Gray of Morpeth came from Norfolk. Four wives came from Yorkshire, three from County Durham, two from Cumberland and one from Lancashire.

The county of origin is known for the wives of 20 of 21 Northumberland gentlemen flourishing in 1586 who held important local civil or military office. Five came from neighbouring counties; one came from Somerset and three came from Yorkshire. One of these Yorkshire women was the first wife of Sir Henry Widdrington (d. 1593), the marshal and deputy governor of Berwick. Sir Henry's second wife Elizabeth was the daughter of Sir Hugh Trevannion of Cornwall.

It is interesting to note that none of the small 1586 sample and only one of the 89 gentlemen heading families in 1615 had a Scottish wife. Before 1603 it was illegal to marry a Scot without first obtaining a licence from the warden and, if one were a prominent person, possibly from the Privy Council as well.[63] Even after the union of the Crowns, most Northumberland gentlemen did not fancy Scottish wives. However, sometime after 1608 Thomas Carr of Ford esquire took a Scotswoman as his second wife. Thereafter he found himself confronted with numerous personal difficulties although admittedly these had little to do with his wife's nationality. During a brief interlude of sobriety Carr had entailed his estates to William Carr, his son by his first marriage. For some reason the second Mrs Carr took a strong dislike to William and tried to persuade her husband to will his estates to her own sons by her previous marriage. The dispute between the second Mrs Carr and young William, who happened to be a recusant, continued after Thomas Carr's death in 1641. However, by the time of his own death three years later, William Carr was seized of the whole of his father's estate.[64]

Fifty-one of the 60 gentlemen flourishing in 1615 who married local Northumberland women took their wives from gentle families. Of the heads of families with annual incomes of over £400 only John Strother esquire married into what was probably a non-gentle family. Mrs Elizabeth Strother was the daughter of the Roger Selby of Grindon who served as constable of Etal Castle and was mentioned in the will of Sir John Selby of Twizel in 1595. However it is not clear how Roger Selby was related to that prosperous North Durham family.[65] But perhaps poorer gentlemen, such as Robert Clennell of Clennell, felt that there was no great disparity between his status and that of his second wife's family. Mrs Isabel Clennell was the daughter of William Hall of Hepple. Until his murder in 1614 Hall was a close associate and friend of Roger Widdrington, the wealthy master of Cartington.[66]

The family size and fertility of Northumberland gentry families is of some interest. Of the heads of the 84 families (*fl.* 1615) for whom we have fairly complete information, five had no offspring and a further three had offspring only by a second marriage. Two of the five men dying without heirs were leading gentry: Sir Claudius Forster, bart, and Sir William Selby of Branxton. Thomas Ogle of Tritlington, Thomas Ogle of Bebside and Robert Collingwood of Eslington, grandson of Sir Cuthbert Collingwood, were the other three gentlemen who had no offspring.

There are two possible measures of fertility, the number of children born of all first marriages and the number of children born of all fertile first marriages. There were 215 boys and 164 girls recorded for the 84 first marriages; an average of 4.5 children per marriage. But as a general rule the number of boys born in any population is only slightly greater than the number of girls. As there is no reason to believe that Northumberland demographic patterns differed in this respect from those elsewhere, the more casual recording of the births of female children probably accounts for the disparity in the figures. If the number of girls is assumed to be equal to the number of boys, the average number of children born to all first marriages increases to 5.1. If we exclude the eight childless first marriages and again assume an equal number of boys and girls, the average number of children per fertile first marriage is 5.66. These corrected figures may be compared to those which Lawrence Stone has calculated for the aristocracy. He found that the average size of 422 aristocratic families was 4.11 children for all first marriages and 5.08 for fertile first marriages.[67] Since the records for aristocratic families are generally more complete than those for gentry families, one might expect such families to appear to be larger rather than the reverse. But considering the small size of our sample, our final figures were skewed by the presence of several exceptionally large families. Mrs Frances Shaftoe of Bavington had five sons and six daughters. Mrs Isabel Radcliffe of Dilston had six sons and seven daughters. Lady Jane Delaval of Seaton Delaval had nine sons and eleven daughters. Free at last after her sanctimonious husband's death in 1628, Lady Jane ran off with his secretary.[68]

*

The possession of a coat of arms bestowed by heralds from the College of Arms was one measure of a man's rank and status. Another, and one which was of personal concern to the heads of most families in Northumberland be they earls, yeomen or simple cottagers, was the quality of their estate or tenure. The most honourable though not necessarily the most financially desirable form of tenure was tenure-in-chief from the Crown by knight's service. Earl Percy, William Fenwick of Wallington and other royal tenants-in-chief owed the Crown various irksome fiscal dues and other obligations which were essentially feudal in origin. These matters were handled on behalf of the Crown by the Court of Wards and Liveries.[69]

As had been the case in the fourteenth century, royal tenants-in-chief might still have under-tenants holding properties from them by knight's service. Thus in 1592 the Grays of Chillingham held the manors of Chillingham, Howick and Doddington from the ninth earl of Northumberland for one knight's fee each. At least in theory, the Grays, the Forsters of Adderstone and other Percy knights still owed the earl homage and the feudal incidents of relief, marriage and wardship.[70]

The position of some men holding of the Crown by knight's service in Redesdale and Tynedale was somewhat anomalous. In 1604 surveyors in the royal manor of Wark wrote that "the principall freehoulders, and all the rest for anythinge that is shewed to the contrary, hould their land of his Majesty, as of his Mannor of Warke by knights service". However, except for young Cuthbert Heron and William Ridley of Willimontswick, the Crown had neglected to take the wardship of these "freehoulders".[71] At the death of a man holding by knight's service, his heir went to the manorial court, paid one year's rent as a fine and was entered as a "freehoulder" in the court rolls. A similar situation prevailed in the manor of Harbottle.[72] Before the dissolution of the wardenries in 1603 the "freehoulders" in both manors served under the command of their keepers "in as strict a manner as the Customarie Tenants."[73]

The overwhelming majority of Northumbrian landholders held their lands by tenures which were clearly not tenures in chivalry. Contemporaries divided such tenures into two categories; frank and base.[74] Of the two, frank tenure is the most readily explained for it was virtually synonymous with freehold tenure and was regulated and protected by the common law. In Northumberland, perhaps the most usual form of frank tenure was free socage in common, held of the lord of the manor or, if the property was itself a manor, held of the lord of the barony or lordship. So favourable was this form of tenure that some gentlemen, and ladies, preferred it to tenure by knight's service. In 1614 Lady Elizabeth Howard, daughter and heiress of the Earl of Dunbar, and her husband, Theophilus Lord Walden, were granted extensive Crown lands in Redesdale to hold "by fealty only, in free and common socage, and not in capite or by knight's service, rendering yearly for the manor of Redesdale

£72 12s. 4d., four pounds of pepper and one pound of cummin".[75] Likewise humbler socagers only owed their lord a small fine when they entered their tenement, court service and a nominal rent in money or kind. Surveyors reported in 1604 that the 43 freeholders in the barony of Langley "houlde their lands in socage tenure by fealtie and suite of Court, and to the Lord of the Mannor at every alienation one yeres rent for a fine."[76] Townspeople often held land by free burgage, a form of tenure in every way comparable to free socage.[77]

The gentlemen who opposed the 1581 bill for fortifying the borders asserted that most of the "inferior sort" who inhabited the border country were "insolent bondsmen".[78] This was their crude way of reminding Members of Parliament that originally – some time in the early Middle Ages – base tenures had derived from the will of the lord. Most customary tenants holding base tenures were copyholders who, when they appeared before their manorial court to enter into their tenements, were given a certified copy of the terms of their tenure as recorded in the rolls of the manor. The security of base tenures depended upon the customs of each manor and the nature of a man's estate. In this context an estate may be defined as the properties or interest in land which a person might enjoy under any of the ancient tenures. With the passage of time some of these estates were, in effect, equivalent to freehold. As Sir Edward Coke, the great common law lawyer, pointed out in the early seventeenth century, the word 'freehold' had a double meaning. In respect of the common law, only frank tenures were freehold. However if a copyholder could demonstrate that he had an estate of inheritance he might be considered a freeholder "in respect to the state of the land". In this case he had relatively little to fear from his landlord.[79] Thus the 327 tenants in the regality of Hexham who in 1608 claimed their land as "copyholders of inheritance to them, their heirs and assigns according to the custom" for rent and a fixed fine were, in respect to the state of the land, freeholders.[80] However, tenants who only held copies for a term of years or lives, generally that of the tenant, his wife and their named heir, had no interest in the land after the term came to an end.

Before the union of the Crowns there was a particular form of customary tenure known as tenant-right[81] which could not be defined in the same way as other customary tenures. As it was found in parts of all the northern counties, authentic tenant-right rested on special obligations of border service. Tenant-right consisted of a constellation of features which were most advantageous to the tenants. These features varied slightly from manor to manor but, in general, rents and fines were low and often fixed. The duties which a tenant owed his lord were minimal. Perhaps the most distinctive feature of this form of customary tenure was the ease with which tenants could transfer their tenant-right. Unlike most customary tenants in other parts of England, tenants could freely sell all or part of their tenant-right for a cash payment. In most cases the practice or fiction of first surrendering the land to the lord, who in turn would regrant it to the new customary tenant, was absent.[82]

In Northumberland authentic tenant-right was only found in the manors of Wark and Harbottle where, as we have already seen, some local freeholders held land by knight's service under rather unusual conditions. It should be noted that in the manor of Wark customary tenants claiming tenant-right were only to be found in North Tynedale. According to the customs of the manors of Wark and Harbottle, a tenant could sell or will his tenant-right to whoever he wished. A widow had the right to a third part of her late husband's land during her chaste widowhood. According to Wark custom if a tenant died intestate the tenement passed to the next heir, male or female. In Harbottle, tenants followed the unusual practice of partible inheritance amongst a man's sons "bee they never so manye, both rent and farme."[83]

Some tenants outside Wark and Harbottle also claimed tenant-right. It is possible that tenant-right tenure had been known on these other manors at an earlier period and that tenants attempted to revive it when they felt threatened by their landlords in the early seventeenth century. During the first two decades of the century tenant-right claims were put forward, but not authenticated, in Netherton (one of the Ten Towns of Coquetdale), in the barony of Bewick, in the regality of Hexham and in the former Percy barony of Langley.[84]

Except for those in North Tynedale and in Tynemouthshire, virtually all of Earl Percy's customary tenants in Northumberland held their lands according to the custom followed on the manor of Cockermouth in western Cumberland.[85] Percy copyholders paid a "fine at the lord's will and pleasure, after the death, alienation or exchange of the lord or tenant".[86] Until about 1560 Percy copyholders thought themselves "well pleased and in good estate".[87] Successive paternalistic earls had placed a higher value on the number of men they could muster for their service than on the size of their income. Rents were low and "land was of small worth and little regarded or respected".[88] Percy copyholders were perhaps in a position to enjoy some of the benefits of inflation when English armies needing food and other necessities were garrisoned in the North during the 1540s and 1550s. As producers of primary goods, farmers could charge consumers high prices for their produce while their operating costs remained relatively stable. However this era of mild prosperity (which had probably passed most Northumbrians by) had already come to an end before the seventh earl rose in rebellion in 1569. In 1570 Hall and Humberston reported that Percy tenants who followed the custom of Cockermouth now felt that their customs were "so odious unto them that they are not able to endure it." Earl Percy had begun to collect fines "sometime ones in two, three or four years or more".[89] Decay reports and muster returns from the 1580s and 1590s suggest that other landlords were similarly charging their tenants high fines and raising rents.[90]

Soon after the ninth earl of Northumberland succeeded to his inheritance in 1585, he cautioned his estate agents to watch carefully for lands which might escheat for want of male heirs and to collect the goods and chattels of all tenants judged to be felons at the common law.[91] In 1594, mindful of his obligations as the largest non-royal landowner in the county, the earl instructed his agents to evict all tenants who were not properly furnished for border service. These cleared tenements were then to be "let for my best profits". The earl confessed to some hesitancy about adopting this policy for it seemed to run counter to paternalistic ideals. His fears were allayed when it was pointed out that by evicting undutiful (i.e. poverty-stricken) tenants "your lordship might both have benefit and better tenants and also no wrong to any man".[92] Accordingly, with a clear conscience, the earl berated tenants on demesne land at Bondgate in Alnwick because they were "naked and unfurnished...neither able to defend [themselves] nor willing as it seems to join in aid of my other tenants as their cause do require." He warned that unless they equipped themselves for service before the end of August, they should "prepare other dwellings and livings" for themselves. After some delays, in March 1596 he ordered his agents to remove the tenants at Bondgate, but especially "such of them...as have not done their due service or be not sufficiently supplied with horse".[93]

Tenants such as those at Bondgate who were on demesne land arrented by copy were neither protected by the common law nor by manorial custom. They were mere tenants-at-will who could be evicted after they had harvested whatever standing crops they had planted.[94] Even if only a part of a tenant's land lay in demesne, its loss could cause him serious hardship. In 1580 muster masters reported that none of the six tenants at Chollerton in Tynedale could afford the horse and gear necessary to perform border service because their landlord, Thomas Swinburn of Capheaton, had withdrawn his demesne land from their use.[95] Another portion of the Northumberland rural population which held land at the will of the lord consisted of cottagers and squatters. Since such people were neither protected by the common law nor by the custom of the manor, their landlords could reclaim their tenancies at short notice.[96]

Leaseholders were in a far more favourable position than cottagers and many customary tenants, for as long as their leases held good they could have recourse to courts of common law to protect their holdings from unscrupulous neighbours or landlords. In Northumberland the great movement towards leaseholding did not begin until after 1603. However, a few sixteenth-century landlords did recognize the advantage of granting leases rather than copies. As early as 1570 leasehold tenants were recorded in the villages of Newton, Mickley, Bromley and Bywell in the middle Tyne valley.[97]

Even after leasehold began to replace customary forms of tenure, some landlords tried to maintain manorial courts for they regarded them as an efficient way to keep their tenantry in order. Some of these emasculated courts barely paid for themselves. In 1608 surveyors reported that since the tenants at Whalton, near Morpeth, had taken leases in 1587/8 the profits of the court had been so small "as they have but sufficed the necessary charge of the court dinner".[98]

Manorial courts were customary courts. They had the authority to entertain actions of trespass, actions of right and all matters involving the tenure, surrender or inheritance of customary land. Moreover, they could hear pleas of debt under 40s. and presentments of nuisance and minor violence.[99] All freeholders and copyholders were suitors before their manorial court and sat as a jury which made the decisions of the court. Among their other tasks, jurors created and enforced by-laws governing the day-to-day management of manorial affairs. Tenants who neglected their duties were amerced and fined by their fellow tenants on the jury. Thus in October 1589 the manorial court of Embleton, near Alnwick, ordered "all tenantes and inhabitantes in Stamford, Emelton, and all other places within this mannour or lordshipp, as well horse as foote, shall all ryse to fray and following, and gyve theire attendance of the bailiffe or other officer to be redye to go with the dogg all together, upon paine of 6s. 8d. every horseman four everye defalte".[100] A more typical entry on the Embleton roll was a by-law passed in 1598 which forbad any of the tenants to dry their oats in the common oven, with a fine of 6s. 8d. for every default.[101]

By-laws also reminded suitors of their obligations to people less fortunate than themselves. In 1587 the manorial court of Seaton Delaval decreed that "everye tenante within this lordship shall send able and sufficient servants, so often as they shall be warned, for the caringe of crepells and impotent persones, uppon payne iiij^d for every defalt." In 1592 the same court ruled that "every of th'inhabitants within Seton Delavale and Hartlowe [Hartley] shall either send or goe to the churche with every corse or dead persone upon warninge, sub pena xij^d." It was also ordered that "every mann's wife within this lordship shall, within half ane howre after warning, presentlie repaire and go to every woman laboring of child, if they be thereto called and invited, sub pena xij^d."[102] In this way the inhabitants of the manor, acting in the manorial court, helped to maintain the social order. The preservation of the social order was also one of the tasks performed by the clergy in the archdeaconry of Northumberland. To these people and their parishioners we now direct our attention.

 4

The education and religious loyalties of Northumbrians

In the year when the seventh earl of Northumberland rose in rebellion, his long-time antagonist Sir Ralph Sadler asserted that there were not ten gentlemen within the northern counties "that do favour and allowe of her majesties procedings in the cause of religion, and the comen people be ignorant, full of superstition, and altogither blynded with tholde popish doctryne".[1] More than half a century later, in 1617, Sir Henry Anderson claimed that the people of Northumberland "are merely led by the example of their masters, which is for the most part Papistry or atheism".[2] And in 1628 Sir Benjamin Rudyard told the House of Commons that "there were places in England which were scarce in Christendom where God was little better known than amongst the Indians, [and] exampled it in the utmost skirts of the North where the Prayers of the common people are more like spells and Charms than devotions".[3]

Comments such as these led George Ornsby, the Victorian cleric who edited the household books of Lord William Howard, to conclude that in the early seventeenth century, as in 1569, "the gentry of Northumberland were, almost to a man, Catholics, and their tenants and dependents, with few exceptions, were doubtless of the same faith."[4] Ornsby's conclusions can no longer remain unchallenged. But in order to counter them we must first investigate Elizabethan and Jacobean religious policies and the intricate manoeuvres which appeared to be a necessary part of their execution in Northumberland. This done, it will be possible to proceed to a more accurate assessment of the religious affiliations and educational experience of the gentlemen of the county as well as of their social inferiors.

The national church to which by law all English people were required to belong was established by the Acts of Supremacy and Uniformity in 1559. Until 1593, when Richard Hooker began to publish his famous apology, *Of the Laws of Ecclesiastical Polity,* the Church of England had no distinctive theology to set it apart from reformed churches elsewhere in Europe. Although by sixteenth century standards England was a reasonably tolerant state, anything resembling full religious toleration was unthinkable. Loyalty to the national church was equated with loyalty to the ruling sovereign.

At a time when the Roman pontiff and the Catholic princes of Europe were attempting to regain control of the peoples they had lost to the Reformation, the position of English Catholics was particularly difficult. Their dilemma was exacerbated in 1570 when Pope Pius V excommunicated Queen Elizabeth and forbad her subjects to obey her commands. Some Catholics protested their loyalty to the queen in secular matters while remaining steadfast in their faith. Others decided that it was politic to attend occasional services in their parish churches. These Church Papists, as they were sometimes called, were often observed to be sleeping or reading Catholic devotional works while ministers read through the appointed services in the *Book of Common Prayer.* It was suspected, and on occasions proved, that Church Papists returned to their country houses or to the homes of their masters and employers to hear Mass celebrated by resident or itinerant Catholic priests.[5]

Without priests to celebrate the Mass, the central mystery of the faith, the Catholic Church in England was doomed to eventual extinction. The situation became critical during the 1560s as priests ordained before the Henrician Reformation died off. In response to this problem, William Allen established a seminary for young Catholics at Douai in northern France in 1568. Six years later missionary priests trained in this seminary, the first of several such schools to be established, began to arrive in England. In 1580 they were joined by the first Jesuits. Some of these priests entered the country through Newcastle or the secluded little ports further up the Northumbrian coast and stayed for a few days in the homes of local Catholics before they made their way south towards the intellectual centres of English Catholicism. One of the best-known protectors of travelling priests and Catholic sailors in the Newcastle area in the early seventeenth century was the Yorkshire widow, Mrs Dorothy Lawson of St Anthony's. In part it was the priestly traffic through the homes of local Catholics such as this which gave Northumberland its reputation as a centre of Catholic activity.[6]

The arrival of Jesuits and other agents of the Counter-Reformation greatly alarmed the English government. Recognizing that the existing statutory authority of parish officials to fine people 12*d.* for non-attendance at church on a Sunday or feast day was insufficient to drive them into conformity, Parliament enacted new legislation in 1581. Thereafter any person convicted of non-attendance at church (a recusant) could be fined £20 a month or £260 a year. This Act also imposed a fine of 100 marks (£66 13*s.* 4*d.*) a month on anyone who heard Mass; any person who celebrated Mass could be fined 200 marks and imprisoned for a year. Furthermore, anybody attempting to convert a Protestant to Catholicism could be tried for treason. Parliament intensified its campaign against recusants in 1587, on the eve of the Spanish Armada. It empowered lay officials to distrain two-thirds of the income due from lands held by recusants who refused to pay their fines.[7] By these persuasive measures the government hoped to convince Catholic sympathizers that they should openly conform to the tenets of the national Church.

All recusants, it should be noted, were not to be found to the right of the *via media* as it was defined by Hooker. Some were radical Protestants – Presbyterians, separatists, Anabaptists – who in the years after 1580 began to dissociate themselves entirely from the national Church. Although there were doubtless some such people in Newcastle,[8] Protestant non-conformists were apparently rare in Northumberland proper. And in 1587 Berwick officials claimed that none of the townspeople or soldiers there could be charged with being an "Anabaptist or of the Family of Love or an undutiful subject".[9] Thus in the absence of evidence to the contrary, the use of the term recusant in Northumberland can generally be taken to mean a Catholic rather than a Protestant non-conformist.

For more than ten years after the passing of the Acts of Supremacy and Uniformity in 1559, Queen Elizabeth and her clerical advisers paid relatively little heed to the condition of the Church north of the Trent. Notwithstanding, it would appear that several prominent Northumberland families, among them the Delavals, Ogles and Widdringtons, willingly accepted the new religious establishment. In 1564 Sir John Forster reported no great difficulty in finding 12 Protestant gentlemen in the Middle March whom he believed to be suitably qualified to serve as justices of the peace. There were only three gentlemen in the wardenry whom Forster did not trust: Sir Robert Ellerker, "a very Papist" and a Yorkshireman, Sir John Mitford of Seghill and Thomas Bates of Morpeth, the Percy estate agent who later joined the seventh earl in rebellion.[10] Doubtless Forster's criteria for judging the suitability of men's religious sympathies were not quite as rigid as those of his stern brother warden, Francis Earl of Bedford. Bedford was of the opinion that in the East March "there is never a justice of the peace nor none that he can commend as mete for that purpose."[11]

The northern earls' abortive attempt to rescue Mary Queen of Scots and to oust Elizabeth's Protestant councillors late in 1569 finally alerted the government to the grave danger of neglecting the spiritual welfare of its northern subjects. Only then did the Privy Council decide to uphold in the uttermost fastness of the North the principle that religious loyalties must be inseparable from allegiance to the queen and the nation state. This new policy was reflected in the appointment of Edmund Grindal as archbishop of York in 1570 and, of more immediate concern to us, the Earl of Huntingdon's appointment as lord president of the Council of the North. Huntingdon and Grindal, like Bedford and Walsingham (appointed Secretary of State in 1573), were sometimes termed Puritans because they earnestly desired and actively worked for a "more thorough Protestant reformation within the Established Church."[12]

During his 23 years in office Lord President Huntingdon earned the grim sobriquet "the hammer of the northern Catholics".[13] In the early 1570s he frequently assisted Grindal when the latter presided over the northern Court of High Commission. This court derived its authority from the Act of Supremacy and had jurisdiction over the counties of Cheshire, Lancashire and Nottingham, as well as the counties under the jurisdiction of the Council of the North.[14] It was a useful instrument with which to convince recusants that they should come to conform at least outwardly to the tenets of the state Church. If gentle persuasion failed, the High Commission imposed fines or prison sentences.[15] In addition to this ecclesiastical court, over which he briefly presided after Grindal was transferred to Canterbury in 1575, Huntingdon had authority as Lord President of the North to compel justices of the peace to enforce the statutes directed against recusants.[16]

For one reason or another, Huntingdon seldom troubled himself about Northumberland and apparently did not use what influence he had to prevent the county's Catholics from holding office. Between 1584 and 1587 a number of gentlemen who were not of assured religion were on the Northumberland commission of the peace. Among them were Sir Thomas Gray of Chillingham and his brother Ralph, who were termed "vehement Papists" by an anonymous informant in 1588. The same informant noted that if another J. P., Sir Cuthbert Collingwood of Eslington, was not actually a Catholic, he was "extremely bent that way". The informant did not directly criticize justice William Fenwick of Wallington, Sir John Forster's son-in-law, but he did mention a mysterious "Mr Fenwick" who lived with the family and was probably a priest.[17]

In the summer of 1587 privy councillors briefly took cognizance of what could be construed to be Lord President Huntingdon's careless disregard of Northumberland Catholics. In June they directed Captain William Carey, Lord Hunsdon's second son, to use some of the garrison soldiers from Berwick to capture David Ingleby and other Jesuits who were thought to be lurking in the vicinity of Dilston in the Middle March. Dilston was the residence of Francis Radcliffe, the eldest son of Sir George Radcliffe (d. 1588), a prominent Northumberland J. P.[18] Four months later Lord Hunsdon was himself in Berwick. As we shall see, the governor was not one of Huntingdon's admirers. In a letter to Lord Burghley he complained about the growing strength of Catholicism in the North:

> from Yorkshire hither, the most part of Richmondshire, the Bishopric, the Middle and this East March, are almost all became Papists, for where in this East March at my going hence I knew not three Papists, I find not

now three Protestants, for though some of them will some time come to the church, and that not past once a quarter, their wives are notorious recusants.[19]

Apparently the government at first took Hunsdon's statements with a pinch of salt. Although he had warned the queen to be especially careful in her choice of sheriff – the officer who collected the recusancy fines levied by J. P.s – in November 1588 the Crown pricked Anthony Radcliffe, Sir George's younger brother. But a short time later Anthony was accorded a second dubious honour; he became one of the first prominent Northumberland Catholics to be indicted for recusancy. He was hastily replaced as sheriff by Henry Anderson, the wealthy Newcastle Protestant who had been his predecessor.[20]

Administrative inefficiency and confusion interspersed with sharp persecutions characterized the relationship between Northumberland Catholics and the government during the next few years. Typically, one of the leading members of a commission to investigate recusancy in 1592 was Sir Cuthbert Collingwood, a gentleman not noted for his fervent attachment to the state Church. After the commission concluded its investigation, Collingwood informed Sir John Forster that the sheriff could not find any of the recusants living in Castle, Morpeth and Tynedale wards whom the commissioners had listed in their report.[21] This was hardly surprising as the sheriff was Ralph Gray of Chillingham whose wife, even then, was suspected of sheltering seminary priests.[22] Forster brought these matters to the attention of the dean of Durham Cathedral, Tobias Matthew. Matthew was a devoted friend of the pious Earl of Huntingdon and preached stimulating sermons which the earl greatly appreciated. On occasion Dean Matthew also preached before the Court, but Queen Elizabeth recognized him for what he was, a well-meaning, loquacious place-seeker.[23] Matthew and several of his colleagues on the northern High Commission held a session in Newcastle in December 1592 at which they intended to discipline Northumberland non-conformists and in particular those whom the sheriff had not been able to track down in Castle, Morpeth and Tynedale wards. But much to Matthew's embarrassment not a single recusant appeared after the court convened. When the dean recovered his composure, he took counsel with Protestant officials. It was decided to humble the Grays and the recalcitrant recusant gentry by sending Sir John Forster's men to search for Jesuits in the house of John Swinburn at Edlingham, a dozen miles south of Chillingham. Sir John's men found the walls of the late fourteenth-century castle so thick and the hiding places between the vaulting of the main hall and the floor above so numerous that they decided that "traitors" could only be "hungered out" after a more prolonged siege than they were prepared to conduct.[24]

Northern Catholics and their priestly guests did not always escape so easily; on occasion a few of them were singled out as examples to the rest. In August

1592 Newcastle officials hanged and quartered Joseph Lambton of South Biddick, County Durham, on the Town Moor. William Waterson suffered a similar fate in January 1594. The following July John Ingram, a Jesuit who had worked in the Northumberland mission field, was tortured on the rack in the Tower of London before being sent to Gateshead for execution. In November 1596 George Errington of the Hurst, possibly the only Northumbrian to die for his faith during this period, was executed at York for attempting to convert a Protestant.[25]

This brief and terrible persecution ended soon after the death of the Earl of Huntingdon in December 1595 and the subsequent appointment of Archbishop Matthew Hutton of York as acting head, rather than as fully empowered lord president, of the Council of the North. Hutton had been a devoted follower of the earl and, like him, had wished to make the established Church more thoroughly Protestant. Yet in his new role Hutton showed himself willing to tolerate recusants and Catholics who went quietly about their daily affairs. This policy was altogether in agreement with that of another of Hutton's aristocratic friends, the royal favourite, Robert Earl of Essex.[26] But it was bitterly opposed by Hutton's subordinate, Tobias Matthew. Matthew had other differences with Hutton. In 1589 the Earl of Huntingdon had encouraged Dean Matthew (as he was then) to hope that he would be given the bishopric of Durham; Hutton got the place instead. Matthew's subsequent elevation to the see after Hutton went on to York was scant recompense for the earlier hurt.[27]

After Tobias Matthew finally became bishop in March 1595, he found himself powerless to proceed as he would have liked against recusants in the archdeaconry of Northumberland. It seemed to him that county justices of the peace and other officials spent more time arguing among themselves about the terms of the penal statutes of 1581 and 1587 than in enforcing them. The northern Court of High Commission was also ineffective. Matthew alleged that the new commission which the Crown had issued after Hutton had assumed control of the Council of the North was much weaker than the old, being "defective in three or four late most material and necessary statutes . . . how we shall do more good with less authority I see not." The new commission stipulated that members could not transact any business unless Archbishop Hutton was personally present at the session; he alone was of the quorum. Considering the strained relations between Hutton and Matthew, it was extremely unlikely that the former would care to travel up to Newcastle to hold sessions. So with the archbishop on the one hand and ineffective county officials on the other, Matthew found himself unable to harass Northumberland Catholics as he would have wished. He argued that true religion could only make headway in the far North if the Privy Council gave him, as bishop of Durham, full authority to proceed against recusants without reference to York.[28] This the Council was not prepared to do. As a result, for almost three years Northumberland recusants enjoyed a considerable degree of toleration.

Then in 1599 the government suddenly reversed its policies. Taking advantage of the absence of the Earl of Essex (who was in Ireland), Robert Cecil secured the dismissal of Hutton and made his own brother, Thomas Lord Burghley, Lord President of the Council of the North. Burghley was given the full powers of the office and ample authority to enforce the penal laws.[29] Upwards of 150 Northumbrians were convicted of recusancy at the Newcastle assize held in August 1600. This was more than the total number which surviving records indicate had been convicted since the penal laws were first enacted in 1581.[30]

Bishop Matthew was delighted with the results of the session. He was also pleased when the Privy Council instructed the lord wardens to co-operate with him in disciplining "such evill disposed subjectes as the Recusantes are in those Northern parts".[31] In accordance with these instructions in 1601 Sir Robert Carey, by then warden of the Middle March, dutifully brought a number of recusants to the church in Newcastle in which the High Commissioners were sitting. Carey found that Bishop Matthew had not seen fit to attend, possibly because he feared a repetition of the embarrassing fiasco of December 1592 when no Northumberland recusants had come before him and his brother commissioners. Despite Matthew's absence, this session proceeded smoothly enough. At the request of one of the ecclesiastical commissioners, Carey read a prayer for the queen's safety. All the recusants except Henry Haggarston, a North Durham man, reverently knelt during the prayer. As for Haggarston, he "stood upon his feet with an obstinate and disloyal behaviour not saying thereto 'amen'". He was imprisoned for this impropriety.[32] For his part, Sir Robert Carey did not relish this close association with Bishop Matthew's friends. A consummate opportunist who attempted to be all things to all men – of influence – Carey knew that Tobias Matthew was cut out of the same cloth as himself. Two days after the Newcastle session Carey asked Sir Robert Cecil to excuse him from further work with the High Commission.[33]

A short time later the commissioners took forceful action against one of the most prominent of the recusant squires in the Middle March, Francis Radcliffe of Dilston. Radcliffe, whom Bishop Matthew termed an "obstinate, dangerous and not unlearned recusant", was imprisoned at York. In 1602 the Crown granted a lease of two-thirds of the annual income of the Radcliffe manors of Dilston and Whittonstall to a County Durham man.[34]

After the discovery of the Gunpowder Plot in November 1605, Parliament passed such stringent anti-Catholic legislation that Northumberland Catholic families must have been compelled to think seriously whether the course of recusancy was worth the cost. One statute empowered lay officials to confiscate two-thirds of a recusant's estate whether or not the recusancy fines had been paid.[35] Another forbad convicted recusants to hold any rank in the army or navy, to be trained in the professions, to serve as guardians of children or executors of estates. Moreover they were forbidden to serve in public office. As we have already seen, during the remainder of King James's reign no convicted recusant is known to have held office in Northumberland as a justice of the peace, sheriff or deputy lieutenant. The 1606 anti-Catholic legislation also stipulated that convicted recusants could not travel more than five miles from their house or go to London on business without a licence such as that granted to John Swinburn of Edlingham in April 1618.[36] According to yet another statute, a recusant who refused to take the oath of allegiance to King James, which was first introduced in 1606, could be deprived of his lands and imprisoned for life.[37]

Possibly with a view to enforcing these strict new recusancy laws, in January 1607 commissioners made a survey of "the state of Northumberland for religion in the principall families, by whom the multitude may safely be ledd in matters of religion and other action."[38] According to this list, by 1607 the heads of two prominent families whose religious affiliation might have distressed conscientious officials in the 1580s did so no longer. Sir Cuthbert Collingwood had died in County Durham in December 1596 and his recusant heir Thomas had died at Eslington early in the following year. Thomas's eldest son and heir, Robert, was a ward of Sir Ralph Gray.[39] Sir Ralph, who had succeeded his brother Thomas on the latter's death in 1590, appears to have lost his enthusiasm for Catholicism after the death of his recusant first wife Jane sometime before 1600. However Ralph's younger brother Edward was "a reputed Church Papist" in 1607 and his sister, a recusant, was married to Francis Radcliffe of Dilston, who had by this time regained his freedom and a pardon from the king. But Sir Henry Widdrington, another of the principal gentlemen about whom the commissioners were concerned, had only recently fallen into disfavour. The commissioners noted that Sir Henry "cometh seldom to church" and that he had recently married the sister of Sir Henry Curwen, a Cumberland Papist. They also noted that he had recently settled his differences with his brother Roger Widdrington, "the most dangerous recusant in that County". However Sir Henry and his brother had already rendered the Crown valuable service and would do so again. Their loyalty equalled if not surpassed that of some of the gentlemen listed as firm Protestants in 1607; Sir William Selby of Branxton, Sir John Selby, Sir Robert Delaval and the Middletons, Mitfords, Muschamps and Strothers.[40]

The 1607 report disproves Ornsby's contention that during the years when Lord William Howard was at Naworth "the gentry of Northumberland were, almost to a man, Catholics".[41] Indeed by 1615, when heralds from the College of Arms visited Northumberland, the overwhelming majority of the heads of gentry families were conforming churchmen. Only 16 of the 89 heads of gentry families were convicted of recusancy at some time in their lives.[42] Only four of the 16 were men of substance with annual incomes of over £400 a year.

They were Francis Radcliffe of Dilston, his son-in-law Roger Widdrington, Thomas Haggarston and Sir William Fenwick of Meldon. During the reign of King James, Fenwick was the only office holder amongst them; he was appointed a deputy lieutenant of Northumberland in 1622. This was not improper for, though Fenwick had long been paying recusancy fines on behalf of his widowed mother Meg of Meldon (commonly regarded as a witch), he was not convicted of recusancy in his own right until 1629.[43]

The 12 other recusant squires who headed gentle families in 1615 were all lesser men whose life style did not differ markedly from that of Protestants of similar financial standing. Only one of their number, Sir Ephraim Widdrington, served as a justice of the peace during James's reign, but he was not convicted of recusancy until after the king's death. In his religious affiliation Sir Ephraim seems to have been led quite as much by his current wife as by his nephew, friend and frequent host at Cartington, Roger Widdrington. In 1607, at a time when Ephraim was possibly still married to a sister of the recusant George Thirlwall, it was noted that he was not careful of any religion.[44] In 1615, about the time that he was first joined to the Northumberland commission of the peace, Sir Ephraim married Eleanor, the widow of the staunchly Protestant squire, Lancelot Strother.[45] By 1625, when he was first recorded as a recusant, Sir Ephraim had married his third wife, Jane, a daughter of the recusant Michael Hebburn.[46]

Only three of the heads of gentry families in 1615 were known to be Church Papists, men who attended their parish churches with sufficient frequency to satisfy the law. All three were substantial gentlemen with incomes of over £400 a year. Some less prosperous gentlemen may also have been Church Papists but, simply because of their lesser standing, their precise status was of little import to government officials. Of the three known Church Papists one, Thomas Swinburn of Capheaton, took no part in local government. Swinburn's wife was convicted of recusancy, as was his son William.[47] The Church Papist Edward Gray of Morpeth was sheriff in 1597–8 and deputy warden of the Middle March under Ralph Lord Eure. He was later a member of the first border commission although he appears never to have been a justice of the peace. After the Protestant Earl of Dunbar began to dominate the local scene in 1606, Gray retired from public life and devoted his energies to managing his own and Lord William Howard's estates in the lordship of Morpeth. Sir Edward's three sons, Philip of Howick, Edward of Morpeth, and Thomas, were indicted for recusancy in the 1620s and 1630s.[48] The third prominent Church Papist was Sir Matthew Forster of Adderstone, high sheriff in 1620–1. His son Thomas, like the sons of Edward Gray and Thomas Swinburn, was indicted for recusancy, as was his wife.[49] This seems to indicate that in Northumberland, at any rate, Church Papists obeyed the dictates of convenience rather than conscience.

Even though Northumberland recusants were occasionally made to feel rather uncomfortable during the reign of King James, they seldom suffered the full force of the law. In order to enforce even the least stringent aspects of the penal statutes the Crown had to rely on the services of inefficient sheriffs and local officials who apparently did not believe that their Catholic neighbours were a serious threat to the established order. Indeed they were a recognized part of this order. Rather than allow a friend to lose lands through confiscation, some Protestants willingly held title to a Catholic's estate in trust.[50]

The government's inability to intervene meaningfully in the personal affairs of recusant gentlemen is exemplified by the case of John Swinburn of Nafferton and Edlingham. In 1615 he informed his only son Thomas that he would be disinherited as he was a Protestant. The elder Swinburn intimated that he would will his estates to his daughter Margaret, wife of William Swinburn of Capheaton, a well-known recusant, and to her son John. Thomas Swinburn protested his father's decision to the bishop of Durham and to the Privy Council. Eventually the Council warned John Swinburn that he would suffer the full force of the penal laws if he disinherited Thomas. Subsequently Swinburn was imprisoned as an "obstinate Papist" and forced to compound for his estates for the annual rent of £50. Nevertheless at Swinburn's death in 1639 virtually all of his property devolved upon his recusant grandson to the exclusion of the Protestant Thomas.[51]

Scarcely was King James cold in his grave when the government, in a desperate search for funds, decided to enforce the recusancy laws far more stringently than the old king had allowed. In 1625 Exchequer officials ordered Sir John Delaval, the sheriff, to distrain the goods of local recusants. County officials seized goods to the value of £621 from Sir Edward Radcliffe bart, by this time the head of the Dilston family. Sir Edward's brother-in-law, Roger Widdrington, suffered the confiscation of 700 head of cattle and 400 sheep worth £909 6s. 8d. Widdrington's friends Richard and George Thirlwall lost goods valued at £756 6s. 8d. Mark Errington of Ponteland and his son Gilbert lost goods worth £519 6s. 8d. John Swinburn of Edlingham lost nothing at all having conveniently, but only temporarily, transferred Edlingham to his Protestant son Thomas. However the sheriff seized from the Swinburns of Capheaton and Black Heddon cattle and sheep valued at £445 16s. In all, goods belonging to 12 gentry families were seized. Sixty-five recusants of a lower social status were also visited by the sheriff's officers and lost goods or paid fines ranging from £2 to £100.[52]

Whether members of the recusant minority, conforming churchmen or staunch Protestants, gentlemen of substance had very considerable influence on the common people in their locality.[53] Roughly half of the 674 recusants whose names were entered upon the rolls kept by exchequer officials during two years of exceptionally severe persecution, 1600 and 1625, lived in the southern part of the ward of Tynedale. This district was dominated by the wealthy Radcliffes of Dilston and such lesser Catholic families as the Carnabys of Halton and the Thirlwalls of Thirlwall. In 1625 29 recusants lived in the immediate neighbourhood of Cartington Castle, home of the recusant Roger Widdrington, and 19 lived nearby in Rothbury. A further 11 lived near Widdrington Castle on the coast, the residence of Roger's brother Sir Henry. Contrary to their enemies' allegations, it does not appear that the Widdrington brothers made any serious attempt to propagate the Catholic faith in Redesdale or North Tynedale. Only four of the 27 highlanders whom Richard Forster alleged in 1617 were the Widdringtons' principal followers were ever indicted for recusancy. The situation in Morpeth town and lordship is also of some interest as the area was under the domination of the powerful Catholic (who was himself never indicted) Lord William Howard. In 1600, at a time when the Howard influence was strong at Court, only two Morpethians were indicted for recusancy. In 1619, after Lord William's brother, Lord Treasurer Suffolk, had fallen from power, eight were indicted. In 1625, when the influence of the Howards was at a low ebb, 12 recusants from Morpeth were indicted.

The scarcity of recusants in certain other areas doubtless reflected the Protestant sympathies of local landowners. Thus the apparent decline in recusant strength in Glendale ward during the first quarter of the seventeenth century, from 19 in 1600 to only five in 1625, is very possibly related to Sir Ralph Gray's decision to dissociate himself from the recusant party. It might be noted that none of Gray's gentle neighbours were recusants. A similar situation prevailed in Bamburgh ward, an area which was under the sway of the Forsters. No recusants were found in the ward in 1600 when Sir John was still alive. In 1625 only 11 recusants were found in this populous ward. In both 1600 and 1625 there were few recusants in Castle ward, thanks perhaps to the influence of the powerful Delaval connection and to the proximity of the predominantly Protestant town of Newcastle.

The exchequer recusancy rolls serve as a source for estimating the total number of Catholics at all levels of society in Northumberland between 1600 and 1625. Earlier exchequer lists are too scanty to be considered. In the belief that people who escaped the snares laid by recusant-hunters in one year might very possibly be caught in succeeding years, it seems appropriate to make a total of all the people who were indicted between 1600 and 1625; 1,255 individuals in all.[54] Taking into account that many of them were husbands and wives, it is perhaps best to use a conservative multiplier, four, when estimating the total number of recusants and people directly influenced by recusant family members. The resulting figure 5,020 is slightly more than 6 per cent of the estimated 83,000 people in the county in 1617. In that year Count Gondomar, the Spanish ambassador, estimated that there were 300,000 recusants in England; 7.5 per cent of an estimated population of 3.8 million.[55] But if no multiplier is used for the Northumberland figure, the resulting number of indicted recusants would be 1.7 per cent of the county's population. This is certainly not a high percentage when compared to the situation in other shires. It has been calculated that in 1604 2 per cent of the population of Yorkshire were recusants and that 1.4 per cent of the people in the diocese of Chester of an age to take communion were recusants.[56]

As the overwhelming majority of the inhabitants of late Elizabethan and Jacobean Northumberland conformed to the established Church, the condition of that Church locally cannot have been quite as precarious as some contemporaries would have us believe. Admittedly the Church did suffer from a serious shortage of funds and of qualified clergy. In the course of his visitation in 1578–9 Bishop Barnes found that there were only 55 churches with resident clergy in the 46 parishes of Northumberland.[57] The whole of Redesdale was served by Elsdon parish church for the chapels at Holystones, on the upper reaches of the Coquet, and at Corsensides, south of Elsdon, were without incumbents. Seven of the 15 parish churches in the deanery of Bamburgh, including those at Tweedmouth, Holy Isle and Bamburgh itself, wanted incumbents or were served by stipendiary priests. Seven of the ministers whom Bishop Barnes called before him were former Catholic priests from Scotland; four were not licensed by an English bishop and one, Andrew Wright of West Lilburn, was excommunicated for non-attendance.[58]

Barnes found that the majority of the 73 vicars, curates and stipendiary priests whom he examined were theologically illiterate. Only 23 could give him a satisfactory account in Latin or English of the gospel story as it was related by St Matthew.[59] Of course, as Samuel Butler's Ernest Pontifex, the Victorian theological student, discovered in his discussions with the fundamentalist Mr Shaw, such a test was not as easy as at first sight might appear. Very few of the clergymen Barnes examined were educated men who could preach the inspiring sermons demanded by advanced reformers.

According to the Earl of Huntingdon's friends and clients, the number of competent preachers in Northumberland did not increase appreciably during the 1580s and 1590s. In 1587 one of them claimed that "there are not passing Three or fowre preachers in the whole shire".[60] In 1595 Sir William Bowes contended that "true religion has taken very little place" in the Middle March "not by the unwillingness of the people to hear, but by want of means, scant three able preachers being to be found in the whole country."[61] But three or four preaching clergymen were, by Queen Elizabeth's standards, quite sufficient. She believed that it was far better that the common people should hear simple homilies on obedience read by 'dumb dogs' than be stirred up by sophisticated preachers who might not be quite in tune with official church policies as she saw them.[62]

It was not to be expected that the archdeaconry of Northumberland would be particularly attractive to educated clergymen. According to Bishop Matthew, writing in 1597, considerations of personal safety dissuaded some able young clerics from remaining in their cures or from accepting livings in the archdeaconry in the first place.[63] In 1596 Warden Ralph Eure recommended that the queen appoint Richard Crakenthorpe (1567–1624) to one of the better-paid livings in the county, that of Simonburn in North Tynedale.[64] Crakenthorpe, an Oxford graduate, was Lord Eure's chaplain, tutor to his son and a noted Puritan preacher. However, when offered the cure, Crakenthorpe declined it. He claimed that he was "unable to live in so troublesome a place and his nature not well brooking the perverse nature of so crooked a people".[65] As Crakenthorpe had been born and brought up in Westmorland, he knew the North well and probably thought that a rural cure in Northumberland would do little to further his career. After the accession of James I, he preached an "inauguration sermon" at St Paul's Cross and was frequently seen about the Court. In 1605 he accepted a living in Essex and later wrote several well-known theological studies.[66]

But one man's poison might be another man's meat. So it was with Bernard Gilpin, the "apostle of the North" and the subject of a hagiographic study published in 1629 by George Carleton, bishop of Chichester.[67] Although ordained a Catholic priest under Queen Mary, Gilpin obediently accepted the authority of the new Elizabethan establishment. Between 1556 and 1584, while he was vicar first of Easington and then of Houghton-le-Spring in County Durham, he annually visited Redesdale and Tynedale. Contemporaries would have us believe that by these visits Gilpin convinced hundreds of Redesdalers and Tynedalers of the truth of the word of God. In 1586, two years after Gilpin's death, William Harrison wrote that by the "diligence chiefly of Master Gilpin, and finally of other learned preachers" the people of the highlands:

> have been called to some obedience and zeal unto the word, it is found that they have so well profited by the same, that at this present their former savage demeanour is very much abated, and their barbarous wildness and fierceness so much qualified that there is hope left of their reduction unto civility and better order of behaviour, than hitherto they have been acquainted withal.[68]

Without in any way disparaging Gilpin's very considerable achievements, it must be remembered that the introduction of reformed religion was only one of the many features in the transformation of western Northumberland during Elizabeth's reign.

Gilpin held a series of good livings in County Durham; to judge from his will he was quite prosperous.[69] This could be said of few clergy resident in Northumberland. In 1597 an anonymous writer asserted that a preacher in that county should be provided with a benefice worth £40 a year. According to Christopher Hill, a clear £30 was probably the minimum annual stipend necessary to maintain a clergyman.[70] But during Bishop Barnes's episcopacy there were only three Northumberland livings (outside Newcastle) worth more than £30 a year: those at Rothbury, Simonburn and Tynemouth. The poorest living, at Ovingham, was worth only £5 8s. 8d.[71]

Queen Elizabeth's ideas about ecclesiastical finance certainly did not contribute to the well-being of the Northumbrian clergy. She frequently used property which before the Reformation had belonged to the see of Durham to reward northern secular officials rather than reserving it for the support of the clergy. In 1559 she seized the temporalities of Norhamshire and Islandshire from the Bishopric and later gave many of them to her cousin, Lord Hunsdon.[72] She leased the tithes of Norhamshire to Sir William Read, the dissolute captain of Holy Isle. In 1591 she compelled the unwilling dean and chapter of Durham to grant William Selby, son of the gentleman porter of Berwick, a lease on very favourable terms to the tithes of Lowick in Glendale.[73]

Sir John Forster was another northern official whom the Crown richly rewarded with ecclesiastical spoils. In the middle of Elizabeth's reign William Camden found this philistine living in considerable comfort in the east end of Hexham Abbey, just above the Saxon crypt. In Forster, St Wilfrid, the turbulent founder of the abbey, had finally met his match.[74] In addition to monastic lands, Forster held the advowsons of the former abbeys at Alnwick and Hexham, the college of Bamburgh and the parsonages of Warkworth and Carham.[75] In 1587 Robert Ardern asked Lord Burghley to persuade Forster that "nowe after he hath so long tyme gathered the fleice, he would ymploie some porcion of every of the same livings for fyneding of preachers: or yf that milde course serve not... Then that nowe in this parliament some good order may be established in that behalf."[76] Despite Ardern's plea, the impropriation of tithes and livings long continued to weaken the church in Northumberland.[77]

All too often impropriators of tithes reserved a very small fixed sum for the upkeep of the incumbent clergyman. During the years of inflation the buying power of this stipend declined while the value of crops and other tithes in kind appreciated. In 1580 speculators received a royal lease to the tithe lands and the rectory of Corsensides in Redesdale and reserved £6 13s. 4d. for the vicar. This lease was conveyed to others in 1592, 1601, 1606 and again in 1628 but the stipend received by the cleric remained the same. In 1628 the vicar, one John Graham, was reported to be in "sharp misery".[78] Emmanuel Trotter, vicar of Kirknewton in Glendale, recognized that he could greatly improve his financial situation if he seized direct control of the tithe crops. In 1609–10 the lay impropriators accused Trotter of "having a covetous desire to increase the living of the said vicarage more than did of right belong" by falsely claiming the tithe corn. In response to charges brought against him in the Star Chamber, Trotter claimed that he only received £30 a year "which is a very small portion for the maintenance of God's service in that place, whereas the commodity which the said complaints have of the rectory of that parish is commonly esteemed worth £300 per annum or thereabouts".[79]

Richard Satherwaite, parson of Ingram and vicar of Whittingham, confronted similar difficulties when he attempted to collect tithe corn due from Fawdon and Ingram. Mindful of the very real danger of Scottish raids in the late Elizabethan period, he decided "for quietude's sake and his own safety" not to antagonize the crypto-Catholic, Sir Cuthbert Collingwood, who controlled the tithes. For a time the vicar seemed content to accept £2 13s. 4d. a year in lieu of tithes. Then in 1613, some years after Sir Cuthbert's death, Satherwaite decided to collect the tithes at Fawdon and Ingram. In this he was bitterly opposed by Sir Cuthbert's younger son, Cuthbert of Thrunton. The matter was brought before the Council of the North but before the case could be decided Cuthbert took direct action. The vicar later informed the Lords of the Star Chamber that in the autumn of 1613 James and Robert Scott had destroyed a hundred cartloads of hay and sizeable quantities of tithe grain. After the manner of the time Robert Collingwood, Sir Cuthbert's grandson, presented counter-charges against Satherwaite in the Star Chamber. Collingwood told the Court that Satherwaite was a pluralist who had not preached a sermon for the last five years. He also alleged that the vicar kept a "common ale-house or tippling house in his parsonage". In spite of all this Satherwaite continued to prosper; he retained his two livings, said to be worth £200 a year, until his death in 1625.[80]

All in all it is not surprising that puritan-inclined observers felt that true religion did not flourish in Northumberland; neither, they thought, did good learning. In 1597 an anonymous critic of Warden Eure's administration linked the spread of Catholicism with the shortage of teachers: "at years of understanding" children "want the Word to establish religion." For, he added:

> in their younger years they shall not find so much as a grammar school in all Northumberland to inform them with literature. Their livelihoods for the most part are either so little, or so dispended, that not one amongst five thousand maintains his son at the university and their good fortunes are less, having so fit towns as Alnwick, Morpeth and Hexham for schools; had never those blessings founded for their youth, to comfort their old age.[81]

But in fact schools were not entirely lacking in the county. Aspiring scholars could attend the grammar school in Newcastle, founded in 1525, that in Morpeth founded in 1552 and later the school in Hexham founded in 1600. There were other schools at Alnwick and Berwick but as these were not endowed, tuition was charged. In 1578 Bishop Barnes found that there were only nine schoolmasters in the county proper; three in Berwick, two at Alnwick, two at Morpeth and one each at Corbridge and Woodhorne. There were 11 in the town of Newcastle.[82] In these respects Northumberland does not compare favourably with contemporary Yorkshire or Lancashire. In the first half of the sixteenth century Yorkshire had 46 grammar schools; between 1545 and 1603 68 new schools were founded. By 1540 there were perhaps as many as 12 endowed schools in Lancashire.[83]

Despite the scarcity of schools and teachers in Northumberland, there is abundant evidence of a lively interest in education in the county. In 1563 Gabriel Hall of Elsdon left money in his will so that his sons Edward and Nicholas could be "sent to the school at Newcastle and when they have learned that their friends think to be done in learning and understanding, every of them to have £20 a piece to make them a stock of merchandise".[84] It is doubtful if Gabriel Hall himself had enjoyed the benefits which a school such as that at Newcastle might bestow.

It is also improbable that many of the first governors of the new school at Hexham had themselves been to a grammar school. The town had lost its earlier school at the time of the dissolution of the local monastery. But doubtless encouraged by the donation of £20 by George Lawson of Little Usworth in County Durham in 1587[85] and by the bailiff, Roger Widdrington, the townspeople petitioned the Crown for a licence to re-establish the school. Permission was granted in 1599. The extent of local patronage for the school is revealed in the list of the first governors, all of whom were required to live in the parish of Hexham. Eight of the 12 first governors were clearly not of gentry status. The other four, John Ridley of Coastley, Philip Thirlwall of Over Ardley, John Swinburn of Blackhall and Gabriel Blenkinsopp of Greenridge, were perhaps members of cadet branches of gentry families.[86] One of the governors, Richard Gibson, may well have been identical with or related to the yeoman of the same name who was admitted to a three acre customary tenement in Hexham in 1613. Tenants with surnames the same as those of the governors, Bell, Spark, Robson, Liddell, also suggest the humble origin of these men.[87] By their licence the 12 governors had authority to choose a schoolmaster, who was then to be approved by the archbishop of York, and to assume responsibility for the revenue of the school. The governors were apparently also responsible for establishing the curriculum; it was fairly typical of that of grammar schools elsewhere in England. As the schoolmaster was required to have an M. A. from either Oxford or Cambridge the curriculum offered at Hexham should have prepared students for the universities.[88]

Similar evidence of local interest in establishing a school was found at Berwick and Alnwick. In 1578 there were two schoolmasters at Alnwick who were supported by an endowment for a pre-Reformation chantry school which yielded only £4 1s. 8d. a year. As this sum was obviously insufficient, in 1588 the townspeople and burgesses petitioned Lord Burghley to restore the original grant of £13. This request was denied. In 1614 the townspeople raised enough money among themselves to found a school. It was established "to the end and intent that the honor and glory of almightie God may be increased, evill maners supplanted and the youth of this borough well instructed and informed in literature and schoole learninge". The schoolmaster was to be "sufficient learned and skillfull in the latyne and greek tonges and perfect in the learninge of poetry, prepared and provided, being allso a man of solidd witt and discreat government".[89]

Sons of people from all levels of society might attend the grammar schools. But many gentlemen's sons had private tutors, a luxury unknown to the lower orders. For example, in his will dated 1594, Edmund Craster left his schoolmaster "Sir Thomas" 10s. The master may have been Thomas Benyon, the rector of Embleton. Benyon had been a fellow of Merton College and had received his M. A. in 1561.[90]

During Elizabethan and Jacobean times the value of attendance at the Inns of Court or a university was increasingly recognized. One family which was outstanding in its concern for higher education was the Delaval family of Seaton Delaval. In 1595 Sir Robert Delaval (c. 1542–1607) sent his two eldest sons, Ralph and John, to Middle Temple. Three of Sir Robert's remaining four sons attended University College, Oxford, in the years around 1600 and then attended Inner Temple. In due course Sir Ralph Delaval (c. 1576–1628) sent his son and heir Robert (1600–23) to University College and Lincoln's Inn. Sir Ralph's fourth son John attended Lincoln's Inn in 1629 and his sixth son William attended St John's College, Cambridge.[91] The Claverings of Callaly were also aware of the value of higher education. Robert Clavering (1530–82) sent his second son John to Queen's College, Oxford, where he matriculated in 1575; his fifth son matriculated from the same college in 1583. John, grandson of Robert and heir to the family fortune, was admitted to Middle Temple in 1608. Sir John's three eldest surviving sons all attended Queen's College and two of them also attended Lincoln's Inn.[92]

In all, only seven of the 89 heads of families flourishing in 1615 had themselves attended either a university or the Inns of Court. Sir Ralph and Sir John Delaval and Sir John Clavering have already been mentioned. Sir William Selby of Branxton went to Cambridge and Sir Henry Widdrington the younger attended Gray's Inn. John Strother and Thomas Ogle of Tritlington, two younger heads of families in 1615, received both university and legal training.[93] It would appear that the heads of families flourishing in 1615 were more cognizant of the advantages of education than their fathers had been, or perhaps they were simply better able to afford the expense. Sons of 22 of the 79 families with traceable male heirs received higher education; 18 of these (20 per cent of the total 89 gentry families) were eldest sons.[94] Considering all that has been written about the educational backwardness of the Northumberland gentry, this does not compare too unfavourably with the situation in Yorkshire. In 1642 (a generation later) the heads of 36 per cent of the Yorkshire gentry families (247 out of 679) had received higher education.[95]

No identifiable Northumbrians are recorded as attending Scottish universities before the Civil War and only one gentleman is recorded as attending a university on the Continent. In the 1630s Claudius Fenwick, the fifth son of

George of Brinkburn, attended St Catherine's College, Cambridge, and then went on to Leiden. In later life he practised as a "doctor of physic" in Newcastle.[96] His eldest brother George matriculated as a fellow commoner from Queens' College, Cambridge, in 1619 and then went on to Gray's Inn. He spent some time in Saybrook, Connecticut, where his first wife is buried; he sat in the Long Parliament from 1643 and was governor of Berwick in 1649.[97]

Like George Fenwick the elder, most Northumbrian gentlemen sent their sons to universities as fellow commoners at a cost of between £40 and £50 a year. But poorer gentlemen might send their sons as sizars or pensioners. Thus Martin and John Fenwick, sons of John Fenwick of Butterlaw, a gentleman whose income cannot have been more than £100 a year, were pensioner and sizar respectively at Christ's College, Cambridge.[98]

Some talented sons of non-gentle Northumbrian families also went to the universities. Thomas Widdrington, the eldest son of the Lewis Widdrington of Cheeseburn Grange who had served as a grand juror at assizes and gaol deliveries on a number of occasions, was admitted as a pensioner to Christ's College in 1617 and two years later was admitted to Gray's Inn. After serving for a time as one of Lord William Howard's legal advisers, Thomas gave his estates at Cheeseburn Grange to his next brother, Henry of Black Heddon. Thomas Widdrington later became a Member of Parliament and in 1656 was elected speaker of the House of Commons.[99] Three sons of Amor Oxley, Charles, Thomas and Amor, attended university. Oxley senior was himself a man of considerable ability; he was parish clerk of Morpeth and the much-respected schoolmaster of Woodhorne in the 1570s and 1580s. His son Thomas matriculated sizar at Christ's in 1597–8, received his B. A. and became curate of Bamburgh in 1601. Later he accepted a cure in Essex and left the advowson of Whalton, west of Morpeth, to his son Amor, who was admitted sizar at Christ's in 1637. Charles Oxley received his B. A. from Christ's in 1606–7 and his M. A. in 1610. Between 1616 and 1636 he was vicar of Chillingham and after 1627 also vicar of Edlingham.[100] The third son, Amor Oxley the younger, matriculated as a pensioner at Christ's in 1615, received his B. A. in 1618 and his M. A. in 1626. He was headmaster of Morpeth school in 1631 and of Newcastle school in 1637. At Morpeth Amor Oxley encouraged Ralph, the fourth son of Lewis Widdrington, to go on to Christ's, following in the footsteps of his famous elder brother Thomas. Ralph later became Regius Professor of Greek at Cambridge.[101]

Although recusants were excluded by statute in 1606 from attending Inns of Court or universities, it was still possible for their sons to do so. Edward and John Radcliffe, sons of the recusant Francis of Dilston, were admitted to Lincoln's Inn in 1605 and 1608 respectively.[102] The three eldest sons of John Clavering of Callaly and his recusant wife Anne received a university and legal education. Two of them were later indicted for recusancy. The Claverings' youngest son, Thomas, was admitted to the English college in

Rome in 1649 under the alias Conyers and became chaplain to the Benedictine nuns at Pontoise.[103] But surprisingly few other young Northumberland Catholics left evidence that they had studied abroad.[104] It may be, however, that this was what Ralph and Cuthbert Carnaby, the two eldest sons of Lancelot Carnaby of Halton, had in mind when they secured a licence from the Privy Council in 1615 to travel abroad for three years.[105]

Putting all the evidence together, we can no longer accept assertions that Elizabethan and Jacobean Northumbrians were unlearned and, as one hostile observer put it in 1597, "an old tradition called Papistry fitteth them best". This understanding prepares us for a study of county politics during the late Elizabethan period when all too often self-seeking outsiders misrepresented the loyalties and attributes of the people of Northumberland.

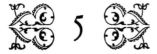

The politics and governance of Northumberland, 1586-95

> "Now the wit of the fox is everywhere on foot, so as hardly a faithful or virtuous man may be found." Queen Elizabeth I[1]

Royal policy towards Northumberland between the years 1586 and 1595 reflects some of the least attractive aspects of Elizabethan statecraft. After the Treaty of Berwick had in effect reduced the formerly hostile kingdom of Scotland to the status of a satellite, the queen and her principal advisers came to regard Northumberland as a backwater which could safely be left under the control of the resident official who almost singlehandedly dominated county affairs: old Sir John Forster (1501–1602), the *custos rotulorum* and warden of the Middle March. Although it should have been obvious that a man as old as the century itself was not really capable of defending the marches from Scottish raiders or of overseeing the conduct of civil affairs, the Crown (except for a brief interlude in 1587–8) supported Forster in his offices until 1595. During the late 1580s the aged warden's competence was questioned by Northumberland gentlemen 40 or 50 years his junior. These men must have known that Queen Elizabeth tolerated and indeed often encouraged a certain degree of rivalry among office holders and potential office holders, for she assumed that such rivalries would allow her to keep a firm grasp on the conduct of affairs of state.[2] But Forster's opponents soon learned that when it came to wardenry affairs, the queen was only prepared to listen to Forster's side of an argument. This forced them to seek their own patrons at Court and at the Council of the North at York. In consequence, for the formulators of royal policy towards Northumberland from 1586 to 1595, the needs of the county were of far less importance than the personal connections of the rival Northumberland faction leaders. Policies based on similar considerations may have been beneficial to some parts of the kingdom, but they profited the people of Northumberland not at all.

Sir John Forster, the central figure in Northumberland affairs during these troubled years, was the second son of Thomas Forster of Adderstone, a Percy squire who had joined Cardinal Wolsey's party in the 1520s. Through his mother Dorothy, the daughter of the third lord Ogle, and through the marriage of his brothers and sisters, Forster was allied to the Carnabys, Herons, Widdringtons, Whartons and other prominent northern Crown families.[3] After Reynold Carnaby, the original leader of the Court party in Northumberland, died in 1543 Forster attracted the favourable attention of Sir Ralph Sadler, the influential privy councillor and long-time antagonist of the Percy family.[4] In 1545 the Crown bestowed its first mark of favour upon Forster with the grant of the ruined cell of the Austin canons at Bamburgh. Knighthood followed two years later. In January 1549 Sir John was chosen high sheriff of Northumberland.[5] Most second sons nearing their fiftieth year might consider such an appointment to be a fitting culmination to a public career; Forster's was just beginning. The accession of Queen Mary Tudor in 1553, the restoration of the Percy lands to Thomas, the Catholic seventh earl of Northumberland, the earl's appointment as warden of the Middle and East marches and the outbreak of war with Scotland all served to give Forster occasion to demonstrate his loyalty to the Crown and his enmity for the Percys.[6] Soon after her accession, Queen Elizabeth came to distrust Earl Percy and dismissed him from his wardenry posts. Sir Ralph Sadler then assured her that Forster was the man to have the Middle March. Yet for some months the young queen hesitated to give this strategically placed post to a person of Sir John's age and reputation. He did not receive his commission until November 1560.[7]

Triumphant at last, the new warden was openly hostile to the Catholic earl during the 1560s. Thus he very possibly contributed to the latter's decision to join the Earl of Westmorland in revolt.[8] For Forster the Northern Rising was a godsend. To reward him for his role in crushing the rebels and maintaining order in Northumberland, the Crown allowed him to confiscate spoils worth an estimated £3,000, granted him leases to lands of an annual value of more than £5,000 and appointed him bailiff and receiver of Bywell and Bulbeck, Northumbrian baronies forfeited by the attainted Neville earl.[9] Forster also appears to have been appointed steward of the Percy lands in Northumberland.[10] While he occupied Alnwick and Warkworth Castles, he stripped them of everything that could possibly be sold or taken away. This behaviour even disgusted the recently appointed warden of the East March, Lord Hunsdon.[11] Hunsdon's distrust of Forster increased in the summer of 1572 when, after he had vainly pleaded with Lord Burghley to spare the life of the attainted Earl of Northumberland, Forster presided over the latter's execution at York. Well might Percy officers remember Forster 20 years after his death as a "sure back friend to that honourable house."[12]

Sir John did not begin to establish his own family until he married Jane Ogle sometime after 1545. Jane was the widow of his cousin Robert, fifth lord Ogle, and the daughter of Sir Cuthbert Radcliffe of Dilston and Cartington.[13] Sir John and Lady Jane had two daughters, Juliana and Grace. While Francis Earl of Bedford was warden of the East March in the 1560s, Forster arranged a marriage between Juliana and the earl's third son, Lord Francis Russell.[14] Grace, his second daughter, married the prominent Northumbrian squire William Fenwick of Wallington sometime after 1575.[15]

In religion Forster was a trimmer, a reasonable enough position for a man who had lived through all the changes made during the reigns of Henry VIII, Edward VI, Mary and Elizabeth. Sir John must occasionally have appeared receptive to advanced religious ideas, for his friends the Earl of Bedford and Secretary Francis Walsingham (Forster's principal patron at Court after the autumn of 1583)[16] were both well-known Puritan sympathizers. James Melvill, the exiled Scottish Presbyterian leader, also thought well of him. After dining with Forster one day in November 1585 the reformer noted in his diary: "we war estonished to heir the mouthe of a warldlie civill man sa opened to speak out the woundarfull warkes and prases of God, wrought for us."[17] Phrases in Forster's will are also suggestive of Puritan influence,[18] yet his life style was that of a man who wore his religion lightly. After his wife's death he lived with a common law wife, one Isabel Sheppard. He sired many bastard children, the best known of whom was Nicholas Forster. In 1595 Sir Robert Carey noted that young Forster, then serving as deputy warden of the Middle March, was "so given over to drunkenness that if he cannot get company, he will sit in a chair in his chamber and drink himself drunk before he rise."[19] A decade later commissioners reported that Nicholas was a "profane libertine".[20] Such then were the Forsters of Bamburgh.

Among the Northumbrian gentry Sir John's most determined opponent was Sir Cuthbert Collingwood of Eslington (c. 1540–96). Sometime before 1570 Collingwood took as his wife Dorothy Bowes, daughter and co-heiress of Sir George Bowes of Dalden and Streatlam Castle, the leader of a prominent Crown gentry family in County Durham. Yet as we have seen, in 1588 Collingwood was suspected of being a Catholic.[21] Unlike Forster, Sir Cuthbert sought advancement by serving both the Crown and the Percy earls. This dual loyalty sometimes led him into difficulties. He was in a particularly awkward position late in 1569 when the seventh earl rose in rebellion for, in addition to being the earl's constable at Alnwick Castle, he was high sheriff of Northumberland. On 18 November, the day after Collingwood's term as sheriff had expired and four days after the main rebel forces had assembled in County Durham, Warden Forster appeared before Alnwick Castle demanding its surrender. Sir John claimed that Percy followers put up a spirited resistance, yet the Crown later knighted Collingwood for his loyalty during the rebellion![22] Sir Cuthbert's apparent ability to serve two masters was further demonstrated in 1580. That September he became Northumberland receiver for the avowedly Protestant eighth earl of Northumberland; two months later he began his second term as high sheriff.[23] But before his term expired he was again in difficulty. The central authorities castigated his patron Earl Percy for demanding that 48 Northumberland gentlemen appear in London to testify in a lawsuit against Forster's ally, the Earl of Bedford. The privy councillors pointed out that by compelling these gentlemen to leave Northumberland, Percy was depriving the lord warden of their assistance in the service of the borders.[24] Collingwood must by now have begun to realize that as long as he retained his ties with the Percy interest, he could make little headway in his campaign to discredit and perhaps replace the octogenarian lord warden.

A few months after the eighth earl died in the Tower under suspicious circumstances, Henry, the ninth earl, dismissed Collingwood from the Northumberland receivership.[25] Deeply hurt, in February 1586 Collingwood vowed: "I will never serve under that subject that so small accounts of me as he has done...He should know that I am able and can live in my country without him, God willing."[26] By this time Collingwood had apparently made two momentous decisions; he would show more enthusiasm for the Established Church and he would seek the patronage of the well-known patron of Puritan preachers and causes, Secretary Francis Walsingham.[27]

Collingwood knew that Nicholas Forster and William Fenwick were in London that February to assure the Privy Council that Forster's march was quiet and well-ordered. But Sir Cuthbert was convinced that it was not. In a letter directed to his influential son-in-law, the Hostman Henry Anderson who was in London as a Member of Parliament for Newcastle, Collingwood reported that Scots surnames were virtually in a state of open war with the men of Redesdale. To protect his own goods Sir John Forster had entered into a personal agreement with the Liddesdale Elliots and allowed no Englishman to seek revenge against them. As these were serious allegations, Collingwood cautioned Anderson only to present them to Walsingham "if you think it convenient, not otherwise".[28]

In April Forster learned that grievous complaints had been lodged against him in the Privy Council. In a tone of injured innocence he wrote to Walsingham that this was "the greatest discouragement that ever came to me".[29] But though he was apprehensive, Forster could console himself with the knowledge that Sir Francis owed him a very considerable political debt. Nine months earlier Sir John had informed the secretary that whilst he and the Scottish warden were amicably exchanging bills at a day of truce at Cocklaw high in the Cheviots an unknown Scottish or English borderer had shot and killed his son-in-law, Lord Francis Russell (27 July 1585). Forster reported that the

Scottish warden had been no less shocked by the murder than he was himself, but that neither of them attached any political significance to the incident.[30] But as this account of the events at Cocklaw would not serve the purposes of Walsingham or the Scottish Presbyterians who were attempting to remove Chancellor Arran, a religious moderate, from power, Walsingham's agent in Edinburgh had asked Forster to write a more suitable account. Forster had obliged. Walsingham's agent had then used Sir John's revised report to persuade King James to remove Arran temporarily from power.[31]

Walsingham remained faithful to the controversial warden during the summer of 1586. He saw to it that the English treaty commissioners at Berwick did not query him about his dispute with Collingwood or his conduct of wardenry affairs.[32] Thus the men who petitioned the commissioners on behalf of the inhabitants of areas which had been cruelly plundered by the Scots since Forster's appointment in 1560 may well have felt that they were wasting their time. After the treaty commissioners had left the borders Sir John sent Walsingham a brace of gyr falcons "giving your honour humble thanks for all your goodness shewed unto me from time to time."[33]

The Council of the North also continued to neglect Northumberland wardenry affairs in the summer of 1586 although in theory they were within its purview.[34] This situation had prevailed ever since Walsingham's friend Henry, third earl of Huntingdon (1536-95), had assumed the presidency of the Council in 1572.[35] Late in the summer of 1575 Regent Morton of Scotland had specifically requested that the English Privy Council place Warden Forster more directly under the Lord President's jurisdiction. Morton had suspected that Forster's secret agreements with border supporters of Mary Queen of Scots had been the cause of the fray at Redeswire (7 July) which had upset his and Walsingham's plans to forge an Anglo-Scottish alliance. Huntingdon shared Morton's suspicions yet he apparently made no effort to make his influence felt in the wardenries until November 1586.[36]

In that month Huntingdon was forced to intervene in Northumbrian affairs because of a serious dispute among the local gentry. On 22 November Sir Cuthbert Collingwood, sheriff Robert Clavering and his brother William, together with their wives and friends, were returning home from Newcastle after attending celebrations commemorating Queen Elizabeth's accession. As they rode across the moor north of Morpeth they were assaulted by a company of 10 to 15 soldiers from Berwick under the command of young William Selby of Branxton, son of Lord Hunsdon's deputy warden for the East March. During the ensuing fray, Sir Cuthbert was shot in the stomach and William Clavering, the sheriff's brother, was killed. Fearing for his life, Selby fled. Upon hearing of this incident Huntingdon, who had himself just left the festivities at Newcastle, rushed back to the town and summoned a grand jury which charged the three soldiers who had fired the fatal shots with wilful murder. Much to Huntingdon's disgust petty jurors later found them guilty only of manslaughter.[37]

Eventually Secretary Walsingham suggested that Huntingdon and Lord Hunsdon settle this local dispute by arbitration. When this course failed Walsingham took matters into his own hands, seeing in this an opportunity to draw more Northumberland gentlemen into his political orbit. The affair dragged on until August 1588 when Sir John Selby, the deputy warden, thanked Walsingham for "ending of my son's troubles" and for his "further-ance in obtaining of his wife": Dorothy Bonham, daughter and heiress of Charles Bonham of Town Malling in Kent.[38] Young William Selby, later one of the most prominent officials in Northumberland, also hastened to acknow-ledge his gratitude to Walsingham.[39]

Queen Elizabeth's fateful decision to permit Mary Stuart to be executed at Fotheringhay Castle on 8 February 1587 once again placed the English marches in jeopardy. No one knew how King James would receive the news of his mother's death.[40] In fact, he accepted it with far better grace than did his rash cousin, Francis Stewart, Earl of Bothwell, the keeper of Liddesdale. Sensing that the king and Chancellor Maitland meant to do nothing which would strain the newly forged alliance with England, Bothwell, normally a militant Protestant, allied himself with Catholic malcontents and the surnames of Liddesdale and Teviotdale.[41] Together they made many savage incursions into the Middle March.[42]

These bloody raids should have come as no surprise to the privy councillors for Sir Cuthbert Collingwood had been warning them for months that Forster could not defend the Middle March even in time of peace.[43] Feeling that they should do something, early in March – no more than a month after Mary Stuart's execution – the Council asked the Earl of Huntingdon to determine whether or not in his estimation Forster should be retained as lord warden.[44] On 20 March Huntingdon talked with Forster in Newcastle and satisfied himself that the lord warden's relations with the Scottish surname groups on the one hand and with the men of Redesdale on the other were quite in order, whatever Sir Cuthbert Collingwood might claim to the contrary. However, Huntingdon did hint that, in view of his advanced age, Forster might con-sider retiring. Forster indignantly refused. He argued that "now when there is some doubt of trouble and unquietness", his presence on the borders was even more essential than before.[45] Huntingdon did not pursue the matter further.

Forster's success in hoodwinking the honourable earl forced Collingwood to resort to desperate courses to gain the ear of the Puritan Secretary of State. On 21 May he confessed in a letter to Walsingham that two of his own kins-men had smuggled several Jesuits and seminary priests through Northumber-land into Scotland. No doubt assuming that such information would encourage Walsingham to read further, Collingwood went on to describe some of the atrocities recently committed by Scots in Forster's wardenry. He warned that unless there was a speedy reformation, all English gentlemen living near the borders would be forced to abandon their habitations.[46]

In July 1587 Edward Talbot, a younger son of the Earl of Shrewsbury, similarly warned that the Middle March was in imminent danger of being ruined by the Scots. As Talbot had been a knight of the shire for Northumberland in the recent Parliament and had generally stood clear of the disputes between Forster and Collingwood, his words should have borne considerable weight.[47] Some privy councillors noticed that reports seemed to indicate that the Scottish terrorists were concentrating almost all of their attention on the English Middle March whilst ignoring the East and West marches. This curious situation clearly called for an investigation into Sir John Forster's conduct of wardenry affairs.

By this time the Council had decided that one of its members should go to Edinburgh to smooth King James's ruffled feelings and restore harmonious relations between the two nations. Their choice was the queen's trusted cousin, Henry Hunsdon (c. 1524-96). A man of action with few intellectual pretensions, Hunsdon was Lord Chamberlain of the Household as well as absentee warden of the East March and governor of Berwick. Thus the councillors thought it appropriate to ask him to take the wardenship of the Middle March upon himself on a temporary basis and then to conduct a public hearing into Forster's administration of that wardenry.[48]

Baron Hunsdon convened the hearing at Newcastle on 27 September 1587. Sir Cuthbert Collingwood and his friends were also present, expecting that the new acting warden would ask them to elaborate upon the written charges they had already filed against Forster.[49] Much to their astonishment and contrary to all their evidence, Hunsdon declared that Sir John was innocent of all but the most trivial of the charges brought against him![50] This decision was all the more unexpected in view of the fact that before Hunsdon had left London he had never publicly favoured Forster.

The surprise outcome of the Newcastle hearing can be directly attributed to Hunsdon's bitter enmity for Huntingdon, the urbane Lord President of the Council of the North. Their quarrel calls into question the generally accepted assumption that the first generation of Elizabeth's advisers (in contrast to men of Essex's generation) kept their animosities under control and thus avoided endangering the security of the commonwealth. Although Hunsdon and Huntingdon had been rivals for at least six years, it was only now that their dispute became significant in border affairs and especially for the unfortunate people of Northumberland.[51]

A day or two before Hunsdon opened the proceedings at Newcastle, he received a letter bearing the date 20 September, in which Lord Burghley intimated that as governor of Berwick Hunsdon was no more worthy of the queen's trust than was Sir John Forster.[52] Burghley's charges were almost certainly based on a report on the condition of the border garrison written by one Robert Ardern. Ardern was a client of the Earl of Huntingdon and his brother-in-law the Earl of Leicester. Although he admitted that he had not actually been in Berwick for some months, Ardern alleged that Hunsdon's incompetent deputy, Sir Henry Widdrington, the head of the well-known Northumbrian family, had allowed the garrison to grow so weak that it could not possibly resist an invading army. While Widdrington spent his time in drinking and dicing, England's northern postern stood wide open. Ardern's report probably reached the Earl of Huntingdon early in 1587.[53] Its whereabouts until September are unknown, but it is possible that Huntingdon or Walsingham held it in reserve until Hunsdon had left London and was no longer in a position to defend his reputation in person. They then presented it to Lord Burghley and sat back to watch the results.

On the day of the Forster hearing Hunsdon wrote to Burghley roundly condemning the man who had informed against him: "I know not upon what zeal or information he did it, but surely it proceeded of light credit, small skill and less discretion, if not of malice, wherein he has done me greater injury than I have given him cause."[54] As Hunsdon now saw it, both he and Forster were victims of plots concocted by the Earl of Huntingdon. Hunsdon apparently reasoned that if he could convince Burghley that Forster had been wrongly accused, he himself was well on the way to proving that nothing was seriously amiss at Berwick. In a letter to Burghley Hunsdon made the improbable allegation that the scheme to overturn Forster "has been long a-laying, hatched by Sir Cuthbert Collingwood, his mortal enemy, and nourished and set on by my lord of Huntingdon".[55] Thinking to slander the Lord President further, he noted in another letter "what will not malice do, the worker being of authority and credit?"[56]

After the privy councillors learned about Hunsdon's unexpected decision in the Forster case they repeatedly pressed him for further details about affairs in the Middle March so that they could make a permanent appointment to the wardenship. In response, Hunsdon claimed that Warden Forster had not been adequately supported by the people of the march. He reminded Burghley that many of the inhabitants of the county were too poor to furnish themselves with horses and weapons. He added that the leaders of local society were commonly so at odds with each other that they would not come to the assistance of neighbouring people who were being pillaged by half a dozen Scots. "This being true, as it is most true", Hunsdon assured Burghley, "how can the warden help it: so, as for anything I can understand, there could no man do more for the stay of this incursion than he has done."[57]

It was to Hunsdon's advantage in these machinations that as he was only acting warden, the Privy Council had appointed the keepers of Tynedale and Redesdale.[58] Thus he had no compunction about ruining these men's reputations. The new keeper of Tynedale, John Heron of Chipchase, a shirt-tail

relation of Sir John Forster who had been county sheriff in 1581–2,[59] was the
first to suffer Hunsdon's wrath. A few days after the Forster hearing 400
Scots led by Kinmont Willie the elder conducted a daytime raid on the
village of Haydon Bridge on the South Tyne. Hunsdon later alleged that
Heron and his fourth son Reginald had had a private agreement with the
Scots and waited until after they had plundered the village before organizing a
rescue party. With unbecoming haste Hunsdon convened a court of wardenry
at Alnwick Castle where a subservient jury found Reginald Heron guilty of
March Treason. Heron managed to save his life by asking for a stay of execution while he appealed to the queen. Meanwhile, Lord Hunsdon asked the
privy councillors to dismiss the elder Heron from the keepership. They
refused.[60]

It was a source of considerable vexation to Hunsdon that the Privy Council
had given the keepership of Redesdale to Forster's great rival, Sir Cuthbert
Collingwood, who, in contrast to keeper John Heron, was overeager to dash
the Scots. On 27 November 1587, acting without Hunsdon's prior knowledge,
he marshalled his household servants and a troop of Yorkshire horsemen sent
up a day or two earlier by the Earl of Huntingdon.[61] Intending to redress the
balance of terror between English and Scottish borderers, Sir Cuthbert led 800
men from his house at Eslington, on the upper Aln, into Teviotdale. Unfortunately the Scots had been forewarned of his approach and carried their goods
and flocks to safety long before his band crossed the border. Sir Cuthbert
returned to Eslington empty-handed. Three days later more than 2,000 Scots
from Annandale, Liddesdale and Teviotdale returned Collingwood's visit.
Led by Robert Ker, laird of Cessford, and Walter Scott, laird of Buccleuch,
the Scots caught the English completely by surprise. During the ensuing
battle the Scots killed 14 Yorkshiremen, injured Sir Cuthbert's eldest son and
took another son prisoner. But as soon as the Scots began to withdraw and
local people came to Eslington to help repel the invaders, Collingwood sallied
out to counter-attack and captured more than 150 prisoners. Even Lord
Hunsdon could not conceal his admiration for the keeper's bravery. Yet, as he
laboriously pointed out to Lord Burghley, Collingwood had very nearly
wrecked his own efforts to effect a reconciliation between King James and the
English government. Had Hunsdon known of Collingwood's plans, he
would have forbidden him to ride into Teviotdale in the first place.[62]

Baron Hunsdon had an opportunity to show Sir John Forster in a particularly good light late in January 1588. On his recommendation Forster was
appointed one of the English commissioners to settle outstanding differences
along the border.[63] On 25 February, a few weeks before he was due to return
south, Hunsdon boasted that Sir John had in large measure been responsible
for the success of the international conference just concluded. No man knew
the ways of the border better than he; without him the other commissioners
would have achieved nothing. He blandly assured Lord Burghley "upon my

credit, that neither he nor any friend of his ever spoke to me herein, but having considered of the matter, I find him the fittest man for the time."[64] Burghley and the Council did not reply. By 15 March Hunsdon began to worry lest they give the wardenship to the man whom he believed was Huntingdon's chief local agent, Sir Cuthbert Collingwood. Deeply perturbed, he informed Burghley that he could have tried Collingwood before a court of wardenry for selling horses to Scots; this was a March Treason and a capital crime. He had only refrained from bringing him to trial lest it appear he had done so "for revenge".[65]

Hunsdon left Northumberland for the last time in April 1588 and later took up command of the 35,000 troops appointed to guard the queen's person against Spanish invaders. But at the time of his departure, the Privy Council still had not decided who was to be the permanent warden of the Middle March.[66] Thus both the Middle March and Hunsdon's own East March were left without resident commissioned lord wardens during the August days when the battered Spanish fleet limped slowly past Tynemouth, Alnmouth and Berwick. It was fortunate that the confusion so much in evidence in Northumberland and indeed throughout the whole area under the command of the Earl of Huntingdon, the lieutenant general of the North, was matched by the blunders of Admiral Medina Sidonia and Philip of Spain.[67]

After the Spanish threat had passed, old Sir John Forster gradually regained official favour. When he appeared in Newcastle at the regular August assize, the judges treated him with respect.[68] By the spring of 1589 he had been restored with full powers as *custos rotulorum* and lord warden. Conditions in the troubled Middle March rapidly returned to normal. Sir Cuthbert Collingwood accused Forster of plotting to deliver his sons into the hands of his hated enemies, the Burnes of Scotland. Forster termed this a "manifest lie". He wrote to his old patron Secretary Francis Walsingham that "if it come to the hearing, I will truly prove that I have dealt more equally with him and his friends than any friend I have!"[69] Forster's position was in no way weakened by Walsingham's death in April 1590 for by then he was fully supported at Court by William Lord Burghley and his ambitious son Robert Cecil.

In the years 1590 to 1592 Forster's principal assistant in wardenry and civil affairs was William Fenwick of Wallington (1550–1613).[70] Fenwick, at one time Forster's son-in-law, had taken Margaret Selby, the daughter of William Selby the prominent Newcastle Hostman, as his second wife after Grace Forster's death. He had pursued an active career in Northumberland politics for many years. He was high sheriff in 1578–9[71] and later apparently served as constable at Alnwick Castle under the absentee ninth earl of Northumberland.[72] Doubtless Percy, a conforming churchman who enjoyed considerable favour at Court, realized that it was better to have an ambitious,

unscrupulous man like Fenwick as an ally than as a foe. The Earl of Huntingdon and many privy councillors also recognized Fenwick's talents. He appears
to have commanded the Northumberland militia in the fateful summer of
1588. In November 1589 he was again pricked high sheriff. The following
April Sheriff Fenwick served as Forster's deputy at a day of truce with Scottish
wardenry officials.[73]

Few Northumbrians openly criticized Sir John Forster's administration
during the early 1590s; indeed, even Sir Cuthbert Collingwood remained
silent.[74] While it is possible that Forster and Fenwick gave no cause to protest,
it is more likely that the men of Northumberland realized that protest was in
vain. Forster was fully supported at Court by Queen Elizabeth and Lord
Burghley, like the warden survivors from an earlier age. Thus we find that
the Earl of Northumberland's estate agents decided not to bring a lawsuit
concerning Howling Close, Warkworth, and other parcels of land before the
judges of assize at Newcastle, "for if it should come to oath [Forster] out of
his own authority might and would have procured men in that country to
swear what he desired."[75] Incidents involving young Reginald Heron, the
Delavals and a number of justices of the peace, substantiate the agents' contention that in Northumberland the influence of Forster's clique was virtually
all-pervasive.

In 1590 Heron was still appealing his sentence of death as a march traitor
for allegedly helping the Scots at Haydon Bridge. His precarious position
encouraged Sheriff Fenwick and his greedy neighbours to claim that they
could legally seize all of his lands and goods. On 30 March Fenwick's under-
sheriff, the unscrupulous Edward Charlton of Hesleyside, and a crowd of about
200 people laid siege to Heron at Prudhoe Castle. Heron later informed the
lords in the Star Chamber that the mob had milled about the castle for a week.
Then on 13 April, a few days after the siege had been lifted, Sheriff Fenwick
himself suddenly appeared in the castle yard. He arrested Heron's servants as
they were threshing grain in the barns and hustled them off to Ovingham
where he kept them incommunicado overnight. The next morning Fenwick
took them to Alnwick where Sir John Forster was to deal with them.[76]

Reginald Heron was on friendly terms with Joshua, Ralph, Clement and
Peter Delaval, members of a cadet branch of the wealthy Protestant family
which had its seat at Seaton Delaval.[77] Like Heron, the four brothers fell afoul
of the Forster-Fenwick alliance. Early in 1590 there had been a fray between a
party led by Gawin Milburn, father-in-law of Clement Delaval, and one led
by Thomas Widdrington of Ashington. Thomas was Forster's nephew and
had married one of his illegitimate daughters. In the course of the fray
Milburn had been killed and Thomas Widdrington had received wounds from
which he died three months later. No proceedings seem to have been taken
against the people who killed Milburn, but immediately after Widdrington's
death, Sheriff Fenwick convened a grand jury which charged Clement Delaval

with murder. Writing about the jurors later, Delaval contended that "the first twelve were all of them either cousin germane by affinity or consanguity unto the said Thomas Widdrington or else servants or tenants unto the said Sir John Forster, uncle and father-in-law and a special friend unto the said Thomas Widdrington".[78] As might be expected this jury indicted Delaval for murder. Sheriff Fenwick then refused to accept bond for Delaval's release pending trial by petty jury. Instead he fettered Delaval with "shackles and bolts as many or rather more as he was then able to bear" and committed him "close prisoner among roughs and thieves in a most filthy prison" in Newcastle although there were better quarters available for gentlemen of Delaval's quality.

Clement Delaval remained in prison for eight weeks until the Court of Queen's Bench ruled that his indictment was faulty. But at the next general session of gaol delivery held on 1 August, Sheriff Fenwick attempted to have Delaval indicted once again. In this however he was frustrated by three jurors related to the late Thomas Widdrington who convinced their colleagues that there was insufficient evidence against Delaval. But Fenwick and Forster were determined to get their man. They met in great secrecy with a new jury and Richard Fenwick of Stanton, at one time a J.P. Forster thought that Richard would appreciate the fact that in the past he had forborne from trying him for March Treason.[79] But even with the threat of a future march trial hanging over his head, Richard Fenwick refused to co-operate in the indictment of the long-suffering Clement Delaval. Notwithstanding, Sheriff Fenwick proceeded with the indictment and swore on his honour that there had been a feud between the Widdringtons and the Milburn-Delaval connection and that Clement Delaval was clearly guilty of murder. Thoroughly cowed and frightened, the jurors obediently indicted Delaval. Later the central law courts ruled that this second indictment was no more valid than the first. But with bull-dog determination Forster, in his capacity as *custos rotulorum*, met at quarter sessions in January 1591 with Thomas Bradford J.P. Together they persuaded a jury to indict Delaval for the third time. At this stage in the drama Clement Delaval appealed to the lords of the Star Chamber for protection.[80]

On 21 January 1591 Joshua and Peter Delaval[81] set out from Seaton Delaval on their way to London to testify on behalf of their brother Clement. In their company was their friend Reginald Heron. As the party drew close to Newcastle, they were ambushed by Robert Widdrington of Plessey, his younger brother Ephraim, and a Newcastle merchant named Randal Fenwick. Heron managed to escape the ambush but Peter and Joshua were captured and imprisoned in Randal Fenwick's house. They later escaped to another house and barricaded the door whilst Randal Fenwick stormed about outside. A short time later the mayor of Newcastle had Fenwick arrested for disturbing the peace. Randal shamefacedly admitted that he was not in the habit of becoming involved in county disputes but as Sheriff William Fenwick had given him a warrant to arrest Reginald Heron on sight and both he and the sheriff were sons-in-law of Alderman William Selby, he had felt that he could not refuse to do him this favour.[82]

In contrast to the Middle March, where the influence of a lord warden was too much in evidence, men in the East March and Berwick suffered because there was no resident governor or warden to maintain a balance between conflicting interests. In March 1593 William Morton, the mayor of Berwick, complained that in Lord Hunsdon's absence, local gentlemen took it upon themselves to "play the king" and oppress and exploit lesser men.[83] As Morton feared, Hunsdon took his complaints as a personal insult. Later that month, after the death of the bungling marshal Sir Henry Widdrington, Hunsdon sent down his second son, John Carey, as deputy governor. The free burgesses of Berwick soon found that young Carey was "touched in the spleen", haughty and overbearing.[84]

Lord Burghley and other senior privy councillors had often been unsympathetic to northerners who found themselves harassed by duly-constituted wardenry officials. But after hearing rumours that King James of Scotland was thinking of using Spanish assistance to seize the English throne,[85] the councillors took a renewed interest in the condition of border defences. In October 1592 Burghley learned from an impeccably reliable informant, Sir John Forster, that no survey of the decay of border service had been made since 1583-4.[86] Burghley feared that there were fewer men able to serve than there had been eight years earlier, but he comforted himself with the thought that responsibility for the maintenance of border defences really lay with the Earl of Huntingdon, either in his capacity as Lord President of the Council of the North, or as lord lieutenant of the several border counties.

Queen Elizabeth let it be clearly known that she was of the same opinion. In February 1593, while she and Huntingdon were in conference with privy councillors at Lord Burghley's house near the Strand, Elizabeth suddenly turned on the earl. Conveniently forgetting that he had no effective authority in Northumberland as long as the government allowed Forster to continue as warden, Elizabeth harshly berated Huntingdon for neglecting the defence of the marches towards Scotland. She then informed him that he was to be placed in charge of a commission to survey and, what is more, to redress the decay of the border service in accordance with the statute of 23 Elizabeth I, c. 4.[87] This incident at Burghley's house marked the beginning of the Lord President's last attempt to bring the county of Northumberland and the wardens under his control.

For a brief period it seemed that the Privy Council would actively assist Huntingdon. In order to make it more difficult for Forster and the other wardens to intimidate the decay commissioners, the Council saw to it that all of the 12 northerners appointed to the commission on 24 February were associated directly or indirectly with Huntingdon's Council of the North and that none of them resided in Northumberland, Westmorland or Cumberland.[88] But in fact several of the privy councillors had no real wish to see the border counties brought under the effective magisterial authority of Huntingdon's council. Lord Keeper Puckering disliked the northern council in principle because in its judicial capacity it drew business away from the common law courts.[89] Robert Earl of Essex, the queen's ambitious young favourite newly sworn to the Privy Council, possibly opposed the February decay commission because it would encourage northern gentlemen to look to the Council of the North rather than to himself for patronage and support. Archbishop Whitgift, the scourge of Puritans, opposed the commission because it would increase the authority of the Earl of Huntingdon, a well-known patron of Puritan preachers. So it was that these privy councillors, together with a few others, had the February decay commission revoked before Huntingdon could make any effective use of it.[90]

In July Chancery put Huntingdon in charge of a much less powerful decay commission. Almost all of its working members were gentlemen resident in the border shires over whom the earl had little control.[91] A few weeks later hostile privy councillors imperiously demanded why Huntingdon had not yet sent in the returns on decay which they thought the new commissioners should have collected. But as the commissioners had not yet had time to convene juries from which to elicit the necessary information, Huntingdon could only send the impatient councillors returns collected in 1583 and 1584. He cautioned them that they should expect to find borderers less able to provide for their own defence than they had been earlier.[92]

Lord President Huntingdon was in Northumberland in September. He listened to accounts of Scottish raids made since 1588 for which Sir John Forster had neglected to seek redress. Huntingdon now realized even more clearly than before that somehow he must take a firmer hand in the affairs of the wardenry. To this end he ordered all wardenry officials to begin to collect bills against Scottish raiders so that the arduous process of seeking redress from Scottish wardens could begin.[93] But three weeks after Huntingdon left the county the sheriff, Robert Delaval, informed him that few men dared to turn in bills or present evidence against the Scots for fear of reprisals.[94]

William Fenwick of Wallington, in his capacity as keeper of Tynedale, also wrote to Huntingdon. He informed him that on 30 September a small band of Liddesdalers had invaded Tynedale. They had killed one of Fenwick's household servants and driven off 60 sheep. A week later more than a thousand members of the Elliot surname had ridden into Tynedale on a daytime foray and stolen goods worth more than £1,000. Fenwick, who only a few months earlier had worked hand in glove with the aged warden, Forster, went on to assure the Lord President that he and most other border gentlemen now looked to him as their sole "refuge and support".[95] One of these other gentlemen was almost certainly Forster's long-silent rival, Sir Cuthbert Colling-wood. As he was a member of the decay commission, although not one of the quorum, it may have crossed his mind that he, no less than Fenwick, could help Huntingdon to prove that Sir John Forster had allowed the military strength of the Middle March to wither away.[96]

Early in October 1593 Huntingdon examined reports showing the decay of the border service in Northumberland. He found the situation was so bad that he despaired of his own ability to restore the service to a level acceptable to Queen Elizabeth. Although he may have had a new set of complete returns in his possession, for some reason he sent only a brief summary up to the Privy Council.[97] He warned the councillors that unless they took forceful action to redress decays "much discontent will rise among those who hope to see faults mended and Northumberland especially will be wasted."[98]

Then in January 1594 Sir John Forster and three other principal decay commissioners contended that they had not conducted any survey and that as far as they knew no survey of border decays had been made since 1584.[99] This statement naturally led some privy councillors to wonder who had given Huntingdon his information about the extent of decay in the Middle March. Some may have suspected Collingwood and the turncoat Fenwick of Walling-ton.[100] However, for the sake of form the councillors ordered Forster to travel in the depth of winter to Durham to satisfy Bishop Hutton that affairs in the Middle March were in order. By April the seemingly indestructible 93-year-old lord warden was back at his house near Alnwick, still in full possession of his various offices.[101] If Huntingdon had covertly attempted to oust him, he had failed.

During the remainder of 1594 and the first half of 1595 conditions in Northumberland unquestionably deteriorated. There was a bad harvest in 1594; in 1595 the harvest was no better. In season and out of season Scottish marauders harassed the county. Robert Carey claimed that Northum-berland gentlemen who lived near routes commonly used by raiders paid black-mail in order to save their lives and goods; others allowed Scottish spies to live on their land. Farmers who were too poor to pay blackmail were entirely at the mercy of the Scots.[102]

The continuing deterioration of Northumberland greatly troubled the Earl of Huntingdon, but he knew that nothing could be done for the county until Queen Elizabeth and Lord Burghley were persuaded to dismiss Forster from the wardenship.[103] To this end Huntingdon seems to have prevailed upon his influential friends to deluge him and members of the Privy Council with dole-ful reports about conditions in Northumberland. In December 1594, at a time when Huntingdon was helping to arrange a marriage between the Earl of Northumberland and Dorothy Devereux, sister of the Earl of Essex, Earl Percy took the unprecedented step of asking Huntingdon to seek redress from Scottish wardenry officials for outrages committed against those of his North

Tynedale tenants who could not receive satisfaction from Forster.[104] The following August Tobias Matthew, recently appointed bishop of Durham, sent the earl a graphic account of an extraordinary incident at the recent assize held in County Durham. Matthew reported that after a Scottish outlaw named David Armstrong, alias Bangtail, had been convicted of eight separate felonies, he had turned to his captor, William Fenwick of Wallington, and had warned him that he should hang for daring to bring a Scotsman to trial. Fenwick gave the appearance of being a thoroughly frightened man and had begged Armstrong to spare his life. Then turning to the astonished judges, he had implored them to declare a mistrial.[105]

Ralph Lord Eure, another of Huntingdon's proteges, also attended the County Durham assize. On 12 August he implored Lord Burghley to rescue the queen's subjects in Durham and Northumberland from "the wild boor that greedily seeks their subversion". He begged Burghley to consider "what distress, calamities, pitiful complaints with the cries of widows and fatherless children even to the skies is enforced in this bishopric of Durham by the great theft, intolerable sufferance of Northumberland and the weakness or rather dastardy (if I may so term it) of the inhabitants there."[106]

Lord Eure's broad hint that the Crown should appoint a new warden for the Middle March was well taken by the aged Lord Burghley. This was not entirely surprising for he had recently recovered from a severe illness and like other men in such circumstances he wished to make provision for his family. In particular, Burghley hoped that his younger son Robert, rather than the scheming royal favourite Essex, would succeed him as the queen's first minister. As Burghley and Cecil temporarily had the upper hand over Essex and controlled patronage, they decided to act while they could. On 20 August 1595 the Council brusquely ordered Sir John Forster to show cause why he should not be dismissed forthwith.[107] On 6 September, much against his better judgment, Lord Eure accepted the wardenship of the Middle March.[108] So it seemed that the Earl of Huntingdon had triumphed over Forster at last.

On 25 November, after several delays, Lord Eure arrived in Newcastle to be formally installed as warden. In his company were the Lord President and a number of councillors from York. They found that Huntingdon's trusted friend, Sir William Bowes, had already taken possession of rolls of presentment and other wardenry papers. Bowes reported that when he had collected these papers from Forster he had queried him about his recent conduct in office, whereupon Forster "did wind like an eel".[109] As other officials had already held musters at three locations in the march,[110] for the first time Huntingdon was able to get an accurate impression of local conditions. The situation was far worse than even he had anticipated. Muster masters William Fenwick and John Featherstone reported that only 38 of the 3,000 foot soldiers in North and South Tynedale, Hexhamshire, Prudhoe and the barony of Langley were adequately furnished.[111] In the Middle March as a whole, fewer than 200 horsemen were service-worthy, although in 1593 Huntingdon had informed Lord Burghley that there were more than five times this number.[112]

On Wednesday 26 November Roger and Henry Widdrington, William Fenwick, Edward Gray, Robert Delaval and other prominent Northumberland squires provided Huntingdon with further disquieting information. They claimed that they knew of at least 200 people who had been murdered by Scots since 1568 for whom Sir John Forster had never sought redress. The Northumbrians graphically described the manner in which Scots tortured English prisoners whom they held for ransom "thrusting hot irons into their legs and other parts of their body".[113] On Thursday, after attending divine service, Huntingdon heard further reports of Forster's gross negligence. That evening in the hearing of John Ferne, the newly-appointed secretary of the Council of the North, the Lord President exclaimed: "Oh, how that man betrayed Queen Elizabeth". His countenance was heavy with sorrow as he reflected that he himself was not without blame for the woes of Northumberland. That night and the following day he was very ill.[114]

Early in December Huntingdon, now in his familiar rooms in the King's Manor in York, attempted to write to Lord Burghley about his recent proceedings in Northumberland. He mentioned the certificates he had received from the muster masters "which I found to differ so far from that which I sent unto my lords last as it did a . . ."[115] He broke off and retired to bed. On Sunday 14 December 1595 the "honourable, religious, faithful and wise" Lord President expired; Sir John Forster heard it said that he had died of a broken heart.[116] With his passing honest Northumbrians of all degrees lost their best-intentioned friend.

6

The Northumberland gentry challenged, 1595-1603

Whatever his faults, former warden Forster had at least one redeeming attribute in the eyes of most of his fellow Northumberland gentry; he was a local man born and bred. So too were the gentlemen who had controlled the East March and the fortress at Berwick after Lord Hunsdon left Northumberland in 1588; the deputy warden, Sir John Selby of Twizel (*d.* 1595) and Sir Henry Widdrington (*d.* 1593), the marshal of Berwick. Indeed for a time in the early 1590s it had seemed that Widdrington's ambitious nephew Henry Widdrington the younger (*c.* 1567–1623) might succeed Sir John Forster as warden. Another likely candidate had been Ralph Gray of Chillingham (*c.* 1552–1623), possibly the wealthiest squire in the county.[1] However, with the appointment of the Yorkshireman, Ralph Lord Eure, in 1595, wardenry affairs slipped from the hands of the Northumbrian gentry. Worse was to follow. Early in 1596 Widdrington, Gray and several other prominent Northumbrians who might normally expect to serve as justices of the peace, found themselves displaced from the local commission of the peace by Eure and other men from south of the Tyne. Thereafter many of the local gentry expended a great deal of energy opposing these strangers, in the hope that they could regain their accustomed hegemony over Northumberland's civil and military affairs.

The challenge which in varying degrees thus confronted the Northumberland gentry during the last eight years of Elizabeth's reign was the result of a deliberate policy decision made by Robert Cecil, his father William Lord Burghley and other great councillors of state. Sometime in 1595 they concluded that though King James of Scotland was only one of several possible claimants to the English throne, he might soon resort to desperate strategems to win it. In consequence, it was no longer politic to entrust the Northumbrian marches to independent-minded wardens drawn from the ranks of the factious local gentry. It would not do to repeat the mistakes made with Sir John Forster. In future wardens must be men of proven competence whom the Cecils and other like-minded councillors could easily control.

Ralph, third lord Eure (1558–1617), appeared to have all the qualifications necessary for a warden. Most of his estates and following lay in Yorkshire and County Durham. Although he held the Northumbrian lordship of Sturton Grange and had been born in Berwick-upon-Tweed during the last few months of his father's deputy wardenship, Eure had not resided in Northumberland for many years.[2] Thus it seemed unlikely that he had any meaningful ties with the Forster connection, the anti-Forster faction or with other groups in the county. The 37-year-old Yorkshireman had other attributes to commend him to the Cecils. He appeared to be as devoted to the Elizabethan religious establishment as was his friend, the Puritan Earl of Huntingdon. Moreover he seemed to be firmly committed to the idea that Northumberland and the border wardenries should be brought under the direct control of the Council of the North. As the Cecils also hoped to bring the borders under the sway of York, Lord Eure's connections with the northern council were most important.

For a few months after Huntingdon's death in December 1595, John Ferne, the secretary and acting head of the Council of the North, co-operated closely with Eure in wardenry affairs. In March 1596 Ferne ordered Yorkshire J.P.s to send 70 soldiers to the Middle March to assist Eure to maintain order. With somewhat less success he also ordered justices in County Durham to send Eure ten soldiers.[3] In April the secretary and some of his colleagues from York went to Hexham to help Eure hold his first court of wardenry and a session of gaol delivery. The northern councillors further made their influence felt in the wardenry by attending musters of footmen and by appointing a jury to survey the decay of border service.[4]

As Eure, possibly with Ferne's advice, had appointed Sir Cuthbert Collingwood of Eslington as his deputy and William Fenwick of Wallington as his keeper of Tynedale, the full implications of his presence in Northumberland did not become apparent until early in 1596. Before that time about 15 of the approximately 40 J.P.s in commission were Northumbrian squires such as Fenwick, Collingwood, Ralph Gray and Sir John Forster.[5] But in a new commission issued in January, Eure replaced Forster as *custos rotulorum* and the number of native Northumbrian justices was reduced to six. Two of these were veteran Crown servants: old Sir John Forster and William Selby the elder who had succeeded his brother as gentleman porter of Berwick in 1595. Neither Gray nor Collingwood were joined to the commission as at this time the Crown was systematically purging all county commissions of convicted recusants and Catholic sympathizers.[6] The four remaining Northumberland J.P.s were gentlemen of assured religion who had earlier attracted the favourable attention of Eure's patron, Huntingdon. They were Robert Delaval of Seaton Delaval, sheriff in 1592–3; Robert Clavering, sheriff in 1586 when his brother was killed by a soldier under the command of young William Selby of Branxton;

George Muschamp, sheriff in 1597 and brother-in-law of the same William Selby; and Thomas Bradford of Bradford, sheriff during most of the period between November 1594 and January 1597. As sheriffs included on a commission of the peace were not allowed to serve as J. P.s during their term of office, the number of native Northumberland justices between January 1596 and November 1597 was reduced to five.[7] And as Forster was too infirm to serve, in practice there were only four active Northumbrian J. P.s during this period.

As this contingent of justices was far too small to serve the needs of 77,000 people spread over 2,000 square miles, the Lord Keeper also included a number of gentlemen from County Durham and Yorkshire on the Northumberland commission in anticipation that they would be active members. One such J. P. was George Lightfoot, a lawyer from County Durham whom Lord Eure appointed Northumberland clerk of the peace. Lightfoot replaced Forster's appointee, John Brown, a volatile lawyer from north-eastern Northumberland.[8] Several of the outsiders placed on the commission were members of the Council of the North. At Lord Burghley's request, Eure nominated some of them to serve on a commission to investigate abuses committed by Forster during his long wardenship.[9] The choice of these men as J. P.s can thus be seen to reflect the Crown's determination to place Northumberland and the Middle March firmly under the direction of the Council of the North and its acting head, John Ferne.

But even as the northern councillors were beginning to find their way in their difficult new tasks, Burghley and his son Robert were forced to jettison the convenient new arrangements between York and the Middle March. This was because their rival Essex had persuaded Queen Elizabeth to put the northern council under the control of Matthew Hutton, the pliant archbishop of York. The Cecils could not prevent the archbishop's appointment, but they did see to it that he was deprived of the full authority of a lord president. Moreover, after Hutton replaced Ferne as acting head in the spring of 1596, the Cecils sought to curtail the Council's magisterial authority in the far North.[10] They no longer encouraged the northern councillors who had been joined to the Northumberland commission of the peace to assist their Northumbrian colleagues at quarter sessions or to oversee wardenry affairs. This new policy greatly increased Lord Eure's freedom of action.

As a fully commissioned lord warden Eure could appoint his own keepers without formal reference to outside authorities. John Brown, Henry Widdrington and other Northumbrians noted that some of the people to whom he gave office were strangers of very questionable repute. One such person was Henry Bowes of County Durham, the penurious younger brother of Sir William Bowes, perhaps the Crown's leading expert on border affairs. It is clear that Henry came to Northumberland to make his fortune. By the autumn of 1596 he had married Anne Heron, the wealthy widow of Cuthbert Heron of Chipchase, and succeeded William Fenwick as keeper of Tynedale.[11] Another of Eure's appointees was Ralph Mansfield, a Yorkshire adventurer whom he made captain of Harbottle Castle after dismissing Captain Nicholas Forster, the old warden's bastard son. Later Mansfield served as Eure's deputy, his keeper in Redesdale and his secret agent in Scottish affairs.[12] Another ill-reputed Yorkshireman who frequently associated with Eure was Thomas Percy (*c.* 1559–1605), the Earl of Northumberland's receiver for the county.[13]

Although Eure was a patron of Puritan preachers,[14] many of his particular allies within Northumberland seemed to be recusants or Catholic sympathizers. Chief amongst these were Ralph Gray of Chillingham and his brother Edward of Morpeth. It may be conjectured that Eure came to an arrangement of convenience with the Grays soon after he took up the wardenship. Eure promised to further the Grays' interests and not to harass them or their Catholic friends if they in turn would support him against the Forster faction. Whether or not such an arrangement actually existed, in September 1596 Eure unsuccessfully petitioned Lord Burghley to give Ralph Gray the treasurership of Berwick. The next month he suggested that either Ralph or Edward be chosen sheriff, and in October 1597 he appointed Edward Gray his deputy warden.[15]

Later that year Bishop Tobias Matthew of Durham complained that Eure, in his capacity as *custos rotulorum*, had not caused a single Northumbrian to be indicted for recusancy.[16] Matthew's none-too-subtle hints and allegations, together with our knowledge that in later years Eure's younger brother as well as his own son and heir were convicted of recusancy, might lead us to suspect that he was a secret Catholic. However, one would not think of accusing Bishop Matthew of secretly adhering to the banished faith simply because his eldest son was a convert to Catholicism.[17] Perhaps in religion Ralph Lord Eure, like his illustrious predecessor in the wardenship, can be best described as a trimmer.

In July 1596, with the death of Henry Lord Hunsdon, the long absent governor of Berwick and warden of the East March, the Crown had the choice of giving these posts to a Northumbrian gentleman or of continuing its new policy of ruling the marches through outsiders. Queen Elizabeth, Lord Burghley and Sir Robert Cecil (appointed principal secretary of state in the month of Hunsdon's death) discarded the first option. But as they were unwilling to decide which non-Northumbrian should have these offices permanently, they appointed Hunsdon's spleenish second son, John Carey, as acting governor and the baron's youngest son, Sir Robert, as acting warden.[18]

During the next 16 months these temporary officers confronted a worsening situation. In 1597 the series of bad harvests which had begun in 1594 culminated in a terrible famine. And as Queen Elizabeth had refused to give King James his annual pension in 1596,[19] he made no effort to prevent his borderers from plundering the English wardenries. Sir Robert Carey repeatedly begged for patents for office, pointing out that Northumbrians were too weak and disorganized to resist the invaders effectively. They urgently needed to be unified under the command of a fully-accredited lord warden who could compel people to perform border service.[20] But in June 1597 Queen Elizabeth rebuked Carey for daring to question the policies which contributed to the misery of Northumberland. "[We] do command you to do as you ought", she wrote, "for we that can judge what is fit for you, will do things as we please".[21] This then was the sovereign whom the Victorian historian and cleric Mandell Creighton claimed "paid as good heed to the remote parts of her realm as she did to those near at hand."[22]

Northumbrians might have thought that the king of Scotland's policies towards them also deserved censure. For beyond a doubt James was well able to control the activities of the two young wardenry officials most odious to Northumberland, Robert Ker of Cessford and Walter Scott of Buccleuch. Cessford, nephew of James's great minister, John Maitland of Thirlstane, was warden of the Scottish Middle March from 1594 to 1602. He was sworn to the Scottish Privy Council in March 1596 and later became a Gentleman of the King's Bedchamber.[23] If Lord Eure's description of him may be trusted, Cessford perfectly fitted the popular image of a Scottish courtier: "wise, quick spirited ... ambitious, desirous to be great, poor [and] not able to maintain his estate to his great mind".[24] He was also bloody-minded. In 1597 it was estimated that he had murdered or been present at the murder of more than 20 men during the previous decade. Cessford's brother-in-law, Scott of Buccleuch, keeper of Liddesdale from October 1594 until 1603, was no less vicious. He was credited with the murder of 16 Englishmen and Scotsmen.[25]

Buccleuch conducted his famous raid on Warden Scrope's headquarters at Carlisle Castle to rescue the notorious thief, Kinmont Willie the younger, in April 1596.[26] Some weeks later John Carey retaliated on behalf of Scrope by sending 50 garrison horsemen into Scotland to hunt down a horse thief named John Douglas. When the troops captured Douglas they hacked him to pieces. These tactics, which Queen Elizabeth censured as "very barbarous and seldom used among the Turks", invited Cessford to reply in kind.[27] Thinking that Selby, the gentleman porter, and his nephews, William Selby of Branxton and Ralph Selby of Weetwood, were chiefly responsible for Douglas's murder, Cessford harried them unmercifully. John and Robert Carey scarcely lifted a finger to help the Selbys lest they again incur the queen's displeasure. Matters came to such a pitch that in November 1596 the elder Selby informed his nephew William, then safely in London, that the latter's friends dared not stay at home at night for fear of being trapped and murdered in their beds by Cessford's followers. The wretched Englishmen slept in the fields.[28]

Sir William Bowes likened the state of the borders on both sides to a "winter war" between opposing garrisons. He claimed that the Scots had 3,000 horsemen under the command of wardens and keepers who "for strength of body, courage and wit or friendship among themselves and reputation with their followers as no man's memory now living can match of borderers at one time in that nation." The opposing English forces were greatly outnumbered and, Bowes thought, lacked "such wickedly disposed generals to perform so memorable attempts as do their opposites." Bowes predicted that if this imbalance were allowed to continue, the English wardenries would "waste by little and little to nothing".[29]

But several Northumbrians were of the opinion that Scotland had no monopoly of "wickedly disposed" wardenry officials. In May 1596 William Fenwick of Wallington and Sir Cuthbert Collingwood began to suspect Warden Eure of double dealing. In strictest confidence the warden had proposed to them and to justice Robert Clavering that Ker of Cessford be given a pension of £100 a year. Fenwick was appalled at this dishonourable suggestion. He himself had recently received an insulting letter in which Cessford boasted that he counted him and his friend Henry Widdrington "as light as the air". Refusing to be a party to Eure's nefarious dealings, Fenwick resigned as keeper of Tynedale.[30] A short time later Collingwood resigned as deputy warden. Perhaps feeling that he was too old to participate in another round of partisan conflict, Sir Cuthbert gave his Northumberland estates at Eslington to his recusant son and withdrew to County Durham.

According to later statements by Henry Widdrington and John Brown, the displaced county clerk of the peace, Warden Eure and his shifty friends Ralph Mansfield and Thomas Percy met secretly at Harbottle Castle with Ker of Cessford a few days before the two wardens were scheduled to hold their first international day of truce at Stawford. Eure allegedly promised that he would not protect Brown or Widdrington from Cessford. This was done with the full knowledge that the Scottish warden wished to avenge the death of one of the leaders of the Burnes surname whom Brown had killed while repulsing a Scots attack on Denwick, the manor which he held from the Earl of Northumberland. Two or three days after Eure and Cessford held their day of truce (17 August 1596) 36 of the Scottish warden's friends and household servants rode into Alnwick searching for Brown. Cessford's toughs missed their man but struck down and seriously injured Robert Clavering.[31]

Cessford was rather more successful in settling scores with Henry Widdrington and his brothers. Ill-will between the Scottish warden and Widdrington had been festering for some time. Earlier that summer Ralph Selby of Weetwood had captured one of Cessford's boon companions, James Young of the Cove. In order to divert the attention of Cessford's raiders from the ill-defended East March to the slightly stronger Middle March, Selby had committed the custody of Young to Henry Widdrington at Swinburn Castle. After Ker of Cessford had secretly met Warden Eure at Harbottle, he rode past Swinburn and decided that it could easily be captured. On 27 August, riding at the head of a party of horsemen, he broke into the castle, rescued Young and forced Roger Widdrington, Henry's younger brother, to promise to surrender himself at Cessford's convenience. To escape similar humiliation Ralph, the youngest of the three Widdrington brothers, "leapt out of his chamber window, being three stories high, upon a pavement where he was almost bruised to death and hardly escaped." In later years Ralph was described as a "simple man".[32]

As Henry and Roger Widdrington could not persuade Warden Eure to avenge Cessford's daring raid, Roger felt honour-bound to become Cessford's prisoner. In November he secured a licence to enter Scotland from Sir Robert Carey, the acting warden of the East March. But Eure claimed that this licence was not valid and charged Roger with March Treason before a court of wardenry. Much to Eure's disgust, the jurors found Roger innocent. Yet a short time later Henry Widdrington learned that the vindictive warden also intended to charge him with March Treason. In January 1597 Henry left the county, claiming that he could not live in Northumberland as long as Eure remained warden.[33] Widdrington was soon joined by his friend Ralph Selby of Weetwood who had fallen out with acting governor Carey as well as with Eure's allies, Ralph and Edward Gray.[34] In July Selby, Henry Widdrington and a number of other Northumbrians joined the Earl of Essex on his ill-fated voyage to the Azores.[35]

Sir Robert Cecil viewed these developments with alarm for he feared that Essex was gathering a party of disaffected gentlemen who might threaten his recently won position as the queen's leading councillor. In order to reduce the number of potential malcontents who might support the temperamental royal favourite, Cecil made it his policy to settle provincial disputes as equitably as possible. In the spring of 1597 he instructed Sir William Bowes and Bishop Matthew, two of the special commissioners earlier appointed to settle outstanding border differences with Scottish commissioners, to convene Northumberland juries of presentment which would provide the Privy Council with information about the country gentlemen's dispute with Lord Eure and John Carey.[36]

The busy principal secretary apparently forgot that Lord Eure had recently antagonized Matthew by supporting the *custos rotulorum* of County Durham in his claim that it was illegal for Durham J. P.s to levy rates to pay for soldiers used in the Middle March.[37] Considering the strained relations between the bishop and the warden, it was not altogether surprising that the Northumberland jurors concluded that Eure had betrayed the queen's trust. They charged that he had acted without the London government's permission or knowledge when he had sent home most of the Yorkshire soldiers earlier assigned to him to help defend the Middle March. He had then given the soldiers' pay and horses to his servants and particular friends in Redesdale. The jurors also asserted that Mansfield, the keeper of Redesdale, had given material assistance to English and Scottish thieves.[38]

Lord Burghley later asked Eure to refute the jurors' allegations. In his own defence Eure claimed that since Henry Widdrington and his friends had refused to sell foodstuffs to the Yorkshire soldiers, he had been forced to send them home. He denied that he or his under-officers harboured thieves, though he admitted that Henry Widdrington, William Selby the gentleman porter and their friends might well be guilty of such March Treasons.[39]

By one means or another the lawyer John Brown discovered what Eure had written to Burghley. Appalled by the man's claims, he drew up a protestation in favour of the dishonoured gentry of Northumberland. He hotly denied that Northumbrians had to be paid or bribed to perform border service and other obligations due from loyal subjects. As for Henry Widdrington and William Selby the elder, Brown affirmed that "they are undoubted right Englishmen . . . they are two of the chief pillars upholding that dwindling people and the honour of the queen on those marches, also accounted by the malicious enemies of this estate as their noted adversaries." Brown added that Eure's friend Ralph Mansfield was in almost daily contact with Sir Robert Ker of Cessford, "Northumberland's arch bloody enemy".[40] After Warden Eure learned that Brown had sent this bold statement to the Privy Council he prudently decided to leave the Middle March, ostensibly to avoid the plague. In his absence, he left Edward Gray as his deputy.[41]

As far as the Northumberland gentry could ascertain in July 1597, Secretary Robert Cecil fully supported Lord Eure, his deputy Edward Gray and John Carey, the troublesome acting governor of Berwick. Cecil, like his aging royal mistress, would tolerate no one who criticized members of the northern administrative hierarchy no matter how incompetent or treacherous they appeared to be. On 29 July the Privy Council sternly warned William Selby, the gentleman porter, that if he continued to criticize John Carey "it will prove a matter of such nature as you will hardly be able to answer."[42] On the same day Cecil sent a curt message to the Earl of Essex ordering him to send Henry Widdrington and other Northumberland adventurers home from the Islands voyage.[43]

Yet even while Cecil was publicly backing Eure and Carey, he and his fellow privy councillors were frantically searching for new wardenry officials and for a person to replace Essex's ally, Archbishop Hutton, the acting head of the Council of the North. As the secretary wearily informed the Earl of Shrewsbury: "if I should make your lordship privy to all our talk of presidents, captains of Berwick and changing of wardens, I should make all the posts northward break their wind".[44] At one point the Cecilian and Essex factions on the Privy Council thought that they had hit upon a compromise candidate for warden; Henry Percy, the ninth earl of Northumberland. As Percy was on friendly terms with the Cecils and was Essex's brother-in-law, it seemed logical for the Council to ask him to accept the wardenship of the Middle March as well as the lord lieutenancies of the three border counties. But the Wizard Earl's main concern was with science, art, architecture and the world of the intellect. He had little interest in national politics and no interest in re-establishing the hereditary influence of the Percy family in Northumberland. Writing to Cecil from the civilized seclusion of Syon House on 28 July he begged to be allowed to continue to enjoy his "quiet, secure, pleasant and easy courses".[45]

The Privy Council's immediate response to Percy's refusal was to order Bishop Matthew and Sir William Bowes to convene new juries of presentment in the Middle and East Marches. The councillors intimated, without saying so directly, that Bowes and Matthew should persuade the jurors that, although there might have been some simple misunderstandings between Lord Eure and the gentlemen of Northumberland, the two parties had no serious differences.[46] These instructions placed Matthew in a difficult position. Although he was completely loyal to Secretary Cecil, he was convinced that Lord Eure had betrayed the cause of true religion and had secretly allied himself with Northumberland's enemies. Confronted with the harsh choice of betraying Cecil or standing by his own convictions, the oft-vilified bishop chose the latter course.[47]

After convening 23 jurors at Newburn-on-Tyne on 21 September Matthew told them that although the Privy Council had suggested that they exonerate Lord Eure, he expected them to be guided by their consciences.[48] Only the maverick Richard Fenwick of Stanton failed to take the hint. The former J. P. perversely contended that Eure had been greatly wronged by the Northumberland gentry and added that "if Jesus Christ were amongst them, they would deceive him, if He would hear, trust and follow their wicked counsels!"[49] The remaining jurors were united in their opposition to Eure even though the warden was personally present at the session. Under the guidance of their chief spokesman and pensman, John Brown, the jurors found Eure guilty of betraying his trust to the queen and to the people committed to his protection.[50] Bishop Matthew dared not openly defame the warden when reporting the results of the Newburn session to Secretary Cecil. Yet he warned that "the while Northumberland ... is in worse case than if it were barbarous, and will yet be worse than it is, if where defaults be found apparent, they be not censured in some condignly and punished in others egregiously."[51]

In spite of the jurors' verdict, the quarrel between Eure and the gentry of Northumberland might well have continued indefinitely had it not been for the heightened rivalry between Cecil and Essex. Perceiving that Cecil's position as the queen's principal adviser was none too secure, both parties entered into correspondence with Essex's followers. On 24 October 1597 Eure candidly asked Anthony Bacon, one of the leaders of the group during Essex's absence on the Islands voyage, to stand as his friend and protector.[52] A few days later John Brown wrote to the privy councillor Sir William Knowles, another prominent Essex supporter, asking for protection against Lord Eure. Brown claimed that the warden's household servants from Witton Castle, County Durham, had assaulted him as he was on his way up to Court to present further evidence against Eure.[53]

Once again Secretary Cecil demonstrated his uncanny ability to remain on good terms with all parties to a provincial quarrel. He retained Bishop

Matthew's confidence by asking him to collect depositions against Eure's servants.[54] Lord Eure was advised to take up his seat in the House of Lords, thus
making it more convenient for him to attend Court to refute the charges made
against him.[55] Brown and Widdrington were allowed to cleanse their spleens
by presenting written statements to the Privy Council.[56] No other action was
taken until late in January 1598 when Eure learned that his deputy, Edward
Gray, had been so humiliated by Henry Widdrington's uncle, Ephraim, that
he wished to resign. Eure used this as a convenient excuse to plead his own
inability to continue serving as warden. Sometime after 22 January he quietly
resigned, his honour and credit with Secretary Cecil still intact.[57] Cecil did not
see fit to chastise the former warden's friends, Ralph Mansfield, the captain of
Harbottle, and Thomas Percy, the Earl of Northumberland's chief agent at
Alnwick, even though Bishop Matthew warned that they were closely allied
with Ker of Cessford.[58] Mansfield remained in Northumberland until late in
1598 when he entered the service of the Earl of Essex and sailed to Ireland.
Thomas Percy, later a Gunpowder Plotter, was still in Northumberland early
in 1603, busy exploiting the Earl of Northumberland's tenants for his own
profit.[59]

During the last half of 1597 relations between Northumbrian and Scottish
borderers steadily deteriorated. Part of the difficulty was that in the Treaty of
Carlisle which had been contracted that May, English and Scottish border
officials had agreed to exchange pledges who would be held in captivity until
the bills outstanding between their respective nations had been satisfied.[60] Cessford and Buccleuch scorned this pledge scheme, fearing that they would lose
face with their followers among the surnames if they allowed them to be used
as hostages. Then at last, Buccleuch consented to surrender himself as a hostage.
Unfortunately, the exchange which took place at Norham Ford on 8 October
increased rather than diminished international tensions. Buccleuch waited until
it grew dark before surrendering himself to Sir William Bowes. A few minutes
later Cessford's followers from Teviotdale surrounded the Anglo-Scottish party
and began to fire off pistols. This enabled some of the pledges to escape. However Buccleuch chose to remain Bowes's prisoner. He was brought back to
Berwick where he was kept in the custody of the gentleman porter.[61]

For some months after the incident at Norham Ford, Ker of Cessford's
followers cruelly harassed Northumberland. Late in October, 30 of them
broke into Sir John Forster's house in Bamburgh intending to avenge ancient
grievances. The old man was rescued after his quick-witted common-law wife
barricaded his chamber door and screamed for help.[62] A month later Forster's
former son-in-law, William Fenwick of Wallington, informed Henry Widdrington that several of the latter's principal friends had been murdered since he had
left the county the previous January. Fenwick was convinced that Scottish
enemies "rather increase than decrease, more nightly roads and robbery than is

continually now in all parts of Northumberland hath not been these many years, God himself send redress."[63] On 12 November John Carey, the acting governor of Berwick, told Lord Burghley that in the course of writing him a short letter he had three times been called into the castle yard to see "the fresh bleeding bloody wounds and hurts that have been given this last night by the Scots". In a parallel letter to Robert Cecil Carey compared Northumberland countrymen to "sheep without a shepherd".[64]

It was perhaps just as well that the Privy Council declined the services of one man who volunteered to shepherd the people of Northumberland: Richard Fenwick of Stanton. In mid-November 1597 this frustrated squire of middling means and less wisdom offered to serve as deputy warden of the Middle March for a three-month trial period. Fenwick promised that if he were given command of 100 professional soldiers he would capture and summarily execute 40 Northumberland gentlemen, including his own sons-in-law and brothers-in-law, whom he alleged regularly harboured Scottish and English thieves. Fenwick suggested that the money derived from the estates forfeited by these march traitors should be used to pay for an additional 100 horsemen to be placed under his command. This done, the queen could withdraw the first contingent of soldiers secure in the knowledge that Northumberland would remain well and truly pacified at no further cost to herself.[65] Fenwick's draconian proposals possibly strengthened the Privy Council's resolve to keep the Northumberland wardenships out of the hands of local men. Late in November they finally gave Sir Robert Carey his long-sought-after commission as warden of the East March. Four months later the Council transfered Carey to the Middle March and gave the governorship of Berwick and the wardenship of the East March to Peregrine Bertie, Lord Willoughby d'Eresby of Lincolnshire.[66]

In Lord Willoughby (1555-1601), a veteran of several campaigns against the Spanish in the Low Countries, the people of Northumberland found themselves confronted with an outsider no less difficult than Ralph Lord Eure had been. In contrast to the former warden, however, there was absolutely no doubt about Willoughby's integrity. He was so honest and straightforward that Sir Robert Cecil, being of a rather different temperament, seldom confided in him and on occasion hoodwinked him. Willoughby was also sometimes duped by his dashing friend and comrade in arms, Robert Earl of Essex, by the earl's secret agent William Eure, the former warden's brother, and by Ker of Cessford, the Scottish warden.[67]

Willoughby took up his post at Berwick on 28 March 1598, almost ten years after Lord Hunsdon, the last fully accredited lord governor, had left the town. He found the garrison in a shocking state. Most of the soldiers would not have passed muster in a contemporary Dutch or Spanish army. Artillery was in short supply and most of the ammunition was stored in a building which could readily be set on fire by a trained sharpshooter from outside the walls. Despite the great sums of money which the queen had lavished on rebuilding the fortifications, they were still far from complete.[68] Yet Willoughby was not easily discouraged. After inspecting his new command he vowed that he would soon knock it into proper military shape.

In this vain endeavour the new governor was ostensibly supported by Sir William Bowes, the impoverished border expert to whom the Crown had recently granted the lucrative treasurership of Berwick in preference to Ralph Gray of Chillingham.[69] However, a more able assistant was Willoughby's own cousin John Guevera (c. 1568–1607). Appointed deputy warden of the East March sometime before August 1599, Guevera was the Protestant grandson of a Spanish mercenary soldier who had settled in Stenigot, Lincolnshire, in the 1550s. As he had attended Gray's Inn and knew something about common law,[70] Guevera's skills nicely complemented those of his cousin. Lord Willoughby himself an expert on martial law.

The two men found that as governor of Berwick, Willoughby controlled what amounted to a private franchise equipped with its own complex of courts. In addition to the King's Council which consisted of the lord governor, treasurer, gentleman porter and other officials and which was solely concerned with local military affairs, Berwick had its own chancery, exchequer and other royal courts which were empowered to hear causes arising from amongst the five or six thousand townspeople. The town's approximately 150 free burgesses constituted a guild which annually elected aldermen and a mayor. The mayor, in company with the bailiff, presided over the court to which the burgesses were suitors and jurors. This court managed the town's civil and agrarian affairs.[71]

Willoughby and Guevera decided that they could at least defend the ancient prerogatives of the governor and warden and the privileges of the town of Berwick, even if they could do little to improve the fighting potential of the garrison soldiers. In October 1600 Willoughby asserted that the town was immune from the jurisdiction of the Council of the North. As the Council was headed by Secretary Cecil's elder brother, Thomas Lord Burghley, Willoughby's assertion was, to say the least, impolitic. In July 1601 the law officers of the Crown ruled that the burgesses of Berwick fell within the jurisdiction of the Council at York.[72]

In the midst of their foolish argument with the Council of the North, Willoughby and Guevera became embroiled in a dispute with William Selby of Branxton. Selby had long since been pardoned for his role in the killing of William Clavering. He had been a Member of Parliament in 1593 and 1597 and in 1600 he was joined in commission with his uncle and eventual benefactor, Sir William Selby the elder, as co-gentleman porter of Berwick.[73] That October the younger Selby charged that although Guevera had not been joined to the commission of the peace, he had begun to exercise the authority of a justice in the East March. This charge again suggests how critical was the shortage of J. P.s in Northumberland. Selby further charged that contrary to custom Guevera was hearing pleas of indebtedness involving considerable sums of money in his courts of wardenry.[74] Selby also let it be known that he resented Willoughby's recent assertion that he was a commanding general who possessed absolute authority over all his subordinates whether they were military men or civilians such as himself.[75] Fearing that Willoughby might vindictively try him before a court martial, Selby left the town early in November. However, he consented to return after Secretary Cecil had assured him that Lord Willoughby would do him no harm.[76]

Queen Elizabeth regarded the authoritarian lord governor as one of the last surviving members of the faithful old guard earlier personified by the Earl of Bedford, the Earl of Huntingdon and Baron Hunsdon. On learning that Willoughby was ill, in March 1601 she cautioned him not to overtax himself with work on her behalf "considering how long it is before men of service be bred in this age."[77] After his death that June the Privy Council decided that Willoughby had indeed been the last of his kind. The governorship of Berwick remained vacant until the office was extinguished with the union of the Crowns.[78] Had he been less the stern soldier and more the courtier-politician Willoughby would doubtless have cut a fine figure at Court, but he always said that he refused to associate with such "reptilia".[79]

One of the best-known examples of this despised species was Willoughby's near neighbour in Northumberland, Sir Robert Carey (c. 1560–1639), youngest and favourite son of Henry Lord Hunsdon. Before his appointment as acting warden of the East March and then as fully-accredited warden of the Middle March, Carey had been employed on diplomatic missions to Scotland and the Low Countries and on military missions to France. As a bachelor, his wit and demeanour made him not unattractive to Queen Elizabeth. Late in 1591, where better men had failed, Carey managed to persuade the queen to allow the Earl of Essex to remain in Normandy where he was in charge of the decaying military force sent over to assist Henry IV to repel the Duke of Parma. After he had been knighted by Essex, Sir Robert knew that he had at least one friend at Court. But of far greater service to him was his own father. In 1593 Lord Hunsdon persuaded his son-in-law Thomas Lord Scrope, recently appointed warden of the West March, to make Robert his deputy. In 1595, much to the disgust of John Carey, the old warden gave Robert lands and offices in Norhamshire which were said to be worth £400 a year.[80] Sir Robert represented Morpeth in the Parliaments of 1586, 1588 and 1593. He sat as a knight of the shire for Northumberland in the Parliaments of 1597 and 1601.[81]

Carey temporarily lost favour with Queen Elizabeth in August 1593 when instead of marrying a great heiress he married Elizabeth Trevannion, widow of the spendthrift marshal of Berwick, Sir Henry Widdrington the elder.[82] This love-match greatly strengthened Sir Robert's position in Northumberland because it allied him with Henry and Roger Widdrington, the late marshal's two able nephews, as well as with William Fenwick of Wallington and other members of the old Forster connection. It was largely due to his alliance with this party that Carey was able to administer the Middle March successfully between 1598 and 1603; although perhaps not quite as successfully as he would have readers of his published memoirs believe.[83]

When Carey became warden of the Middle March Queen Elizabeth and Secretary Cecil still had not given King James VI cause to hope that he would eventually accede to the English throne. As the Scottish sovereign did not know how best to win this elusive prize, his policies fluctuated wildly.[84] On some occasions he seemed willing to humour the English government. On others he played along with the Earl of Essex in his various schemes to topple Cecil from power. No less fickle were the king's policies towards the border wardenries. Sometimes it seemed that he was encouraging his borderers to terrorize Northumberland in order to force Elizabeth to recognize his claims. On other occasions he seemed to be doing his best to tame the Scots surname members in Liddesdale and other troubled areas. A master of deception, it was not unlike James to pursue two contradictory policies simultaneously.

In the summer of 1598 Ker of Cessford, the king's able assistant in border affairs and warden of the Scottish Middle March, promised Sir Robert Carey that he would co-operate amicably with him in the administration of the international frontier. Carey was half prepared to take Ker at his word; however, Henry Widdrington and William Fenwick urged him to be cautious.[85] Their caution was well advised. On 2 August Widdrington and Fenwick learned that a party of Scots variously estimated at between 60 and 200 strong had ridden into Redesdale ostensibly to hunt and to cut wood. The two squires hurriedly assembled a counterforce of horsemen. While pursuing the intruders north of the border they killed four or five of them.[86] This spilling of blood put a new complexion on the whole affair.

Since James did not wish to hazard his growing reputation as a responsible ruler or lose an instalment of his English pension, he decided not to countenance a retaliatory raid as he might have done two or three years earlier. As the Scots had been slain north of the border, James and Cessford saw a way to humiliate the English government at no cost to themselves. Accordingly, James demanded that Widdrington and Fenwick be tried for murder before English and Scottish assize jurors who would almost certainly find them guilty. Cecil's border agents tried to negotiate a compromise, but to no avail; James and Cessford remained adamant. Cecil attempted to propitiate the Scots on 6 November, at the height of the raiding season, by ordering Widdrington and Fenwick to enter the protective custody of Bishop Tobias Matthew in Durham. In this way the secretary deprived the Middle March of perhaps the only two influential private gentlemen who, in Sir Robert Carey's words "pack not neither palter with Scots".[87] Carey's pleas that the two men be released so that they could organize resistance to a new wave of incursions by Cessford's followers were seconded by Bishop Matthew and Lord Scrope, the warden of the West March. However Cecil did not allow Fenwick and Widdrington to regain their freedom until May 1599.[88] Thus Cessford and King James had made Cecil dance while they called the tune. For their part, Widdrington and Fenwick must have wondered if the Earl of Essex would have treated them so shamefully had he rather than Cecil been in control of the queen's government.

In September Widdrington, now deputy warden and keeper of Redesdale under his friend Carey, was involved in another painful international incident. Riding at the head of a large force of horsemen, he entered Liddesdale and captured the brother of the laird of Langholm, a notorious patron of thieves over whom King James apparently had no control. Later the laird himself posted bond with Sir Robert Carey and promised to bring his followers to heel. But James asserted that Widdrington's raid was an affront to his sovereign dignity and allowed Cessford to challenge him to a duel to the death at Hare Crag. The fierce Scottish warden warned Widdrington that if he did not appear at the appointed time and place, which in fact he did not, the world would know him for a "prattling coward".[89]

During the following months, Cessford's continuing hostility towards Henry Widdrington masked King James's policy towards most other border gentlemen. Since he was determined that he should be the prince who rode down the Great North Road to claim the throne of England after it passed from Elizabeth's hands, he thought it imperative to build up a following in Northumberland. As if by magic, Cessford began to discipline thieves as zealously as any honest Englishman could wish.[90] William Selby of Branxton clearly understood the meaning of the king's subtle policies. Writing from Berwick in May 1600, he advised Sir Robert Cecil:

> Thus much I have from Scots of good credit, that the king makes no less reckoning of all the borderers from Newcastle to Berwick and of their chief officers ... than if they were his natural subjects, saving of a very few ... And I fear this persuasion of the king's is not altogether vain ... How dangerous the king's haste to this Crown and the drawing away of her subjects may be to her Majesty's good estate your honour can wisely consider.

Selby assured Cecil that despite other men's eagerness to espouse the king's cause, he would always remain loyal to Queen Elizabeth: "worship the sun rising who shall, I will while I live, without regard of present or future peril, worship the sun shining".[91]

That same May the secretary allowed himself to be half-persuaded by Sir Robert Carey that Henry Widdrington and William Fenwick were as loyal as the gentleman porter of Berwick professed himself to be. In June the warden's two assistants received special letters from the queen thanking them for their good service.[92] However, Cecil continued to receive reports that Widdrington was prepared to be of service to the reckless Earl of Essex.[93] At this juncture it was a matter of particular concern to Cecil that he maintain the respect of influential landed gentlemen, for it was common knowledge that the royal favourite might soon resort to desperate means to displace him as the queen's first minister. Indeed, early in February 1601, discontented squires and yeomen from many parts of England began to congregate about the earl's town house in the Strand.

Before Widdrington travelled up to London early in 1601 he apparently thought it advisable to secure a letter from Bishop Tobias Matthew commending him to the Principal Secretary. In his letter which, perhaps in error, he dated 8 February, Matthew wrote that no northern gentleman was better suited than Widdrington to serve Cecil. He added that "that ambitious and malicious generation" then gathering in London hated Widdrington no less than they did Cecil or Matthew himself.[94] However, when Henry Widdrington and his uncle Ephraim joined the armed gentlemen and soldiers assembled at the Earl of Essex's town house on Sunday morning 8 February, they were apparently accepted as genuine allies. After all Henry had sailed with Essex on the Islands voyage and had been shabbily treated in recent years by Secretary Cecil. Moreover Ephraim Widdrington was in the employ of one of Essex's leading aristocratic supporters, Edward Earl of Bedford, old Sir John Forster's spendthrift grandson.

The question of Henry Widdrington's loyalty was finally resolved after Essex had been captured. At the trial Widdrington served as Attorney General Coke's first witness for the prosecution. Perhaps thinking that he could best cement his relationship with his new patron by helping to destroy his former one, Widdrington testified that before Essex had left his house for the City on that fateful Sunday morning he had threatened to kill the two great officers of state whom his followers had taken hostage: Lord Keeper Egerton and Lord Chief Justice Popham. Widdrington further testified that he had personally tried to dissuade Essex from having the two men killed. However, as Popham and Egerton had not come to any harm and no witnesses could be found to substantiate Widdrington's tale, no more was heard of it.[95] Essex was found guilty of treason on other grounds and executed on Tower Hill. As for Henry Widdrington, he returned to Northumberland secure in the knowledge that he would be well rewarded in the future by the triumphant principal secretary of state.

Cecil found another convenient if rather unlikely ally in Henry's younger brother, Roger Widdrington (c. 1573–1642), one of the undoubted leaders of the Catholic community in Northumberland. Through their mutual friend, Sir Robert Carey, Cecil learned that Roger had considerable influence in the lands in Cumberland which were still disputed between Francis Dacre and the Catholic Lord William Howard. By this time the principal secretary had decided to employ as his assistants at Court various Protestant-inclined members of the Howard family who had not enjoyed Queen Elizabeth's favour for many years. Among his new associates were Lord Henry Howard, later Earl of Northampton (1540–1614), Lord William's uncle, and Thomas Howard, later Earl of Suffolk (1561–1626), Lord William's elder brother. Cecil's new friends quite naturally wanted Lord William to be granted the disputed northern inheritance. All that was needed, or so it seemed, was evidence that Francis Dacre was engaged in subversive activity. On 13 November 1600 Lord William's acting bailiff at Brampton advised Lord Thomas Howard to consult with Roger Widdrington about a dangerous new alliance in Cumberland between Francis Dacre and English malcontents at the Scottish Court. No man, the bailiff claimed, knew better than Roger how to smash this league, "and so politicly wrought as Mr Secretary never to be seen in it."[96] Cecil, Widdrington and the Howards left no record of their subsequent actions in this affair. Perhaps it was a coincidence that in 1600 officials serving under Cecil's brother, the Lord President of the Council of the North, made no apparent attempt to persecute Catholics in Roger Widdrington's bailiwick of Hexham. Yet at the assize held in that year more than 150 people living elsewhere were indicted for recusancy.[97] At any rate, sometime in 1603 Lord William Howard and the Lady Elizabeth took up residence in Naworth Castle. Thus, less than 70 years after the third duke of Norfolk attempted to become a magnate along the borders, the Howard presence in Cumberland and in Morpeth ward in Northumberland became a reality.[98]

Secretary Cecil's intervention in the Dacre-Howard dispute and the collapse of the Essex rebellion coincided with the beginning of his famed secret correspondence with King James. Some days or weeks after Essex was executed Cecil concluded that of all possible candidates for the English throne James was the most acceptable. In April 1601 he entered into confidential negotiations with Scottish agents in London and soon began to correspond directly with King James. Cecil promised to prepare the way for James's accession if he in turn would not upset Queen Elizabeth with further rash deeds. This agreement brought to an end the politically-inspired raids and counter-raids across the Anglo-Scottish border. Thereafter Cecil's chief concern was to prove to James that he alone controlled both patronage and the keys to the "promised land".[99]

Among the great English magnates who were victims of Cecil's scheme to monopolize power in the next reign was Henry Percy, the ninth earl of Northumberland. Though a Protestant, the earl regarded himself as the champion of oppressed Catholics. In his correspondence with King James, which he always showed to Cecil and which he sometimes sent to Scotland through his agent Thomas Percy, the earl pleaded that James give English Catholics a certain amount of toleration should he ever come to the throne.[100] To Cecil such a policy, proposed by such a man, was unthinkable. In May

1602 his ally Lord Henry Howard warned King James that Earl Percy "is beloved of none, followed by none, trusted by no one nobleman or gentleman of quality within the land."[101]

Despite these cross-currents at Court, rivalry between Catholics and Protestants in Northumberland itself was of little consequence.[102] However, the county was plagued by the continuing rivalry between the lord wardens on the one hand and Northumberland-born justices of the peace on the other. This rivalry had been gaining in intensity ever since 1595–6 when the Crown had given the wardenships to outsiders and then appointed special border commissioners to carry out some of the tasks usually reserved for wardens.[103] Recognizing that their influence in international affairs was in irreversible decline, wardens reacted by asserting their prerogatives over the inhabitants of the English marches more aggressively than in the past. In this they sometimes seemed to be supported by the central government. For example, the 1601 Act against blackmail clearly stated that nothing in the statute should be construed to "abbridge or impeache the Jurisdicc[ti]on or Authoritie of any the Lordes Wardens".[104]

Lord Willoughby, warden of the East March and governor of Berwick, contended that wardens still in effect administered martial law.[105] But an anonymous writer argued that "wardens govern not by martial law . . . it is as convenient for the good government of the borders, the wealth and safety of the borderers and the prince's service there that wardens should have no iota of martial authority in this happy time of peace". This critic then asserted that borderers deserved to be governed by the laws and customs common to the rest of the realm and that local affairs should be entrusted to J. P.s and other regular civil officials.[106] Willoughby countered such assertions by complaining to Secretary Cecil in October 1600 that Northumberland J. P.s had challenged the authority of his wardenry court to try an Englishman who had murdered an inhabitant of his march. Perhaps unaware that his court had no such authority, Willoughby warned that March Law would be clearly overthrown if impudent J. P.s were allowed to continue their clamour against the wardens.[107] In June 1602 Sir John Carey, Willoughby's successor as warden, urge Cecil to strengthen the office or else it was "likely to go to wrack and decay".[108] Two weeks later Carey disparaged each of the J. P.s in the East March, excepting of course himself. William Read of Holy Isle was blind and senile; Thomas Bradford was bedridden with palsy; George Muschamp dared not show his face in public for fear of assassination at the hands of Oswald and Henry Collingwood of Etal.[109]

It may well be that Northumbrian J. P.s were partial to their friends and neglected some of their responsibilities. It was said that they seldom attempted to regulate the price of grain in local markets or to collect rates for road and bridge repairs.[110] As late as 1599 they disclaimed responsibility for administering any system of poor relief, asserting that the borderers' common obligation to serve in defence of the border freed them "from contributions of this sort which other counties do afford".[111] In 1602 an assize judge was shocked to discover that more Northumbrian murderers and felons had been executed during the last four years than during the preceding decade. He took this to mean that there was a marked increase in lawlessness.[112] On the other hand these figures may show that local law enforcement agencies and juries were more efficient in 1602 than they had been during the administrations of wardens Forster and Eure. It is not perhaps without significance that the first extant records of indictments kept by the county clerk of the peace date from the late 1590s. Thus, in spite of the absence of any other documentary evidence it seems reasonable to assume that local J. P.s were operating effectively in Northumberland in the years immediately before the union of the Crowns.[113]

At last the long era of the lord wardens was drawing to a close. In January 1603 Sir John Carey sourly noted that English and Scottish gentlemen were crossing the border to make merry with their friends in open disregard of the laws of the marches and the authority of the wardens.[114] On Saturday 26 March, learning that Queen Elizabeth was failing rapidly, but unaware that she had died two days earlier, King James VI issued a proclamation enjoining his subjects along the border to keep the peace upon pain of death during any subsequent change of government.[115] That night James was roused from his sleep by an unauthorized messenger from London. Sir Robert Carey joyfully saluted him as king of England.[116]

7

From Border to Middle Shire, 1603-11: the dream and the reality

"Those confining places which were the Borders of the two Kingdomes...
that lay waste and desolate, and were habitations but for runnagates, are
now become the Navell or Umbilick of both Kingdomes". King
James I, March 1607[1]

King James VI and I was a visionary and an idealist. Believing that his accession was only the first step towards a closer union between England and
Scotland, in the spring of 1603 he was confident that there would soon be one
people, one faith, one law and one Parliament in a unified kingdom of Great
Britain. No longer would the Scottish and English border counties lie at the
extremities of two independent sovereign states. Instead they would be the
'Middle Shires' of a united and tranquil realm.[2] But though the king might
use the term 'Middle Shires', his prerogative powers were not in themselves
sufficient to consummate the marriage between his two kingdoms. English
constitutional theory demanded that he obtain parliamentary approval for the
union. This in turn meant that he must convince English sceptics that
Englishmen and Scotsmen were destined to be, and should be, one people. It
was at this level that the Middle Shires assumed great political and symbolic
importance. Doubters must see that ordinary Northumberland, Cumberland
and Westmorland justices of the peace and sheriffs could co-operate amicably
with Scottish magistrates in tracking down thieves who crossed the border and
in other matters of mutual concern. Acting together and in their several
separate capacities, English and Scottish officials should make the Middle
Shires as peaceful as any other shires in the realm. Once pacified, the Middle
Shires could be regarded by all men of good will as a symbol of the new

harmony and as a microcosm of the yet unborn united kingdom of Great Britain.[3]

In his own words, James's programme was "utterlie to extinguishe as well the name, as substance of the bordouris, I meane the difference betwene thaime and other pairts of the kingdome."[4] While in Newcastle in April 1603 he abolished March Law by proclamation and let it be known that he would not allow the lord wardens appointed by Queen Elizabeth to continue in office.[5] Although in strict constitutional theory the laws, customs and treaties which together constituted March Law continued in force until they were formally abolished by Act of Parliament in 1607, in practice March Law slipped quietly into oblivion as there were no wardens to enforce it.[6] The warden of the Middle March, Sir Robert Carey, resigned soon after his famous ride to Edinburgh. Before the end of June Sir John Carey, warden of the East March, had followed suit.[7]

Some months later King James further reversed Queen Elizabeth's policies towards Northumberland. Rather than keeping the county under the control of strangers and outsiders as it had been since 1596, he enabled the leading gentry to resume their traditional roles in local civil affairs. Of the 30 members of the commission of the peace issued in mid-1604, 11, including the newly-dubbed knights Sir Henry Widdrington, Sir Ralph Gray, Sir William Fenwick, Sir Robert Delaval and Sir William Selby the elder, were resident Northumbrian gentry. Seven of the 11 were members of the quorum. Aside from the Lord Chancellor and other honorary members, most of the remaining members of the commission were intimately connected with the Northumbrian scene. They included the absentee Earl of Northumberland, the *custos rotulorum* Edward Talbot and Bishop Tobias Matthew of Durham.[8]

The working members of the county's new commission of the peace must have realized that in the absence of wardenry officials they could no longer excuse their own deficiencies by claiming that their authority had been over-ridden by a lord warden. Aside from George Clifford, Earl of Cumberland (1558–1605), appointed lord lieutenant of the three border counties early in June 1603, and Sir Henry Widdrington, the earl's deputy in Northumberland, there was now no local person in authority to protect J.P.s from the criticism of the lords of the king's Privy Council. Yet during the first few months of the new reign the *custos rotulorum* and his colleagues appear to have managed local affairs competently and efficiently. Meeting together with grand jurors at quarter sessions, they indicted rioters and murderers, cattle and sheep thieves as well as men and women accused of lesser offences. County coroners such as Joshua Delaval of Rivers Green held inquests in all corners of the county, even in Redesdale.[9]

Then in the autumn of 1604 the Northumberland justices realized that they had been altogether too successful in removing the differences between Northumberland and more prosperous counties further south. Before this time, as we have seen, the Crown had generally assumed that the inhabitants of Northumberland, Cumberland, Westmorland, North Durham and the town of Berwick needed every shilling they could find to maintain themselves in fighting trim, ready to repel Scottish thieves. In consequence the Crown had exempted them from paying parliamentary subsidies and forced loans.[10] But now that Scotland and England were united under one king and Northumberland was apparently tranquil, King James saw no reason why Northumberland gentlemen should not contribute to a loan under the Privy Seal.

Late in October Edward Talbot, Sir Robert Delaval and 17 other gentlemen of local prominence met in Morpeth to discuss ways to avoid complying with the Crown's unwelcome request. They decided to argue that godless bandits were so impoverishing men of substance that they could not possibly contribute to the loan. Talbot and his colleagues supported this fiction by claiming that in the absence of courts of wardenry and international days of truce at which victims of theft could obtain redress by time-honoured procedures, thieves had grown desperate: "for whereas before it was but paying the goods again, it is now imagined by the malefactors that nothing will satisfy but life." The gentlemen also asserted that many local officials had shown themselves unwilling to accept responsibility for maintaining law and order. The sheriff, for instance, had often pleaded his inability to locate suspected malefactors whom J. P.s had ordered him to capture.[11] Talbot and his friends were politic enough not to name the erring sheriff, Sir William Selby of Branxton, the younger co-gentleman porter earlier so favoured by Cecil, or to mention that Selby had obtained the Lord Chancellor's permission to attend to his private affairs in Town Malling, Kent, during his shrievalty.[12] The gentry also claimed that some J. P.s, similarly unnamed, had privately released suspected felons on bail, knowing full well that they would not come in to stand trial at a session of gaol delivery. They further asserted that judges of assize did not hold sessions frequently enough to keep potential malefactors in fear of punishment. Because of an outbreak of plague the judges had held no session at all in 1603. In view of all these difficulties, Talbot, Delaval and the other gentlemen concluded that "our estate [is] in no sorts bettered since his Majesty entered".[13] The central authorities in London apparently accepted this argument. No Northumbrian names appear in the registers of receipt for the Privy Seal loan of 1604. Two years later the county was again exempted from payment of the subsidy voted by Parliament.[14]

It would appear that Talbot and his friends decided that they could safely argue that Northumberland was in the grip of a crime wave after they had conferred with the lord lieutenant of the three northern counties, George Earl of Cumberland. When the earl met them at Morpeth he might well have reminded them that a year and a half earlier the Grahams and other well-organized surname groups in the valleys of the Sark and Esk in north-western Cumberland had had their last great fling, the affair known as the

Busy Week which had lasted from 27 March to 7 April 1603. Convinced by some English anarchists that the laws of both kingdoms were in abeyance until King James was actually crowned in Westminster Abbey, surname members and thieves had "assembled themselves together in divers troops by great numbers (three or four hundred in a company) in a warlike and most rebellious manner with their colours displayed and so invaded the inland parts of the east part of the county of Cumberland".[15] The rebels stole or destroyed goods worth an estimated £10,600 in the English and Scottish West Marches before they were finally dispersed by Sir William Selby the elder, Sir Henry Widdrington, Sir William Fenwick and a troop of soldiers from Berwick.[16] But it must be emphasized that this contagion did not spread to Northumberland. The only serious crime reported in that county during the Busy Week occurred on 29 March when one Edward Blenkinsopp of Bellister in South Tynedale burnt down a house and barns belonging to Alexander Liddell of Town Green.[17]

King James's response to the outrages in Cumberland had been to appoint Earl Clifford lord lieutenant of the three border counties and guardian or warden of the English West and Middle marches. As domestic and international border law had fallen into abeyance, the basis of Cumberland's legal authority was a series of commissions of oyer and terminer which empowered him to try suspected malefactors by the forms used in common law.[18] However, despite these apparent marks of royal favour, Cumberland's position at Court was none too secure. He was ill-regarded by the powerful principal secretary of state, Sir Robert Cecil, soon to be created Earl of Salisbury, and by Cecil's allies, Lord Henry Howard and Thomas Howard, Earl of Suffolk.[19] Thus it is not surprising that Cumberland felt it best to exaggerate the complexity of the problems he faced in the North so that more credit would reflect on him when he resolved them. After the earl met the Northumberland gentry at Morpeth he began to assert that Northumbrian jurors were just as fearful as those in Cumberland who, for fear of retaliation, had recently convicted of capital crimes only seven of the 600 men standing trial.[20] In reporting the results of the assize held in Newcastle in August 1604, the earl noted that jurors had refused to convict one suspected offender whom the judges were convinced was guilty. The judges had sent the erring jurors to answer charges in the Star Chamber. But rather than assuming that by this means the judges had brought the situation in Northumberland well under control, the earl argued that "plainly ... the most part of the country, yea even the better sort, stands affected by one means or another [to] favour thieves."[21]

Later in 1604, when the Earl of Suffolk and Henry Howard, now Earl of Northampton, had almost persuaded King James to recall the lord lieutenant and warden in disgrace, Cumberland wrote a spirited defence of his administration. As had become his practice he contended that honest gentlemen in Northumberland as well as in Cumberland agreed that as it had long been an uncivil place, "so can it not now be expected that these people can yet for some few years (notwithstanding what good men say) be reduced to like civil obedience as the other parts of this kingdom are, that have ever lived in subjection to law and justice". He went on to assert that J. P.s, sheriffs, and other regular officials "neither so conveniently may nor indeed so well dare or will strive to do justice of these tribes of thieves as may the lieutenant or his deputies for fear of secret burning their houses or barns or other revenges which hath been too common and for a time will be a practice among those wicked people."[22] The earl did not cite specific Northumbrian examples to support this contention, perhaps because there were so few. The records of the county clerk of the peace suggest that a horse stolen from Sir Henry Widdrington, the deputy lieutenant, was the only loss suffered by a Northumberland J. P. during the months while the Earl of Cumberland was on the borders.[23] However King James, Robert Cecil and the Howards chose to accept the earl's contention that extra-ordinary officials of some sort would be needed for a time to supplement J. P.s, sheriffs and other regular civil officials in Northumberland and neighbouring counties. Yet they were not convinced that Cumberland was the man best qualified to pacify the English Middle Shires in preparation for the final transfer of power to local authorities. Before 4 December they removed him from the commission of oyer and terminer for Northumberland and dismissed him from most of his other border offices. Cumberland died a few months later.[24]

While the earl was still active along the borders, King James embarked upon two projects which were of considerable concern to Northumbrians. His first task was to demilitarize the fortress at Berwick-upon-Tweed which had long symbolized England's military superiority over Scotland. In December 1603 the Crown commissioned Sir Ralph Gray of Chillingham to preside over the dissolution of the garrison. But as Gray profited from the sale of foodstuffs to the soldiers, he was unwilling to see the garrison reduced to a mere skeleton force. He suggested that it be cut back only slightly and hinted that he himself would not disdain command over the new establishment. In the end the garrison was reduced to 100 able-bodied men and pensioners who were placed under the command of Captain William Bowyer, a man much despised by his subordinates. In July 1604 all the ordnance was shipped to the Tower of London. Thereafter the fortress at Berwick stood naked and empty, a monument to ancient hostilities now happily forgotten.[25]

While these changes were taking place in Berwick, King James began to educate Members of Parliament. At the opening of the session on 19 March 1604 he made a long, somewhat confusing speech in which he delineated the benefits of closer union for himself and for his subjects in both realms. Less the impractical visionary than he had been a year earlier, James told Members that he did not expect them to alter the ancient fundamental laws and customs of England all at once, but that he did expect them to remove any obstacles to closer union.[26] That summer Parliament created a General Committee for the Good of Both Kingdoms to study the problem. Among its members were the knights of the shire for Northumberland, Sir Ralph Gray and Sir Henry Widdrington.[27] However, the Earl of Cumberland insisted that Widdrington could not be spared from his tasks as deputy lieutenant in Northumberland.[28] Talbot and other responsible county gentlemen considered this to be a great blunder, especially in view of a recent royal proclamation in which James, anticipating parliamentary acceptance of the union, let it be known that henceforth he was to be styled "King of Great Britain".[29] Realizing that the sovereign considered the matter of the union to be of supreme importance, the Northumbrian gentry urged Cumberland to give Widdrington leave to join the committee, adding that "to promote the same we are and will be contented rather to sustain such home-bred prejudices as may befall us in his absence than to hazard the hindrance and utter undoing of us and so posterity for ever".[30] It is likely that Widdrington was among the English and Scottish committeemen who made their preliminary report in December 1604.

Among other things, the committee recommended that mutual redress be made for all wrongs committed by English and Scottish borderers between the conclusion of the Treaty of Carlisle in 1597 and Queen Elizabeth's death. This was no small undertaking for English borderers asked redress for goods valued at £30,000 and Scottish claims were no less exorbitant. Yet the committee members felt that tempers all round might be sweetened if redress were made before Parliament reconvened for the session at which it was scheduled to debate the union more fully.[31] James concurred and recognized that it was also advisable to establish good order in the Middle Shires before Parliament reassembled. With a sense of urgency he wrote that "the readdiest and surest meanes" to make the borders as peaceful and answerable as any other part of the kingdom "are now to be thocht upon and embraced without any regairde to the honoure, commoditie or contentment of any subject quhatsomeever."[32]

After the general committee had made its report, the king turned for advice to the most able and trusted of his Scottish favourites, George Home, later Earl of Dunbar (1548–1611). This quiet, ruthlessly efficient man had more influence in shaping policy towards Northumberland and the Middle Shires than did any other single councillor of state with the possible exception of Secretary Robert Cecil. Dunbar was the scion of a well-known border family. By 1586 he was a Gentleman of the Bedchamber; by 1590 Master of the Wardrobe. He accompanied James on his journey south in 1603 and soon became a personage of some importance at the English Court. In June he was appointed Keeper of the Great Wardrobe. The next year, after he had been naturalized by a private Act of Parliament, he was sworn to the English Privy Council and created Baron Home of Berwick. In July 1605 he was granted the earldom of Dunbar in the Scottish peerage. Thereafter, until his death early in 1611, Dunbar shared with Lord Alexander Dunfermline the chief management of Scottish affairs.[33]

To help Dunbar support his titular dignity, King James granted him extensive estates in the former English Middle and East marches. In 1603 Cecil persuaded Sir Robert Carey to sell Dunbar his estates in North Durham for £6,000. About the same time James granted Dunbar Berwick Castle and its appurtenances as well as the Crown's lands in the manors of Wark and Harbottle, in Etal and in the Ten Towns of Coquetdale. In the summer of 1604 Dunbar was joined to the Northumberland commission of the peace.[34] Thereafter the stern Protestant councillor was able to counterbalance the local influence of the absentee ninth earl of Northumberland on the one hand and that of the Catholic lord of Morpeth, William Howard, on the other. Moreover, Dunbar served as a convenient intermediary between the Scottish Privy Council and the Northumbrian gentry. For example, in June 1605 he persuaded the Scottish Privy Council that Sir John Carr, a Scot, had wrongly tried to seize some lands debatable between England and Scotland which were claimed by Ralph Gray of Chillingham.[35] By such deeds and by his occasional presence in Northumberland and Berwick, Dunbar reminded the gentry and the common people of the king's firm determination to pacify the Middle Shires.

The techniques which the government might use to effect this end were the subject of many discussions between Dunbar and King James in December 1604 and January 1605. In mid-January, after leaving the "little beagle", Secretary Robert Cecil, at Court, the two Scots went to the king's hunting lodge at Huntingdon. While there they drew up rough plans for a special Anglo-Scottish border commission. On the thirteenth the king commanded one of his travelling secretaries, Sir Thomas Lake, to send Cecil detailed instructions for a new commission for the Middle Shires. However, his Majesty was so eager to be away to his pleasures that Lake could hardly make head or tail of his instructions.[36] The confusion thus in evidence at the conception of the first Jacobean border commission surrounded it until its demise.

On 25 February 1605 Chancery gave five northern English gentlemen a special commission of oyer and terminer. On the same date the Scottish Chancery issued a similar commission to five Scots. Together the ten border commissioners were instructed to pacify the Middle Shires.[37] To assist them in this task the two sets of commissioners were each provided with a force of 25 paid horsemen. Fifteen of the English horsemen were to be used in Cumberland and Westmorland and were placed under the command of Sir Henry Leigh. Sir William Selby of Branxton, the principal commissioner in Northumberland, assumed command of the remaining ten horsemen.

By virtue of their commissions of oyer and terminer, the border commissioners could hold frequent sessions of gaol delivery. The English commissioners had legal authority to try malefactors inhabiting Berwick, North Durham, Westmorland, Cumberland and the whole of Northumberland, while the Scottish commissioners had similar authority in their half of the Middle Shires. However, there was some doubt whether Englishmen who were captured in England after committing offences in Scotland should be tried in Scotland or in England. In December 1604 many members of the parliamentary committee to study the union had argued that Englishmen and Scotsmen should "be governed by the common laws and statutes of either kingdom where they shall dwell". This would suggest that Englishmen must be tried by English judges.[38] Notwithstanding, King James instructed the border commissioners to try offenders in the country where they had committed their crime. Typically he did not clearly state whether English or Scottish commissioners should try Englishmen accused of crimes in Scotland.[39]

In addition to running down and trying suspected criminals, the English commissioners were instructed to remove all the obstacles which people like the Earl of Cumberland and many southerners thought might prevent border justices of the peace from assuming full control of their respective counties. The border commissioners were to compile lists of outlaws and suspected wrongdoers and to expel all vagabonds, idle and ill-mannered people. They were also instructed to send full and frequent reports of their proceedings up to the Privy Council.[40] To compensate them for their troubles, each of the commissioners was given a stipend of 100 marks a year. Sir William Selby and Sir Wilfrid Lawson, the two leading English commissioners, were given an additional allowance for travel.[41]

In choosing the English members of this powerful international commission, the Privy Council attempted to effect a balance among the various interest groups. Sir William Selby (c. 1559–1638), variously of Branxton, Twizel and Barmoor in Northumberland and Town Malling in Kent, represented what perhaps may best be called the Protestant Court Party; in large measure he was dependent upon the Earl of Salisbury for favour and advancement. During the early months of 1605 this strong-willed and forceful man seemed determined to open the whole of Northumberland to regular civil officials as quickly as possible. Success would enhance his reputation with Salisbury and the king and, no less important, enable him to retire permanently to his estates in Kent.

It may be assumed that Selby was on only tolerable terms with the second of the new border commissioners, Edward Gray of Howick and Morpeth (1557–1631), a Church Papist and younger brother of Sir Ralph Gray of Chillingham. Edward Gray was an even-tempered man of modest means who served as Lord William Howard's principal estate agent in the lordship of Morpeth.[42] No doubt the Court Howards, the Earls of Suffolk and Northampton, would have preferred to see their kinsman Lord William Howard on the border commission, but as he was an avowed Catholic, this was impractical.

Edward Gray's sister Dorothy was married to the third of the Northumbrian border commissioners, Sir Robert Delaval of Seaton Delaval (c. 1542–1607).

A devout Protestant, Delaval had attracted the Earl of Huntingdon's favourable attention in 1592 while he was Northumberland sheriff. Four years later he was one of the few county gentlemen on the local commission of the peace. In February and June 1602 he alone among the Northumberland gentry was included in a commission of oyer and terminer for the northern counties.[43] A wealthy, righteous man, Delaval was more at ease when attending to public business in his own county than in London. In 1600, for instance, he was worried what local gossips would say if he extended his stay in the ill-reputed capital. He wrote to his son Ralph: "I must be content and give the wicked leave to vomit out their venom which if they did not, I judge they would burst, but God amend them and so lend them garlic to chew if it be their pleasure."[44]

Sir Wilfrid Lawson of Isell (1545–1632), one of the two border commissioners resident in Cumberland, was closely tied to the Earl of Northumberland's interest. The second son of a minor Yorkshire family, Lawson acquired Isell through his third wife, Maud Redmain. Around 1591 the ninth earl appointed Lawson his lieutenant in the honour of Cockermouth in Cumberland. In 1605 it was suggested that Sir Wilfrid owed his recent knighthood, his seat in Parliament and his place on the border commission to Earl Percy. This malicious informer added that the earl's receiver, Thomas Percy, had been Lawson's dinner guest as well as "his bedfellow (for such is the public rumour)".[45] Joseph Pennington of Muncaster, the other commissioner resident in Cumberland, contributed little to the work of the commission in Northumberland except to keep copies of all the commissioners' correspondence relating to the county from February 1605 to mid-1607.[46]

It soon became apparent that the competence and patience of the border commissioners, Scottish as well as English, would be rigorously tested. Pleading illness, Sir William Selby did not see fit to attend the first general meeting which was held in April at Carlisle. In his absence the other commissioners debated the merits of remanding: whether Englishmen who committed felonies in Scotland should be tried in Scotland or in England. They recognized that trial in Scotland by Scottish judges and jurors was contrary to March Law. However, since King James had abolished March Law by proclamation, the commissioners felt that they could ignore customary border practices with impunity. But one of the English commissioners timidly pointed out that according to the common law men could only be convicted of a capital crime by jurors resident in their own shire. The Scots retorted that King James considered the Middle Shires to be a special case. He had instructed the commissioners to send malefactors "to the country and place where they offended to receive their condign punishment". Surely the king's instructions bore greater weight than mere legal custom. The four English commissioners did not press the matter further.[47]

Sir William Selby cleverly avoided confronting the remanding issue during the next four months. Then on 4 August two Scottish commissioners asked him to join them on the bench at Hawick in Roxburghshire while they held a session of gaol delivery. At first Selby protested that English judges had no business conducting court in Scotland. But after learning that the Earl of Dunbar had sent some Redesdalers to Hawick for trial, he agreed to go. It appears to have been a most inharmonious session. Selby was shocked to find that "the commissioners of Scotland made no bones to kill such fugitives or felons as made resistance". He later wrote to Lawson that he hoped the English commissioners and their provost marshal would never use such harsh measures "albeit in strict law such men may with us peradventure be forcibly dealt withal, yet force would be charitably used and never but in case of extreme extremity".[48] At the conclusion of the Hawick session Selby made an agreement with his heavy-handed Scottish colleagues. In future English commissioners would attend court sessions in Scotland to see that English defendants received fair trial by Scottish legal procedures. However, they would not lay themselves open to criticism by common law judges and lawyers by joining the Scottish commissioners on the bench.[49]

Selby was more successful in staying clear of another controversial issue, the removal of the Grahams from the valleys of the Sark and Esk in Cumberland. Although the Grahams were only one of the surnames which had caused a disturbance during the Busy Week, King James had singled them out for special punishment, intending to grant their lands to the Earl of Cumberland or whoever would pay him an improved rent.[50] Accordingly, the Privy Council ordered the border commissioners to round up 150 young Graham men for 'voluntary' military service in Brill and Flushing. Early in June 1605 Delaval, Gray, Lawson and Pennington met to discuss this project in Berwick, only a few miles from Selby's residence. However Sir William and his government-paid horsemen were far away in Kent. Ten days after the other commissioners had sent 72 Grahams—78 short of their quota—off to the Low Countries, Sir William, his wife Lady Dorothy and the soldiers returned to north-eastern Northumberland.[51]

During the next few weeks Selby tried to convince the justices of the peace in his neighbourhood that they could permanently get along without the assistance of a resident border commissioner such as himself. It served his purpose well that in August 1605 assize judges George Snigg and Sir John Sayle announced that J. P.s in all parts of England were to be separated into divisions so that they could deal more effectively with administrative business out of quarter sessions.[52] In September Selby notified the Earl of Salisbury that he had recently convened the first "six week meeting" or petty session ever held in Northumberland. Together with other J. P.s he had appointed high constables, petty constables and other lesser officials heretofore unknown in that division. Selby reported that he and his colleagues had also reduced the number of alehouses in the district from 105 to 15 and had ordered vagabonds to leave the area. He had asked his fellow J.P.s to consider whether it would be appropriate to levy a rate of 12*d*. a plough to pay for sleuth dogs and they had agreed that the inhabitants of the division should maintain night watches between August and Christmas. Delighted with his own achievements, Selby predicted that "before one year be expired these shires may as well be governed by the ordinary service of justices of the peace as the rest of England."[53] Selby was mistaken. So profound was the impact which the Gunpowder Plot was to have upon leading figures in the English Middle Shires and at Court that the Crown would decide that the border commissioners must be retained indefinitely to assist justices of the peace and other regular county officials.[54]

The revelation that Thomas Percy, Guy Fawkes and other desperate Catholics intended to blow up the king, Lords and Commons "all at one thunderclap and in one horrible and diabolical Doomsday"[55] served Salisbury as a convenient pretext to cut short the public career of Henry Percy, ninth earl of Northumberland, the largest private landowner in that county. When the earl was interrogated before the Privy Council he steadfastly maintained that he had no prior knowledge of the plot. He admitted that his receiver for Northumberland, the traitor Thomas Percy, had been his dinner guest at Syon House on 4 November, but he insisted that they had confined their conversation to matters related to the management of the earl's northern estates. The privy councillors found these disclaimers unconvincing; they had the earl warded in the Tower of London and fined him the enormous sum of £30,000.[56]

Sir Henry Widdrington M. P. returned to Northumberland a day or two after news of the "horrible and graceless conspiracy" (as Sir William Selby called it)[57] had reached the county. He carried with him instructions from the Earl of Salisbury to interrogate everyone who had recently been associated with Thomas Percy and to seize the Earl of Northumberland's castles at Alnwick, Warkworth and Tynemouth. After Widdrington had forced the Percy agent, George Whitehead, to rise from his sick-bed and leave Tynemouth Castle on the night of the thirteenth, Whitehead ominously noted that Sir Henry "is likely to get cold entertainment here for no man living is more hated than he is in this country."[58]

Sir Wilfrid Lawson probably came to share this sentiment after he learned that Widdrington had a warrant to wrest the Percy castle at Cockermouth from his control. He still did not know what measures the government might take against him when he joined his fellow border commissioners at Newcastle for a session of gaol delivery which lasted from 11 to 14 November. Edward Gray and Sir Robert Delaval were also rather apprehensive for they too had recently been in contact with Thomas Percy and the suspect Earl of Northumberland.[59] In fact all five commissioners were worried lest they be summarily dismissed and disgraced, for it was widely believed that more crimes were now being committed in the Middle Shires than before the border commission had been established.[60]

The commissioners discussed this problem amongst themselves and decided to inform Salisbury and the Privy Council that they had been frustrated in their work by circumstances beyond their control. Part of their difficulty was that they were not certain which suspected criminals lay within their jurisdiction and which lay within that of regular assize judges.[61] Adding to this confusion was the third earl of Cumberland's recent reminder that they were not to deal with any person who had committed what might be construed as a felony or misdemeanour while in the service of himself or his deputy lieutenant and keeper of Redesdale, Sir Henry Widdrington.[62] Nobody knew the limits of the border commissioners' authority and, in consequence, most people simply ignored them. Many men negotiated directly with the thieves who had victimized them. Northumberland J.P.s ordered suspects whom they released on bail to report to the regular assize judges for trial. Although the border commissioners held a special commission of oyer and terminer for this very purpose, they had not been able to try a single notorious Northumbrian malefactor at any of the three sessions of gaol delivery which they had held in the county.[63]

However the commissioners were confident that they would be able to serve the Crown better in the near future. They saw the Earl of Northumberland's malevolent receiver, Thomas Percy, as a convenient scapegoat and argued that he had prevented them from bringing evil-doers to justice; he had shielded malefactors and intimidated potential witnesses and jurors. But now that Percy was out of the way there was nobody (or so it seemed) to prevent them from capturing, trying and executing all of his thievish dependants.[64]

To demonstrate the ease with which he and his colleagues could now pacify the county, Sir William Selby captured William Orde and Fergus Storey, two Percy estate agents who owed their places to Thomas Percy and whom he had allegedly converted to Catholicism. But Salisbury's special agent, Sir Henry Widdrington, ordered Orde and Storey released after he had interrogated them and found, to his own satisfaction, that they knew nothing about the Gunpowder conspiracy.[65] Sir William Selby was not a man who could readily forgive Widdrington this affront; thereafter there would always be bad blood between them.

In the short term the border commissioners were more successful in dealing with four Coquetdale men who were also thought to have been Percy's associates, Thomas, Percival and John Davidson and John's son, Michael. As it happened these men owed service to Sir Henry Widdrington in his capacity as captain of Harbottle Castle and keeper of Redesdale.[66] On the morning of 18 November, six days after Thomas Percy had been killed in Warwickshire, Henry Guevera, a J.P. who worked closely with Selby at quarter sessions, appeared before John Davidson's house in Biddlestone and demanded that he be allowed to search for Percy. As the Davidsons were already on bad terms with Guevera and had no reason to trust him, they refused him admittance. That evening, after Guevera's men had secured a ladder from the next village and began to remove the turf roof from the house, the Davidsons finally surrendered. They found themselves charged not with harbouring Thomas Percy, but with the murder of one John Collingwood in 1597. Guevera's wife was a Collingwood.[67]

Sir William Selby, Sir Wilfrid Lawson and the other border commissioners held a session of gaol delivery at Newcastle on 20 January 1606 at which they sentenced 18 Scotsmen and Englishmen to death, including the four Davidsons. Selby later boasted to the Earl of Salisbury that this session had been far and away the most successful ever held in Northumberland. By proving that malefactors would be brought to justice, it had deterred many potential wrongdoers. Selby was of the opinion that theft was now no more common in Northumberland than it was in any other shire in England.[68]

Roger Widdrington of Cartington, the most prominent Catholic in the county, viewed the border commissioners' proceedings at Newcastle in a rather different light. As he saw it, the real reason why Sir William Selby was going to so much trouble to convict the Davidsons and other men in Sir Henry Widdrington's keepership, was to undermine the latter's credit with Salisbury and the king. In a secret letter Roger warned Sir Henry that Selby fully intended to win control of Northumberland for his own and the Protestant interest. Roger suggested that his elder brother counter Selby's nefarious schemes by persuading his patrons at Court that Parliament should issue a general pardon for all crimes, except murder, which had been committed before the king's accession in March 1603. Roger reasoned that if Northumbrians knew that their past offences were forgiven, they would settle down and become law-abiding citizens. He also recommended that Sir Henry remind the Earl of Salisbury that two of the border commissioners, Delaval and Lawson, had been closely identified with the fallen Earl of Northumberland. Sir Henry should suggest that he himself be appointed a commissioner in their place.[69] In the event, Sir Henry was never joined to this border commission. However on 2 February he was pricked Northumberland high sheriff,[70] a position which might enable him to influence the choice of jurors and witnesses and thus to shield some of his friends from Commissioner Selby.

While Sir Henry attended to his business at Court, Roger Widdrington appears to have gone to work behind the scenes in Redesdale. Late in February or early in March 1606 Thomas Hall of Branshaw in Redesdale and William Wanless, bailiff of Harbottle, appeared before the lords of the Privy Council. Speaking on behalf of the people of Tynedale as well as those of Redesdale and others who owed service to Harbottle Castle, they bitterly denounced the border commissioners' treatment of highlanders during the recent Newcastle session of gaol delivery. Hall asked the councillors point-blank if they approved of the death sentence meted out to Michael Davidson for a murder allegedly committed by his father in 1597 at a time when Michael was not yet 12 years old.

The privy councillors made their answer on 11 March in a letter addressed to the border commissioners which they gave to Hall to take back to Northumberland.[71] A fortnight later, no doubt after first acquainting himself with its contents, Hall delivered the letter to Commissioner Robert Delaval.[72] Delaval was appalled to learn that the Privy Council was extremely critical of the border commissioners' proceedings at Newcastle and warned them never again to try men for crimes committed before March 1603 without its express permission. Delaval also learned that Selby and his pliant accomplice Lawson had endangered his own reputation, as well as that of commissioners Gray and Pennington, by writing privately to the Earl of Salisbury to request a reprieve for young Michael Davidson.[73] Sir William Selby later tried to play down the importance of the Privy Council's reprimand. On 27 March he cheerfully wrote to his fellow commissioners "we have great cause to rejoice and give thanks to God that we can be accused of nothing but for that which is well and justly done".[74] But at heart this dissembler must have known that the careers of all the border commissioners were once again in jeopardy.

The English commissioners had clearly lost whatever influence they might have had in Northumberland and along the Scottish side of the border by the time they convened a session of gaol delivery at Newcastle on 24 April 1606. Only two of the 36 named suspects whom Selby had imperiously demanded that the Scottish commissioners send down for trial actually appeared. Jurors chosen by Sir Henry Widdrington or his under-sheriff found only one man guilty and acquitted 13 of the crimes with which they had been charged.[75]

Infuriated by this set-back, on 3 May Selby sent off a letter to Lord Treasurer Dorset in which he complained that the Northumberland sheriff was obstructing the orderly processes of civil administration; as he did not account to the Exchequer he could not be trusted with recognizances and fines.[76] In a second letter, directed to the Privy Council at large, Selby sought to discredit Thomas Hall of Branshaw, Roger Widdrington's friend from Redesdale who had prompted the Council to forbid the border commissioners to try men for crimes committed before March 1603. Selby claimed that Hall and many of his near relations were guilty of serious crimes and that "the name Hall hath according to the number been little less offensive to their neighbours of Northumberland than the Grahams to the people of Cumberland, and heretofore few or none of them punished, the people not daring to give information against them."[77] In a third letter Selby asked the Earl of Salisbury to support him and his fellow commissioners or to allow them to resign. He stated that he and his colleagues:

are so far from that ambition that having now served more than a year in this painful province, we do rather desire that others worthier than ourselves may take upon them this burden which we evidently perceive is laboured by some here, as well by discountenancing us in our service, as by seeking to make some of ourselves discoverers of our servants and opposers against the rest, in which point they have not a little prevailed.[78]

Of course Sir William had no intention of resigning. By the time he had sent off the three letters he had rallied a party in support of a policy known to be opposed by the Widdringtons but much favoured by Salisbury. He had conferred with Edward Charlton of Hesleyside, John Brown and other reliable Northumberland gentlemen about the Privy Council's directive of 11 March. These gentlemen had then drawn up a petition requesting that wrongdoers be punished for crimes committed in Queen Elizabeth's time.[79] Later, Salisbury requested Attorney General Coke to consider the possibility of adding a proviso exempting the Middle Shires from the general pardon bill then before Parliament. Coke decided that this was not possible as the Middle Shires were not yet known to the law. However the general pardon approved by Parliament before it rose on 27 May 1606 did not extend to the crimes most prevalent on the borders in the years before James's accession: murder, horse theft, burglary and arson.[80] A month later the Privy Council officially advised the border commissioners that the king's clemency did not "extend to malefactors in exorbitant crimes or to such as proceed still in their ill life and therefore you are to proceed against them with that distinction according unto law and as you see cause for the same".[81] Notwithstanding, at their next general meeting, at Carlisle, the commissioners decided that rather than be the cause of further controversy, they would only try men for crimes committed since March 1603.[82]

This was the last time that the five English commissioners agreed on a common policy. After the conference Sir William Selby went up to Court. In his absence, Edward Gray and his patron Lord William Howard tried to wean Wilfrid Lawson from his alliance with Selby. Early in November Gray informed Lawson that according to reports reaching Howard:

Sir William Selby is very much busied about in proceeding to overthrow the commission now in force and has been catching in particular at his lordship [Lord William Howard] so far as he dare adventure, and snapping at us the rest of his fellow commissioners but covertly, but my lord hopes he shall miss of his purpose for as his lordship saith, some of his plots have been returned upon himself, little to his comfort and less to his credit...[83]

Soon after Lawson was pricked Cumberland high sheriff on 17 November, Lord William wrote to him directly: "Mr Sheriff, I tell you in plain terms, if Sir William Selby might have had his will...your commission had been dissolved and a new established whereby himself had been sole commissioner in Northumberland and Mr Thomas Salkeld sole commissioner in Cumberland".[84] Thus was Selby's alliance with Lawson broken.

The session of Parliament at which the fate of King James's proposal for closer union with Scotland was finally decided convened on 18 November 1606 and was to last until 4 July 1607. When the session began many Members were still not convinced that the king's scheme would be beneficial for England. Even a privy councillor felt bound to admit that the English and Scottish border commissioners had found it virtually impossible to co-operate in enforcing law and order in the Middle Shires.[85] This being the case, how could English and Scottish officials hope to work amicably together governing a united Great Britain? James and his advisers decided that the analogy of the Middle Shires as a microcosm of a united Great Britain might be made to serve their purposes, rather than those of opponents of the union, if an efficient administrative hierarchy were immediately superimposed on existing county organizations. The king hoped that before the proposed union came up for a final vote in the House, he could truthfully tell Members that special English and Scottish officials had brought "happy quietness" to the Middle Shires. Members should thus be confident that great English and Scottish officials of state could no less conveniently govern a united Great Britain.[86]

In practice administrative efficiency in the Middle Shires meant putting the entire area under the control of a single supremely competent border commissioner.[87] The king believed that the English magnate best qualified for this post, save in respect of his religion, was Lord William Howard. In recent months Howard had greatly assisted Sir Wilfrid Lawson and Bishop Henry Robinson of Carlisle (who had been added to the border commission that spring) by running down and capturing malefactors in Cumberland.[88] However, as Howard was a Catholic he was legally barred from office.[89] The Protestant fourth earl of Cumberland did not appear to have the strength of character necessary to bring order to the Middle Shires. Thus James had little alternative but to entrust this onerous responsibility to his stern Scottish favourite, George Earl of Dunbar.

In mid-December 1606, while Dunbar was busy in Linlithgow intimidating those dissident Scottish Presbyterian ministers who had not already fled into exile, James empowered him to supervise the English border commissioners as well as J.P.s, sheriffs and other regular civil officials then serving in Northumberland, Cumberland and Westmorland. Mindful that legalistic Members of Parliament might object if they thought that a Scotsman was presiding over English sessions of gaol delivery, the king cautioned Dunbar that "our meaning is not to give you any authority to proceed as a judge or commissioner, but to reserve that power to them only where we have enabled in that kind to determine all those things by a commission under our great seal".[90] During the next few months, while Sir Henry Widdrington and other Members of Parliament debated the merits of the proposed union, King James kept close tabs on Dunbar's activities in the Middle Shires, feeling that the success or failure of his parliamentary project in no small measure rested in his favourite's hands.

Dunbar greatly enjoyed the sport of running malefactors to earth and seeing that they were brought to justice. But as he was nearly 60 years old and in poor health he was not as efficient as King James hoped and expected. On 16 January Sir Thomas Lake reported to Salisbury that the king was boasting of Dunbar's capture of "the most ancient thieves and receivers of thieves that were there abiding; and many of them such as durst not before times be meddled [with] which his Majesty thinks by this time to have suffered the law".[91] The king was wide of the mark. Six weeks later Sir William Selby informed Sir Wilfrid Lawson and Bishop Robinson that prisoners "of all sexes and for all causes", who had been incarcerated in Newcastle jail since the assize held the previous August, were still awaiting trial. Selby reported that the prisoners were all confined in one foul room and had told him that death upon the scaffold was preferable to life in "so vile a place".[92] Dunbar's ill-health caused their trial to be put off repeatedly; it was not held until 9 April. Sir William Selby could not then preside as a judge because he was now sheriff of Northumberland; Dunbar could not serve because of the king's prohibition.

From what Selby had told them trial judges Lawson and Robinson expected to find more than 100 notorious and dangerous criminals at the bar. However grand jurors indicted only 30 men, most of them for relatively minor crimes. After sitting for four days and until 10 p.m. on Saturday night, Lawson and Robinson finally condemned 11 men to death.[93] In reporting their proceedings to the Earl of Salisbury they cryptically noted that the session had been most "confused".[94] But Sir William Selby professed himself well pleased with its results. He informed Salisbury that all the Redesdalers and Tynedalers summoned to the bar of the court had appeared and that there was now greater obedience to lawful authority in Northumberland than at any time since the border commission was first established. He credited these remarkable developments to his new friend the Earl of Dunbar.[95] A few weeks later Selby had further cause to praise Dunbar when the latter dismissed Sir Henry Widdrington from the keepership of Redesdale and gave the post to Selby's ally, Edward Charlton of Hesleyside.[96]

Meanwhile in Westminster, Members of Parliament were mulling over suggestions made in November 1606 by the parliamentary committee which had been considering the proposed union with Scotland. Of these suggestions, the most significant from the point of view of local administration in Northumberland was the recommendation that Parliament make provision for the mutual extradition of suspected criminals so that Englishmen who committed crimes in Scotland would be tried in Scotland. This recommendation was strongly opposed by Sir Henry Widdrington, knight of the shire for Northumberland. As an alternative Widdrington proposed that Englishmen who stole goods from Scots be sent to Berwick so that they could make arrangements to restore stolen property to its rightful owners.[97] From his own recent experience and from what his brother Roger had told him, Sir Henry was convinced that Sir William Selby had used remanding simply to further his own devious ends. Sir Henry feared that if Parliament gave legal sanction to remanding, the scheming border commissioner would send the Widdringtons and many of their friends north of the border to certain death before Scottish courts of law.[98] Sir Henry and his supporters in Parliament then asked whether it was proper to allow freeborn Englishmen who stood accused of felony to be tried by the forms used in Scottish courts, which were based on the principles of Roman law rather than English common law. This in turn raised the question of whether the archaic forms still used in all English courts in such cases were not unnecessarily prejudicial to men on trial for their lives. As matters stood an Englishman accused of felony was neither allowed the use of counsel nor might sworn witnesses testify on his behalf.[99]

A bill which, among other things, would prohibit remanding and give Northumbrian defendants an opportunity to use witnesses in their defence was given its first reading in the House on 2 May. On 16 June the speaker, Sir Edward Phelips, informed the Earl of Salisbury that Sir Henry Widdrington was willing to sacrifice the clauses about witnesses as they appeared to be endangering the passage of the remainder of the bill.[100] Later that month Sir William Selby, Francis Earl of Cumberland, Bishop William James of Durham and other northern worthies petitioned the Commons to delete the anti-remanding clause so favoured by Widdrington. They claimed that a parliamentary ban on remanding would be "unserviceable for the Rooting out of Theft, and of apparent and especial Disadvantage to England". They concluded their petition by begging the House that "being Members with you of the same Kingdom, to be careful, in your Wisdoms and Charities, either not to mislike the present Form of Proceedings, whereof so great Good hath ensued; or else to provide us a better Way instead thereof, quick in Execution, and such as may disappoint Offenders of all Escapes, Shifts and Subterfuges."[101] A few days later one of the Scottish border commissioners, Sir William Seton, a tall man of bold speech and countenance, spoke for half an hour before the bar of the House in favour of Selby's petition. Seton claimed that the Scottish border commissioners had executed only seven Englishmen while the English had executed 30 Scots. Thus for Englishmen, "the Fear were greater than the Hurt".[102]

Since remanding would appear to minimize the differences between English and Scottish judicial practices, King James greatly favoured it and advised the committee appointed to study the matter to do the same. Angered by his meddling, on 18 June the committee decided that the letter which the sovereign had sent to Speaker Phelips in support of remanding should not even be entered into the journals of the House.[103] Thus, in part because of his own tactlessness, King James was defeated on this vital issue. The bill which passed its third reading in both houses and to which the king gave his reluctant assent early in July 1607 ordained that Englishmen who had committed offences in Scotland before or after the king's accession were to be tried in England by English judges of assize, commissioners of oyer and terminer or commissioners of gaol delivery.[104]

In addition to banning remanding, the new statute, 4 James I, c. 1, gave defendants resident in Northumberland, North Durham, Westmorland and Cumberland greater protection from malevolent judges and juries than Englishmen enjoyed elsewhere in the realm. Perhaps Parliament at last recognized that borderers deserved some compensation for the gross injustices they had so long endured at the hands of Sir John Forster, William Fenwick of Wallington, Ralph Lord Eure, Peregrine Lord Willoughby and most recently Sir William Selby. According to the new law members of a jury were now allowed to reject witnesses "either in regard of their hatred and malyce, or their favour and affeccion, either to the Partie persecutinge or to the Partie arraigned, or of their former evill Life and conversacion." In contrast to the forms used south of the River Tyne, sworn witnesses were now allowed to testify on behalf of defendants. Another clause stated that jurors in cases involving felony must be freeholders in possession of lands to the value of £5 a year in the county where the trial was held.[105] Elsewhere in England 'substantial freeholders' from the hundred or shire in which the defendant committed the crime might serve as petty jurors, but until 1664 there was apparently no general agreement as to what constituted a 'substantial freehold'.[106]

The only positive legislative result of months of discussion and controversy about the union, the statute of 4 James I, c. 1, also extinguished the Laws of the Marches by abolishing all laws hostile to Scotland. But most Members were not prepared to do more than this in support of King James's long-cherished scheme. As far as they were concerned the union was now a dead issue.

After Parliament rose on 4 July government informants noted that Sir Henry Widdrington's Northumbrian friends went home rejoicing. Thomas Hall of Branshaw and William Wanless, the Redesdale petitioners of March 1606, happily announced to whomever would listen that thanks to their brave patron, "Scotland will be Scotland, borders will be borders and [that] they will live in the country in despite of any that are evil doers."[107] King James had other ideas. Angered by Widdrington's opposition, he had him removed from the Northumberland commission of the peace and confined to the town of Boston in Lincolnshire. Widdrington remained in confinement until January 1610, just before the opening of the next session of Parliament.[108]

As the king's advisers had written evidence to show that Sir Henry's Catholic brother Roger had covertly encouraged him to oppose remanding and other government measures,[109] they decided that he too must be banished from Northumberland. The Earl of Dunbar confessed: "I can never deny but I have a particular spleen in this matter against him".[110] Dunbar had hoped that Roger would be confined in England so that government spies could keep an eye on him. However it appears that Lord William Howard and his co-religionist Queen Anne persuaded the king to allow Roger to slip quietly away to France. He remained in exile until he learned of Dunbar's death in 1611.[111]

Most notable of the several other Northumbrian gentlemen who were warded outside the county in the autumn of 1607 was Thomas Carr of Ford. As Carr was Commissioner Selby's brother-in-law and as recently as 1606 had been joined to a commission to inquire into the lands of the traitor Thomas Percy, it is not entirely clear why he fell into disfavour at this time. Perhaps he had publicly opposed remanding. It is also possible that the Earl of Salisbury bore Carr a deep-seated grudge. In 1601 a household servant whom Carr had just dismissed for pilfering (certainly not a very reliable informant) notified the hunch-backed Principal Secretary that Carr had said that he wished he had Cecil's "deformed body [in his hands] that he might tear him in pieces!"[112] In January 1607 commissioners investigating the state of religion in Northumberland found that Carr was "yet a Protestant" but noted that he was a "dissolute man and a favourer of ill men".[113] It was on the pretext that this very substantial landed proprietor harboured thieves that he was warded outside the county. In September the Earl of Dunbar informed Salisbury that Carr was "one of the worst of all them that are confined."[114]

In the same letter Dunbar went on to assert – in direct contradiction to the evidence of records compiled by the Northumberland clerk of the peace[115] – that "if the course of confining those gentlemen that are warded had not been taken, stealing and harbouring by all likelihood had been at such a height this ensuing winter as your lordship and the Council would have held it marvellous in a country of any government."[116] Thus did the authoritarian Scottish earl casually depreciate the work of Edward Talbot, Sir Robert Delaval, Thomas Middleton and other Northumbrian justices of the peace who had been regularly holding quarter sessions and performing the other functions normally expected of justices.[117]

King James was obviously seeking to avenge his defeat in Parliament when, late in August 1607, he revoked the existing border commission and established a new one dominated by Dunbar. This was the first time that the Scottish earl had been given the power of life and death over Northumbrians who had been indicted in English courts. A short time later Dunbar was also appointed lord lieutenant of Northumberland, Cumberland, Westmorland and the town of of Newcastle. Doubtless as a sop to English public opinion, the Crown gave equal rank to Francis, fourth earl of Cumberland, knowing that he would acquiesce to anything which the Earl of Dunbar suggested.[118]

In Northumberland, Dunbar's chief assistant on the new border commission was of course Sir William Selby. Aside from *custos rotulorum* Talbot, all the other Northumbrians associated with this new commission in a subordinate capacity were beholden to Dunbar for past favours or looked to him for future patronage. Sir Ralph Gray of Chillingham M. P. was grateful to Dunbar for helping him to obtain redress from Scottish thieves some years earlier and other favours. Captain Sir William Bowyer owed him his recent knighthood. It was due to the earl that Commissioner Edward Charlton had recently been appointed keeper of Redesdale and that Commissioner Sir William Fenwick had been allowed to continue as keeper of Tynedale. Though not joined to the commission, John Fenwick (*c.* 1579–1658), Sir William's opportunistic son by his first wife Grace Forster, rightly regarded Dunbar as a source of future patronage. So too did Arthur Delaval, a younger brother of Commissioner Sir Ralph Delaval; Ralph had assumed the leadership of the Seaton Delaval branch of the family after the death of his father, Sir Robert, the former border commissioner, on 1 January 1607.[119] Thomas Swinhoe of Goswick, the last of the new special commissioners of oyer and terminer, was a squire of very modest means whose North Durham estates lay very close to those held by Dunbar.[120] It is perhaps significant that Edward Gray of Morpeth, a gentleman whose religion was suspect, was not joined to the new commission. Neither was another former border commissioner whose presence Dunbar might have found embarrassing, Joseph Pennington of Muncaster. Pennington had kept copies of all the commissioners' correspondence ever since the first border commission was established in February 1605.[121] Dunbar worked best when his proceedings were not recorded. Even his most fervent admirers admitted that he was a man of few words, "the most difficult affairs he compassed without any noise and never returned when he was employed without the work performed that he was sent to do."[122]

Few Englishmen had the courage to protest Dunbar's appointment as the Crown's leading official in the English Middle Shires. Indeed some profit-minded men openly welcomed him. On 1 October 1607 George Whitehead, the Percy agent whom Sir Henry Widdrington had so rudely evicted from Tynemouth Castle in November 1605, informed the ninth earl that "my lord of Dunbar is coming down lieutenant with my lord of Cumberland . . . I trust by this means we shall have theft clearly banished, the country and our bangsters holden short, that we shall have less trouble to make your lordship's profits than we had."[123]

Before Dunbar left the Court for Northumberland he had already decided how he would deal with the common people in those districts in which Sir Henry and Roger Widdrington allegedly had had the greatest influence, Redesdale, Tynedale, Coquetdale and 'Tynewater'. He generously decided that the bulk of the population, "the less harmful sort", were to be "suffered to remain for manuring the ground and exercising all kinds of husbandry" under the watchful eyes of the landlords (of whom Dunbar was one of the greatest) and Northumbrian justices of the peace. One hundred outlaws, "bangsters of evil surnames" and their followers were to be required to volunteer for military service in Ireland. Before they embarked they were to be warned that they would be executed if they ever dared to return to their homes.[124]

On 26 October Dunbar, in company with Selby, Bishop James of Durham and the Earl of Cumberland, convened a session of gaol delivery in New-castle which was reminiscent of the wardenry courts and quarter sessions held in the early 1590s by Sir John Forster. The grand jurors, headed by Sir William Selby's brother Sir Ralph, indicted 110 men. Later petty jurors decided that only four of them were guilty of the crimes with which they had been charged.[125] However most of the 106 acquitted men then found them-selves eligible, according to Dunbar's plans, for deportation to Ireland. Writ-ing of this unsavoury business later, Sir William Selby claimed that Dunbar had made every effort to appear impartial. He had called the leading Northum-berland gentry before him and heard "the allegations as well of the friends as of the ill-wishers of every particular person".[126] Bishop James also thought it appropriate to inform Salisbury that Dunbar had carried out this service with such "justice, equability and clemency that no man have or hath just cause . . . to complain of cruelty in . . . pressing any for his Majesty's service".[127] Several years later Lord William Howard hinted that Dunbar and his cohorts had acted out of "private spleen", but he dared not say so in 1607.[128] Dunbar had no difficulty in finding his self-allotted quota of 100 volunteers although never before in living memory had any Northumbrian been pressed into service. Indeed so smoothly did this business proceed that at the last moment he decided to send an additional 40 men to Ireland.[129] A fortnight after the 140 unfortunate Northumbrians had embarked at Workington, Sir William Selby boasted that the county "is become peaceable and well freed from theft since the sending of our men into Ireland, their followers left behind abstaining from their trade of stealing through fear of a new press."[130]

Thereafter nobody questioned Dunbar's authority to do what he wanted with the border commission and with the criminal element in Northumberland, such as it was. In June 1608 the Crown gave him an allowance for 25 addi-tional mounted men to supplement those under the command of the Earl of Cumberland.[131] In the same month the Crown reorganized the border commis-sion to enable Dunbar to control his subordinates more effectively. Sir William Selby and Sir John Fenwick (Sir William Fenwick's son) became the earl's chief assistants in Northumberland while old Sir Wilfrid Lawson and Sir Christopher Pickering were made deputy commissioners for Cumberland.[132]

In 1609 Dunbar kept St George's Day at his magnificent new palace in Berwick-upon-Tweed. Attended by his blue-liveried servants, Captain Bowyer's ancient garrison soldiers and accompanied by 30 Scottish peers, knights and gentlemen and by those of the Northumberland gentry who were not in exile, the earl provided the townspeople with a spectacle the likes of which they had not seen since King James passed through Berwick in 1603.[133] A short time later Dunbar presided over his second recorded session of gaol delivery in the High Castle in Newcastle.[134] No doubt bothersome legal safeguards made it less successful for Dunbar than the famous session which he held in Dumfries two months later. After learning of the Scottish session, Lord Dunfermline, the Scottish chancellor, assured King James that Dunbar "has purgit the Borders of all the chiefest malefactors, robbers, and brigands as were wont to reign and triumph there, as clean, and by as great wisdom and policy, as Hercules sometime is written to have purged Augeas, the king of Elide, his escuries".[135] An English observer who was probably more objective than Dunfermline admitted that the English border shires were far more tranquil than they had ever been in Queen Elizabeth's time. After presiding over the local assizes in 1608 and 1609, Sir Edward Phelips, the speaker of the House of Commons during the troubled session of 1606–7, advised the Earl of Salisbury that "Northumberland, Cumberland, Westmorland and Lancashire are as free from the spilling of blood and other felonies and outrages as any other counties within the kingdom".[136]

The comments of this assize judge should have convinced King James that the English Middle Shires were at last pacified and that he could begin to think of committing them solely to the charge of the resident justices of the peace.[137] In Northumberland J. P.s had, after all, been competently handling most aspects of local administration for several years. Yet to James's way of thinking, the border counties would not be satisfactorily pacified until the English Parliament had reversed its decision to prohibit the remanding of suspected criminals. Thus, after a chastened Sir Henry Widdrington and other Members of Parliament assembled in February 1610, the government presented a bill to permit commissioners of oyer and terminer, judges of assize or J. P.s in the border counties to examine Englishmen accused of committing offences in Scotland. If they were satisfied there was "pregnant proof" that the defendant had committed a felony known to the English law, they were to send him to Scotland for trial. At some stage in the proceedings a clause was added to the effect that the measure would not be valid until the Scottish Parliament passed reciprocal legislation. Another provision stipulated that should the bill become law it would only remain in effect until the end of the first session of the next Parliament. Thus even had the Scottish Parliament passed the required legislation, which it did not, the English statute would have expired in 1614 with the dissolution of the Addled Parliament. Some peers opposed the measure until James, who was very keen on it, assured them that none of them would ever be remanded to Scotland. On 16 July 1610 committees from the Lords and Commons met to iron out their differences. The next day the bill passed its third reading in both houses and became the statute of 7 James I, c. 1.[138] This Parliament also passed the first lay subsidy within living memory which did not exclude Northumberland and the border counties.[139]

George Home, Earl of Dunbar, did not long survive his royal master's parliamentary triumph in the remanding controversy. After his death on 30 January 1611,[140] he was remembered as a champion of law and order and the Protestant religious establishment. His "survivor in the government of the Middle Shires on both sides", Francis Earl of Cumberland, spoke of him as an "upright, careful justiciar, a most painful and faithful servant to his sacred Majesty".[141] Some years later John Smaithwaite, parson of Elsdon in Redesdale, still revered Dunbar as a just man by whom "great captains had their deserts, some by death, others by banishment, others by imprisonment".[142] Yet there is some doubt whether Dunbar's activities, in themselves, did lead to an appreciable decrease in the local crime rate. According to the records kept by the clerk of the peace, 39, 40 and 32 people were indicted in 1605, 1606 and 1607 respectively. In 1607 and 1608 Dunbar deported 175 Northumbrians of doubtful character. Yet in each of the three succeeding years approximately 25 people were indicted for cattle theft and similar offences.[143] Though it must be admitted that this level of crime compared favourably with other parts of England, it was higher than statements by Chancellor Dunfermline, Commissioner Selby and parson Smaithwaite would lead one to expect.

Perhaps the Earl of Dunbar should be seen as only one of several agencies in the transformation of Northumberland into a relatively tranquil and peaceful county; another was the first Jacobean border commission. But of far greater importance was the lessening of tensions between inhabitants of the shires on either side of the border after the personal union of the Crowns. Within Northumberland relative domestic tranquillity was assured (except for a few confused weeks after the discovery of the Gunpowder Plot) by the cadre of hard-working justices of the peace headed by Edward Talbot, the *custos rotulorum*. Although southerners might still regard Northumberland as virtually ungovernable, Talbot saw to it that local justices kept their quarter sessions with remarkable regularity. This unsung hero of Jacobean Northumberland generally attended at least three of the four sessions held each year. Talbot's record was only matched by that of justices Sir William Fenwick of Wallington and Thomas Middleton of Belsay.[144]

The work of these justices was made considerably easier, not by anything within their own control, but by good fortune. Between the years 1603 and 1611 harvests were generally good or excellent. As Northumbrian farmers had enough for their own sustenance, they felt little need to covet their neighbours' flocks or stores of grain. So it seemed that the gods themselves looked favourably upon King James's noble dream of bringing peace and quietness to the Middle Shires. With pardonable exaggeration he told Members of Parliament in 1607 that in recent years the borders had been:

planted and peopled with Civilitie and riches: their Churches begin to bee planted, their doores stand now open, they feare neither robbing nor spoiling: and where there was nothing before heard nor seene in those parts but bloodshed, oppressions, complaints and outcries, they now live every man peaceably under his owne figgetree, and all their former cryes and complaints turned onely into prayers to God for their King, under whom they enjoy such ease and happy quietnesse.[145]

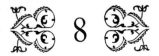 8

An agrarian economy, 1603-25

Despite King James's proud boast to the contrary, the economy of Northumberland as a whole was not noticeably affected by the end of border hostilities until around 1610. Of course there were local exceptions. As early as the spring of 1604 farmers in upper Coquetdale decided that it was now safe to resume the use of pasture lands and wastes which had long lain deserted because of Scottish raids.[1] On the other hand, the end of raiding played havoc with the economy of a village such as Bywell on the middle Tyne. Famed in earlier days for its trade and manufacture of the buckles, stirrups and other iron goods used by border horsemen, by 1608 Bywell consisted of only 17 "small sheds for smiths to work in and in very small request by reason there is little trade there".[2] The new harmony also dislocated the economy of Berwick-upon-Tweed for, as a contemporary pointed out, it was closely linked to the money which the Crown paid the garrison soldiers "which, as the blood through the veins, was conveyed into every part thereof for other commodities". After all but 100 members of the old garrison were dismissed and sent away in 1604, many Berwick merchants faced ruin.[3] But in most of Northumberland proper, economic conditions steadily improved as the effects of the raids, famines and plagues of the 1590s were gradually erased by the passage of time and a series of good harvests. By about 1610 landlords noted that many of their tenants were flourishing and began to feel that it was worth their while to challenge customary tenures and to regularize encroachments made on to the waste.

The gradual conversion of customary tenures to leasehold was the most notable change which occurred in the agrarian economy of Northumberland during the first quarter of the seventeenth century. Surveys made in 1604 and 1608 show that only 13 per cent of the tenants on royal land were leaseholders. Sixty-eight per cent were customary tenants, 2 per cent were cottagers and 17 per cent were freeholders.[4] These figures are probably representative of the county as a whole. In 1607 Members of Parliament were informed that "uppon the Borders there are few or no Freeholdes all their Estats being tenant rights a Kind of Copyhold."[5] But 30 years later Sir William Widdrington could point out that most of the 'poorer sort' in Northumberland now held leases.[6]

The extent of the conversion of customary tenures to leasehold can best be studied by examining records concerning properties held by the ninth earl of Northumberland and other leading landholders. As G. R. Batho has shown, Earl Percy was rather careless of estate management and something of a spendthrift during the first few years after he succeeded to his estates in 1585. But by the 1590s he was taking a keen interest in his lands and was in frequent correspondence with George Whitehead, William Orde, Robert Delaval, Thomas Fotherley and other northern estate agents. After the earl was accused of being privy to the Gunpowder Plot, imprisoned and fined £30,000, he may have felt that any additional income he might receive would only go towards paying off the fine which, in any case, would probably be pardoned should his enemies die or fall from power. Indeed, a few months after the death of Robert, Earl of Salisbury, Percy was pardoned the remainder of his fine on the immediate payment of £11,000. Although he remained in the Tower until 1621, after November 1613 whatever profits he made from his Northumberland estates were his own.[7]

Earl Percy had a good deal of latitude in dealing with his Northumbrian customary tenants for, except for those in Tynemouthshire and North Tynedale, almost all of them followed the custom of the manor of Cockermouth. In 1570 Hall and Humberston had interpreted the Cockermouth custom, as it applied to the barony of Alnwick, to mean that copyholders "make fine at the lord's will and pleasure after the death, alienation or exchange of the lord or tenant". However, lands which tenants had forfeited, escheated or otherwise lost could be demised for a term of years or "in such sort as to the lord shall seem best for his benefit."[8] After the discovery of the Gunpowder Plot a northern clergyman claimed that he had heard rumours that Earl Percy was contemplating forcing all his tenants to exchange their copies for leases. The cleric warned of the political dangers of such a "designment, than which there can be no greater corrosive to his whole country nor any thing of like moment to cause a commotion and cause all the yeomen and husbandmen of that country to take armour and rise up as one man."[9] But as the earl was still uncertain about the respective merits of copyhold and leasehold, no such change was imminent.

One apparent advantage of copyhold from a landlord's point of view was the high fine which a tenant paid at the death of the lord or tenant. In 1586 the ninth earl received from his Northumberland tenants (excluding those in Tynemouthshire) £1,763 in fines, bringing his total receipts from the county to more than £2,600. His receipts did not again reach this level until 1636.

Over the long run it would appear that the earl received roughly half as much in fines as he received in rents from those of his Northumbrian tenants who followed the custom of Cockermouth.[10] Another advantage of copyhold was that it was hallowed by long usage and custom and was generally well accepted by tenants. Robert Delaval noted the reluctance of copyhold tenants in Long Houghton to accept new-fangled leases at an economic – or rack – rent.[11] Although payment of an entrance fine might be a hardship at first, in subsequent years the low rent made it easier for a tenant to weather a debilitating illness or a run of bad harvests. In the course of a normal lifespan a tenant who owed a high entrance fine and a low rent paid less for his tenement than he would have done had he paid an economic rent and no fine. Indeed the ninth earl eventually came to realize that high fines were much the same as a loan to the Percy estate at current interest rates.[12]

In January 1608 William Orde argued that the earl would profit if he granted 21-year leases rather than copies for new enclosures of waste ground in Rothbury Forest. Orde admitted that the first lease to a new tenement would not be particularly profitable for as the tenant would have to pay for the planting of hedges and other improvements he could not be expected to pay a high rent. However, after the first lease had expired the next lessee could, Orde reasoned, be charged an economic rent.[13] Six months later the earl rejected the idea that leases, first for an increase in rent of 2s. in the pound and later for double the old rent, would yield him greater profits than the copies currently held by customary tenants in Warkworth. He recalled occasions when fines might be levied, the services rendered by the copyholders and the possibility of the properties escheating to the lord. Perhaps he was right when he said that such new leases would "in effect . . . give away my land for nothing and touch me in honour."[14]

Later the earl allowed his hardworking estate agents to force some customary tenants holding according to the custom of Cockermouth to accept leases on terms more favourable to himself. Yet the bargaining and cajoling which accompanied each individual change was slow and tedious. What was really needed was a court decision showing that all such tenants held for life only. The first breakthrough occurred early in 1609 when Margaret, Countess of Cumberland, brought a case in Chancery in which it was found that copyholders liable to a fine at the death of the lord and tenant did not hold customary estates of inheritance. This decision greatly alarmed the Earl of Northumberland's tenants who held by the custom of Cockermouth. A few of them told Robert Delaval that they were now willing to accept leases. He in turn asked the earl for permission to grant leases for 21 years at double the old rent.[15] In June 1610 50-year-old William Bowden of Long Houghton accepted a lease at double the old rent and no fine; eight years earlier he had paid an entrance fine for his copy. Perhaps with tongue in cheek, Delaval wrote to his employer: "if it maye please your honour, I would not have anye denyed a lease upon the like condyssyons that be coppye houlders, that arr so likelye to leve as he is, and hath paid a fyne so latelye."[16]

After considerable delay the earl finally resolved to act on a suit which would be a "leading case to all my tenant rights in Northumberland".[17] At the summer assize in 1613 the earl's agents challenged the tenure of one John Hunter of Rothbury, a copyholder holding by the custom of Cockermouth.[18] After the assize Thomas Fotherley reported that the judge had found for the earl because the "estates being but for life of lord and tenant, the one deceasing they hold no estate at all but such as the lord would be pleased to grant them".[19] George Whitehead noted that "copyholders are down the wind, after death in your lordship's power... it was a good day for your lordship... for now I make no doubt now to see your lordship's estate bettered by five hundred pounds a year."[20]

The position of the man who had been the defendant in this important test case was rather better than that of many Percy tenants who were subsequently to take leases. Hunter had protested in court that he would be reduced to utter poverty if he lost his copyhold. In response Judge Altham suggested that Percy agents grant him a lease for his old rent and accept £8 as an entrance fine. If this fine was double the old rent, then over a 21-year period Hunter would pay the earl £92 for his tenement, as opposed to the £84 in rent he had paid previously. Fotherley agreed to these terms in order to encourage the jury to consider the case favourably but he clearly did not think himself bound to treat other tenants as generously.[21] A later estate memorandum recommended that on the death of a tenant, copies be replaced by leases at treble the old rent. In the case of a £4 old rent this would amount to £252 over a 21-year period. If the son or other heir was unable or unwilling to pay the new rent, the memorandum suggested that the earl lease the land to a new tenant "for your lordship's best advantage".[22] However George Whitehead, a Percy agent with family connections at Boulmer, north of Alnmouth, cautioned the earl that it would be a "course very profitable and honourable both to your lordship to use mercy with conquest, for I assure your lordship, the country is much troubled with this overthrow of copyhold estate".[23]

The Hunter decision paved the way for the gradual demise of the custom of Cockermouth in Northumberland as on the death of a copyholder his heir now had no choice but to accept a lease or be dispossessed. However the earl's agents failed in their attempt to challenge existing copyholds at the 1614 assize. At a time when anti-Catholic feelings were at a level unknown since 1605,[24] they should have realized that it was folly to bring a case of this sort. The sheriff responsible for empanelling the jurors was Ralph Selby of Weetwood, brother of Sir William Selby, the militant Protestant border commissioner. Sir Henry Widdrington, the only Catholic sympathizer in the county with sufficient influence to bridle the Selbys, was, as Thomas Fotherley cryptically noted, unable to attend the assize because of "his illness of health, as was reported".[25] A Hertfordshire man himself, Fotherley noted that "such are the conditions of these northern jurors as that they respect their friends before oaths or evidence".[26] This temporary respite notwithstanding, some Percy copyholders deemed it prudent to accept leases rather than stand trial at a later assize. In 1615 Fotherley informed the earl that two Lesbury men against whom a case was pending, George and Gawen Salkeld, were willing to surrender their copyholds and take 21-year leases at double their old rents if the earl would pardon the fine which should have been paid seven years earlier.[27]

In July 1617 the earl ordered Fotherley and Whitehead to summon all tenants who had "no estates in their tenements", as well as the heirs of all tenants "holding for term of life" and to compound with them for 21-year leases "at treble the ancient rent or for such fines as you shall think fit to impose on them". If tenants refused to accept a beneficial lease (with an entrance fine and a relatively low rent) or a lease at rack rent, Fotherley and Whitehead were to expel them and give 21-year leases at treble the old rent to whomever they saw fit.[28]

In July 1619 an assize jury headed by a gentleman who was friendly to the earl's interest, Sir William Selby of Shortflatt, found against Percy tenants claiming copyhold of inheritance at Newham. The jury found that one of the tenants had forfeited his copy because he had let his tenement without licence. Fotherley informed his employer that "this trial has stricken a great terror into all your lordship's pretended copyhold tenants, and I believe that most of them will come in without further suit, for the case received a fair trial upon a full hearing".[29] Thereafter the custom of Cockermouth gradually came to an end as copyholders were persuaded to exchange their copies for leases or died and were replaced by leaseholders.

In contrast, some of the Crown's copyholders in the manor of Tynemouth succeeded in halting the erosion of their customary tenure. Their struggle was of considerable interest to the Earl of Northumberland, particularly as he leased most of the non-customary land in Tynemouthshire and had the right to conduct the local manorial court.[30] In 1608 Bartholomew Haggatt and George Ward surveyed the area on behalf of the Crown. They found that tenants in the manor of Tynemouth proper claimed:

> to hold their land to them and their heirs, by fine rent and service. And that their fines are certain, viz. one year's rent upon the admittance of a tenant's heir, and two years' rent upon a surrender. But we find a great discord in the payment of their fines, having been sometimes more, sometimes less, they allege my lord of Northumberland's officers be the cause thereof.[31]

And because Percy officers had neglected to keep the court records, the surveyors could not tell whether tenants in outlying parts of the manor, at Elswick, Benwell, Amble and Hauxley, could justifiably claim customary estates of inheritance.[32] Tynemouthshire copyholders were perceptive enough to realize that the Crown had ordered the survey with a view to making two interlinked changes: challenging customary tenures and selling the land to contractors. In November tenants from all the towns except North Shields and Tynemouth town itself petitioned Robert Earl of Salisbury for permission to compound for their copyholds.[33] The following April the Court of Exchequer confirmed these Tynemouthshire copyholds as estates of inheritance with forms of surrender and admittance as they had existed before 1577/8. In return for confirmation, the copyholders agreed to make an aggregate payment of £789 13s. 4d. This sum was nearly six times the copyholders' ancient monetary rent. As at least 110 tenants compounded, the fine worked out at about £7 a tenement.[34] This was not an unreasonable sum; Hunter of Rothbury would pay an £8 fine for his new lease in 1613.

Less fortunate were the 50 or more Tynemouthshire copyholders in North Shields. At the beginning of the sixteenth century the Prior of Tynemouth had rented these tenements to the fishermen who presumably had supplied the monks with fresh fish. Each tenement consisted of only a cottage and a small forecourt on which nets could be dried. The cottages fell into disrepair after the Dissolution and in 1565 they were let by copy of court roll according to the custom of the manor of Tynemouth. The Crown's surveyors examined the status of the tenants in 1608 and concluded that as their copies were only of 30 or 40 years' standing they should accept leases.[35]

Haggatt and Ward also surveyed the regality of Hexham on the occasion of the expiration of the 40-year lease which Queen Elizabeth had granted to Sir John Forster and which in 1608 was held by Forster's wily grandson, Sir John Fenwick. The surveyors found that 375 copyholders and customary tenants in the regality "claim their lands as copyholders of inheritance to them, their heirs and assigns according to the custom of rent, fine and border service." The tenants claimed their fines were certain; one year's rent at each change of tenant.[36] After Fenwick's lease expired part of the regality was purchased by contractors in fee simple and part in fee farm. Around 1610 the contractors unsuccessfully challenged the validity of some of the tenants' claims to customary estates of inheritance in the Court of Exchequer.[37] Fifteen years later the court again looked favourably on Hexham people. Claiming that their manorial records had been lost in a Scottish raid in 1546, petitioners representing 300 men, women and children in Wall and Acomb asked the Exchequer to confirm them in their customary estates of inheritance with fixed fines.[38] Copyhold survived in Hexham into the nineteenth century.[39]

Improvement was the order of the day in western Northumberland in the early years of the seventeenth century. As Joan Thirsk has pointed out, throughout England as a whole "the assumption was commonplace that the test of a country's worthiness was the abundance of its cornfields ... the furrows that followed the ploughshare were deemed the only reliable sign of agricultural progress."[40] So it was that absentee Northumberland landlords felt that now that bloody-minded Scottish raiders were no longer systematically plundering the highlands, Redesdale and North Tynedale would prove attractive to enterprising settlers from lowland Northumberland and perhaps even from south of the Tyne. These settlers could establish permanent farmsteads and plant crops on the thousands of acres of land which were currently used as common pasture by the shiftless highlanders whose winter farms were located in the valleys.[41] No less important, the settlers would pay economic rents.

In 1604 King James ordered a survey to be made of all the Crown's lands in Redesdale and Tynedale. Later that year John Goodwin and John Johnson, as well as the lowland Northumbrian gentlemen who were also members of the survey commission, made their report. It was clear from the variations they found in existing rents that many Redesdalers could reasonably be expected to pay a higher rent than they were actually paying. George Hall, for example, paid 5s. per annum for a house, eight acres of meadow, six acres of arable and a fifth share in a 830-acre pasture, while Jenkin Brown paid nearly twice as much, 9s. 2d., for a house, barn, three acres of meadow, five acres of arable land and a tenth share in a 222-acre pasture.[42] The commissioners did not entirely agree amongst themselves what rents should be charged. Johnson and Goodwin argued that in the manor of Harbottle the 21,200 acres of highland pasture for which an annual rent of only £3 17s. was currently paid could be made to yield £353 6s. 8d. This was calculated at the rate of 4d. an acre, the same rate which was commonly charged for newly enclosed lands along the middle Tyne and in Coquetdale.[43] But the men of Redesdale thought that this valuation was utterly preposterous. In a letter to the Privy Council they wrote that "if the commissioners will find men to take those lands according as [they] have valued them, let them be thought honest officers. Those of the commission who best know the nature of the country, finding their producings ridiculous, refused to set [their] hands to the same." From personal experience the Redesdalers knew that most of the land there was "barren heath, high mountains and desert wastes so that in ten miles of grounds there will not be a hundred acres of arable".[44] Perhaps the Earl of Dunbar (to whom King James granted these lands later in 1604) was of the same opinion. No systematic attempt was made to challenge the claims of resident highlanders to their summer pastures or to their lowland farms until after Dunbar's death in 1611.

The Earl of Northumberland handled his highland tenants rather differently. In May 1604 he directed Edward Charlton of Hesleyside, collector for the Talbot lands (most of which lay within the bounds of the manor of Wark), to take possession of parcels of pasture land called Bolls and Blacksop which were illegally occupied by Scottish followers of the laird of Buccleuch.[45] A few months later, in exchange for what he took to be a promise to pay an annual rent of 40s., Percy granted Cuthbert Charlton, Matthew Charlton and other Charltons some waste ground "according to the Tynedale custom". The Charltons perversely took this to mean that they should pay no rent at all.[46] By 1608 the earl was a wiser man and was contemplating leasing highland pasture to individuals rather than to extended families. Edward Errington of Walwick Grange, who had succeeded Charlton as collector for the Talbot lands,[47] offered to take a 21-year lease to some of the Tynedale uplands at an annual rent of £40 and a fine of £200. He promised that he would erect permanent "winter houses where yet never any have been" and enclose pastures which were currently used in common by local customary tenants and freeholders. Percy's receiver, Robert Delaval, urged him to accept Errington's offer and reminded him that in neighbouring Cumberland Lord William Howard was said to be greatly increasing his income by enclosing his great upland commons and granting leases to individuals.[48]

Earl Percy decided not to accept Errington's offer but in the spring of 1609 he allowed William Orde to enter into direct negotiations with the English customary tenants. After much haggling Orde got them to offer £20 a year for the upland pastures then occupied by the Scots. With ill-concealed disgust he noted that the prospective tenants intended to use the land for summer pasture in the traditional fashion, "whereas if tenements could be raised and people planted according as the ground would very well bear, that rent [£20] would be first doubled if not trebled."[49] That July Earl Percy commissioned Orde to survey the lands and let them to the highest bidder.[50] Unfortunately he had failed to consult the Earl of Dunbar in this matter. In September the Scottish earl warned that he would go to law if Percy began to grant leases to the Tynedale wastes to which his tenants claimed customary rights.[51] By May 1610 Dunbar's threats and the intransigency of the Tynedale tenantry convinced Orde that it was futile to pursue the matter further.[52] No more was done until after the death of the Earl of Dunbar.

Then in the spring of 1611 Earl Percy commissioned Thomas Fotherley to survey all his lands in North and South Tynedale.[53] Obscure transactions concerning the "higher lands of Tynedale" took place in the following months. An estate memorandum from 1613 recorded that an unnamed sublessee, possibly Sir Henry Widdrington, "is willing upon reasonable terms to pass over the lease secretly to whom your lordship please or, because he is a man [who] can do more than any man, he, upon your lordship's agreement with him, will cause the most of the obstinate [to] turn tenants to your lordship and take leases from you, so shall you be possessed of all and no man can challenge any part".[54] At the 1614 assize Earl Percy succeeded in winning a case on behalf of his lessees Sir Henry Widdrington, Robert Delaval and William Orde. After the session Fotherley reported that "the trial for Tynedale is passed in your lordship's behalf albeit all the tenants swore strongly for their tenant-right estates, but their grounds being but wastes and commons and no part of their tenements, as was proved, it went clearly".[55] After the trial Roland Milburn, "on behalf of some forty others of his name", complained to the earl that the new leases were forcing them from their upland pasture.[56]

It should be stressed that this leased land was to be used for pasture rather than as arable. Although ten years earlier Earl Percy and his agents had hoped that colonists could be induced to establish permanent farmsteads, they now realized that this was impractical. Given the current level of farming technology, it was not even possible to grow enough grass to maintain cattle all the year round. Pasture management was not sufficiently advanced to allow this higher ground to be used for permanent settlement until the eighteenth century. Even then it was often uneconomic. In recent years much of this land has been planted in coniferous trees by the Forestry Commission.[57]

After Earl Percy challenged the claims of Tynedale extended families to their customary upland pastures, he preferred to allow the Howards, the Crown and other northern landlords to lead the way in the costly campaign against tenant-right.[58] These landlords argued that now that tenants claiming tenant-right had long since ceased to be called upon to perform their special obligations of service on the borders, their tenures were no longer valid. In July 1620, after Lord William Howard and others had begun suits in the central law courts and there had been a number of disturbances in Cumberland, King James issued a proclamation abolishing tenant-right.[59] Subsequently non-royal tenants in the barony of Kendal in Westmorland, who might have served as examples for people claiming tenant-right in Redesdale and North Tynedale, found that it was possible to preserve the essence of their tenure. In November 1622, the Westmorland tenants were accused in the Star Chamber of "unlawful assemblies, and publishing a libellous book ... to oppose his majesty's proclamation for abolishing of the tenure and name of border service".[60] The possibility that the case might be resolved in the tenants' favour greatly alarmed certain northern landlords and in May 1623 they requested the king to punish severely all tenants who combined against the proclamation.[61] Later the Westmorland tenants pleaded not guilty to the charges laid against them in the Star Chamber. Rather than claiming tenant-right they asserted that they held customary estates of inheritance. The judges accepted this argument and limited their inquiry to two considerations. Firstly, were the Kendal estates descendable from ancestor to heir and secondly, were fines on alienation certain or arbitrary at the will of the lord. In June 1625 Justice Sir Henry Hobart announced that border service had not been mentioned in the Kendal tenants' admittances or entries and that they held customary estates of inheritance. Although in common parlance the Kendal tenants' tenure might thereafter be known as tenant-right, strictly speaking it had been shown to be a customary tenure of inheritance.[62]

The issue was resolved rather differently in Northumberland. Here the most active landlord was Theophilus Lord Howard de Walden (1584–1640), after 1626 second earl of Suffolk. In 1614, after his marriage to Elizabeth Home, daughter of the Earl of Dunbar, Walden and his wife received a royal grant of the whole of Dunbar's former properties in the manor of Wark in Tynedale and in the manor of Harbottle in Redesdale.[63] Soon afterwards Walden began to challenge his tenants' claims to tenant-right for both their winter farms and their summer pasture in the Court of Exchequer. This court was nominally under the supervision of his father, Lord Treasurer Suffolk. The position of Walden's tenants was rather weak. Harbottle tenants explained the absence of written records pertaining to their lowland tenements by pointing out that they had never had to pay entrance fines.[64] Ingenious as they were in certain instances, the Wark and Harbottle tenants did not realize that after the Crown had issued the proclamation abolishing tenant-right, it was imperative to drop their claims to this form of tenure and instead claim that they held customary estates of inheritance. In 1621 judges ruled that, in the light of the 1620 proclamation, the Reads were tenants-at-will for summer pasture known as Redeshead and that they must either compound as tenants-at-will or accept leases. The Reads managed to put off the day of reckoning until July 1622, when the Court of Exchequer ordered the sheriff of Northumberland to throw them off their lands.[65] Subsequently the court declared that Walden's customary tenants in Wark and Harbottle held their winter farms as well as their summer pasture at the will of the lord and that he could require them to take leases or could replace them with other tenants.[66]

If we are to accept a report sent to the Earl of Northumberland in the 1630s, Walden reached a compromise with his tenants. Some of those in Harbottle agreed that they should have two-thirds of their former tenements at the whole of the ancient rent and that a third part should be leased for Walden's "best profit".[67] Indeed, in a few cases something resembling such a division had already taken place before the court ruled against the Reads. Although in 1604 there had been no leaseholders in the manor of Harbottle, in 1618 14 lessees were paying rent for a third part of ancient tenements.[68] Earl Percy's correspondent also reported that those of Walden's tenants who had not taken such leases had agreed to buy their tenements at 80 years' purchase, that is 80 times their ancient rent. At the time this correspondent was writing many of Lord Walden's tenants had not yet paid the full purchase price and apparently had no intention of so doing. He calculated that if these properties were rented at the rack they could not yield more than £200 a year "with the royalties added to it."[69] By his general tone the correspondent showed that he, for one, did not believe that Lord Walden had been able to gain a financial return commensurate with the money and effort he had expended in overturning tenant-right in Wark and Harbottle.

Perhaps the Earl of Northumberland was wise to be cautious in his dealings with the tenants who had lowland farms in his manor of Charlton. In the autumn of 1629 Percy agent Clark recommended that rather than engaging the Tynedalers in litigation, the earl should recognize them as customary tenants of inheritance. The agent noted that the tenants, whom he described as "miserably poor", were willing to pay a £14 fine on the death of the lord or tenant or on the alienation of a tenement. Clark added that because of recent bad harvests Percy would find it difficult to recruit tenants from elsewhere if he chose to supplant those already in occupation.[70]

The bad harvests of the 1620s emphasized the marginal nature of the physical resources of the Northumberland uplands and dashed landlords' hopes that these areas could be made to yield substantially greater profits over the long term than they had while they were being raided by Scottish terrorists. In 1628 John Forster and Herman Nicholson agreed to pay a fine of £11 10s. and an annual rent of £6 8s. to continue a lease to a tenement in the manor of Harbottle which had been deserted "by reason of the great dearth which was about four or five years since." They claimed that the bailiff there "careth not who were tenants so that they were honest men".[71] Deserted tenements in Redesdale and North Tynedale can also be interpreted as reflecting the absence of population pressure in Jacobean Northumberland. There was no land hunger which might tempt people to settle on marginal lands. But in the transitional zone and in the lowlands there was reasonably attractive land which could be enclosed and let for relatively low rents to the mutual advantage of landlords and tenants.

There are remarkably few records of Northumberland landlords engaging in depopulating enclosure between the years 1603 and 1625. It may be that contemporary commentators neglected the problem because it only affected people at the bottom end of the social scale whose rights were not protected by manorial custom or common law courts. Yet in 1610 the ninth earl of Northumberland was warned that he might be involved in a "suit of law and great clamour" if he ignored the rights of 14 tenants, four freeholders and four cottagers to property which he wished to lease to Robert Clark. Clark later secured the lease but only on the understanding that he would respect the customary rights of local people.[72] It is possible that families who were displaced by enclosure found it relatively easy and inexpensive to rent other land. But it seems more likely that because of far-reaching changes in agricultural land use, there was actually far less depopulating enclosure after 1603 than there had been during the troubled 1590s. After that critical decade of grain shortage and high grain prices most farmers recognized that rather than concentrating their resources on producing wool, they should diversify their farming. The advantages of diversified farming were especially apparent in the south-east where there was ready access to the markets which supplied

Newcastle and the Tyneside coal areas with grain, dairy products and meat.[73] Then too, by the mid-Jacobean period many farmers realized that money invested in sheep did not always bring them the returns they might win from grain production. Because of changes in the national and international wool market there was only a modest demand for wool which was not of the highest quality.[74] And if market conditions failed to convince a conservative farmer of the unprofitability of continuing to rear large numbers of sheep, a serious outbreak of disease might finally drive the lesson home. This was certainly the case with Sir Ralph Delaval. Around 1610 Sir Ralph completed the task begun by his father, the conversion of the 2,500-acre estate at Hartley from arable to pasture. However, even before 1627, when a third of his flock died of disease, Sir Ralph had decided to return to more diversified farming. By the time of his death in 1628 he had begun to re-divide Hartley into farms which he leased to tenants for use as arable.[75]

Most of the enclosure which did take place in Jacobean Northumberland can be divided into two kinds. The first consisted of encroachments on to waste and commons, and took place mainly in the transitional zone. In such areas grazing land was generally unstinted and there was little shortage of pasture. Evidence from royal and Percy lands indicates that there was a move to regularize the position of people of all ranks who had made encroachments by granting them leases at relatively low rents. For the lesser sort the availability of such leases meant that they were not generally affected by any scarcity of opportunities to find employment as wage labourers. Though as a rule commercial farmers from the lowlands did not feel it was worth their while to make encroachments in the transitional zone, a few did so. In 1606 Robert Lawson of Cramlington – who lived only 20 miles from Rothbury as the crow flies – claimed copyhold for an unenclosed pasture known as Newbiggin in Rothbury Forest on which he had built a small stone house.[76]

The Earl of Northumberland was concerned that gentlemen who engrossed land from the waste by taking advantage of a "poor man's weakness" paid him suitable rents.[77] He was no less concerned that this poor man also paid his due. In Rothbury Forest the earl found that his tenants clung to their claim that they had a customary right to enclose land from the common for a rent of 4d. an acre.[78] William Orde tried to persuade such tenants to accept leases but at first he made little headway. In 1608 he noted that "the common sort of our country, who as they will know nothing but their particular profit and the ordinary and accustomed means that lead to it, so are they much subject to clamour if they be pressed to move [other] than usual."[79] In 1611 Timothy Elkes noted that certain Rothbury freeholders were complaining that they had lost their customary rights to part of the Forest, while at the same time they were covertly making enclosures of their own.[80] In 1613, shortly after the Hunter decision, an estate memorandum recommended that the earl's commons be "let by lease in parcels as may be best improved." The tenants should take leases at reasonable rents and enclose and hedge the land themselves; later, rents could be substantially increased.[81]

Other landlords were coming to similar arrangements with encroachers in the transitional zone. In the 1608 survey of the royal baronies of Bywell and Bulbeck there is a long list of rents which the surveyors suggested might be charged for recent encroachments or for those which people anticipated making in the future. These intakes varied in size from a 50-acre intake which George Boultflower wished to make to a one-acre intake which William Frende of Slaley had already made. Four tenants of Riding had made an intake "for summer kine" and Thomas Lawson "has built two houses on the king's common and thrusteth out his hedge into the king's ground." The rent suggested by the surveyors for most of these intakes was 4d. an acre, the same rent customarily paid by Percy tenants for intakes in Rothbury Forest.[82] It appears that, with the exception of George Boultflower of County Durham and Francis Radcliffe from nearby Dilston, the men who had made or planned to make encroachments on to the waste in Bywell and Bulbeck were small local farmers, either freeholders, lessees or tenants-at-will.[83]

The other type of enclosure most common in Jacobean Northumberland involved the division of lowland common field villages and the gradual establishment of self-contained individually-held farms. As we have seen, before 1603 a form of division had taken place which limited a farmer's holdings to one part of a village but generally preserved co-operative strip cultivation. In a policy note written in 1607 Percy agent Robert Delaval reiterated the main agricultural advantages such a division would have for a large village. He observed that it would result in farmers having land only in that part of the village closest to their farmsteads and that they would thus be able to manure all of their fields more easily. The agent only took into account tenants with a full husbandland and did not consider men for whom depopulating enclosure might still be a reality, cottagers with tenuous rights to a few rigs or selions in the common fields. Delaval regarded a division of the common fields as the best way to initiate the complete consolidation of the scattered strips into individual fenced farms whereby the tenants would "remove their houses to the midst of their several farms and that part they now have most barren may be thereby as fertile and good" as any other fields. Moreover this redistribution would enable Earl Percy to consolidate his demesne and either lease it at an improved rent or use it for grain production or for cattle breeding.[84]

Enclosure of the kind described by Delaval was in some ways attractive to both landlords and tenants. Yet the number of common field villages which actually were enclosed during the Jacobean period was not as large as one might suppose. Though the formal end of border hostilities did enable landlords to forget about the needs of local defence when assessing estate management policies, there were other important considerations to be taken into account when deciding whether enclosure was feasible and, if so, when it should be effected. Some 24 villages for which we have information still retained their common fields in 1625; at least ten of these were enclosed by 1700.[85] Thus, although comparatively few Northumberland villages remained to be enclosed in the eighteenth century, it is incorrect to imply that there was a rapid acceleration in the rate of enclosure in the years immediately following the accession of the first Stuart king. Rather, enclosure was a gradual process which continued throughout the entire seventeenth century.

The process of enclosing the common fields might take several forms, depending upon local circumstances. A short time before 1622, the common fields of Harlow Hill, a village on the Roman Wall north of Prudhoe, were divided into four parts on the tenants' initiative. It appears that these tenants (who continued to share a common pasture) divided each of the new fields into half and enclosed their individual plots. As a result of this division they were able to pay higher rents than they had earlier. By 1625 five of them had taken 21-year leases.[86]

Somewhat different was the situation in nearby Prudhoe where, according to William Orde, the tenants were troubled by neighbouring villagers who pastured their cattle on outlying parts of the unfenced common. In addition, the tenants lived too far from some of their fields to be able to manure them properly. In 1625 Orde recommended that a division be made so that the tenants could move their houses closer to their enclosed fields which, he implied, should be held individually. He also suggested that the tenants exchange their copies for leases.[87] By 1651 Prudhoe had been divided into two equal parts. A Mr Fenwick held a lease to the west side and Percy tenants and four freeholders held the east side. It would appear that strips in the half belonging to the freeholders and the Percy tenants were still intermingled, for an estate agent noted "we cannot have a division between your worship's tenants and the four freeholders this year so conveniently as after by reason that they have sown their seeds."[88]

Another example of a township which was enclosed in very gradual stages was nearby Ovingham. In 1622 Orde informed the ninth earl that during the eighth earl's time (he died in 1585) most of Ovingham had been held by freeholders and Percy tenants who, although they were on demesne land, had always been treated as if they were copyholders. Sometime before 1622 each of the several parties had been assigned separate arable and pasture land, although one great common field still lay undivided. Orde reported that the Percy tenants "humbly desire" that this field now be divided and allotted in several to better enable them to pay their rents.[89]

As the inhabitants of the Percy manor of Long Houghton learned to their cost in 1619, there were occasions when the interests of landlord and tenant conflicted. Sometime before 1603 Long Houghton's common fields had been divided into two parts but the various common pastures which together constituted half of the area of the township had remained unfenced. Over the years cattle belonging to Sir Edward Gray of Morpeth and his tenants at Howick strayed on to the small common which lay just north of Long Houghton village. Around 1619 the earl thought to end this petty dispute by enclosing the common and granting Gray a lease to half of it. Percy then informed his own tenants that they would have to take leases to individually-enclosed pasture lands at the rate of 2d. an acre. The tenants responded by tearing up the hedges. They were later pardoned for this indiscretion and granted leases to the pasture. However, they continued to resent the fact that their cattle no longer had access to their accustomed water supply at Howick Burn and that they themselves could no longer reach the seashore to collect the seaweed which they used to manure their fields.[90]

There were other cases in which lowlanders found that their customary rights were threatened with extinction. About 1605 Ralph Carr brought a case against Sir Ralph Gray and his under-officers in defence of his tenants' right to dig turfs on the moor between Detchant and Belford. Carr's tenants used the turf for fuel and as a roofing material.[91] For his part Gray brought a case against his neighbour George Muschamp. Gray claimed that squire Muschamp had led a gang which had set upon his tenants at Doddington shortly after they had cut and dried 400 wainloads of turf worth £3 6s. 6d. Gray informed the lords of the Star Chamber that Muschamp's men had burned the turfs to ashes "to the great hurt of the tenants, having no other fuel or better means to warm themselves in the winter season".[92] And as a result of an agreement reached after another Star Chamber case, tenants of Sir William Selby of Branxton, Sir Nicholas Forster and his son Claudius lost their customary rights to summer pasture in the Forest of Cheviot. In 1605 Sir William and Sir Nicholas had agreed to divide the pastures into two parts before "indifferent" observers. Forster paid Selby £200 for the privilege of first choice and then selected the western half of the Forest. At about the time that Claudius Forster purchased his baronetcy in 1620, he noted that his Cheviot lands, which had been of small value before 1603, now netted him a clear £200 a year.[93]

Just how much the landholding class as a whole profited from agricultural improvements made in the years 1603 to 1625 is difficult to ascertain. But we do know that there was a very considerable increase in the rental value of some of the lands to which Scottish raiders had formerly had ready access. It was said, doubtless with some exaggeration, that the Gray estates in the Till valley and in the eastern lowlands which had yielded less than £1,000 a year in the 1590s were yielding between £7,000 and £8,000 a year by the 1620s.[94] The Carrs' manor of Hetton, located a few miles north of the Grays' seat at Chillingham, was said to be worth between £80 and £100 a year in 1627; in Queen Elizabeth's time Hetton had yielded only £16 a year.[95] Other examples demonstrate the same trend. In 1596 the Earl of Northumberland granted the township of Alnham to a lessee for £17 a year. In 1613 an agent described it as a "handsome manor" which could be let for £100 a year, an increase of more than 500 per cent over the previous rental.[96] Again, in 1612 the annual rent of the manor of Fawdon near the River Breamish was only £10 6s. An agent viewed it in September 1620, "at a time when the grass and corn best be seen", and decided that as it lay "far from any market, neither is it enclosed, nor wood or field for cattle in winter", the manor could not be made to yield more than £50 a year. But this represented an almost fivefold increase in the rental value since 1612.[97]

Lands near the now tranquil border or along routes formerly used by Scottish raiders were not of course typical of the situation in the county as a whole. Far more representative were the widely scattered Percy estates, taken in their entirety. Decay reports and literary evidence might lead one to assume that the earl had derived little financial benefit from his Northumberland lands before Thomas Percy was dismissed from the receivership in 1605, but that subsequently, following a generation of peace and efficient estate management, the earl's profits had increased phenomenally. However, a study of the estate account records shows that the rate at which the earl's income actually did increase was not out of the ordinary when compared with the changing incomes of aristocratic families whose lands were located south of the Tyne. M. E. James has shown that between 1586 and 1605 the Percy receipts from Northumberland (excluding Tynemouthshire) increased from £971 to £1,350. By 1611 they had increased to £1,560 and by 1636 to £2,723. The earl's income from his estates in Sussex and elsewhere in England also approximately doubled in the period 1604 to 1636.[98] This rate of increase was about the same as that recorded over roughly the same time span for the Cavendishes for their estates in Derbyshire and Yorkshire, the Brudnells for their estates in Northamptonshire and the Lumleys for their estates in Sussex.[99]

If certain allowances are made, it would appear that the percentage increase in income which Lord William Howard received from his lands in and around Morpeth was comparable to that received by Earl Percy. Howard's receipts from the town and lordship were £948 in 1613. Included in this total was the £500 which he received from the burgesses of Morpeth as rent for Clifton Field, a great pasture two miles south of the town. However the burgesses felt that Howard had tricked them into leasing this pasture and when the lease expired in 1619 they refused to renew it. Thereafter the field apparently lay idle. Howard's receipts from Morpeth town and lordship were £588 in 1620; by 1625 they had risen to £644.[100] By excluding Clifton Field it can be said that Howard's annual income between 1613 and 1625 increased by 43 per cent.

One gentleman whose actual landed income increased greatly as a result of the union of the Crowns was the new lord of Norhamshire, the Scottish courtier-politician, George Home, Earl of Dunbar. The mansion house which he built in Berwick-upon-Tweed was described in 1607 as "the greatest squadron by much in England; and of that exceeding heyght, and yet magnificent turrets above that heyght, a goodly front, and a brave prospect open to the meanest and most distant roome, and that uniforme proportion everye waye generally, as wold stodye a good architector to describe."[101] In comparison, even the new mansion at Denton which the *nouveau riche* coal magnate Anthony Errington built in 1622 was old-fashioned; following the medieval pattern, Denton was centred round a great hall.[102] Indeed, when it came to domestic building, most of the Northumberland gentry were conservative and cautious. Aside from Errington, none of them built entirely new houses in the years before 1625.

Perhaps Sir Ralph Delaval of Seaton Delaval would have done so had he not had to provide for his 20 children. A gentleman with a genuine interest in building who was "never without work-people either within or without doores", he contented himself with putting new windows and wainscoting in the old peel tower and its attached Tudor manor house and with building brewhouses, barns and other outbuildings. A hundred years later all of Sir Ralph's work was swept away by Vanbrugh, the architect of the house at present on the site.[103] During the 1620s extensive renovations were carried out at Chillingham, probably by Sir Ralph Gray's ambitious son William, Lord Gray of Wark. Among other things Gray rebuilt the northern entrance wing and provided it with a fashionable three-storied frontispiece with coupled columns.[104] Cuthbert Heron made extensive additions to the fourteenth-century peel tower at Chipchase in 1621. The three-storied E-shaped manor house which he built adjoining the tower is, according to Professor Pevsner, "easily the best example of its time in the county."[105]

Francis Radcliffe, the wealthy Catholic master of Dilston Hall, also engaged in building activities but, as we shall see, he lived to regret them. It remained for his son to build a new range of domestic buildings at Dilston. In January 1622 young Edward Radcliffe signed a building contract for a large three-storied block, consisting of a kitchen and servants' quarters on the ground floor, lodgings and a great chamber on the first floor, and lodgings and a long gallery on the top floor. The use of the ground floor for services was a relatively new idea which had recently been brought over from France. This arrangement, in marked contrast to the older plan centred round a great hall such as that at Denton Hall, can be linked to the diminishing size and scale of gentry households and the increasing physical separation of members of the family from their servants.[106] Roger Widdrington, like his brother-in-law Radcliffe, built extensive additions to his chief dwelling house. By the time of the Civil War his mansion at Cartington must have been one of the largest and most impressive houses in Northumberland.[107]

During the Jacobean period a few families who were not of gentry status found it possible to build additions to their cramped peel towers. In 1614

William Welton added a range to the tower at Welton in Ovingham parish. Eight years later Robert and Jane Fenwick added a range to Bitchfield Tower.[108] It is likely that some of the heavy-walled single-family stone bastles which are found in Redesdale and North Tynedale were also built during this time.[109] But all in all, few buildings of outstanding architectural merit were constructed in Northumberland during the first quarter of the seventeenth century. This fact reminds us of the remoteness of the county and the relative poverty of many of its leading families.

Inventories of household goods also show that prosperity continued to elude many Northumberland gentlemen. In 1617, two years after his arms were entered at the College of Arms, John Burrell of Howtel left household goods worth only £1. They included six "old puther dishes" worth 2s., one "old fether bed, one paire of sheetes" and other bed fittings worth 8s 6d.[110] In 1632 Alexander Selby of Biddlestone, the head of a staunchly Catholic family, left "household stuff" worth only £3 6s. 8d.[111] At the other end of the social scale a few gentlemen were able to surround themselves with costly possessions. At the time of his death in 1642 Roger Widdrington and his second wife Rosamund owned three pairs of gold and silver embroidered gloves, two purses wrought with gold and silver, five pairs of silk stockings, three gold watches, ten bloodstones and a gold toothpick.[112] In contrast, the apparel of Widdrington's Protestant counterpart, Sir Ralph Delaval, was characterized as "ever decent, not rich".[113] Widdrington's study contained mathematical instruments, books, pictures, a desk and cushioned chairs, a silver cup and some brass candlesticks, valued in all at £60. The chamber used by Roger's uncle, Sir Ephraim Widdrington, was comfortably furnished with bedsteads, sheets and blankets valued at £5 10s. 1d.[114] In common with Widdrington, several gentlemen of substance had sizeable collections of plate. That left by Sir William Muschamp of Barmoor in 1613 was valued at £100.[115]

Some of the status symbols which would be found in the house, chapel or stable of every self-respecting southern gentleman were conspicuously lacking in Jacobean Northumberland. Even Roger Widdrington, certainly one of the most sophisticated and well-travelled gentlemen in the shire (thanks to Dunbar), apparently did not feel that it was necessary to own a coach. Similarly there is no indication that any contemporary Northumberland gentleman or lady ever sat for a portrait, though Widdrington may well have seen Cornelius Johnson's portrait of his wealthy friend, Lord William Howard of Naworth.[116] Possibly the only county gentleman to be commemorated by an ostentatious funerary monument following the fashion which prevailed south of the Tyne was Sir William Selby of Branxton, the border commissioner. Selby's monument, together with that of his uncle, Sir William the elder, is to be found in Ightham church in Kent.

No less impressive is the literary monument which Thomas Delaval wrote to commemorate his father soon after the latter's death in 1628. According to Thomas, Sir Ralph Delaval:

> kept an open, great and plentiful house for entertainment, his own family consisting daily in his house of three-score persons and above. He was a justice of the peace, of the quorum ... His life was religious. He kept a chaplain ever in his house that read public prayers daily in his house ... and taught and educated his children. He governed his people in excellent order, and stocked and managed his whole estate himself, directing his servants daily their several labours. He kept also the books of his cattle, corn etc. and how they were disposed. He never rode to any public assembly without five or six men in liveries and two or three of his sons to attend him. He never affected drinking. Cards nor dice, he never could abide them.[117]

With the death of the Earl of Dunbar late in January 1611, it remained to be seen whether this old-fashioned squire and other leading Northumbrian gentlemen had the skill and ability necessary to bring the county through the crises which were sure to confront it in the months and years immediately ahead.

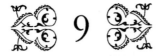

9

Factionalism revived:
Northumberland, 1611–25

"now as heretofore, the Men of the Time are, in most cases, unprincipled, and act from motives of interest, of passion, of prejudice cherished and unchecked, of selfish hope or unworthy fear." Lord Acton[1]

By 1611 the overwhelming majority of the inhabitants of Northumberland were as law-abiding and as deferential towards those in authority as people in any other part of England. Even in Redesdale and North Tynedale it was rare to find local men committing offences more serious than "petty and secret stealings of a very few cattle and sheep".[2] Northumberland behavioural patterns were not affected by the death of the Earl of Dunbar, the local lord lieutenant and chief border commissioner, in January 1611. But with the death of Salisbury, the king's principal English minister, 16 months later, the complexion of Northumberland county politics changed and, as we shall see as this chapter unfolds, changed for the worse. In the absence of a supremely competent councillor to assist the indolent Stuart sovereign, militant Protestant privy councillors vied with their Howard rivals for control of state policy and patronage. This vicious rivalry was of great importance on the local level, for by early in 1614 aristocrats belonging to both factions were flourishing as major landowners and office-holders in Northumberland and the border counties. In short, local politics had become inextricably linked with the corrupt politics of the Court. Northumbrian Protestants and their northern allies perceived themselves to be insecure and tried to discredit their recusant and Catholic-sympathizing rivals by claiming that they were in league with the thieves and brigands whom they alleged had found friendly refuge in Redesdale and North Tynedale. These allegations and counter-allegations billowed into great clouds of confusion, half-truth and myth and eventually enveloped the Court. King

James, like most of his southern-educated advisers, did not perceive any great difference between the allegedly lawless inhabitants of western Northumberland and people in the rest of that shire. Indeed he was quite prepared to believe that law and order were seriously threatened everywhere in the far North. Now that parliamentary approval for a closer union with Scotland was impossible, this threat gave James a rationale for preserving the special institutions found in the area he still wished to be known as the Middle Shires of Great Britain. But whether outlaws and thieves were actually present in sufficient numbers to threaten the social order of Northumberland, or whether that order was more seriously threatened by people of rather higher social standing, are questions which the reader can better answer after examining in some detail the course of events in Northumberland between 1611 and 1625.

Even in 1611 no one could deny that many of the Scottish surname members whom the Earl of Dunbar had supposedly pacified were still prone to violence. A few months after the favourite's death a company of Liddesdale Elliots and Armstrongs rode into Leaplish in North Tynedale. They shot and killed Lionel Robson and Elizabeth Yearowe, injured several other English people and hewed down Robson's house with heavy axes. Old Sir William Fenwick considered this "the most horrible and grievous outrage that ever hath been done in my time in these parts either before his Majesty's entrance to the kingdom or since."[3]

By this time the Earl of Salisbury (earlier rather overshadowed in such matters by Dunbar) had quietly resumed full responsibility for affairs in the far North. Although King James had been cold and haughty towards him ever since the autumn of 1610 when he had failed to persuade Parliament to accept the Great Contract (a plan to put government finances on a secure footing), Salisbury was determined not to allow the English Middle Shires to relapse into incivility. Early in February he saw to it that Dunbar's associate in the supervision of border affairs, Francis Earl of Cumberland, was appointed sole lord lieutenant of Northumberland, Westmorland and Cumberland and given charge of the border commission. Sir William Selby of Branxton and Sir John Fenwick were confirmed as assistant border commissioners for Northumberland.[4]

But the following April King James professed to be ignorant of Salisbury's sensible arrangements. While at his hunting lodge in Royston he blandly informed Dunfermline, the Scottish lord chancellor, and other Scottish councillors that as far as he knew the border commission had not been renewed after it had fallen into abeyance on Dunbar's death. The king went on to assure the Scots that they were far better qualified than Salisbury to advise him about the future governance of the Middle Shires. The Catholic-inclined chancellor heard the king out and then, feeling that he could speak freely, suggested that of all the English border commissioners who had served under Dunbar, only Sir Wilfrid Lawson had been worth his pay. He recommended that the king grant a new commission to Lawson, Sir Henry Widdrington and to their avowedly Catholic friend Lord William Howard. James was led to believe that if he did appoint these men to a commission they would be certain to work in harmony with the Scottish border commissioners and in this way would help to strengthen and revitalize the concept of the Middle Shires. Accordingly, around midday on Saturday 6 April, the king instructed his travelling secretary, Sir Thomas Lake, to find out by Monday at the latest if a border commission was currently in force and if Salisbury approved of the commissioners nominated by Dunfermline.[5] Given the opportunity, Salisbury would surely have replied in the negative. But late on the night of the sixth Lake wrote him a second letter stating that, on reflection, his Majesty had decided that the choice of new border commissioners could wait until his return to Court.[6]

Salisbury fully approved of all the members of the new border commission which was finally issued in July 1611. Under the new arrangement Sir William Selby and Sir John Fenwick remained in commission for Northumberland. Sir Wilfrid Lawson remained in commission for Cumberland and Westmorland whilst Christopher Pickering was replaced by a militant Protestant much detested by Lord William Howard, Sir William Hutton of Penrith.[7] Hutton's natural ally was the Earl of Cumberland. Although the earl was no longer directly attached to the international border commission, he continued to exercise a considerable influence in all the English Middle Shires. As lord lieutenant, it was his prerogative to appoint the provost marshal and the 25 government-paid horsemen used by the commissioners. After the Crown pensioned off the remaining soldiers at Berwick in the summer of 1611, he controlled the only serviceable military force in the English Middle Shires.[8] This was as Protestants thought it should be.

The government in London instructed the four squires to whom they granted the extra-ordinary commission of oyer and terminer to apprehend malefactors and to see that they were tried in the country in which they had committed their crime. This was not quite in accord with the terms of the recent remanding statute, 7 James I c. 1, since the Scottish Parliament had not yet passed the reciprocal legislation necessary to give effect to that statute. The government might also have given offence when it advised the commissioners to accept the testimony of Scotsmen against English felons on trial for their lives. This was contrary to the spirit, but not to the letter, of the statute of 4 James I, c. 1 (1607). Less controversial was the supplementary authority which the Crown gave the border commissioners over agents of local government, for it was much the same as that given in 1605 to members of the first border commission. The commissioners could compel J. P.s to help them disarm Redesdalers and Tynedalers who held lands worth less than £100 a year. They were to deprive such people of all horses except the 'mean nags' they used for ploughing. The Crown also authorized the commissioners to compel local justices to help them prevent the theft of horses. As it was said that many people travelled on foot searching for unattended horses, travellers were now forbidden to walk about the countryside unless they carried a licence issued by their local J. P. Moreover the justices were to assist the commissioners to chase away all prosperous-looking vagabonds and unemployed persons with no visible means of support on the assumption that they were thieves.[9] Had Selby and Fenwick enforced all these rules and regulations strictly, Northumberland would soon have been inhabited solely by saints and grave-diggers.

But if Lord William Howard's friends among the Scottish border commissioners are to be believed, the English commissioners did not take their onerous responsibilities very seriously. In October 1612 the Scots complained that Sir John Fenwick was more concerned with his private affairs than his public employment and that Sir William Selby spent most of his time at Ightham Mote, his newly-inherited Kentish estate. Sir Wilfrid Lawson and Sir William Hutton were so old and infirm that they could scarcely mount their horses, let alone track down thieves. And in contrast to the Scottish mounted police under Lord Cranston who were "vigilant, parsimonious and industrious, as night or day a thief cannot stir but he is presently punished", the English border police were virtually useless. According to the Scottish commissioners, they were "base, idle, cowardly fellows and of bad conversation; for these five years that they have had his Majesty's pay they have not brought in five malefactors of any reckoning or done any one day's service worth one week's pay yet the meanest of them receives." The Scots claimed that this idleness could not be justified by the argument that there were few thieves, "for since his Majesty's happy entrance there was never more stealing in these parts than at this instant."[10] Yet if the record of indictments made by Richard Pearson, the Northumberland clerk of the peace and of the assize, is an accurate reflection of conditions in the county, there was less crime in 1612 than in the previous year. The number of indictments for cattle and sheep theft was down by a third and the number of indictments for murder dropped from four to one.[11] These figures suggest that Howard's Scottish friends found fault with the Protestant border commissioners not because the latter were particularly inefficient, but because Howard wished to take advantage of the weakened position of the Protestant party at Court.

After the Earl of Salisbury's unlamented death in May 1612, King James frequently turned for advice to privy councillors who belonged to the Howard family or who supported the Howard interest. Chief amongst them were Lord William of Naworth's unscrupulous uncle Henry, Earl of Northampton (d. 1614), his brother Thomas, Earl of Suffolk, and his cousin Charles, Earl of Nottingham, the lord high admiral. Among other things, the Court Howards tried to persuade James that he could rule without parliamentary interference, follow a pro-Spanish foreign policy and allow English Catholics a greater degree of toleration. In these policies the Howards were opposed by a group of aggressively Protestant councillors. This group was headed by Thomas Lord

Ellesmere, the Lord Chancellor, Sir Ralph Winwood, the English ambassador at the Hague and later secretary of state, and George Abbot, the archbishop of Canterbury. Before Abbot's elevation to the episcopacy in 1609 he had served as the Earl of Dunbar's domestic chaplain and had travelled with him in Scotland and the borders.

Early in 1613 Northampton and Suffolk discovered that Robert Carr, the king's current bachelor favourite, had fallen in love with Suffolk's unscrupulous daughter Frances Howard. Realizing that the men and women who controlled the king's favourite could probably control the king, Northampton hastened to capitalize on his good fortune. Although Lady Frances was already married to Robert, third earl of Essex, the son of Queen Elizabeth's rash favourite, Northampton believed that she could easily get a divorce. However, things did not go quite as smoothly as Northampton had expected. Carr's secretary, Sir Thomas Overbury, distrusted the Howards and vehemently opposed the divorce. The king grew annoyed at Overbury's interference and commanded him to be warded in the Tower of London. There the poor man died of poison. Notwithstanding, Lady Frances obtained her divorce and married the king's favourite. In July 1613 James appointed her father lord treasurer of England and gave her husband, now Earl of Somerset, Suffolk's place as lord chamberlain.[12]

The Court Howards then proceeded to make their impact felt in Northumberland. In January 1614 Lady Frances's brother, Theophilus Lord Walden, and his wife Elizabeth received a grant of all the Earl of Dunbar's former possessions in Redesdale, Tynedale, Coquetdale and North Durham. Northumberland's newest territorial magnate was not a particularly agreeable fellow. He apparently combined in his own delicate person his mother's boundless greed and his father's gentlemanly sloth.[13] Although Lord Walden in no way resembled his uncle, Lord William Howard, he probably did consult him about the choice of estate agents. Roger Widdrington, only recently returned from banishment at the hands of the Earl of Dunbar, became Walden's learned steward in Tynedale, Redesdale and the Ten Towns. William Wanless, one of the two Redesdalers whom Widdrington had sent to London in March 1606 to protest Sir William Selby's brutality at the Newcastle session of gaol delivery, became bailiff of the manor of Harbottle. George Thirlwall became keeper of Harbottle Castle. Although Lord Walden was apparently a conforming churchman himself, militant Protestants noted with dismay that all of his estate agents were recusants or Church Papists. So too were Lord William Howard's principal estate agents in Morpeth: Edward Gray, the former border commissioner, and his son-in-law, Randal Fenwick of Blagdon.[14]

As there was no resident magnate who could protect the Northumberland Protestant interest from the Howard following, this dubious honour fell to the lord lieutenant, Francis Earl of Cumberland (1559–1641) and later to his son, Lord Henry Clifford. The earl was a quiet self-effacing man whose primary concern was to salvage and strengthen the Clifford inheritance in Cumberland,

Yorkshire and other northern counties which had been squandered by his spendthrift brother George, the third earl. The fourth earl's niece Lady Anne Clifford, who usually had a deft hand at drawing characters, found virtually nothing about him worthy of comment except that he was governed by his son during the last 20 years of his life.[15] Lord Henry Clifford (1592–1643), like his near contemporary Lord Walden (1584-1640), was a frequent participant in the festivities at Court. Lady Anne portrayed him as "endued with a good natural wit . . . a tall and proper man, a good courtier, a brave horseman, an excellent huntsman [who] had good skill in architecture and mathematics."[16] He was also a vicious and vindictive Protestant. Lord Henry had been drawn into the network of staunch Protestant families in 1610 when he married the Earl of Salisbury's daughter, Lady Frances Cecil. The following year his ties with this group were strengthened when his sister married Sir Thomas Wentworth, the prominent Yorkshire squire. Lord Henry recognized Wentworth's superior intellect and felt honoured to serve him. Wentworth in turn found Clifford competent, if uninspiring. On one occasion he noted that provided Lord Henry was given a full set of plans and a skilful assistant he could perform any simple task well enough.[17]

King James and his councillors precipitated a clash between the Northumberland Protestant establishment and the restless recusant party when they joined Lord Walden and the Earl of Cumberland in commission as co-lord lieutenants of Northumberland, Cumberland and Westmorland in February 1614. In October, after learning of the bitter rivalry between the two aristocrats, the Privy Council suggested that Lord Walden assume responsibility for military affairs in Northumberland and Westmorland while Cumberland attended to such matters in his titular county.[18] As much of Cumberland lay under Lord William Howard's influence, this suggestion was clearly intended to favour Lord Walden. Later that month Walden was appointed vice-admiral of the three northern counties under his elderly cousin, Nottingham. As his chief assistant he chose Sir Henry Widdrington, a man much suspected by local Protestants.[19]

With the dissolution of the Addled Parliament in June 1614,[20] the statute which had provisionally sanctioned the remanding of criminals to Scotland (7 James I, c. 1) quietly expired.[21] Perhaps by coincidence Northumberland's crime rate soared. There had been only 19 incidents resulting in indictments in 1613; there were 47 in 1614 and 59 in 1615.[22] This increase might have reflected greater efficiency on the part of local law enforcement officials and juries though, considering local circumstances, this is improbable. It might also have reflected a genuine upsurge in crime now that men knew that Sir William Selby and the other border commissioners appointed in 1611 could no longer practice remanding. It could also be argued that, as a greater proportion of the indictments in 1614 and 1615 were for livestock theft than in any year since 1608, the increase in crime was related to an appreciable increase in cattle prices.[23] However some of the crimes reported in 1614 and 1615 were certainly related to the sharpening of religious tensions in the county. At a time when Protestant officials were increasingly suspicious of Catholics, a ne'er-do-well like Arthur Radcliffe of Rothbury presumably thought that he could with impunity murder William Hall of Hepple, one of Roger Widdrington's chief supporters during the anti-Catholic persecution of 1605–6. Radcliffe was pardoned for this crime in 1618.[24] Religious tensions were also reflected in allegations made by the archdeacon of Northumberland, Dr John Craddock.[25] Early in 1614 Craddock accused John Lisle of Acton in Coquetdale of plotting with other unnamed people "who have a secret purpose and intentment (as it seems) to prejudice, abridge, diminish and suppress so far as in them lieth, the ancient rights, liberties and jurisdictions of the said archdeaconry."[26] And in the spring of 1615 John Smaithwaite, vicar of Elsdon in Redesdale, asked Bishop James of Durham for permission to give up his cure, claiming that he was constantly being harassed by Roger Widdrington and his followers.[27]

That August the Court Howards persuaded the Crown to issue a new commission of oyer and terminer for the northern counties. It was a measure of the Howards' strength that the special border commissioners Sir William Selby and Sir William Hutton were omitted from this commission entirely and that Sir John Fenwick was not a member of the quorum. In Northumberland this privilege was for all intents and purposes reserved for Theophilus Lord Walden, Sir Henry Widdrington, the recusant lawyer Thomas Riddell, the mild-mannered moderate Sir Ralph Delaval and Edward Talbot, the *custos rotulorum*.[28] But before the northern Howards could capitalize on this triumph, disaster virtually overwhelmed their relatives at Court.

For some months the Howards' Protestant opponents – Archbishop Abbot, Chancellor Ellesmere and Principal Secretary Winwood – had been trying to arouse King James's paternal and sexual interest in George Villiers, their dashing young protégé from Leicestershire. They naively assumed that if Villiers replaced the Earl of Somerset as the king's favourite, they could continue to control him and through him, control the king. Meanwhile Secretary Winwood suspected that Frances Countess of Somerset had played some part in the death of Sir Thomas Overbury two years earlier. Winwood had no concrete evidence to support this suspicion until September 1615. Then he learned that an apothecary's apprentice named William Reeves had confessed – on what he had assumed was his death-bed – that Lady Frances had paid him £20 to put mercury sublimate into an enema subsequently administered to Overbury; Overbury had died a few hours later. After authenticating Reeves's evidence Winwood laid the case before the king. James was flabbergasted for it seemed likely that his favourite Somerset had been an accessory to his wife's crime. However he agreed that the Somersets must both go on trial for murder. Later it was rumoured that Lord Treasurer Suffolk would also go on trial as Lady Frances's accessory. But King James was determined not to be brought entirely under the domination of Winwood and his friends. Early in 1616 he appointed Thomas Lake, a loyal Howard supporter, as co-secretary of state.[29] The Somersets' trial was put off until May.

This delay gave Sir Ralph Winwood time to build up a case against the Somersets and their relations.[30] In November 1615 he saw to it that one of the northerners whom he regarded as a particularly useful ally was pricked high sheriff of Northumberland. This man was Sir Henry Anderson of Newcastle (c. 1583–1659). Anderson was the eldest son of Henry Anderson, the great coal magnate, by his second wife Fortuna Collingwood. Sir Henry had matriculated from Puritan-dominated Christ Church, Oxford, in 1602 and married Mary Remington, daughter of the Puritan archdeacon of the East Riding of Yorkshire.[31] Later Anderson associated closely with Dr John Craddock, the archdeacon of Northumberland, and with William Morton (c. 1560–1620), the vituperative vicar of St Nicholas's in Newcastle and archdeacon of Durham.[32] Anderson was also active in secular politics. He was mayor of Newcastle in 1613–14 and represented the town in the Addled Parliament and in many succeeding Parliaments. In the late 1620s Sir John Eliot, the fiery Cornish M.P., noted that Anderson always put his own interests before those of either the Court group or of the various opposition groups in Parliament.[33] But in November 1615 this opportunist recognized that his own interests pretty well coincided with those of Secretary Winwood and the anti-Catholic, anti-Spanish, anti-Howard faction in the Privy Council.[34]

On learning that Anderson had been pricked sheriff of Northumberland, Lord William Howard acted on the assumption that the best way to protect himself and his recusant friends and dependants was to seize the initiative locally and at Court. Although he had no official role in the administration of the English Middle Shires, early in February 1616 Lord William, together with his nephew Lord Walden, appeared before the board of the Privy Council. Lord William advised his brother Thomas Earl of Suffolk, Secretary Lake and other councillors that there had recently been an alarming increase in criminal activity in the far North.[35] He asserted that responsibility for this distressing state of affairs rested squarely on the shoulders of the ageing and incompetent Protestant border commissioners and the venal government-paid horsemen. Later Lord William privately told Secretary Lake that if he were given permission to recruit and command a fresh troop of horsemen to replace those now under the command of the Earl of Cumberland, he would stamp out thievery within a few months. Mindful of Protestant sensibilities, Lord William suggested that this troop should officially be under the command of Lord Walden.[36]

The Earl of Cumberland also spoke to the privy councillors. He did not deny that theft was more common along the borders than it had been for some time. But he claimed that this was because so few sessions of gaol delivery had been held in recent months "partly by reason the commission of oyer and terminer have lately been subject to alteration, the persons therein named not being (as he conceived) fully resolved on." Cumberland implied that this situation could be remedied if the border commissioners and other reliable Protestants were restored to the regular commission of oyer and terminer and held frequent sessions of gaol delivery.[37]

After Howard and Cumberland had presented their testimony, the privy councillors decided to effect a compromise between the rival parties. Warning that King James considered it "a kind of idolatry to bestow entertainment upon [those mounted policemen] who have but the show and shadow of soldiers", the councillors asked the two co-lord lieutenants to nominate additional commissioners of oyer and terminer.[38] A short time later Chancery issued a new and enlarged commission. In contrast to the 19-man Howard-dominated commission of August 1615, the new commission was directed to 37 northern gentlemen who represented a broad spectrum of interests. Among its members were the militant Protestants Sir William Hutton and Lord Henry Clifford, son of the Earl of Cumberland. Sir John Fenwick of Wallington was given the full authority of a member of the quorum. As Sir William Selby was apparently still busy about his affairs in Kent, he was omitted from this commission.[39]

But Sir Henry Anderson and other local Protestants were in no mood to accept a compromise with members of the Howard connection especially at a time when they thought that it might be possible to make the Countess of Somerset's brother Theophilus and her uncle William share in her humiliation. Early in March 1616 Northumberland church wardens and clergymen sent Archdeacon Craddock reports about the number of recusants in each parish. By comparing these totals with those of earlier years, Craddock, Morton and Anderson proved to their own satisfaction that the number of recusants in Redesdale, Tynedale, Coquetdale and in the area around Morpeth had increased alarmingly in the years since the death of the Protestant champion Dunbar.[40] They asserted that responsibility for this lamentable situation rested squarely on the shoulders of Walden's Catholic estate agent, Roger Widdrington of Cartington. John Smaithwaite, the parson of Elsdon, had told them that Widdrington insisted on conducting the public business of Redesdale and Tynedale in Elsdon churchyard on Sunday mornings during divine service.[41] So it was largely because of this wicked man that the greater part of the people of western Northumberland "are become professed Papists, thieves or atheists and so live without fear of God, or regard of any wholesome laws."[42] A Newcastle man himself, Sheriff Anderson warned Winwood that "the country will never be reformed whilst any of the natives have to do in the government".[43]

Shortly after Easter Anderson reported that he had just received some important information concerning Philip Thirlwall of Hexham and his former master, Roger Widdrington. Thirlwall had known that Widdrington and the Howard estate agent Randal Fenwick had been in London early in November 1605. Around Michaelmas 1614 Thirlwall had fallen out with Widdrington about the custom of a mill and had parted from him with the ominous words, "if you Roger know as much by me as I know by you, I must hang for it." But what Anderson was most interested in was Thirlwall's death-bed confession; it was no less sensational than that made earlier by the apothecary's apprentice, Reeves. While *in extremis* Thirlwall had reportedly whispered that he bitterly regretted not having told the authorities about Roger Widdrington's connections with Thomas Percy, the Gunpowder Plotter. This statement naturally led Anderson to assume that Widdrington himself had been one of the plotters.[44] And in the light of this assumption, the sheriff now saw sinister meaning in angry words spoken during a recent quarrel between Widdrington's Radcliffe in-laws and members of the Thirlwall family. After Radcliffe's eldest son had reprimanded a local innkeeper for entertaining two disorderly young Thirlwalls and Thomas Fenwick, one of the youths had spread the word that squire Radcliffe was paying for the building of a new chapel at Dilston Hall with money he had received from Thomas Percy in 1605.[45] Piecing all this information together, Sir Henry Anderson concluded that Francis Radcliffe as well as Roger Widdrington and Randal Fenwick had clearly been party to the Gunpowder Plot. He suspected that Fenwick's employer, Lord William Howard, had also been party to the plot but he dared not denounce him directly.[46] In mid-April he sent Secretary Winwood and Archbishop Abbot all of the evidence and pseudo-evidence he could find to incriminate the three lesser men.

The militant Protestant councillors fell on these revelations of hidden conspiracy ten years cold like a flock of hungry vultures. They hoped against hope that before the Somersets went on trial it could be proved that Lady Frances's near relations were employing unregenerate traitors. Accordingly they ordered Anderson to send the three suspects up to Court along with any witnesses he could find to testify against them.[47] Winwood and Abbot began to examine Alexander Ridley, Thomas Fenwick, Richard Copeman,[48] parson John Smaithwaite and other witnesses on 2 May. Much to their disappointment they found little that could be used to influence the course of the Somersets' trial.[49] But five days after Lady Frances and Lord Robert (who by now could not stand the sight of each other) were found guilty of conspiring to poison Overbury and imprisoned together in the Tower of London, Abbot and Winwood interrogated Roger Widdrington at Lambeth Palace. As they were not entirely satisfied with his answers they placed him under house arrest. On 18 November they again examined witnesses unfriendly to Widdrington and the northern Howard connection.[50] To understand why they failed to link them with Thomas Percy and the Gunpowder Plotters it is only necessary to look more closely at the character of some of these witnesses and the quality of the evidence which they presented.

It is perhaps an understatement to say that Alexander Ridley of Whit Shields near Haydon Bridge was not a very reliable witness. In 1615, after he had discovered that Edward Talbot, the *custos rotulorum*, had commanded bailiffs to distrain some of his goods, Ridley, together with his sons and a group of friends, had argued with the bailiffs and then captured all of the cattle which the latter had just distrained from neighbouring farms. In the heat of the riot a yeoman named Nicholas Crane of Crow Hall shouted that "Talbot and all the rest should kiss his arse and if the justices should come with a thousand men to drive away their goods, if he had but one hour's warning, he did not care one pin for them all."[51] Fearing that Crane's noisy challenge to constituted authority might jeopardize his own future, Alexander Ridley must have agreed that if Sheriff Anderson shielded him from the law, he would go before the Privy Council to testify against Roger Widdrington. Ridley presented his first testimony in May (1616); in June the Council ordered judges of assize to take appropriate action against Crane of Crow Hall.[52]

After interrogating Ridley the privy councillors realized that most of his testimony was secondhand information he had had from his drinking partner, Thomas Fenwick. In his own testimony Fenwick told the councillors that he had entered Thomas Percy's service in October 1605. After the discovery of the Gunpowder Plot he and several other Percy followers had hurriedly left London carrying some £200 or £300. Fenwick claimed that this money had been collected from Northumberland recusants to finance the conspiracy and that later it had somehow come into the hands of Francis Radcliffe of Dilston. As Fenwick seemed a bit vague about some of the details of his story, the councillors suggested that he refresh his memory and then come back at a later date. That summer Fenwick spent a considerable amount of time in the company of his current employer, Sir John Fenwick of Wallington, and Sheriff Henry Anderson while the two gentlemen helped him to reconstruct the events surrounding the Gunpowder Plot. The following November young Fenwick was able to tell Archbishop Abbot and Secretary Winwood precise details about the movement of Percy agents, when and where they had met Roger Widdrington and so on. Fenwick now claimed that Radcliffe had received recusant money to the value of £600 rather than the two or three hundred pounds he had mentioned earlier.[53]

By this time Secretary Winwood and Archbishop Abbot had learned that Fenwick had had a personal grudge against the squire of Dilston and his family ever since Edward Radcliffe had had him thrown out of a tavern in 1615. They noted the inconsistencies in Fenwick's testimony and indeed in the testimony of all the witnesses who had appeared before them in person or who had sent them evidence in writing. With regret Winwood and Abbot concluded that it was utterly fruitless to try to implicate Roger Widdrington, Francis Radcliffe or Randal Fenwick in the Gunpowder Plot. All that could be said against them was that they were Catholics and very clever men.

After the ghost of Thomas Percy had finally been laid to rest, the northern anti-Howard faction found that they had to adopt more conventional means to destroy their opponents. In this they were assisted by our old friend Sir William

Selby of Branxton who was chosen to succeed Sir Henry Anderson as sheriff in November 1616.[54] The following spring a retired Northumbrian thief and former recusant named Richard Forster came before the board of the Privy Council to present a list of 27 vicious thieves and murderers whom he claimed were servants or followers of Roger Widdrington or his brother Sir Henry. Forster boasted that Sir Henry Anderson, Archdeacon Morton, Archdeacon Craddock and Sheriff Selby could readily corroborate his information.[55] But if one turns to the records of indictments kept by the Northumberland clerk of the peace one finds only three of the men on Forster's list were accused of stealing sheep or cattle after 1603; two others allegedly committed similar offences before that date. Only one, George Hall of Burdhope in Redesdale, stood indicted for murder, a crime which he had allegedly committed in 1594. There is no evidence that the other 21 men could justly be accused of any crime.[56] Though moderate members of the Privy Council probably did not have the Northumberland records before them, they thought it strange that Forster had difficulty in answering some of their questions. Growing impatient, they asked one of their clerks, George Calvert, to interrogate him more closely. Calvert, a secret Catholic, had little difficulty in reducing Forster to a state of utter confusion. In desperation, he confessed that he was illiterate and that he now realized that the scribe to whom he had dictated the list of Widdrington followers had played him false; these men were not really criminals after all! Calvert reported Forster's antics to the lords of the Privy Council who later had him thrown into prison for daring to abuse them with false information.[57]

After this set-back Sir Henry Anderson lost all sense of proportion. In a long diatribe in which he skilfully played on and strengthened southerners' misconceptions about affairs in Northumberland, he warned the Privy Council that all Northumbrians of wealth and influence "do participate of their country humour, which is cunning and their own ends, without respect of God or goodness." He was convinced that most of them were in league with thieves and that the master-mind behind them all was Lord William Howard. In Northumberland Howard's chief agent was Sir Henry Widdrington "the only man of action in all the shire and therefore most followed, to which his command under my Lord Walden helps him, for he carries the country absolutely as he will". Under such conditions, Anderson went on to claim, regular civil government was a mockery, "sessions of peace and court of the county kept, but without any manner of legal proceedings, and more in name than substance".[58] As it happened, one of Anderson's *bêtes noires*, Theophilus Lord Walden, was also feeding southerners' misconceptions about local people, but for entirely different reasons. In a typical outburst, in 1616 Walden informed the lords of the Star Chamber that people in Hexhamshire whose tenures he was challenging were "not as yet reclaimed from that barbarous course of life wherein they have heretofore, especially in the time of your Majesty's predecessor, been nursed up with in those remote parts".[59] Sir Henry

Anderson could not have put it better! Yet the records of the county clerk of the peace suggest that there was considerably less criminal activity when Anderson was writing than at any time since the eruption of factionalism in February 1614. The 29 indictable offences recorded in 1617 compare favourably with the 37 in 1616, 59 in 1615 and 47 in 1614.[60]

In the spring of 1617 King James had an opportunity to see conditions in the county for himself. Yielding to what he called his salmon-like instincts, he travelled by easy stages up to Scotland; he was in Northumberland from the fifth to the tenth of May.[61] As he had heard almost nothing but bad reports about the inhabitants of the county during the last three years, he was fully convinced that they had all reverted to the lawless behaviour supposedly so common in the 1580s and 1590s. The king brought with him certain suggestions for the future administration of the Middle Shires which he discussed with Sir John Fenwick, Theophilus Lord Walden, Lord William Howard and other prominent northerners. Yet he made it quite clear that he had no intention whatever of altering his programme in any fundamental way.[62] Like thousands of lesser men James only learned from his travels what he had known before he set out.

As usual the king's interest in the governance of the Middle Shires soon lagged. That of the privy councillors did not. Shortly after the royal entourage had passed through the county the Council sent the Northumberland gentry a six-point questionnaire about the problems of local law enforcement and instructed them "to assemble and deliver their answers in writing".[63] That June 48 justices and other gentlemen met in Berwick-upon-Tweed. They discussed the feasibility of augmenting the county's standing commission of oyer and terminer with lawyers and judges from the Council of the North and whether the controversial troop of 25 mounted policemen used by the border commissioners should be disbanded. But most of their discussions were devoted to the problems of western Northumberland where, as we have seen, no firmly Protestant gentleman of quality actually lived. Forty-five of the assembled Northumbrians were clearly hostile to the Howard interest. They adopted a resolution asking the Crown to require Lord Walden to assume financial responsibility for the good behaviour of his tenants and under-tenants in Redesdale and Tynedale. The gentry argued that it was unfair of Walden and his predecessor Dunbar to expect that lowland J. P.s "should at their own charge make good other men's lands, being noblemen and gentlemen of great worth and very able to do it themselves."[64]

Sir Henry Widdrington, the gentleman whom only a month earlier Anderson had claimed "carries the country absolutely as he will", vigorously opposed the majority report. Seconded only by two recently appointed justices, Sir Ephraim Widdrington and Sir William Selby of Shortflatt, he presented as an alternative to the majority report a plan to administer western Northumberland in a manner compatible with reasonably enlightened Jacobean concepts of social justice and administrative efficiency. With impeccable logic Widdrington argued that "it is most fitting the governors of the country be resident in the places most defective and which stand most need to be governed". He proposed that the Crown require suitable J. P.s to live in Elsdon, Bellingham and other centres in Redesdale and Tynedale. Such justices could punish a thief while his misdemeanour was still "green and before it grow so old as the thief shall have means to labour for himself". Resident justices could provide dalesmen with ever-present examples of civilized behaviour and thus "will be a great means of reforming their uncivil and rude manners". Sir Henry's proposal was also designed to encourage and instruct Northumberland J. P.s. As he put it, "when particular quarters are allotted to particular justices, it will stir up the justices themselves in a good and zealous emulation in striving who shall do good, his Majesty and his country best service, whereas the country remaining as formerly, no justice thinks himself engaged more than the other. The want of a particular magistrate will have the former experienced effect of a general neglect of the service."[65]

Sir Henry Widdrington realized that lowland justices would not care to live in western Northumberland as long as they and certain highly-placed people at Court chose to believe that he and his friends protected the thieves who allegedly infested the area. In order to gain a favourable response for his scheme he knew that he must explode this time-honoured myth once and for all. Accordingly, in November 1617 he rode into western Northumberland accompanied by only a handful of household servants. He arrested a number of men of ill-repute, most of whom appear to have been innocuous semi-retired sheep thieves. After receiving the Privy Council's approbation, Widdrington returned to the area and continued his self-appointed task.[66] In December and January he arrested more highlanders, cast out "the wives and children of such fugitives as were not outlaws themselves" and destroyed their rude habitations. Several frightened fugitives and outlaws came to Widdrington voluntarily to give in bond for their future appearance at a court of law; "choosing" as Sir Henry put it, "rather to hazard their lives upon trial than to see their dwelling houses spoiled and their wives and children cast out this winter to go a-begging". By 15 January he was able to inform Lord Treasurer Suffolk that "I have brought these highlands . . . to that pass at this instant that, in a manner, all these people are answerable . . . so great an effect has so small a course produced in so short a time."[67]

Widdrington no doubt hoped that his optimistic reports would encourage King James to re-assess his basic assumptions about the state of law and order in the western highlands. But by this time the king and his leading advisers had become quite inflexible; they were convinced that the highlands were inhabited by barbarians and they were not prepared to argue the point further. On 23 December 1617 the Crown issued a proclamation which was nicely calculated to deal with conditions in Northumberland as they might have existed during the Pilgrimage of Grace in 1537 or during the early years of Sir John Forster's wardenship. One clause in this proclamation extended to Hexhamshire and to what it termed the 'liberty' of Redesdale the provisions of a late-fifteenth-century statute (11 Henry VII, c. 9) relating to the old liberties of North and South Tynedale. This long-forgotten statute had ordained that a landlord could only let or lease his Tynedale lands to a Tynedaler if the latter found two 40-shilling freeholders who were not resident in the liberty to post a £20 bond to guarantee that the tenant would report to local or royal officials for questioning on eight days' warning. Only marginally less oppressive than the revival and extension of the Tynedale statute was the clause in James's proclamation which stated that "all landlords in the several wards of the county" were to post bond to guarantee the restitution of goods stolen by their tenants.[68] The rationale behind this sweeping measure was clearly related to Sir Henry Anderson's recent assertion that all Northumbrians "do participate of their country humour, which is cunning and their own ends".

The proclamation of 23 December 1617 was only one result of a series of Privy Council conferences on northern affairs which had been held the previous month. In addition, the Council created three special commissions for the Middle Shires. The first was a large Conjunct Commission which in effect replaced the international border commission which had been established in July 1611. The second was a greatly enlarged commission of oyer and terminer and the third was a commission to survey vagabonds and unemployed persons.[69] In setting up and staffing these new commissions, the king's ministers hoped to be able to satisfy as many of the Northumberland gentry as possible in order to restore harmony in the county. But unforeseen events frustrated these intentions.

On 8 February 1618 death removed one of the leading moderates in Northumberland, Edward Talbot, the eighth earl of Shrewsbury. In his capacity as *custos rotulorum* Talbot had for many years provided local J. P.s with efficient and competent leadership – whatever Sir Henry Anderson might have implied to the contrary. Talbot's successor as *custos rotulorum* was Sir Ralph Delaval (*c.* 1576–1628).[70] As we have seen, Delaval was a wealthy, well-educated, prudent Protestant squire who ruled his very considerable family and household with an iron hand. But in public affairs he showed himself to be excessively timid. Perhaps this was because he had no influential friends at Court to shield him from the raging fury of ultra-Protestant extremists or from magnates who were sympathetic to Catholics.

Delaval was particularly apprehensive about the future after the Crown ill-advisedly joined headstrong young Lord Henry Clifford in a commission of lieutenancy with his father and Lord Walden on 25 February 1618.[71] Sir Ralph's apprehensions were echoed by other Northumberland justices and gentlemen who met with him in Newcastle on 25 April. In a joint letter to the Privy Council they noted that "it is a great grief that his most great sovereign and the state should be so much troubled with the government of this people." But despite the king's concern, local administration was still frustrated "through opposition and private ends". The gentlemen earnestly begged the Council to appoint a single powerful lord lieutenant who would reside in the county until the "height of impiety and iniquity be suppressed in these parts".[72] But few such model governors existed in late Jacobean England.

Indeed so variable were the shifting alliances at Court in the spring of 1618 that most sensible politicians opted to stay as close as possible to the king in order to protect their own interests. Part of the difficulty was that the Protestant privy councillors were without effective leadership. Lord Chancellor Ellesmere had been laid in his grave in March 1617, followed in October by Secretary Winwood. The two councillors were unmourned by their former client, the unscrupulous and talented George Villiers, who by now had become the king's sole favourite. Villiers had been sworn to the Privy Council in 1617 and on New Year's Day 1618 had been created Marquis of Buckingham. Thereafter only the Court Howards prevented him from monopolizing the favours and patronage distributed by the Crown. It was obvious that if Villiers should succeed in destroying Lord Treasurer Suffolk, the career of Lord Walden would also be in jeopardy.

It was against this background that the three special commissions mentioned earlier came into existence. The most prestigious but least useful was the Conjunct Commission which was established on 23 January 1618. This commission was created to give new strength and substance to James's idealistic concept of the Middle Shires of Great Britain. It closely resembled the border commissions which had been established in 1605 and 1611 except that its membership was much larger; it was directed to 29 Englishmen and 30 Scots.[73] Among its members were five leading Northumberland J.P.s, Sir Ralph Delaval, Sir Ralph Gray, Sir John Fenwick, Sir Henry Widdrington and Sir William Selby,[74] as well as the three co-lord lieutenants. Sir Henry Anderson, Archdeacon Craddock and Archdeacon Morton, the leaders of the recent anti-Howard crusade, were not at first members.

The principal task assigned to these unpaid commissioners was to capture and remand malefactors who had committed crimes in one country and fled across the border to the other. As this policy was patently illegal, Sir Henry Widdrington and many other northern gentlemen refused to have anything to do with it. This was one reason why the Conjunct Commission did not really begin to function for several months. Then too, as part of Lionel Cranfield's economy campaign after King James's costly sojourn in Scotland, the London government abolished the controversial troop of 25 mounted policemen which had been an integral part of the machinery of law enforcement in Northumberland and Cumberland since 1605.[75] Thereafter if conjunct commissioners chose to employ ordinary bailiffs or constables to capture suspected criminals, Northumberland gentlemen could quite legitimately ask why regular J.P.s should not be given legal authority to oversee the task and, indeed, all the other duties assigned to the special commissioners.[76] To which the Crown could only have replied that J. P.s could not give institutional reality to the metaphysical concept of the Middle Shires of Great Britain.

For a time the work of the conjunct commissioners was also frustrated by the privy councillors of Scotland. The Scots found the 1611 commission and William Lord Cranston's 25-man police force perfectly satisfactory and persuaded the Crown to allow them to continue. As a result, on the Scottish side of the border the two commissions co-existed for many months. Following directions from Edinburgh most of the newly-appointed commissioners remained inactive whilst Cranston and the old Scottish commissioners continued to police the area so long under their jurisdiction.[77] Thus between them the Scots councillors and the northern English gentlemen made a mockery of the concept of the Middle Shires.

For some months it appeared that the greatly enlarged commission of oyer and terminer for the northern counties which was issued early in 1618 would be no more operative than the Conjunct Commission. This second commission was directed to the lord president of the Council of the North, Edmund Lord Sheffield, and 41 other northern gentlemen.[78] They were instructed to preside over auxiliary courts which would supplement those held annually by judges of assize and those which in theory, but not often in practice, were held every Lenten term in Newcastle or Carlisle by members of the Council of the North. The stated intention of these frequent sessions of gaol delivery was to remind potential criminals that they would be quickly and severely punished if they dared to offend against the king's peace.[79] The new commission also appeared to reflect the Crown's determination to bring Northumberland, Cumberland and Westmorland once again under the firm control of the Council at York. In earlier years Thomas Cromwell and the Earl of Huntingdon had attempted to pursue this policy in the interests of greater administrative efficiency. But seen within the context of Court politics in 1618, it can be argued that the Crown ordered Sheffield to repeat these earlier experiments, not in the interest of efficiency, but rather to build up a convincing case for his dismissal.

Among his other tasks, Sheffield was to compel Northumberland justices of the peace to enforce all the clauses contained in the "Proclamation for the better and more peaceable governance of the Middle Shires" which had been issued on 23 December 1617. As we have seen, according to this proclamation J. P.s were required to collect bonds from all landlords to guarantee the restitution of stolen goods. In addition they were to review all licences held by ale-house keepers and make certain that publicans were people of "honest conversation" who could find two reputable men to stand surety for them. Justices were also to ensure that slaughtered animals were sold in their branded skins so that their ownership could be easily determined. Sheffield was to caution justices that they would be dropped from the commission of the peace if they granted bail to suspected offenders outside regular quarter sessions. Further, he was to warn them that they must compel all outlaws and felons to surrender themselves before 23 January 1618.[80]

But nearly two months after this deadline had passed Sheffield still professed himself ignorant of the exacting new role which the privy councillors expected of him as head of the enlarged northern commission of oyer and terminer.[81] On 21 April the Council sent him and his fellow commissioners a stinging reprimand. They warned that:

> informacion is given to his Majestie that so little care is had by you that are trusted with the government of those partes as noe one article contayned in the aforesaid proclamacion is yet observed or put in execution, to the generall prejudice of the peace and quiett of the country, and the frustrating of his Majesty's gracious and princely intention in that behalf...his Majestie did not expect any such grosse or willfull neglect upon so cleere and expresse directions in a cause of this waight and consequence.[82]

Sheffield must now have realized how precarious was his hold on the lord presidency. Early in May he was in Northumberland begging local justices to co-operate with him in enforcing the royal proclamation. Much to his delight he found "the gentlemen of those parts very forward and ready to give of their best assistance to settling of peace and government amongst them."[83] *Custos rotulorum* Delaval, Sir Henry Widdrington, Sir Ralph Gray and other well-intentioned J. P.s began to enforce the royal proclamation with a will. They collected bonds from landlords, issued licences to innkeepers and interrogated people who had witnessed criminal incidents.[84] The Northumberland J. P.s thus demonstrated that if they felt they were protected from factious local magnates by Lord President Sheffield and his colleagues on the Council of the North, they could accomplish almost anything usually required of justices.

This brief period of administrative efficiency came to an end in the autumn of 1618 when it became known that the Spanish ambassador and the Marquis of Buckingham were persuading King James to dismiss Sheffield because of his anti-Catholic sentiments. In July 1619 Sheffield was succeeded in the lord presidency by a suspected Catholic, Emmanuel Lord Scrope. This change was only one of the crises which confronted the Council of the North during these troubled months. Split asunder by a controversy between its legal members and its administrative members, the Council lost whatever magisterial interest it had earlier had in the English Middle Shires.[85] In consequence ultimate authority under the Crown for the supervision of Northumberland's affairs devolved upon the co-lord lieutenants. In February 1619 Lord Walden, Lord Clifford and the Earl of Cumberland commanded their deputy lieutenants to see that local J. P.s fully enforced the terms of the controversial royal proclamation. They implied that they should do so without reference to the Council of the North or to any of the special commissioners of oyer and terminer who were not resident in Northumberland.[86]

The third of the commissions established early in 1618, the commission to make semi-annual surveys of all notorious, idle and misbehaved persons, was superficially more successful than the other two, for it centred on a concern of equal interest to all landowners and was composed of a balanced number of Catholic sympathizers, militant Protestants and moderates. The recusant-Catholic element was represented on the 47-man commission by Sir Henry Widdrington and Sir William Selby of Shortflatt, men who were never indicted as recusants, by Sir Ephraim Widdrington, a conforming churchman in 1618 who was later indicted, and by Lord William Howard, the great Catholic magnate.[87] This was the first time that Howard had been joined to a commission for the Middle Shires. His appointment can be interpreted as a fitting recognition of his zeal in upholding law and order on the borders or as an act of political folly which was certain to exacerbate religious tensions.[88] Militant Protestants were represented on the commission by Lord Henry Clifford, Sir Henry Anderson and Sir William Selby of Branxton. However, more than half of the survey commissioners were moderate churchmen and political neutrals such as Sir Ralph Delaval who hoped to stay clear of extremists on both sides. As the moderates recognized that the work of the commission was almost certain to be controversial they apparently hoped that the Crown would forget all about it. When the Privy Council queried them about the progress of their survey early in the spring of 1618, they replied that, as they had not yet received copies of their commission, they had deemed it wise to await further instructions.[89]

The moderates' understandable reluctance to begin work enabled Lord William Howard to seize the initiative. As soon as the weather permitted he made a comprehensive survey of "lewd and idle" people in eastern Cumberland and then surveyed the inhabitants of Redesdale and Tynedale on behalf of his nephew Lord Walden.[90] By proving that it was possible to make such a survey Lord William removed one of the moderates' most plausible excuses for remaining inactive. Now they had no alternative but to meet Howard and militant Protestant commissioners and decide which of them should survey each of the several wards of the county. Before 12 May six commissioners had surveyed Bamburgh ward and others had surveyed Morpeth, Coquetdale and Castle wards.[91] The following October the commissioners conducted the second of their semi-annual surveys. On this occasion Roger Widdrington helped his brother Henry to compile a list of 30 fugitives and "lewd persons". Most of them were men of small means who had stolen a few sheep or cattle or had illegally returned home after they had been deported to Ireland in 1607 or 1608 by the Earl of Dunbar. One such person was Bartholomew Wilkinson of Alwinton in upper Coquetdale. After he had returned from Ireland Wilkinson had twice been tried for petty theft and had then been branded on the hand. According to the Widdrington brothers he was "a bad-reputed fellow and an idle liver who has nothing to live upon but by stealing and such misdemeanours." Another listed person was Nicholas Read of the Bog, who was accused of stealing 24 sheep from Cuthbert Dodd of the Crag in Redesdale in November 1616. Then there was John Hall of Elsdon, alias Long Process John, who had also spent some time in Ireland. He was "much-suspected . . . ill-reputed, a notorious liver, having nothing to maintain himself but by keeping a common ale-house."[92]

Several of the commissioners who compiled these lists claimed that they did so at great risk to their persons.[93] They hoped that they would now be allowed to send "the said notorious ill-livers and misbehaved persons to Virginia or to some other remote parts to serve that they might no more infest" Northumberland.[94] Indeed, this had been King James's intention in May 1617 when he had first informed border gentlemen that a survey commission would shortly be established.[95] However Lord William Howard pointed out that in earlier years many "innocent soules" had been sent away "either out of private spleene, or for greedy gaine" and that royal officials had "winked at . . . barbarous offenders".[96] It would seem that the ageing British Solomon understood Howard's meaning for he decided that "much suspected" Northumberland paupers should not be deported. Although the survey commission was renewed in March 1619, it was not until the spring of 1624, when effective control of the central government had passed from the generous but rather lazy king to Prince Charles and Buckingham, that arrangements were made to send 100 Northumberland 'volunteers' to Ireland.[97]

Lord William's success in persuading the king to change his policies was the last triumph achieved for many years by any member of the Howard family except Thomas Earl of Arundel, the leading connoisseur of the fine arts at Court.[98] Earlier in 1618 Buckingham had decided that office-holders who were not dependent upon him for their places must be swept from Court. High on his list of intended victims were the Earl of Suffolk, the Earl of Nottingham, Secretary Lake and Theophilus Lord Walden. Lionel Cranfield, a financial genius and former City merchant who was now in Buckingham's service, brought it to his patron's attention that Lord Treasurer Suffolk was none too careful about the handling of affairs in his department. Cranfield also reported that Suffolk's wife was making a tidy fortune from the gifts and gratuities which her agents required of suitors to the Court of Exchequer. Buckingham had no difficulty in persuading the king to order an investigation of treasury affairs. In July Suffolk was suspended from office and nominally replaced by his old enemy, Archbishop Abbot. But Suffolk, as the leader of an honourable aristocratic family which was being systematically ruined by a parvenu, managed to elicit a good deal of sympathy and thus to delay facing a formal trial for several months. Meanwhile Cranfield and Buckingham convinced the king that the management of the Admiralty also left much to be desired. In January 1619 James graciously allowed the elderly Earl of Nottingham to retire.[99] In consequence Lord Walden lost his sinecure as vice-admiral of the counties of Northumberland, Cumberland and Westmorland.

Walden lost a good deal more than this when his parents finally went on trial. In November 1619 the Earl and Countess of Suffolk were found guilty of misappropriating treasury funds, fined £30,000 and imprisoned in the Tower. There they were joined by Lord Walden and his brother Thomas. The four Howards were freed after ten days. Walden agreed to give up his post as Captain of the Gentlemen Pensioners and to absent himself from Court and other public places.[100] Like Sir Edward Coke and other good men, Walden came to realize that he could only regain the king's favour by toadying to Buckingham. In February 1620 the Duke of Lennox stood proxy for the favourite and the king at the christening of Walden's son at Audley End.[101] However, Walden's further rehabilitation progressed slowly. He was omitted from the Northumberland commission of the peace issued in 1621 and did not participate in the usual round of activities at Court until 1622.[102] In that year he was joined to a commission of oyer and terminer for Northumberland. Later the Crown gave him a free gift of £5,000 and restored him to his former positions as vice-admiral of the northern counties and co-lord lieutenant of Northumberland. Yet in practice, after mid-1618 the Jacobean Privy Council regarded Henry Lord Clifford and his ageing father, the Earl of Cumberland, as the leading aristocratic authorities on Northumberland.[103] Henry Percy, the ninth earl of Northumberland, was released from his long confinement in the Tower in 1621 but was not allowed to return to his titular county.[104]

Lord Henry Clifford marked his growing ascendancy in Northumberland by attempting to break the strength of the local recusant community. Seconded by Archbishop George Abbot, a cleric who knew the transgressions of Lord Walden's recusant estate agents and their followers like the back of his hand, late in 1618 Clifford persuaded the Crown to appoint a five-man commission to deal with recusants. Two of the commissioners, Thomas Ogle of Tritlington and Sir John Fenwick of Wallington, were crude, grasping opportunists who no doubt offended the sensibilities of their more moderate colleagues, Sir Ralph Delaval, Sir Francis Brandling and Thomas Middleton.[105] In the 12-month period following Michaelmas 1619 these commissioners indicted 358 people in Northumberland, the highest total for any year during King James's reign.[106] This sudden surge of recusant-hunting activity in the archdeaconry of Northumberland was in marked contrast to the situation in the archdeaconry of Durham where Bishop Neile was able to prevent the persecution of most Catholic non-conformists. In the neighbouring diocese of Carlisle Bishop Snowden was likewise discouraging the persecution of recusants.[107]

Clifford attempted to weaken the Northumberland recusant community still further by persuading the Crown to force Lord Walden to dismiss his principal estate agent, Roger Widdrington. Already in disgrace himself, Walden responded by saying that all of his agents in Redesdale and Tynedale were "honest and sufficient men" who gave no one cause to complain. He pointed out that no lowland gentleman was willing to venture into those dales in broad daylight, far less to live there permanently. Even the border commissioners who "have power by his Majesty's commission and special direction, neglect the same."[108] Widdrington managed to continue in his estate management duties until April 1622 and perhaps longer.[109] However in December 1625 his mean-spirited employer insisted that he had not entrusted Roger Widdrington with office for five or six years. To substantiate this claim Walden recommended that the privy councillors consult the deputy secretary for Scottish affairs at Court "that it may the plainer appear unto your lordships how curious I have been to employ any man of his religion."[110] Curious indeed!

Despite Clifford's continuing hostility towards Widdrington, between the years 1620 and 1625 his Protestant zeal was held in check by Lord President Scrope, the Council of the North (to which he was admitted in July 1619)[111] Bishop Neile of Durham and the Crown. Only 14 Northumbrians were indicted for recusancy between Michaelmas 1620 and Michaelmas 1621. In July 1621 Archbishop Abbot accidentally killed a game warden while out hunting; following this unfortunate incident he was forced to retire permanently from Court.[112] In part this may explain why no Northumbrian recusants were indicted in 1621/2 or in the two succeeding 12-month periods. Only one person was indicted in 1624/5.[113]

Probably sensing that the Crown did not look favourably on his recusant-hunting activities, Clifford decided to reactivate the virtually defunct Conjunct Commission. In September 1619 he invited William Lord Cranston and other Scottish border commissioners to join him at Newcastle to discuss peacekeeping in the Middle Shires.[114] The issuance of a new Conjunct Commission soon followed. Despite the statute to the contrary (4 James I, c. 1), the government explicitly commanded the newly-appointed commissioners to remand English borderers who had committed offences in Scotland to that kingdom for trial.[115] As might be expected, the Scottish commissioners found remanding very much to their liking and tried to coax the English to follow the London government's directive. For instance on 18 May 1620 Cranston asked the English to send one Andrew Storey north of the border for trial.[116] But as long as Commissioner Sir Henry Widdrington retained control of his faculties, the English seldom if ever did remand prisoners. Instead they chose to have men suspected of committing offences in Scotland tried by regular English judges and juries during the autumn session of assizes.[117]

Even after Northumberland and the northern counties began to suffer the effects of bad harvests in 1623, the English conjunct commissioners – Clifford and his minions excepted – insisted that remanding would not deter criminals. Indeed it seemed to many of them that there was no present threat to law and order. In September 1623 Commissioner Sir John Delaval reported that the "estate of this country is reasonable quiet and though small thefts be done, they are occasioned by reason of the great dearth and scarcity in these parts than that great thieves dare adventure to disquiet."[118] But Lord Henry Clifford, thinking only of his own standing with the king, encouraged the government to proceed on the assumption that the "fires of disorder, partiality and contempt of justice and peace" would be certain to ravage Northumberland if the border commissioners did not remand thieves to Scotland.[119] Assured of Court backing, Clifford ignored Widdrington and other commissioners who opposed the practice. In April 1623 he boasted that he had just sent eight Englishmen to Scotland for trial.[120] A few months later the Privy Council instructed Clifford to report the names of all the English members of the Conjunct Commission who had refused to remand prisoners or who were otherwise negligent of their duty, warning that they would be prosecuted in the Star Chamber.[121] Clearly, the councillors were determined to provide their ageing sovereign with at least one functioning institution to give substance to his nebulous concept of the Middle Shires of a united Great Britain.

In this they were only partially successful. In the summer of 1625 the Council was informed that instructions sent to the English commissioners some time ago had not been obeyed "by reason that many of the said commissioners near inhabitants to the English side were dead".[122] The noble Sir Henry Widdrington died on 4 September 1623. His one-time rival Sir Ralph Gray of Chillingham died three days later. In the same month Sir George Selby (d. 1625) was so ill that he was unable to mount his horse. Sir John Delaval reported that his brother, Commissioner Sir Ralph Delaval (d. 1628), was seriously ill and unable to leave his house at Seaton Delaval. Sir John also noted that Commissioner Robert Cowpen had recently died. In December Sir John Fenwick of Wallington (d. 1658) wrote that "being by illness unable to do any journeys or to ride from home" he was unable to serve the Conjunct Commission except in an advisory capacity. As for Sir William Selby of Branxton, for so many years the leading border commissioner and Protestant plotter in Northumberland, he lived "altogether in the South", at Ightham Mote.[123] Thus for all practical purposes the Conjunct Commission for the Middle Shires had ceased to function some months before King James expired on 27 March 1625. With his death this commission, like all the other special and regular commissions for Northumberland and the Middle Shires, automatically lapsed.[124] An era of Northumberland history had come to an end.

Northumbrians doubtless looked back on the reign of King James I with mixed feelings. To some, the hardships they had endured far outweighed the benefits they had received. Many had friends who had been unjustly imprisoned or executed for crimes which they had never committed. But thoughtful men realized that the county suffered less from the misplaced zeal of a few spleenish gentlemen holding commissions of oyer and terminer than from the shocking negligence of local justices of the peace in the years after the death of *custos rotulorum* Talbot and the dismissal of Lord Sheffield. Although nowhere in England were justices and other local authorities able to cope with the problems associated with famine and poverty entirely satisfactorily, those in Northumberland seem to have made little effort to face the problem at all.

Typical of their ostrich-like attitudes are the comments of John Astell. In a letter dated 20 January 1624 and directed to Sir Ralph Delaval, the *custos rotulorum*, Astell wrote that he had just read Lord Treasurer Cranfield's directive on poverty and poor relief:

> Yet I cannot dream what should be the drift hereof if it be not severally to have punished idle persons and such as have no means to live or, having some small means, do spend that they have in riotous living, for when all is gone yet they will go on with their former course they have begun and out of want become fit persons to entertain any villains whatsoever.

Astell noted that Cranfield had also commanded that ale-houses should be licensed "according to the law as it is ... and done in all shires but Northumberland." This comment strengthens the suspicion that after Lord Sheffield's dismissal, Delaval and other J.P.s neglected most of their administrative responsibilities. Astell's further remarks lead to the same conclusion. He commended Delaval for at least pretending to study Cranfield's directives on social and economic problems, saying: "Therefore you have begun well to require a meeting of the justices ... but if it be as the usual custom hath been to meet and so end, it is to be feared that this custom will not be well taken, nor allowed for current in the end, for it is to be doubted that some cloud appears which, if it break, it may prove a dangerous storm."[125]

Delaval need not have worried that Lord Treasurer Cranfield or any other government efficiency expert would sweep him out of office in order to re-establish sound administrative practices in the county. Quite the contrary; in April 1624 Cranfield was himself impeached and suspended from office. Thus many of the administrative innovations earlier introduced into Northumberland by Edward Talbot and Sir William Selby of Branxton were neglected and lost.[126] Although North Durham, Dilston township and a few other localities in Northumberland might have made some provision for poor relief, J. P.s appear to have made no concerted effort to enforce the Elizabethan poor laws or other social and economic legislation on a county-wide basis. Even during the years of King Charles I's personal rule, Northumberland justices apparently never put into effect the clear and concise instructions contained in the Book of Orders.[127]

During the famine-pinched years which marked the close of King James's reign and the beginning of that of his son, indigent Northumbrians had to be content with private charity, if such could be found. In October 1625 it was reported that "the late bad harvests by-passed and small increase of corn with this now unseasonable harvest, has begot a general great loss to the gentlemen and almost utter undoing of the meaner sort... the multitude of poor people... would starve if they were not relieved out of the bounties and charge of the gentlemen and others here."[128] But random charity was not enough. That same autumn the mayor of Newcastle complained that hundreds of poor people from Northumberland were congregating around the High Castle begging for food.[129]

Custos rotulorum Delaval and other Northumberland J. P.s were no doubt quite as aware of their administrative responsibilities as justices anywhere in England. It would seem that they failed to enforce the Crown's social and economic policies not so much because of ignorance or of the continued public poverty of Northumberland,[130] but because they were fearful of antagonizing powerful aristocratic faction leaders. Between the years 1614 and 1625, and indeed well into the reign of Charles I, Francis Earl of Cumberland and his son Lord Henry Clifford, the non-resident co-lord lieutenants, were far less interested in fostering sound administrative practices in Northumberland than in dashing their rival, Theophilus Lord Walden. To this end they stirred up lowlanders' half-forgotten suspicions about the outlandish life styles of the inhabitants of Redesdale and Tynedale. In April 1623, at a time when people in the lowlands were starving, Clifford brazenly asserted that Redesdalers and Tynedalers "are the most cunning thieves and make best appearance in clothes and well liking bodies, for they work but little and steal much."[131] Strange that less than two years later the 'volunteer' soldiers enlisted from these areas were "for the most part naked, save coats."[132] Clifford also played upon men's religious sensibilities. In September 1625, after militant Protestants in Parliament had fiercely attacked Arminian and pseudo-Catholic innovations in religion, Clifford warned that: "in the county of Northumberland, the Papists are so powerful in themselves and are so adhered unto by thieves that his Majesty cannot find one man amongst them which may be trusted to do him service, and I do hear of late that there is such a faction and division amongst the gentlemen as if these that are firm in religion be not encouraged, his Majesty's best servants will come to the worse."[133] The following month Clifford's father contended that "there are divers malefactors and ill-disposed persons in this country, especially in Tynedale and Redesdale, whose life shows them to be of no religion."[134] In December 1625 six justices subservient to the Cliffords arrested Anthony Wanless, collector of Lord Walden's rents in Redesdale, on the pretext that he had stolen some goods several years earlier. Walden soon learned of his hated rivals' activities. Mustering up his courage, which was in short supply, he wrote to the six justices demanding to know on what warrant and upon "what just ground" they had apprehended

Wanless and three members of the Hall family. He warned the justices to "be careful of your work that you walk the way of ordinary justice ... the proceedings in this kind without my party is somewhat extraordinary".[135]

In 1604 King James had piously written:

> The worke we have presentlie in hande is utterlie to extinguishe as well the name, as substance of the bordouris ... For doing quhairof it is necessarie that all querrellis amoungst thaim be reconcyled ... and that no factions be forstered among thaime ... and fynally that that pairt of the kingdome maye be maid as peaceable and ansourable as any other pairt thairof. The readdiest and surest meanes for bringing this to pass are now to be thocht upon and embraced without any regairde to the honoure, commoditie or contentement of any subject quhatsomeever.[136]

The deeds of the sovereign's chosen representatives in Northumberland during the last ten years of his reign belied these noble words.

Notes

Note The figures given in diamond brackets at the top of each recto text page refer to the page on which the notes will be found.

Introduction

1. M. E. James, *A Tudor Magnate and the Tudor State; Henry Fifth Earl of Northumberland* (1966); *Change and Continuity in the Tudor North; the Rise of Thomas First Lord Wharton* (1965); 'The First Earl of Cumberland, 1492–1542, and the Decline of Northern Feudalism', *Northern History*, I (1966); 'The Concept of Order and the Northern Rising 1569', *Past and Present*, LX (August 1973); B. W. Beckingsale, 'The Characteristics of the Tudor North', *Northern History*, IV (1969). See also Alan Everitt, *Change in the Provinces: the Seventeenth Century* (Dept of English Local History, Leicester University, Occasional Papers, 2nd ser., no. 1, 1969).
2. Northumberland County History Committee (eds), *A History of Northumberland* (15 vols, 1905–40; hereafter N. C. H.); John Hodgson, *A History of Northumberland* (3 parts in 7 vols, 1820–5); George Tate, *History of the Borough, Castle and Barony of Alnwick* (2 vols, 1866–9); James Raine, *The History and Antiquities of North Durham* (1852).
3. Nancy Ridley, *A Northumbrian Remembers* (1970); George MacDonald Fraser, *The Steel Bonnets; the Story of the Anglo-Scottish Reivers* (1971); chapter I of James Reed's *The Border Ballads* (1973).
4. Thomas I. Rae, *The Administration of the Scottish Frontier, 1513–1603* (1966), 35. This is the best recent study of the Scottish borders.

Chapter 1

1. For general political history before 1603 see George Ridpath, *The Border History of England and Scotland* (1776); D. L. W. Tough, *The Last Years of a Frontier: a History of the Borders during the Reign of Elizabeth* (1928); Rachel R. Reid, *The King's Council in the North* (1921).

2. The standard account of Anglo-Scottish relations in the 1560s is Conyers Read, *Mr Secretary Cecil and Queen Elizabeth* (1955), chapters VII and VIII. For the period 1570–85 see Read's *Mr Secretary Walsingham and the Policy of Queen Elizabeth* (3 vols, 1925), II, chapter IX.

3. Gordon Donaldson, *Scotland, James V to James VII* (1965), 187–8, 214sqq. This is the best recent history of Scotland during this period. For a less sympathetic appraisal of James's character see David Harris Willson, *James VI and I* (1956), 116–37, and Robert Ashton (ed.), *James I by his Contemporaries* (1969).

4. S. P. 14/5/4; S. P. 14/5/5 I; Thomas Rymer, *Foedera* (1727–35), XV, 803; Charles A. Coulomb, *The Administration of the English Borders during the Reign of Elizabeth* (New York, 1911), 114–15; Frederick Dietz, *English Public Finance, 1558–1641* (New York, 1932), 36, 108; Frederick Dietz, *The Exchequer in Elizabeth's Reign* (Smith College Studies in History, VIII, no. 2, Northampton, Mass., 1923), 96; Ridpath, *op. cit.*, 667–8.

5. B. M. Lansdowne MSS. 49/62, reprinted in James Raine, *The History and Antiquities of North Durham* (1852), xxxviii.

6. *Ibid.*

7. N. C. H., II, 41–2; Hist. MSS. Com., *Salisbury*, III, 150.

8. C. G. Cruikshank, *Elizabeth's Army* (1966), 130sqq.; Tough, 173.

9. 23 Elizabeth I, c. 4, *Statutes of the Realm*, IV, i, 664; S. P. 15/28/80, fos. 104–20, 142.

10. S. P. 15/28/80, fos.104–20, 142; S. P. 59/22/181. S. P. 59 refers to the documents in the Public Record Office printed fairly fully in the *Calendar of Border Papers* (2 vols, ed. Joseph Bain, 1894, 1896).

11. B. M. Cotton MSS. Titus F. xiii 249, reprinted in Raine, *op. cit.*, xli.

12. S. P. 59/31/323. For mention of the other decayed tenancies see chapter 2, p. 25.

13. S. P. 59/36/853; Thomas I. Rae, *The Administration of the Scottish Frontier, 1513–1603* (1966), 2–3. See also G. H. Thomson, 'Some Influences of the Geography of Northumberland on its History' (Historical Association Leaflet no. 28, 1912).

14. S. P. 15/32/76.

15. Hodgson, III, ii, 203. Hodgson printed in full the survey of the borders by Sir Robert Bowes in 1550, and that by Sir Robert Bowes and Sir Ralph Ellerker in 1541.

16. *Ibid.*, III, ii, 203–4.

17. *Ibid.*, 203.

18. N. R. O., Delaval Papers, letter 31.

19. S. P. 59/35/745.

20. Hodgson, III, ii, 171–245; *Cal. S. P. For.*, 1561–2, 217. Instructions to the commissioners in 1583–4, their survey of fortifications and Christopher Dacre's comments and map (S. P. 15/48/95 IV; S. P. 15/27/44 I) are printed in Cadwallader John Bates, *The Border Holds of Northumberland* (Arch. Aeliana, N.S., XIV, 1891), 69–80.

21. S. P. 15/28/95 iv; Nikolaus Pevsner and Ian A. Richmond, *The Buildings of England: Northumberland* (1957), 140–2; N. C. H., II, 196–216.

22. N. C. H., XIV, 156–9.
23. Sir William Selby of Branxton, a major figure in Northumberland during virtually the whole of our period, must be distinguished from his uncle, Sir William Selby of the Mote in Kent, *d.* 1612. A third Sir William Selby, of Shortflatt, was the second son of William Selby, the Newcastle Hostman; see Appendix 3, Selby.
24. S. P. 59/32/431; Hodgson, III, ii, 183.
25. S. P. 15/28/95 iv; Hodgson, III, ii, 212; N. C. H., XV, 476.
26. See especially the 1584 map, printed in Bates, *op. cit.*, between pp. 78 and 79.
27. Hodgson, III, ii, 216–17; *Cal. S. P. For., 1561–2*, 217.
28. Hodgson, III, ii, 231–3.
29. For bastles see H. G. Ramm, R. W. McDowall and Eric Mercer, *Shielings and Bastles* (1970), 61–94, esp. 61–6.
30. 2 & 3 Philip and Mary, c. 1, *Statutes of the Realm*, IV, i, 266–9; 23 Elizabeth I, c. 4, *ibid.*, IV, i, 666; Ramm, *et al., op. cit.*, 63.
31. S. P. 59/32/410.
32. S. P. 15/27/44 I.
33. *Extracts from the Records of the Merchant Adventurers of Newcastle-upon-Tyne* (Surtees Society, CI, 1899), 27–9, 303.
34. *Extracts from the Records of the Company of Hostmen of Newcastle-upon-Tyne* (Surtees Society, CV, 1901), 285–90.
35. E 167/37 f. 110.
36. *Ibid.*, f.379.
37. On the general problem see Isabel Thornley, 'The Destruction of Sanctuary', in R. W. Seton Watson (ed.), *Tudor Studies* (1924), 182–207.
38. Hodgson, II, i, 65–6. See also S. P. 14/109/6.
39. E 134, 18 James I, Easter 13. See also S. P. 14/124/132.
40. Hodgson, II, i, 5sqq.
41. 11 Henry VII, c. 9, *Statutes of the Realm*, II, 575–6. See also S. P. 14/109/6. Throughout this study we make a distinction between North and South Tynedale. North Tynedale is coterminous with the seventeenth-century ecclesiastical parishes of Simonburn and Bellingham; South Tynedale with the parishes of Haltwhistle, Knarsdale, Kirkhaugh and Whitfield: S. P. 179/158/88; Roundell Sanderson (ed.), *Survey of the Debateable and Borderlands adjoining the Realm of Scotland and Belonging to the Crown of England* (1891), 50; Hodgson, III, ii, 231. Forms of tenure and agriculture in that part of the manor of Wark lying in North Tynedale appear to differ from those in that part of the manor lying in South Tynedale in which there are lease-holders rather than customary tenants and no clear contemporary records of summering; see chapters 2 and 3. Bowes, Ellerker, Dacre and other contemporaries often used the term Tynedale when it is quite clear from the context that they only refer to North Tynedale.
42. Hodgson, III, ii, 223–4.
43. Rae, *op. cit.*, 4–7.
44. Joseph Bain (ed.), *Calendar of Documents Relating to Scotland, 1108–1503* (1881–8), IV, no. 1649.
45. Hodgson, III, ii, 228–30, 243–4.

46. Raine, *op. cit.*, xiii; N. C. H., XV, 160.
47. N. C. H., IX, 154–5; Allen Mawer, *The Place Names of Northumberland and Durham* (1920), 144.
48. *L. & P. Hen. VIII*, XII, i, 351, 395; Madeleine H. and Ruth Dodds, *The Pilgrimage of Grace, 1536–37, and the Exeter Conspiracy, 1538* (2 vols, 1915), I, 195.
49. N. C. H., IX, 155–6.
50. S. P. 59/31/228.
51. George F. S. Elliot, *The Border Elliots and the Family of Minto* (1897), 479.
52. S. P. 59/30/76; S. P. 59/30/77; S. P. 59/30/80.
53. Arthur Clifford (ed.), *The State Papers and Letters of Sir Ralph Sadler* (2 vols, 1809), II, 16.
54. S. P. 59/39/1310.
55. Lansdowne MSS. 49/62.
56. Req. 2/186/27.
57. 43 Elizabeth I, c. 13, *Statutes of the Realm*, IV, ii, 980.
58. Rae, *op. cit.*, 8, 79–82.
59. See S. P. 59/37/1008; George M. Fraser, *The Steel Bonnets; the Story of the Anglo-Scottish Reivers* (1971), 337sqq.
60. S. P. 59/22/197.
61. S. P. 14/6/43.
62. S. P. 14/27/23.
63. Hodgson, II, i, 74–5.
64. C. H. Hunter Blair, 'Wardens and Deputy Wardens of the Marches of England toward Scotland in Northumberland', *Arch. Aeliana*, 4th ser., XXVIII (1950), 74.
65. *Cal. S. P. For., 1566–8*, 167, 170, 182.
66. *Ibid., 1569–71*, 49.
67. Lansdowne MSS. 49/62; S. P. 59/24/451.
68. S. P. 59/25/494.
69. Lansdowne MSS. 49/62.
70. S. P. 15/28/80 fos.109–10.
71. S. P. 59/27/743.
72. *Wills and Inventories from the Registry at Durham* (Surtees Society, 1835, 1900, 1906, 1929), II, 254–6.
73. S. P. 59/23/341.
74. C 181/2 f. 48; S. P. 14/33. See also Req. 2/186/27.
75. E 134, 18 James I, Mich. 20; E 134, 18 James I, Easter 13; Sanderson, 52, 104.
76. 1 Elizabeth I, c. 21; 5 Elizabeth I, c. 31; 8 Elizabeth I, c. 18; 13 Elizabeth I, c. 27; 18 Elizabeth I, c. 23; 23 Elizabeth I, c. 15; 27 Elizabeth I, c. 29; 29 Elizabeth I, c. 8; 31 Elizabeth I, c. 15; 35 Elizabeth I, c. 13; 39 Elizabeth I, c. 27; 43 Elizabeth I, c. 18.
77. 23 Elizabeth I, c. 4, *Statutes of the Realm*, IV, i, 663–7.
78. For the relationship between the parliamentary controversy over 23 Elizabeth I, c. 2 (the Sedition Bill) and the passage of the border bill see *Journals of the House of Commons* (1803), I, 125, 133, 134; *Journals of the House of Lords*

(1846), II, 33a, 46a, 51sqq.; Simon D'Ewes, *The Journals of all the Parliaments during the Reign of Queen Elizabeth* (rev. edn, 1682), 270, 272, 273, 300, 305–6; Hist. MSS. Com., *Salisbury*, XIII, 189; John Neale, *Elizabeth I and her Parliaments* (2 vols, 1953, 1957), I, 393–8.

79. S. P. 59/21/82.

80. See *Acts of the Privy Council, 1580–1*, 72; *1581–2*, 349; *1589–90*, 170; *1590*, 359; *1595–6*, 369.

81. S. P. 15/28/23; S. P. 15/32/83; Hist. MSS. Com., *Salisbury*, XIII, 250.

82. For earlier wardens see R. L. Storey, 'The Wardens of the Marches of England towards Scotland, 1377–1489', *E. H. R.*, LXXII (1957), 593–616, which supersedes Rachel Reid, 'The Office of Warden of the Marches; its Origin and Early History', *E. H. R.*, XXXII (1917), 479–96. See also Hunter Blair, 'Wardens and Deputy Wardens'.

83. S. P. 15/32/59; *Cal. Pat. Rolls, 1559–60*, 37, 144; *1566–9*, 327; Helen Wallace, 'Berwick in the Reign of Queen Elizabeth', *E. H. R.*, XLVI (1931), 80–1. Tough, chapter IV; Coulomb, *op. cit.*, chapter III, and Fraser, *op. cit.*, 129sqq., contain valuable insights into the role of Elizabethan wardens.

84. For March Law see William Nicholson (ed.), *Leges Marchiarum or Border Laws . . . from the Reign of Henry III to . . . K. James I* (1705); Tough, chapters VI and VII; Rae, *op. cit.*, 47–9.

85. S. P. 59/39/1310; S. P. 59/23/343; Tough, chapter VIII; Rae, *op. cit.*, 50, Raine, *op. cit.*, xiii; Coulomb, *op. cit.*, 69sqq. For examples of bills see S. P. 59/26/668; S. P. 59/33/521.

86. Rae, *op. cit.*, 52–4; S. P. 59/28/983.

87. S. P. 59/34/622; Nicholson (ed.), *op. cit.*, 133–5.

88. S. P. 59/32/400; S. P. 59/33/481; S. P. 59/33/515; S. P. 59/33/519; *Acts of the Privy Council, 1596–7*, 202.

89. S. P. 59/21/81; S. P. 59/39/1309; Nicholson (ed.), *op. cit.*, 175sqq.; Tough, 161sqq.

90. S. P. 59/28/834; *Acts of the Privy Council, 1597–8*, 614.

91. S. P. 59/39/1309 fos.3–4.

92. S. P. 59/21/81.

93. S. P. 59/25/546.

94. *Ibid.*; S. P. 59/35/746; S. P. 59/39/1309 f.29; 1 & 2 Philip and Mary, c.10, *Statutes of the Realm*, IV, i, 255–8; William S. Holdsworth, *A History of English Law* (15 vols, 1922–65), IV, 542.

95. S. P. 59/35/746; S. P. 59/36/881; S. P. 59/39/1309 f.19. The statute of 27 Henry VIII, c.24 specifically reserved all pardons of felons and treasons to the Crown: *Statutes of the Realm*, III, 555–8.

96. Lansdowne MSS. 49/62.

97. Hist. MSS. Com., *Salisbury*, V, 65–6.

98. S. P. 59/30/122; S. P. 59/39/1309 f.39; S. P. 14/109/6; Hist. MSS. Com., *Salisbury*, V, 65–6.

99. *L. & P. Hen. VIII*, XII, i, 595.

100. S. P. 59/20/74.

101. S. P. 59/21/81.

102. E 163/14/8; S. P. 13/F/11; S. P. 59/28/893; S. P. 59/41/1546; G. R. Elton, *The Tudor Constitution* (1965), 453.
103. Reid, *op. cit.* (n. 1 above), 494–6.
104. For all this see *ibid.*, pt III; F. W. Brooks, *The Council of the North* (Historical Association, 1966), *passim*.
105. Alnwick Castle, Syon MSS. P II, 2 e; *Acts of the Privy Council, 1589–90*, 217.
106. S. P. 15/14/42; S. P. 15/14/69; B. M. Cotton MSS. Caligula C III, 538; *Cal. S. P. For., 1561–2*, 145; *1562*, 55, 215; Hist. MSS. Com. *Salisbury*, VI, 93; Claire Cross, *The Puritan Earl; the Life and Times of Henry Hastings, Third Earl of Huntingdon, 1536–1595* (1966), 164; Richard Welford, *History of Newcastle and Gateshead* (3 vols, 1884–7), III, 97.
107. Reid, *op. cit.* (n. 1 above), 215–24.
108. S. P. 15/28/23; S. P. 15/32/81; S. P. 15/32/83; S. P. 15/32/87; S. P. 59/28/904; Hist. MSS. Com., *Salisbury*, XIII, 250.
109. C 66/1302; Cross, *op. cit.*, 197–8, 207–8; Elton, *op. cit.*, 451–2. As the 1580 commission does not survive it is uncertain whether Northumberland was included.
110. S. P. 59/27/743. See also S. P. 59/25/565; S. P. 59/25/569; S. P. 59/25/572.
111. S. P. 59/39/1309 f.1.

Chapter 2

1. William Camden, *Britannia* (trans. Philemon Holland, 1610), 799; B. W. Beckingsale, 'The Characteristics of the Tudor North', *Northern History*, IV (1969), 79; William Weaver Tomlinson, *Life in Northumberland during the Sixteenth Century* (1897), esp. chapters V, VI, VII.
2. Roger B. Manning, *Religion and Society in Elizabethan Sussex; a study in the enforcement of the religious settlement 1558–1603* (1969), 3.
3. S. P. 14/31/40.
4. S. P. 14/216/79.
5. S. P. 16/8/48.
6. Syon MSS. R IV, 1 c.
7. S. P. 14/151/14; S. P. 14/152/51; *Acts of the Privy Council, 1623–5*, 278.
8. S. P. 59/35/776.
9. Cumbria County Record Office, Carlisle, Pennington-Ramsden MS., f.114d.
10. S. P. 59/29/5.
11. S. P. 59/39/1299.
12. S. P. 59/40/1388; S. P. 59/40/1389.
13. S. P. 59/21/82; D. C. Coleman, 'Labour in the English Economy of the Seventeenth Century', *Ec. H. R.*, 2nd ser., VIII no. 2 (Dec. 1955), 280–95; W. G. Hoskins, 'Harvest Fluctuations and English Economic History, 1480–1619', *Ag. H. R.*, II (1953–4), 31.
14. E. J. Buckatzsch, 'The Geographical Distribution of Wealth in England, 1086–1843', *Ec. H. R.*, 2nd ser., III no. 2 (Dec. 1950), 180–202.

15. S. P. 59/24/435. See also B. M. Cotton MSS. Titus B., v. 8; Hist. MSS. Com., *Salisbury*, I, 274.
16. S. P. 59/30/184; *Cal. S. P. Dom., Addenda, 1580–1625*, 231.
17. E. E. Rich, 'The Population of Elizabethan England', *Ec. H. R.*, 2nd ser., II no. 3 (1950), 252.
18. Tough, 26–7.
19. W. G. Hoskins, *Local History in England* (1959), 146–7.
20. Roger Howell, *Newcastle upon Tyne and the Puritan Revolution: A Study of the Civil War in North England* (1967), 1–2.
21. C. M. L. Bouch and G. P. Jones, *A Short Economic and Social History of the Lake Counties, 1550–1830* (1961), 16.
22. Tough's muster figure, 8,350, excluded the 9,000 people whom he estimated lived in Carlisle, Kendal and Penrith: pp. 26–7. The 9,000 was subtracted from the 73,000 given by Bouch and Jones.
23. S. P. 59/20/47; S. P. 59/20/50 (1580 musters); S. P. 59/30/169; S. P. 59/30/170 (1595); S. P. 46/20, fos. 96–101d, 105–18; S. P. 12/256/27 XVII (1596); S. P. 15/32/77 (1593).
24. S. P. 59/23/255. As per the Act for taking musters, 4 & 5 Philip and Mary, c. 3, charter towns were listed separately.
25. S. P. 16/66/86.
26. Tough, 27.
27. 1584 East March muster returns list 598 in North Durham, multiplied by 6.5, gives 3,744: S. P. 59/23/253.
28. Bouch and Jones, *op. cit.*, 16–17.
29. J. T. Cliffe, *The Yorkshire Gentry from the Reformation to the Civil War* (1969), 2.
30. Julian Cornwall, 'English Population in the Early Sixteenth Century', *E.C. H. R.*, 2nd ser., XXIII no. 1 (April 1970), 43–4.
31. Hodgson, III, ii, 238.
32. S. P. 15/28/80 fos.108–10.
33. Hodgson, III, ii, 233, 237.
34. Camden, *op. cit.*, 802, 800.
35. E 112/112/208; E 134, 18 James I, Mich. 22; Sanderson, 50; Hodgson, III, ii, 231.
36. Sanderson, 47–112.
37. *Ibid.*; E 134, 18 James I, Easter 13.
38. E 134, 18 James I, Easter 13; Sanderson, 104.
39. E 134, 18 James I, Easter 13.
40. Hodgson, III, ii, 221; Ramm *et al.*, *Shielings and Bastles* (1970), 1–4, 9–25; Camden, *op. cit.*, 806.
41. E 134, 18 James I, Mich. 20; Sanderson, 52, 104.
42. C 2 S/8/13; Sta. Cha. 8 261/20.
43. L. R. 2/223 fos.103, 189–90, 243sqq.
44. *Wills and Inventories*, II, 125–6.
45. *Ibid.*, II, 76.
46. *Ibid.*, II, 29–30.
47. *Ibid.*, II, 76.

48. W. G. Hoskins, *The Midland Peasant; the Economic and Social History of a Leicestershire Village* (1965), 296.
49. See chapter 3.
50. S. P. 16/410/99. See also Hunter MSS. 23, fos.120–9 (a 1631 rental of Norhamshire) and the 1561 survey of Norhamshire printed in James Raine, *The History and Antiquities of North Durham* (1852), 15–25.
51. S. P. 59/26/668; S. P. 59/33/521; S. P. 59/36/841; S. P. 15/28/80 fos. 104–10.
52. See especially chapters 3 and 14 in A. R. H. Baker and R. A. Butlin (eds.), *Studies of Field Systems in the British Isles* (1973).
53. For the problem caused by such 'masterless men' see Christopher Hill, *The World Turned Upside Down* (1972), 35–40.
54. 23 Elizabeth I, c. 4.
55. Baker and Butlin, *op. cit.*, 138–9.
56. L. R. 2/223 fos.21–6, 34–8.
57. *Ibid.*, fos.295–316.
58. Baker and Butlin, *op. cit.*, 113–14, 138–9; N. C. H., II, 44, 369.
59. Baker and Butlin, *op. cit.*, 112, 122, 133.
60. Joan Thirsk, 'The Common Fields', *Past and Present*, XXIX (December 1964), 20.
61. N. C. H., XII, 157.
62. *Wills and Inventories*, III, 165.
63. Hoskins, *The Midland Peasant, op. cit.*, 154–6.
64. *Wills and Inventories*, II, 53, 303.
65. *Ibid.*, II, 325.
66. Peter Bowden, 'Agricultural Prices, Farm Profits and Rents' in Joan Thirsk (ed.), *The Agrarian History of England and Wales*, vol. IV, *1500–1640* (1967), 651.
67. N. C. H., V, 424.
68. *Ibid.*, V, 200–1.
69. E 134, 23 Elizabeth I, Hilary 6.
70. L. R. 2/223, fos.310–13.
71. N. C. H., X, 141, 266.
72. *Ibid.*, V, 212.
73. *Ibid.*, I, 274.
74. R. A. Butlin, 'Enclosure and Improvement in Northumberland in the Sixteenth Century', *Arch. Aeliana*, 4th ser., XLV (1967), 149–51.
75. For tenants' possible attitude towards division see Thirsk (ed.), *op. cit.*, 27–8.
76. N. C. H., XIV, 211–13; Butlin, 'Enclosure and Improvement', *op. cit.*, 151–2.
77. Syon MSS. Q II, 66; N. C. H., II, 368–76, 378–84.
78. N. C. H., V, 424. Shilbottle was enclosed in 1758; *ibid.*: V, 430.
79. N. C. H., V, 369. In 1702 the township was divided into a north and south side: *ibid.*, V, 372.
80. N. C. H., II, 416–25.
81. N. C. H., I, 350–1.
82. *Ibid.*, V, 212.
83. *Cal. S. P. Dom., Addenda, 1580–1625*, 92.

84. S. P. 59/20/47. Mentioned by Maurice Beresford, *The Lost Villages of England* (1954), 373, 375.

85. E 178/1761, 42–3 Elizabeth I.

86. S. P. 15/32/76; Raine, *op. cit.*, 19.

87. Mentioned in Raine, *op. cit.*, 197–8; N. C. H., I, 275; Eric Kerridge, *Agrarian Problems in the Sixteenth Century and After* (1969), 128, and R. H. Tawney, *The Agrarian Problem in the Sixteenth Century* (new edn, New York, 1967), 260.

88. S. P. 15/28/80, f.105; N. C. H., IX, 124–5, 201–2; Kerridge, *op. cit.*, 128. This example is also quoted by Tawney, *op. cit.*, 257–8, 260.

89. N. C. H., IX, 91.

90. S. P. 59/31/323. Beresford and Butlin found relatively little depopulating enclosure in Northumberland before 1603: Butlin, 'Enclosure and Improvement', *op. cit.*, 157; Beresford, *op. cit.*, 175.

91. S. P. 12/262/10; S. P. 59/29/15; Hist. MSS. Com., *Salisbury*, VII, 295–6.

92. *D. N. B.* For enclosure in Oxfordshire see E. F. Gay, 'The Midland Revolt and the Inquisitions of Depopulation of 1607', *E. H. R.*, xviii (1904), 223; Hoskins, 'Harvest Fluctuations', *op. cit.* (n. 13 above), 40.

93. S. P. 12/262/10. For other letters to the same effect written by Dean James see S. P. 12/262/11; S. P. 12/263/55; S. P. 12/265/36.

94. See Maurice Beresford, 'Habitation versus Improvement', in F. J. Fisher (ed.), *Essays in the Economic and Social History of Tudor and Stuart England* (1961); John Neale, *Elizabeth and her Parliaments*, vol. II (1957), 337–45; William Cobbett, *Parliamentary History*, I, 899, and the bill itself, 39 Elizabeth I, c. 2, *Statutes of the Realm*, IV, i, 893–6.

95. 43 Elizabeth I, c. 9, *Statutes of the Realm*, IV, i, 974.

96. Simon D'Ewes, *The Journals of all the Parliaments during the Reign of Queen Elizabeth* (rev. edn, 1682), 674.

97. Hayward Townshend, *Historical Collections: or, An exact account of the last four Parliaments of Elizabeth* (1680), 300; C. H. Hunter Blair, 'Members of Parliament for Northumberland and Newcastle upon Tyne, 1559–1831', *Arch. Aeliana*, 4th ser., xxiii (1945), 109.

98. *Wills and Inventories*, II, 53.

99. Thirsk (ed.), *op. cit.*, 27.

100. *Acts of the Privy Council, 1617–19*, 445, 468–70; *1623–5*, 120, 185; Wallace Notestein *et al.* (eds), *Commons Debates 1621* (7 vols, New Haven, 1935), VI, 488.

101. S. P. 14/61/73; S. P. 14/153/92; S. P. 14/155/72.

102. S. P. 59/28/824; S. P. 59/28/825.

103. S. P. 59/30/77; S. P. 59/33/571; Helen Wallace, 'Berwick in the Reign of Queen Elizabeth', *E. H. R.*, xlvi (January 1931), 81–3.

104. Alan Everitt, 'The Marketing of Agricultural Produce' in Thirsk (ed.), *op. cit.*, 468–9.

105. E 164/37, f.365, printed in N. C. H., VI, 83.

106. See John U. Nef, *The Rise of the British Coal Industry* (2 vols, 1932). His conclusions have recently been summarized and reappraised by Howell, *op. cit.* (n.20 above), 1–34.

107. Nef, *op. cit.*, I, 36.
108. Sanderson, 77, 112.
109. Sta. Cha. 8 224/21; Sta. Cha. 8 224/19; Sta. Cha. 8 224/22; S. P. 14/6/42; Nef, *op. cit.*, I, 40, 42, 339.
110. Nef, *op. cit.*, I, 394, 396.
111. Lawrence Stone, *The Crisis of the Aristocracy, 1558–1641* (1965), 340. See also his 'An Elizabethan Coal Mine', *Ec. H. R.*, 2nd ser., III no. 1 (1950), 97–106.
112. Nef, *op. cit.*, I, 42.
113. M. E. James (ed.), *The Estate Accounts of the Earls of Northumberland, 1562–1637* (Surtees Society, CLXIII, 1948), xlvii.
114. Syon MSS. Q II, 52; Q II, 92; James (ed.), *op. cit.*, xlv-xlvii; Nef, *op. cit.*, I, 32.
115. L. R. 2/233, f.285; Syon MSS. P X, 2 i, P X, 2 m; L. C. Duke of Nd's MSS. Aln. 4 9a/23/6 fos. 199, 218; Lawrence Stone, *The Crisis of the Aristocracy 1558–1641* (1965), 377; N. C. H., VIII, 18.
116. Nef, *op. cit.*, I, 207.
117. Newcastle Public Library, 'Craster Transcript', II, 29. See also N. C. H., IX, 352.
118. Nef. *op. cit.*, I, 176–7; William Brereton, *Travels in Holland, England, Scotland and Ireland in 1634 and 1635* (Chetham Society, I, 1844), 88; *V. C. H., Durham*, II, 287.
119. Delaval Papers, letters 25, 29.
120. S. P. 14/58/19; N. C. H., IX, 353.
121. E 123, 39 Elizabeth I, Hilary 11; E 123/25/20; E 123/25/139; E 134; 41 Elizabeth I, Easter 19; N. C. H., IX, 227, 230, 323–5; Nef, *op. cit.*, I, 307; *Cal. S. P. Dom., 1595–7*, 16. For Huntingdon Beaumont see Richard Smith, 'Huntingdon Beaumont: Adventurer in Coal Mines', *Renaissance and Modern Studies*, 1 (1957), 91–114.
122. E 134, 8 James I, Trinity 1; E 134, 8 James I, Hilary 1; E 134, 9 James I, Easter 16; L. R. 2/223, f.135; S. P. 14/58/18; N. C. H., XIII, 34, 194.
123. N. C. H., XIII, 185, 186, 191; Nikolaus Pevsner, *The Buildings of England: Northumberland* (1957), 137.

Chapter 3

1. R. L. Storey, 'The Wardens of the Marches of England towards Scotland, 1377–1489', *E. H. R.*, LXXII (1957), 609–15.
2. M. E. James, *A Tudor Magnate and the Tudor State: Henry Fifth Earl of Northumberland* (1966), 6–9, 20; idem, 'The First Earl of Cumberland, 1492–1542, and the Decline of Northern Feudalism', *Northern History*, 1 (1966), 48–50. See also idem, *Change and Continuity in the Tudor North: the Rise of Thomas, First Lord Wharton* (1965).
3. Storey, *op. cit.*, 614; *L. & P. Hen. VIII*, VI, 367; XII, i, 595; J. M. W. Bean, *The Estates of the Percy Family, 1416–1537* (1958), 151; James, *Thomas, First Lord Wharton*, 11.
4. *L. & P. Hen. VIII*, IV, ii, 3119, 4603, 4698; James, *Thomas, First Lord Wharton*, 10–11; *Wills and Inventories*, I, 107; N. C. H., I, 222.

5. James, *Thomas, First Lord Wharton*, II, 30–1; N. C. H., XII, 496.
6. *Cal. S. P. For., 1569–71*, 568.
7. Lawrence Stone, *The Crisis of the Aristocracy, 1558–1641* (1965), 252. Our conclusions on this matter are much the same as those in M. E. James's article 'The Concept of Order and the Northern Rising 1569', *Past and Present*, LX (August 1973), which appeared after our book was in the hands of the publisher.
8. Hodgson, I, i, 370; N. C. H., VII, 470–1; IX, 86; X, 408; M. E. James (ed.), *Estate Accounts of the Earls of Northumberland, 1562–1637* (Surtees Society, CLXIII, 1948), 104.
9. Cuthbert Sharp (ed.), *Memorials of the Rebellion* (1840), 185; Tough, 208–9; Hodgson, I, i, 369.
10. E 164/37 fos.385sqq.; L. R. 2/223 fos.44–119; *Cal. S. P. For., 1569–71*, 640, 661, 657, 658.
11. S. P. 15/15/126; *Cal. S. P. For., 1569–71*, 598, 600; *1572–4*, 56, 111, 218, 340, 384. At least one northern Catholic treasured hair cut from the beard of the dead earl: Philip Tyler, *The Ecclesiastical Commission and Catholicism in the North, 1562–1577* (1960), 67.
12. Samuel Haynes and William Murdin (eds), *Collection of State Papers . . . left by William Cecil, Lord Burghley* (1740–59), I, 555; Conyers Read, *Mr Secretary Cecil and Queen Elizabeth* (1955), 309; James (ed.), *Estate Accounts*, xxi.
13. Syon MSS. P I, 3 d; *Acts of the Privy Council, 1571–5*, 51; Haynes and Murdin (eds), *op. cit.*, II, 21–2; N. C. H., VIII, 163–4; *N. D. B.*, Henry Percy, 8th earl of Northumberland; James (ed.), *Estate Accounts*, xx–xxii.
14. *Ibid.*, xxii–xxiii.
15. S. P. 14/169/43; S. P. 15/28/66; S. P. 15/30/19; S. P. 15/30/20; S. P. 15/30/26; Neville Williams, *Thomas Howard, Fourth Duke of Norfolk* (New York, 1964), 116sqq.; Tough, 210–12; Sharp (ed.), *op. cit.*, 117; James, *Thomas, First Lord Wharton*, 29; George Ornsby (ed.), *Selections from the Household Books of the Lord William Howard of Naworth Castle* (Surtees Society, LXVIII, 1878), viiisqq; Hodgson, II, ii, 380–1.
16. James, *Thomas, First Lord Wharton*, 29; *L. & P. Hen. VIII*, XII, i, 594, 857, 1162; XII, ii, 650, 732; M. H. and R. Dodds, *The Pilgrimage of Grace, 1536–37, and the Exeter Conspiracy, 1538* (2 vols, 1915), II, 251–3, 265.
17. James, *Thomas, First Lord Wharton*, 28; Tough, 211.
18. S. P. 15/30/26; S. P. 15/28/66; S. P. 14/169/43; S. P. 15/50/26; Tough, 211–12.
19. George Cokayne, *The Complete Peerage of England, Scotland and Ireland* (13 vols, rev. edn, 1949), XI, 8.
20. William Harrison (ed. George Edelen), *The Description of England* (Ithaca, New York, 1968), 114.
21. *Visitations, 1615, 1666; Visitations, 1575* (Surtees Society, CXLVI, 1932). Fuller pedigrees for these families and further information about them is found in N. C. H. and Hodgson.
22. Information about the 1586 gentry, in addition to that found in the next

note: feodaries list of Northumbrians who held *in capite* of the crown, 1568, Hodgson, III, iii, lxsqq.; list of gentlemen at the day of truce at which Lord Russell was killed in 1585, S. P. 59/33/331; gentlemen appearing at musters in 1580 and 1584, S. P. 59/20/50; S. P. 59/20/47; S. P. 59/23/259.

23. J. P.s: March–July 1584–7, E 163/14/8; 1596, S. P. 13/F/11; Feb. 1602, C 181/1, p. 19; 1604, B. M. Add. MS. 38139; April 1608–11, S. P. 14/33; 1621, C 193/13/1; 1625, Rymer, *Foedera*, XVIII, 597; Jan. 1626, B. M. Harley MSS. 1622 f.58d; 1626, E 163/18/12; Feb. 1632, S. P. 16/212; July 1636, S. P. 16/405. Commissions of oyer and terminer: Feb. 1602, C 181/1, p. 19; May 1603, C 181/1, p. 44; 1604, C 181/1, p. 166; April 1606, C 181/2 f.4; Aug. 1607, C 181/2 f.48; Feb. 1611, C 181/2 f.137d; Aug. 1615, C 181/2 f.235d; March 1616, C 181/2 f.246; 1622, C 181/3 f.83; Feb. 1624, C 181/3 f.106; June 1624, C 181/3 f.120; 1626, C 181/3 f.181; Jan. 1630, C 181/4 f.37. Sheriffs: *Lists and Indexes*, 99; C. H. Hunter Blair, 'The Sheriffs of Northumberland to 1603', *Arch. Aeliana*, 4th ser., xx (1942), 11–90; C. H. Hunter Blair, 'The Sheriffs of Northumberland, 1603–1942', *Arch. Aeliana*, 4th ser., xxi (1943), 1–92. Escheators: *Lists and Indexes*, List of Escheators for England, 124. For M. P.s C. H. Hunter Blair, 'Members of Parliament for Northumberland and Newcastle upon Tyne, 1559–1831', *Arch. Aeliana*, 4th ser., xxiii (1945), 102–55, and *idem*, 'Members of Parliament for Berwick and Morpeth, 1558–1832', *Arch. Aeliana*, 4th ser., xxiv (1946), 71–112, are both more reliable than W. M. Bean, *The Parliamentary Representation of the Six Northern Counties of England* (1890). Commission for recusants, Feb. 1618, Delaval Papers, Box 29 A. Judges and jurors, 1605–17, from the typescript by H. A. Taylor in N. R. O., 'Vetera Indictamenta: Criminal Records of the General Gaol Delivery and General Quarter Sessions of the Peace for Northumberland, 1594–1630'.

24. James Raine, *The History and Antiquities of North Durham* (1852), *passim*. One North Durham family, the Reveleys of Ancroft, appear in *Visitations, 1615, 1666*, 100. For the list of gentry families in 1615 see Appendix 2.

25. These criteria broadly follow those of Cliffe, and thus the gentry of both counties can be usefully compared; J. T. Cliffe, *The Yorkshire Gentry from the Reformation to the Civil War* (1969), 4–5.

26. Talbot, 150–3.

27. William Gray, 'Chorographia: Or a Survey of Newcastle-upon-Tine', *Harleian Miscellany*, XI (1810), 466–7.

28. Two individual exceptions were Claudius and Sir John Delaval. Claudius, the fifth son of Sir Robert Delaval of Seaton Delaval, was town clerk of Newcastle for some years before his death in 1623 and was succeeded in this office by Sir John, Robert's second son: N. C. H., IX, 171, 172; Roger Howell, *Newcastle upon Tyne and the Puritan Revolution: A Study of the Civil War in North England* (1967), 28, 35sqq.

29. Mary F. Keeler, *The Long Parliament, 1640–1641: a Biographical Study of its Members* (Philadelphia, 1954), 86.

30. S. P. 59/31/217.

31. N. C. H., X, 348.

32. C 193/13/1; C 4211; John Nichols, *Processions, and Magnificent Festivities*

of King James I (4 vols, 1828), III, 281; Hunter Blair, 'Members of Parliament for Northumberland . . .', 109–10.

33. *Cal. S. P. Dom., 1603–10*, 525; Richard Welford, *Men of Mark 'Twixt Tyne and Tweed* (3 vols, 1895), I, 375; H. A. C. Sturgess, *Register of Admissions to the Honourable Society of the Middle Temple*, 103. For Robert's quarrels in the 1620s and 1630s see S. P. 16/175/120; L. C. Duke of Nd's MSS. Aln. 13/23/6, p. 177; Syon MSS. P I, 3 n; P II, 24 k; *Acts of the Privy Council, May 1629–May 1630*, 20; William Longstaff (ed.), *The Acts of the High Commission within the Diocese of Durham* (Surtees Society, XXXIV, 1858), 53–68.

34. S. P. 14/33; S. P. 14/67/163; E 179/158/98; Delaval Papers, 17K; Martin, 37–8; N. C. H., XV, 252.

35. S. P. 16/105/71; 47th *Deputy Keepers Report*, 132; N. C. H., I, 156; X, 280, Raine, *op. cit.*, 225.

36. Wallace Notestein *et al.* (eds), *Commons Debates for 1621* (New Haven, 1935), V, 109; Hodgson, II, i, 330; Hunter Blair, 'Members of Parliament for Northumberland', 111.

37. Exceptions are the Delaval and Swinburn papers in the N. R. O.

38. C 142 II, 256; Martin, *passim*; Talbot, 151; Sanderson, 57–9; H. E. Bell, *An Introduction to the History and Records of the Court of Wards and Liveries* (1953), chapter III; Cliffe, *op. cit.*, 132.

39. Hunter MSS. 23, f.108.

40. 7 James I, c. 23, *Statutes of the Realm*, IV, ii, 1187–1201. Berwick alone was exempt: S. P. 14/56/42; E 179/158/88; Elizabeth Read Foster (ed.), *Proceedings in Parliament, 1610* (2 vols, 1966), II, 286.

41. E 407/35 f.143; Sheffield Public Library, Strafford MSS. 12/137.

42. S. P. 16/357/21; P. C. 2/47/478.

43. E 179/158/88. Other Northumberland subsidy lists are E 179/158/92; E 179/158/96; E 179/158/97; E 179/158/98.

44. Cliffe, *op. cit.*, 139–40.

45. Thomas Wilson (ed. F. J. Fisher), *The State of England Anno Domini 1600* (Camden Miscellany, XVI, 3rd ser., LII, 1936), 23–4.

46. N. R. O., 'Thomas Delaval's Book', quoted in N. C. H., IX, 158.

47. S. P. 59/25/574; S. P. 59/26/601.

48. Talbot, 151.

49. Hodgson, II, ii, 325.

50. C 4211, p. 207; Joseph Foster (ed.), *Alumni Oxonienses, 1500–1714* (1891), I 1257.

51. S. P. 59/33/523; Thomas Garden Barnes, *Somerset, 1625–40, a County's Government during the 'Personal Rule'* (1961), 124–42; J. S. Cockburn, *A History of English Assizes 1558–1714* (1972), 61–2, 104–7.

52. S. P. 15/32/59; 43 Elizabeth I, c. 13.

53. See Forster pedigrees: N. C. H., I, 159, 228. Nicholas Ridley was the uncle of William of Willimontswick (*fl.* 1615).

54. S. P. 15/29/88. Ridley's inventory etc: *Wills and Inventories*, II, 121.

55. S. P. 59/33/466; S. P. 59/33/523; *Lists and Indexes*, 99.

56. S. P. 12/284/56; C 181/1 f.1; *Lists and Indexes*, 99.

57. C 193/13/1; E 163/14/8.
58. S. P. 59/40/1335; S. P. 59/40/1413; Hunter Blair, 'Members of Parliament for Berwick and Morpeth', 77.
59. S. P. 59/26/662; S. P. 59/35/763; S. P. 59/36/830; S. P. 59/36/860; Sta. Cha. 5 F/15/11; Sta. Cha. 5 F/2/34; C 4211, p. 193; Hodgson, II, ii, 113.
60. Vetera Indictamenta, *passim*. For the Goftons see Sta. Cha. 8 130/19; N. C. H. XII, 468–70.
61. Strafford MSS. 12/137.
62. N. C. H., I, 228.
63. Tough, 158.
64. N. C. H., XI, 391, 395–9.
65. *Ibid*., XI, 113, 462; Hodgson, I, i, 374; Raine, *op. cit.*, 338.
66. Vetera Indictamenta, f.135d; Hist. MSS. Com., *Salisbury*, XVIII, 458.
67. Stone, *op. cit.* (n.7 above), 768.
68. N. C. H., IV, 418; IX, 159, 170; X, 280.
69. Cliffe, *op. cit.*, 132; Joel Hurstfield, *The Queen's Wards: Wardship and Marriage under Elizabeth I* (1958). For a list of Northumbrians holding *in capite* of the Crown in 1568 see Hodgson, III, iii, lxsqq.
70. Syon MSS. E IV, 3 h; O I, 2 d; P II, 1 b; P II, 1 d; P II, 2 i; E 164/37 f.109d. See also L. R. 2/223 f.50; Raine, *op. cit.*, 23.
71. Sanderson, 57.
72. *Ibid*., 90.
73. *Ibid*., 57, 90; E 134, 18 James I, Easter 13.
74. Eric Kerridge, *Agrarian Problems in the Sixteenth Century and After* (1969), 32–64, is a useful guide to sixteenth- and seventeenth-century tenures but must be used with caution. See also C. M. Gray, *Copyhold, Equity and the Common Law* (Cambridge, Mass., 1963).
75. Hodgson, II, i, 78.
76. Sanderson, 124. See also the 1608 survey of Langley: L. R. 2/223 f.271.
77. Kerridge, *op. cit.*, 34. For Langley free burgages see L. R. 2/223 f.237.
78. S. P. 59/21/82.
79. Kerridge, *op. cit.*, 32sqq; R. H. Tawney, *The Agrarian Problem in the Sixteenth Century* (new edn, New York, 1967), 287sqq.
80. L. R. 2/223 f.231; E 134, 9 James I, Mich. 22; N. C. H., III, 59; IV, 137.
81. E 112/112/170. For Northumberland tenant-right see S. J. Watts, 'Tenant-Right in Early Seventeenth Century Northumberland', *Northern History*, vi (1971), 64–87.
82. Gray, *op. cit.*, 13–16. In 1620 Percival Hall of Elsdon reported that according to the custom of the manor of Harbottle tenants "may sell and alien the land without licence of the lord of the manor": E 134, 18 James I, Mich. 21.
83. Sanderson, 85, 51. In Wark court cases the custom of partible inheritance was explicitly denied: Req. 2/285/28.
84. Watts, *op. cit.*, 82–3.
85. C 2 L/6/28; Syon MSS. Q II, 98; Q III, 10.
86. E 164/37 f.109.
87. *Ibid*., f.20.

88. Syon MSS. P II, 2 z.
89. E 164/37/ f.20.
90. S. P. 59/20/50 (1580 musters); S. P. 15/28/80 f.105 (1584 decay report); S. P. 59/31/323 (1596 decay report).
91. Syon MSS. O V, 1 a; P I, 1 a; P II, 1 g; P II, 1 h; P II, 2 e; Q I, 24; Q II, 69; James (ed.), *Estate Accounts*, 140–1.
92. Syon MSS. P II, 1 a; P II, 2 g; P II, 2 q.
93. Syon MSS. P II, 2 k; P III, 3 b. See also *ibid.*, P II, 2 g; P III, 1 c.
94. Kerridge, *op. cit.*, 86–7. The assumption being that both lord and tenant clearly recognized what was and what was not demesne land.
95. S. P. 59/20/50.
96. Kerridge, *op. cit.*, 46. For cottagers in Norham see Sanderson, 129; in the baronies of Bywell and Bulbeck, N. C. H., VI, 93, 150; XII, 245 (L. R. 2/223 fos.57-9, 73, 75, 84).
97. N. C. H., VI, 92, 133, 150; XII, 244. For other examples see *ibid.*, XII, 462, 547.
98. L. R. 2/223, f.344.
99. Sir Edward Coke, *The Complete Copyholder* (1650), sections 48, 51, 56.
100. N. C. H., II, 42.
101. *Ibid.*, II, 43.
102. *Ibid.*, IX, 200.

Chapter 4

1. Arthur Clifford (ed.), *The State Papers and Letters of Sir Ralph Sadler* (2 vols, 1809), II, 55.
2. S. P. 14/92/17.
3. J. A. Manning (ed.), *Memoirs of Sir Benjamin Rudyard* (1841), 135-6; quoted by Roger Howell in 'Puritanism in Newcastle before the Summoning of the Long Parliament', *Arch. Aeliana*, 4th ser., XLI (1963), 138, and by Lawrence Stone in *The Causes of the English Revolution, 1529-1642* (1972), 80-1.
4. Ornsby, xxxiii. For a convenient summary of contemporary Elizabethan opinion see Tough, chapter III.
5. For general statements about the lay contribution see Wm R. Trimble, *The Catholic Laity in Elizabethan England, 1558-1603* (Cambridge, Mass., 1964), 239sqq.
6. B. W. Beckingsale, 'The Characteristics of the Tudor North', *Northern History*, IV (1969), 77-8; Claire Cross, 'Berwick on Tweed and the Neighbouring Parts of Northumberland on the Eve of the Armada', *Arch. Aeliana*, 4th ser., XLI (1963), 133; Father William Palmes, *The Life of Mrs Dorothy Lawson of St Anthony's near Newcastle-upon-Tyne in Northumberland* (1851), *passim*.
7. J. T. Cliffe, *The Yorkshire Gentry from the Reformation to the Civil War* (1969), 210; 1 Elizabeth I, c. 2; 23 Elizabeth I, c. 1; 29 Elizabeth I, c. 6.
8. Howell, *op. cit.*, 138.
9. S. P. 15/30/61.

10. *Camden Miscellany*, IX (1859), 66.
11. *Ibid.*, 65.
12. Claire Cross, *The Puritan Earl: the Life and Times of Henry Hastings, Third Earl of Huntingdon, 1536–1595* (1966), xiv. See C. H. George, 'Puritanism as History and Historiography', *Past and Present*, XLI (December 1968), 101sqq.
13. J. Morris, *The Troubles of our Catholic Forefathers* (3 vols, 1872–7), III, 152.
14. Philip Tyler, *The Ecclesiastical Commission and Catholicism in the North, 1562–77* (1960), 118, 120; R. A. Marchant, *The Church under the Law* (1969), 33–4.
15. S. P. 15/15/25 VI; Cross, *Huntingdon*, 227–34; Tyler, *op. cit.*, 94; *Acts of the Privy Council, 1575–7*, 203; *1577–8*, 79–80.
16. Hist. MSS. Com., *Salisbury*, V, 203; Claire Cross, 'The Third Earl of Huntingdon and Trials of Catholics in the North, 1581–85', *Recusant History*, VIII no. 3 (1965).
17. S. P. 15/30/16; E 163/14/8. For similar statements see S. P. 59/30/171; S. P. 59/36/881; Cross, 'Berwick', 133.
18. *Acts of the Privy Council, 1587–8*, 127.
19. B. M. Cotton MSS. Titus F xiii 249, printed in James Raine, *The History and Antiquities of North Durham* (1852), xli.
20 *Ibid.*; Martin, 175; C. H. Hunter Blair, 'The Sheriffs of Northumberland to 1603', *Arch. Aeliana*, 4th ser., XXVIII (1950), 87; N. C. H., X, 276–8.
21. S. P. 15/30/61; S. P. 15/32/50; S. P. 12/243/59; Talbot, 152.
22. Talbot, 59, 151.
23. *D. N. B.*, Matthew.
24. S. P. 15/32/62; S. P. 15/32/62 I; Nikolaus Pevsner, *The Buildings of England: Northumberland* (1957), 143–4; Talbot, 57. Swinburn was first indicated in 1589: Martin, 216.
25. Richard Challoner, *Memoirs of a Missionary Priest of the Roman Church* (1924), 96; Hodgson, II, ii, 540; Richard Welford, *Men of Mark 'Twixt Tyne and Tweed* (3 vols, 1895), III, 86–7. For the Erringtons of the Hurst see N. C. H., IV, 227; Martin, 76.
26. Rachel R. Reid, *The King's Council in the North* (1921) 227, 230n., Hugh Aveling, *Northern Catholics: the Catholic Recusants of the North Riding of Yorkshire, 1558–1790* (1966), 118.
27. S. P. 59/25/548; Reid, *op. cit.*, 230; Hist. MSS. Com., *Salisbury*, IX, 317; XIV, 312.
28. S. P. 59/32/442; S. P. 59/34/631; S. P. 12/263/55; S. P. 59/34/646.
29. Reid, *op. cit.*, 231sqq.
30. E 377/9; Martin, *passim*; *Acts of the Privy Council, 1600–1*, 5–7, 26. See also *Acts of the Privy Council, 1598–9*, 111–12; S. P. 12/270/36.
31. *Acts of the Privy Council, 1600–1*, 28, 26–30.
32. S. P. 12/278/53.
33. S. P. 59/40/1331.
34. S. P. 59/36/862; N. C. H., X, 276.
35. 3 & 4 James I, c. 4, *Statutes of the Realm*, IV, ii, 1071.
36. 3 & 4 James I, c. 5, *ibid.*, IV, ii, 1077; *Acts of the Privy Council, 1617–19*, 125.

37. 7 James I, c. 6, *Statutes of the Realm*, IV, ii, 1162; Joseph Tanner (ed.), *Constitutional Documents of the Reign of James I* (1930), 90–1, 105–9.

38. Talbot, 150.

39. *Ibid.*, 152; N. C. H., XIV, 524.

40. Talbot, 150–3.

41. Ornsby, xxxiii.

42. Sources for the analysis of recusancy: Martin; Talbot, lists for 1595, 1607, 1629 and 1632, pp. 54–60, 150–3; 339–40, 357–9. 1607 list also in Hist. MSS. Com., *Salisbury*, XIX, 3. The gentry of Northumberland in 1588: S. P. 15/30/61 or *Cal. S. P. Dom., Addenda, 1580–1610*, 231. Schedule of goods seized from Catholics 1625: Delaval Papers, Box 17 K. Recusants and non-communicants in Northumberland, 1610: S. P. 14/56/17. Inventory of arms found in the houses of Northumberland recusants in 1625: S. P. 16/10/64.

43. S. P. 16/10/64; Delaval Papers, Box 17 K; Martin, 90–1; Hodgson, II, ii, 11; Talbot, 339–40.

44. Delaval Papers, Box 17 K; Martin, 223; Talbot, 152; Hodgson, II, ii, 237.

45. C 2 0/1/30; C 193/13/1; Rymer, *Foedera*, XVIII, 597; N. C. H., XI, 133; Talbot, 153.

46. Delaval Papers, Box 17 K; Martin, 115.

47. Martin, 217, 218.

48. *Ibid.*, 103–5.

49. *Ibid.*, 94, 95; C. H. Hunter Blair, 'The Sheriffs of Northumberland, 1603–1942', *Arch. Aeliana*, 4th ser., xxi (1943), 6.

50. S. P. 14/17/20; E 112/228/23; E 134, 14 James I, Mich. 11; N. C. H., XV, 420, 492.

51. *Acts of the Privy Council, 1615–16*, 368–9; *1621–3*, 125; Talbot, 340; N. C. H., VII, 137–9; Martin, 216, 218.

52. Delaval Papers, Box 17 K.

53. See R. C. Richardson, *Puritanism in North-west England* (1972), 115–52; Cliffe, *op. cit.*, 206–7; Roger B. Manning, *Religion and Society in Elizabethan Sussex* (1969), 262.

54. Martin, *passim*. The records were kept from Michaelmas (29 September) of one year to Michaelmas of the following year. For example, what Martin terms '1599' thus represents the period 29 September 1599 to 28 September 1600. The August 1600 assizes account for many of these indictments.

55. Cliffe, *op. cit.*, 182; Martin Havran, *The Catholics in Caroline England* (Stanford, 1962), 83.

56. A. G. Dickens, 'The Extent and Character of Recusancy in Yorkshire, 1604', *Y. A. J.*, xxxvii (1948), 24–48; Talbot, 147. See also Richardson, *op. cit.*, 169–70.

57. James Raine (ed.), *The Inquisitions and other Ecclesiastical Proceedings of Richard Barnes, Bishop of Durham, 1575–87* (Surtees Society, XXII, 1850), 7–10.

58. *Ibid.*, 41. For other comments on Scottish priests in Northumberland see B. M. Harl. MSS. 595.

59. Raine (ed.), *Richard Barnes*, 7–10.

60. Cross, 'Berwick', 133.

61. S. P. 59/30/171.
62. Patrick McGrath, *Papists and Puritans under Elizabeth I* (1967), 150.
63. S. P. 59/34/631.
64. S. P. 59/32/357; Hodgson, III, iii, p. xlvi.
65. S. P. 59/32/421.
66. *D. N. B.* See also Hugh Kearney, *Scholars and Gentlemen: Universities and Society in pre-industrial Britain, 1500–1700* (Ithaca, New York, 1970), 83–5, 105, 148.
67. George Carleton, *The Life of Bernard Gilpin, a Man Most Holy and Renowned among the Northern English* (1629). See also A. L. Rowse, *The Expansion of Elizabethan England* (1955), 15.
68. Quoted in Hodgson, II, i, 75.
69. *Wills and Inventories*, II, 83–94.
70. S. P. 59/35/746; Christopher Hill, *The Economic Problems of the Church from Archbishop Whitgift to the Long Parliament* (1965), 205.
71. Hodgson, III, iii, p. xlvi.
72. Raine, *North Durham*, 14–15, 28, 30.
73. *Ibid.*, 134–5; *Acts of the Privy Council, 1591*, 61, 161; *1592–3*, 353.
74. William Camden, *Britannia* (trans. Philemon Holland, 1610), III, 803.
75. E 134, 23–4 Elizabeth I, Mich. 19; E 134, 23 Elizabeth I, Easter 27; E 134, 23–4 Elizabeth I, Mich. 20; N. C. H., IV, 269.
76. Cross, 'Berwick', 134.
77. S. P. 15/33/1; S. P. 59/35/746. See also Hill, *op. cit.*, 115.
78. Hodgson, II, i, 163.
79. Sta. Cha. 8 266/11; N. C. H., XI, 119–20.
80. Sta. Cha. 8 103/18; Sta. Cha. 8 225/18; Vetera Indictamenta, f.137d; Hunter MSS. 6/151; S. P. 59/25/535.
81. S. P. 59/36/881.
82. Raine (ed.), *Richard Barnes*, 45, 46.
83. A. G. Dickens, *The English Reformation* (1964), 211; W. K. Jordan, *The Social Institutions of Lancashire, 1480–1660* (1962), 40.
84. Richard Welford, *History of Newcastle and Gateshead* (3 vols, 1884–7), II, 388.
85. General description of the founding of Hexham school in N. C. H., III, 211–18.
86. For John Ridley see L. R. 2/223 f.172; N. C. H., IV, 14. For Philip Thirlwall see S. P. 14/57/37; N. C. H., IV, 54.
87. L. R. 2/223 fos.175–7; Spec. Coll. 2/195/113.
88. On the curriculum see Joan Simon, *Education and Society in Tudor England* (1967), 378; Foster Watson, *The English Grammar Schools to 1660: their curriculum and practice* (1908), *passim*. Joan Simon's study, in Brian Simon (ed.), *Education in Leicestershire, 1540–1940* (1968), 21, shows how local men supported schools in other parts of the country.
89. George Tate, *History of the Borough, Castle and Barony of Alnwick* (2 vols, 1866–9), II, 82, 78; Syon MSS. R II, 2 b; R II, 2 e; Alnwick MSS. Q III, 1 y. For Berwick school see John Scott, *Berwick-upon-Tweed; the History of the Town and Guild* (1888), 392–5.

90. N. C. H., II, 69, 175. The John Craster who received his M. A. from Oxford in 1577 might have been the son and heir of Edmund, but probably was his brother: Joseph Foster (ed.), *Alumni Oxonienses, 1500–1714* (1891), I, 345.

91. N. C. H., IX, 169–71; H. A. C. Sturgess, *Register of Admissions to the Honourable Society of the Middle Temple*, 68, 69; Foster (ed.), *Alumni Oxonienses*, I, 393. For the value of training at the inns of court see Wilfrid Prest, *The Inns of Court under Elizabeth I and the Early Stuarts* (1972), 137–73.

92. N. C. H., XIV, after p. 536; Sturgess, *Register of Middle Temple*, 90; *idem*, *The Records of the Honourable Society of Lincoln's Inn, 1420–1799*, 234, 246.

93. Ogle received a B. A. from University College, Oxford, in 1613 and was at Lincoln's Inn in 1614: Sturgess, *The Records of Lincoln's Inn*, 168. John Strother went to King's College, Cambridge, in 1611 and Gray's Inn in 1614: John and J. A. Venn, *Alumni Cantabrigienses* (1922–7), I, iv, 176; Joseph Foster (ed.), *The Register of Admissions to Gray's Inn, 1521–1887* (1889), 132. Selby matriculated fellow commoner at Peterhouse in 1573 and very possibly was at Gray's Inn in 1576: Foster, *Register of . . . Gray's Inn*, 49; Venn, *Alumni Cantabrigienses*, I, iv, 41. Widdrington: Foster, *Register of . . . Gray's Inn*, 77.

94. The main sources for the analysis of higher education are Joseph Foster (ed.), *Alumni Oxonienses, 1500–1714* (1891); John and J. A. Venn, *Alumni Cantabrigienses* (1922–7); H. A. C. Sturgess, *The Records of the Honourable Society of Lincoln's Inn, 1420–1799; idem, Students Admitted to the Inner Temple, 1547–1660;* Joseph Foster (ed.), *The Register of Admissions to Gray's Inn, 1521–1887* (1889).

95. Cliffe, *op. cit.*, 73. For an unfavourable view of gentry education in Northumberland see Christopher Hill, 'Puritans and the "Dark Corners of the Land" ', *Trans. R. H. S.*, 5th ser., XIII (1963), 95–6.

96. Venn, *Alumni Cantabrigienses*, I, ii, 131; N. C. H., VII, 472–3.

97. *D. N. B.*; Venn, *Alumni Cantabrigienses*, I, ii, 132; Foster (ed.), *Register of . . . Gray's Inn*, 165; Hunter Blair, 'Members of Parliament for Berwick and Morpeth', 79, 99.

98. Venn, *Alumni Cantabrigienses*, I, ii, 132.

99. Vetera Indictamenta, *passim*; Venn, *Alumni Cantabrigienses*, I, iv, 401; Foster (ed.), *Register of . . . Gray's Inn*, 153; Mary F. Keeler, *The Long Parliament, 1640–1, a Biographical Study of its Members* (Philadelphia, 1954); N. C. H., XII, 325; *D. N. B.*

100. N. C. H., I, 95; Venn, *Alumni Cantabrigienses*, I, iii, 292–3.

101. *D. N. B.*; Venn, *Alumni Cantabrigienses*, I, iii, 292.

102. Sturgess, *The Records of . . . Lincoln's Inn*, 110, 116. See Prest, *op. cit.*, 175–86.

103. Martin, 39, 185; N. C. H., XIV, facing 536; Hodgson, I, i, 378.

104. The Catholic Record Society has printed the registers for Douai, 1598–1654 (vols X and XI); for Madrid, 1611–1767 (vol. XXIX); Valladolid, 1589–1862 (vol. XXX); Rome, 1579–1783 (vols XXXVII and XL). These do not list any identifiable members of Northumberland gentry families.

105. *Acts of the Privy Council, 1615–17*, 53.

Chapter 5

1. John Neale, *Essays in Elizabethan History* (New York, 1958), 79.
2. See Wallace T. MacCaffrey, 'Place and Patronage in Elizabethan Politics' in S. Bindoff, J. Hurstfield, C. H. Williams (eds), *Elizabethan Government and Society; essays presented to Sir John Neale* (1961), 95sqq.
3. *Visitations, 1575*, 79, 88–9; N. C. H., I, 156–7, 228–31; James Raine, *The History and Antiquities of North Durham* (1852), 306–9; Appendix 3, Forster.
4. See Arthur Clifford (ed.), *The State Papers and Letters of Sir Ralph Sadler* (2 vols, 1809); A. J. Slavin, *Politics and Profit; a study of Sir Ralph Sadler, 1507–47* (1966); Michael Burn, *The Debatable Land: a study of the motives of spies in two ages* (1970), 90sqq; Gerald Brenan, *A History of the House of Percy* (2 vols, 1902), I, 263.
5. *List of Sheriffs*, 99; Raine, *op. cit.*, 306; N. C. H., I, 92, 154.
6. M. E. James (ed.), *Estate Accounts of the Earls of Northumberland, 1562–1637* (Surtees Society, CLXIII, 1948), xviii–xix; N. C. H., XI, 189–90; Raine, *op. cit.*, xxx.
7. Clifford (ed.), *op. cit.*, II, 9, 82, 154; *Cal. Pat. Rolls, 1558–60*, 37, 144.
8. James (ed.), *op. cit.*, xix–xx, xxii; *Cal. Pat. Rolls, 1566–9*, 231, 250–2, 389.
9. S. P. 15/27/84 I; S. P. 59/30/122; L. R. 2/223 f.44sqq.
10. Cuthbert Sharp (ed.), *Memorials of the Rebellion* (1840), 332.
11. S. P. 59/22/250; Syon MSS. P II, 2 b; N. C. H., V, 67; Gordon Batho, 'The Percies and Alnwick Castle, 1557–1632', *Arch. Aeliana*, 4th ser., xxv (1957).
12. Syon MSS. Q II, 73.
13. *Visitations, 1615, 1666*, 57; Raine, *op. cit.*, 306; N. C. H., I, 156. *Visitations, 1615, 1666*, 99, states that Forster married Margaret, sister of Sir Cuthbert Radcliffe, but this contradicts all other evidence.
14. As Lord Francis was predeceased by his two elder brothers and his father, his son Edward became the third earl of Bedford. See S. P. 15/29/44; S. P. 15/29/56.
15. N. C. H., I, 156; Raine, *op. cit.*, 306.
16. S. P. 59/22/177; S. P. 59/22/180.
17. Robert Pitcairn (ed.), *The Autobiography and Diary of Mr James Melvill* (1842), 227.
18. N. C. H., I, 158.
19. S. P. 59/30/129.
20. Talbot, 152.
21. *Ibid.*, 152; S. P. 15/25/556; D. N. B., George Bowes.
22. S. P. 15/15/51; *List of Sheriffs*, 99. M. E. James suggests that Collingwood may in fact have been a follower of the cautious 'loyalist' Sir Henry Percy, the 7th earl's brother, rather than of the rebellious earl himself; see 'The Concept of Order and the Northern Rising 1569', *Past and Present*, LX (August 1973).
23. *List of Sheriffs*, 99; James (ed.), *Estate Accounts*, 69.
24. Syon MSS. P I, 3 c; P I, 3 d; S. P. 59/21/118.
25. James (ed.), *Estate Accounts*, 90.
26. S. P. 15/29/89.

27. For a discussion of Walsingham's role in formulating English policy at this time see Conyers Read, *Mr Secretary Walsingham and the Policy of Queen Elizabeth* (3 vols, 1925), III, 179.

28. S. P. 15/29/89; S. P. 15/29/89 I.

29. S. P. 59/24/421. See also B. M. Lansdowne MSS. 49/62.

30. S. P. 59/22/175; S. P. 59/22/177; S. P. 59/23/330; S. P. 59/24/439.

31. S. P. 59/23/337; S. P. 59/23/341; S. P. 59/23/348; Tough, 237–40.

32. For their interest in another northern dispute see Hist. MSS. Com., *Rutland*, 208.

33. S. P. 59/24/445.

34. Rachel R. Reid, *The King's Council in the North* (1921), 229.

35. Sharp (ed.), *op. cit.*, 187.

36. *Cal. S. P. For.*, *1575–7*, 83; Claire Cross, *The Puritan Earl: the Life and Times of Henry Hastings, Third Earl of Huntingdon, 1536–1595* (1966), 204; Tough, 224–7; Thomas I. Rae, *The Administration of the Scottish Frontier, 1513–1603* (1966), 200–1.

37. S. P. 15/29/160; S. P. 15/29/161; S. P. 15/29/162; S. P. 15/29/163; S. P. 15/29/165; S. P. 15/30/33; S. P. 15/30/36; S. P. 15/30/97; S. P. 59/25/521; Hist. MSS. Com., *Salisbury*, XIII, 353–6. Lawrence Stone sees the Collingwood-Selby dispute as "merely the latest episode in a long blood feud between the two families ... in areas as remote as these ... blood money and personal vengeance were still accepted as alternatives to prosecution in the courts of law": *The Crisis of the Aristocracy, 1558–1641* (1965), 228. We disagree. We have defined what Scots and Northumbrians meant by a blood feud in chapter 1. Five years before the incident on Morpeth Moor the Collingwoods and the Selbys had "developed neighbourly friendship": S. P. 15/29/162. A misunderstanding over a dispute with the Burnes, a surname group in east Teviotdale, precipitated the Morpeth Moor fray. In such matters the behaviour of Northumberland gentlemen differed only in degree from that of gentlemen elsewhere in Elizabethan England: see F. G. Emmison, *Elizabethan Life: Disorder* (1970).

38. S. P. 59/26/618.

39. S. P. 59/26/617.

40. S. P. 59/25/494.

41. Gordon Donaldson, *Scotland, James V to James VII* (1965), 190; Rae, *op. cit.*, 245.

42. S. P. 59/25/522. See also S. P. 59/25/494; S. P. 59/25/515; S. P. 59/25/535; Hist. MSS. Com., *Salisbury*, III, 555, 572.

43. S. P. 59/25/475; S. P. 59/25/493.

44. S. P. 59/24/451.

45. S. P. 59/25/501; S. P. 59/25/507.

46. S. P. 59/25/515. See also S. P. 59/25/522.

47. Hist. MSS. Com., *Rutland*, 221.

48. S. P. 59/25/534; *Acts of the Privy Council, 1587–8*, 221, 223, 226; F. H. Mares (ed.), *The Memoirs of Robert Carey* (1972), xiv.

49. S. P. 59/24/453. Joseph Bain, editor of *Cal. B. P.*, affixed a tentative date 27 September 1586, to lists of charges and Forster's answers. These documents should probably be dated *c.* 27 September 1587, the day Hunsdon tried Forster

in Newcastle: *Cal. B. P.*, I, 232–4, i. e. S. P. 59/24/452–5. Compare these with charges and answers firmly dated 27 September 1587: S. P. 59/25/546; S. P. 59/25/547.

50. S. P. 59/25/556.
51. S. P. 59/23/267; S. P. 59/25/548; Tough, 232; Conyers Read, *Lord Burghley and Queen Elizabeth* (1960), 289; MacCaffrey in Bindoff *et al.* (eds), *op. cit.*, 108. According to Hunsdon's biographer in *D. N. B.*, Henry Carey "held himself aloof from the factions which divided the noblemen and statesmen of the day". In her excellent biography of Huntingdon, Claire Cross only mentions his rivalry with Hunsdon in passing: *op. cit.*, 214, 225.
52. S. P. 59/25/548.
53. Claire Cross, 'Berwick on Tweed and the Neighbouring Parts of Northumberland on the Eve of the Armada', *Arch. Aeliana*, 4th ser., XLI (1963), 123–4.
54. S. P. 59/25/548.
55. S. P. 59/25/552.
56. S. P. 59/25/556.
57. B. M. Cotton MSS. Titus F. xiii 249, printed in Raine, *op. cit.*, xl.
58. However, acting warden Hunsdon was told that he might appoint a deputy warden in his absence: S. P. 59/25/537.
59. Forster's sister Margaret was the third wife of John Heron's father, Sir George Heron: N. C. H., I, 228.
60. S. P. 59/25/563; S. P. 59/25/574; S. P. 59/26/601; Sta. Cha. 5 H/53/21; *Acts of the Privy Council, 1591*, 30; N. C. H., IV, 340.
61. Predictably Hunsdon alleged that the Yorkshire troops were poorly furnished and virtually useless: *Acts of the Privy Council, 1587–8*, 267. See also *ibid.*, 232, 274; S. P. 15/30/45.
62. S. P. 59/25/570; S. P. 59/25/571; S. P. 59/25/574; S. P. 59/25/578; Hist. MSS. Com., *Rutland*, 232; Samuel Haynes and William Murdin (eds), *Collection of State Papers . . . left by William Cecil, Lord Burghley* (2 vols, 1740–59), II, 591sqq.
63. S. P. 59/26/586; Haynes and Murdin (eds), *op. cit.*, II, 591; Tough, 246–7; Donaldson, *op. cit.*, 185.
64. S. P. 59/26/596.
65. S. P. 59/26/601.
66. S. P. 59/26/602; *Cal. S. P. Dom.*, *1583–8*, 517. The Yorkshire gentleman Ralph Eure was made acting warden but it does not appear that he attended to this office in person: S. P. 59/26/630; C. H. Hunter Blair, 'Wardens and Deputy Wardens of the Marches of England toward Scotland in Northumberland', *Arch Aeliana*, 4th ser., XXVIII (1950), 75.
67. S. P. 59/26/604; S. P. 59/26/611; S. P. 59/26/620; Cross, *Huntingdon*, 215sqq.
68. S. P. 59/26/627.
69. S. P. 59/26/646; S. P. 59/26/691; S. P. 15/31/23.
70. Sta. Cha. 5 D/16/17; *Visitations, 1615, 1666*, 55.
71. E 163/14/8; *List of Sheriffs*, 99; *Wills and Inventories*, II, 246.
72. Syon MSS. O II, 1 b; P II, 1 b; Alnwick MSS Q III, 2 f; James (ed.), *Estate Accounts*, 108, 136.

73. S. P. 59/26/630; S. P. 59/26/668; *List of Sheriffs*, 99.
74. S. P. 15/32/50; S. P. 59/26/691.
75. Syon MSS. Q II, 73.
76. Sta. Cha. 5 H/53/21. See also Sta. Cha. 5 E/6/39.
77. They were sons of Edward Delaval, 2nd son of Sir John Delaval of Seaton Delaval who died *c.* 1571: N. C. H., VIII, 171; Appendix 3, Delaval.
78. Sta. Cha. 5 D/2/24.
79. *Ibid.*; S. P. 59/26/662.
80. Sta. Cha. 5 D/2/24.
81. Peter Delaval, a London merchant, was at that time keeper of Tynemouth Castle under Lord Hunsdon's son Robert: S. P. 15/30/68; N. C. H., VIII, 167, 170, 171.
82. Sta. Cha. 5 D/16/17; Sta. Cha. 5 D/19/15; Sta. Cha. 5 D/42/6.
83. S. P. 59/28/806.
84. S. P. 59/28/825; S. P. 59/28/836; S. P. 59/28/837; S. P. 59/28/814; *Acts of the Privy Council, 1592–3*, 136.
85. David Harris Willson, *King James VI and I* (1956), 110–11; Donaldson, *op. cit.*, 193.
86. S. P. 59/27/786.
87. S. P. 15/32/81; S. P. 15/32/83; S. P. 15/32/87; *Acts of the Privy Council, 1592–3*, 103–7.
88. S. P. 15/32/81; *Acts of the Privy Council, 1592–3*, 103.
89. Reid, *op. cit.*, 340, 344.
90. For some of his attempts to collect information under the February commission see S. P. 15/32/76; S. P. 15/32/77; S. P. 15/32/83; S. P. 59/28/833.
91. S. P. 15/32/81.
92. S. P. 15/32/83.
93. S. P. 15/32/87; S. P. 59/28/893; S. P. 59/28/903.
94. S. P. 59/28/904.
95. S. P. 59/28/903.
96. S. P. 15/32/81.
97. S. P. 15/32/87. Full returns had been sent up to the Privy Council in 1584: S. P. 15/28/80 fos.104–20, 142.
98. S. P. 15/32/87.
99. S. P. 15/33/1.
100. Collingwood's tenants appear at the top of a note on spoils made in the Middle March (1593): S. P. 59/29/998.
101. S. P. 59/29/931; S. P. 59/29/939.
102. S. P. 59/30/119; S. P. 59/30/129.
103. Hist. MSS. Com., *Salisbury*, V, 135.
104. Syon MSS. P IX, 3 b; Cross, *Huntingdon*, 167–8. See also Syon MSS. P II, 2 g; Q II, 8; U II, 16.
105. S. P. 59/30/97.
106. S. P. 59/30/103.
107. S. P. 59/30/111.
108. S. P. 59/30/119; S. P. 59/30/131; S. P. 59/30/133; S. P. 59/30/154; Tough, 281.

109. S. P. 59/30/184.
110. S. P. 59/30/168; S. P. 59/30/169; S. P. 59/30/170; S. P. 12/256/27; Hist. MSS. Com., *Salisbury*, V, 458–60.
111. S. P. 12/256/27.
112. S. P. 59/30/171; S. P. 59/30/172; S. P. 59/30/173.
113. Hist. MSS Com., *Salisbury*, V, 477; S. P. 59/30/184; Thomas Birch (ed.), *Memoirs of the Reign of Queen Elizabeth from the year 1581 till her death* (2 vols, 1754), I, 335–8.
114. S. P. 59/30/184.
115. S. P. 59/30/173.
116. S. P. 59/31/233; S. P. 59/30/184; Cross, *Huntingdon*, 271.

Chapter 6

1. Gray was Northumberland high sheriff in 1582–3, 1591–2, 1593–4. In August 1593 Lord Burghley and Lord Hunsdon stood by proxy as godparents to his infant son: E 163/14/8; S. P. 59/28/877; *List of Sheriffs*, 99; *Wills and Inventories*, II, 172sqq.; N. C. H., II, 42; N. C. H., XIV, facing p. 328. Henry Widdrington was the eldest son of Edward Widdrington of Swinburn and Cartington (*d.* 1577) and Ursula Carnaby, daughter and co-heiress of Sir Reynold Carnaby. He attended Gray's Inn in 1590: Joseph Foster (ed.), *The Register of Admissions to Gray's Inn, 1521–1887* (1889), 77; N. C. H., IV, 280; *Visitations, 1575*, 93; Hodgson, II, ii, 237; *Visitations, 1615, 1666*, 126. For the violent dispute between Gray and Widdrington in 1592–3 see Sta. Cha. 5 G/9/5; Sta. Cha. 5 G/5/21; S. P. 15/32/53; S. P. 59/28/840; S. P. 59/29/940.
2. N. C. H., V, 243.
3. S. P. 12/256/83; S. P. 59/31/226; S. P. 59/31/232; S. P. 59/31/239; S. P. 59/35/764; Hist. MSS. Com., *Salisbury*, VI, 92; Rachel R. Reid, *The King's Council in the North* (1921), 228.
4. S. P. 59/31/248; S. P. 59/31/249; S. P. 59/31/268; Hist. MSS. Com., *Salisbury*, VI, 148–9. For the 1596 decay returns see S. P. 59/31/323 and chapter 1.
5. E 163/14/8; S. P. 38, vol. 3, 24 February 1591/2.
6. This point was brought to my attention by Dr Trevor Cliffe.
7. S. P. 13/F/11 (January 1596 *liber pacis*); *List of Sheriffs*, 99; *Statutes of the Realm*, IV, i, 207; Reid, *op. cit.*, 495sqq.
8. Syon MSS. P II, 1 c; P II, 1 f; S. P. 59/31/194; S. P. 59/31/219; S. P. 59/36/360; S. P. 13/F/11; Hist. MSS. Com., *Salisbury*, VI 92, 171; Foster (ed.), *The Register of ... Gray's Inn*, 71; M. E. James (ed.), *Estate Accounts of the Earls of Northumberland, 1562–1637* (Surtees Society, CLXIII, 1948), 131; Charles Sisson (ed.), *Thomas Lodge and Other Elizabethans* (Cambridge, Mass., 1933), 211.
9. S. P. 59/31/211.
10. S. P. 59/31/225; Reid, *op. cit.*, 230sqq.
11. C. H. Hunter Blair, 'Wardens and Deputy Wardens of the Marches of

England toward Scotland in Northumberland', *Arch. Aeliana*, 4th ser., XXVIII (1950), 76; N. C. H., IV, 340. For Bowes's dispute with Reginald Heron see S. P. 59/31/217; S. P. 59/34/652; S. P. 59/38/1047; *Wills and Inventories*, II, 200; Hist. MSS. Com., *Salisbury*, VIII, 244. Bowes succeeded William Fenwick of Bitchfield, successor to William Fenwick of Wallington in the Tynedale keepership.

12. S. P. 59/30/159; S. P. 59/31/234; S. P. 59/33/543; S. P. 59/36/902.
13. S. P. 59/36/862; Francis Edwards, *Guy Fawkes: the Real Story of the Gunpowder Plot?* (1969), 29.
14. See above, p. 87.
15. S. P. 59/32/370; S. P. 59/32/422; S. P. 59/35/779; *List of Sheriffs*, 99; N. C. H., II, 354.
16. S. P. 59/36/862. There are no Northumberland entries in the recusancy rolls during the years Eure was in office.
17. *Acts of the Privy Council, 1616–17*, 202; J. T. Cliffe, *The Yorkshire Gentry from the Reformation to the Civil War* (1969), 243; *D. N. B.*, Matthew.
18. S. P. 59/32/326; S. P. 59/32/329; Hunter Blair, *op. cit.*, 74, 77.
19. David Harris Willson, *King James VI and I* (1956), 140sqq.; Thomas I. Rae, *The Administration of the Scottish Frontier, 1513–1603* (1966), 218.
20. B. M. Harleian MSS. 851 f.7; S. P. 59/32/333; S. P. 59/32/373; S. P. 59/32/431; S. P. 59/34/643; S. P. 59/34/651; S. P. 59/36/810; S. P. 59/36/812; S. P. 59/37/903; Hist. MSS. Com., *Salisbury*, VI, 297.
21. S. P. 59/34/651.
22. Mandell Creighton, *Carlisle* (1889), 144.
23. Rae, *op. cit.*, 215–18.
24. S. P. 59/32/343; S. P. 59/31/265; S. P. 59/32/347.
25. S. P. 59/33/507; B. M. Harleian MSS. 851 f.7.
26. Tough, 261; Rae, *op. cit.*, 216–17.
27. S. P. 59/32/329; S. P. 59/32/327; S. P. 59/32/438.
28. S. P. 59/32/431.
29. S. P. 59/33/508.
30. Syon MSS. P III, 3 e; S. P. 59/31/265; S. P. 59/31/294; S. P. 59/36/861.
31. S. P. 59/32/351; S. P. 59/32/366; S. P. 59/36/860; S. P. 59/36/861.
32. S. P. 59/36/861; S. P. 59/32/366; S. P. 59/36/359; Talbot, 151.
33. S. P. 59/33/483.
34. S. P. 59/31/306; S. P. 59/32/353; S. P. 59/33/498; S. P. 59/33/499; S. P. 59/33/500; S. P. 59/33/555; S. P. 59/33/573; S. P. 59/35/697. The dispute between the Grays and the Selbys was still not settled in April 1601: S. P. 59/38/1171; S. P. 59/40/1363.
35. S. P. 59/34/652; John Taylor, *The Pennyles Pilgrimage* (1618), no pagination; N. C. H., XII, 142n.
36. S. P. 59/34/646; Tough, 264.
37. S. P. 59/36/862; S. P. 12/260/20; S. P. 59/32/382; Hist. MSS. Com., *Salisbury*, VI, 411.
38. S. P. 59/34/646; S. P. 59/34/631; S. P. 59/34/638; S. P. 59/34/652.
39. S. P. 59/34/652; Hist. MSS. Com., *Salisbury*, VII, 276.

40. S. P. 59/34/672.
41. S. P. 59/35/779.
42. S. P. 59/35/706.
43. S. P. 46/21/123; S. P. 15/264/61; Taylor, *op. cit.* (under Widdrington Castle).
44. Edmund Lodge, *Illustrations of British History* (3 vols, 1838), II, 505.
45. Hist. MSS. Com., *Salisbury*, VII, 322; Thomas Birch (ed.), *Memoirs of the Reign of Queen Elizabeth, from the year 1581 until her death* (2 vols, 1754), II, 331.
46. S. P. 59/35/743; S. P. 59/35/758.
47. For J. E. Neale's opinion of Matthew see his *Essays in Elizabethan History*, 64.
48. S. P. 59/35/758; S. P. 59/36/805.
49. S. P. 59/35/763 quoted by George M. Fraser on his title page to *The Steel Bonnets* (1971).
50. S. P. 59/35/764; S. P. 59/35/772; S. P. 59/36/820; S. P. 59/36/860.
51. S. P. 59/36/794. See also S. P. 59/37/922.
52. S. P. 59/36/805. See also Birch (ed.), *op. cit.*, II, 248, 296, 311.
53. S. P. 59/36/813; S. P. 59/36/841. For a fuller account of this incident and its aftermath see Sisson (ed.), *op. cit.*, 200sqq.
54. S. P. 59/36/820; S. P. 59/36/836; S. P. 59/36/838; S. P. 59/36/841; *Acts of the Privy Council, 1597–8*, 203.
55. *Journals of the House of Lords*, II, 198.
56. S. P. 59/36/860; S. P. 59/36/861.
57. S. P. 59/36/854; S. P. 59/36/894; Hist. MSS. Com., *Salisbury*, VIII, 73–4. For further rivalry between Eure and Henry Widdrington see Sta. Cha. 5 W/67/11; Sta. Cha. 5 W/77/19; Sisson (ed.), *op. cit.*, 175–9. For Eure's later career at Bremen and on the Welsh marches see S. P. 59/39/1268; Hist. MSS. Com., *Salisbury*, X, 303; XIX, 212; Lawrence Stone, *The Crisis of the Aristocracy, 1558–1641* (1965), 239.
58. S. P. 59/36/841; S. P. 59/36/862; Hist. MSS. Com., *Salisbury*, VII, 452.
59. S. P. 59/38/1050; Syon MSS. P I, 1 a; R II, 2 a; R II, 2 c; Hist. MSS. Com., *Salisbury*, VIII, 504–5, 520; Gordon Batho (ed.), *The Household Papers of Henry Percy, Ninth Earl of Northumberland, 1564–1632* (Camden Society, 3rd ser., XCIII, 1962), xx.
60. For the Treaty of Carlisle see S. P. 59/34/622; Tough, 124–5, 264–6; William Nicholson (ed.), *Leges Marchiarum or Border Laws* (1705), 149–73.
61. S. P. 59/35/784; S. P. 59/35/785; S. P. 59/37/924; S. P. 59/37/1022; Hist. MSS. Com., *Salisbury*, VIII, 23; Rae, *op. cit.*, 218.
62. S. P. 59/36/815; Hist. MSS. Com., *Salisbury*, VIII, 452.
63. S. P. 46/21/123.
64. S. P. 59/36/826; S. P. 59/36/827.
65. S. P. 59/36/830.
66. S. P. 59/32/338; S. P. 59/35/783; S. P. 59/36/913; S. P. 59/36/920; Birch (ed.), *op. cit.*, II, 383; Hunter Blair, *op. cit.*, 74–6; Tough, 280.
67. S. P. 59/37/991; S. P. 59/39/1289; S. P. 59/39/1298; S. P. 59/40/1327; D. N. B.; Georgina Bertie, *Five Generations of a Loyal House* (1845), 324sqq. In January 1601 Willoughby's men entered Carey's Middle March and arrested John Ogilvy, laird of Poury, on the assumption that he was a sub-

versive enemy agent. Cecil commended Willoughby but Carey intimated that Ogilvy was really in Cecil's employ, as indeed he was before the year was out: S. P. 59/40/1314; S. P. 59/40/1318; S. P. 59/40/1319; S. P. 59/40/1331; S. P. 59/40/1409; Hist. MSS. Com., *Salisbury*, XI, 15; Willson, *op. cit.*, 143–5.

68. S. P. 59/37/936.
69. S. P. 59/37/933; S. P. 59/39/1273; Stone, *op. cit.*, 461; *Acts of the Privy Council, 1601–4*, 451–2.
70. S. P. 59/39/1094; Hunter Blair, *op. cit.*, 77; Foster (ed.), *Register of . . . Gray's Inn*, 65; John and J. A. Venn, *Alumni Cantabrigienses* (Pt I, 4 vols, 1922–7), I, ii, 273; N. C. H., II, 126; Bruce Dickens, 'The Gueveras of Stenigot; Spanish Squires in Tudor Lincolnshire', *Bulletin of Hispanic Studies*, XXXVII, iv (October 1960), 215–21.
71. Helen Wallace, 'Berwick in the Reign of Queen Elizabeth', *E. H. R.*, XLVI (January 1931), 79–88; Sydney and Beatrice Webb, *English Local Government*, III, *The Manor and the Borough* (1908), 504–29.
72. S. P. 59/39/1268; S. P. 59/39/1269; S. P. 59/39/1271; B. M. Harleian MSS. 6996 f.250; Reid, *op. cit.*, 333–5; *Acts of the Privy Council, 1600–1*, 285; *1601–4*, 9–12.
73. C. H. Hunter Blair, 'Members of Parliament for Berwick and Morpeth', *Arch. Aeliana*, 4th ser., XXIV (1946), 75, 76; *Acts of the Privy Council, 1599–1600*, 24.
74. S. P. 59/38/1153; S. P. 59/39/1267.
75. S. P. 59/38/1152.
76. S. P. 59/39/1272; S. P. 59/39/1273; S. P. 59/39/1275; S. P. 59/39/1277; S. P. 59/40/1313.
77. S. P. 59/40/1343.
78. Tough, 280.
79. S. P. 59/39/1294; Birch (ed.), *op. cit.*, I, 325.
80. S. P. 59/28/893; S. P. 59/30/157; S. P. 12/231/90; F. H. Mares (ed.), *The Memoirs of Robert Carey* (1972), 15–18, 22, 32.
81. Hunter Blair, 'Members for Berwick and Morpeth', 95; 'Members of Parliament for Northumberland and Newcastle upon Tyne, 1559–1831', *Arch. Aeliana*, 4th ser., XXIII (1945), 109.
82. James Raine, *The History and Antiquities of North Durham* (1852), 30, from Berwick parish registers.
83. Mares (ed.), *op. cit.*, 47–57.
84. See Helen Stafford, *James VI and the Throne of England* (New York, 1940), esp. 26sqq., 193sqq.; Willson, *op. cit.*, 150sqq.
85. S. P. 59/36/909; S. P. 59/36/911; Hist. MSS. Com., *Salisbury*, VIII, 87; X, 60.
86. S. P. 59/37/974; Hist. MSS. Com., *Salisbury*, VIII, 314.
87. S. P. 59/37/1020.
88. S. P. 59/37/978; S. P. 59/37/986; S. P. 59/37/998; S. P. 59/37/1006; S. P. 59/37/1020; S. P. 59/37/1025; S. P. 59/37/1028; S. P. 59/38/1042; *Acts of the Privy Council, 1598–9*, 68, 269, 444. For Carey's later recollections of this incident see Mares (ed.), *op. cit.*, 55–7.

89. S. P. 59/38/1103; S. P. 59/38/1102; S. P. 59/38/1124; S. P. 59/38/1125.
90. S. P. 59/38/1103; S. P. 59/38/1116; S. P. 59/38/1121; S. P. 59/40/1383.
91. S. P. 59/39/1172.
92. *Acts of the Privy Council, 1599–1600*, 372, 373.
93. Henry Savile told Cecil early in 1601 that Widdrington had recently been of service to Essex: S. P. 12/274/2; Hist. MSS. Com., *Salisbury*, XI, 654.
94. S. P. 59/40/1329.
95. S. P. 12/278/56; James Spedding, *Life of Francis Bacon* (2 vols, 1878), I, 324. Spedding thought that, as Widdrington was personally implicated in the Essex plot, he had presented this testimony to clear himself. Robert Lacey accepts Essex's opinion that Widdrington's evidence was mere hearsay: *Robert Earl of Essex* (New York, 1971), 303–4.
96. S. P. 59/39/1282; S. P. 59/39/1281.
97. S. P. 14/86/125; S. P. 14/87/4; *Acts of the Privy Council, 1600–1*, 5–7; Martin, *passim*.
98. Ornsby, xvii–xviii.
99. Willson, *op. cit.*, 153sqq.; John Bruce (ed.), *Correspondence of King James VI of Scotland with Sir Robert Cecil and others in England during the reign of Queen Elizabeth* (Camden Soc., LXXVIII, 1861), *passim*.
100. S. P. 59/41/1520; Willson, *op. cit.*, 148; Phyllis M. Handover, *The Second Cecil: the rise to power 1563–1604 of Sir Robert Cecil, later first earl of Salisbury* (1959), 284–6.
101. *Ibid.*, 285.
102. Except just prior to the August 1600 assize at which 150 recusants were indicted.
103. *Acts of the Privy Council, 1596–7*, 182; *Cal. S. P. Scot., 1619–22*, 386–7.
104. *Statutes of the Realm*, IV, ii, 981. See also S. P. 12/274/118; S. P. 59/41/1546.
105. S. P. 59/38/1152.
106. S. P. 59/39/1309 fos.20–1.
107. S. P. 59/39/1250.
108. S. P. 59/41/1466.
109. S. P. 59/41/1470; S. P. 59/41/1477; Hist. MSS. Com., *Salisbury*, XI, 345.
110. For a Northumberland book of rates pre-dating 1663 see Hodgson, III, i, 243–320.
111. *Acts of the Privy Council, 1598–9*, 261; S. P. 59/35/746.
112. S. P. 12/284/56.
113. Vetera Indictamenta, fos.1–44.
114. S. P. 59/41/1537.
115. *Reg. Privy Council of Scotland, 1599–1604*, 548.
116. Mares (ed.), *op. cit.*, 60–5.

Chapter 7

1. *The Workes of the Most High and Mightie Prince, James . . . King of Great Britaine* (1st edn, 1616), 517.

2. Rymer, *Foedera*, XVI, 506; *Register of the Privy Council of Scotland, 1599–1604*, 560. The Middle Shires consisted of North Durham and the counties of Northumberland, Westmorland, Cumberland, Berwickshire, Roxburgh, Peebles, Selkirk, Dumfries and the stewartries of Kirkcudbright and Annandale. For a sound brief treatment of the Middle Shires see Penry Williams, 'The Northern Borderlands under the Early Stuarts', in *Historical Essays 1600–1750 presented to David Ogg*, ed. H. E. Bell and R. L. Ollard (1963).

3. Rymer, *Foedera*, XVI, 506.

4. Hist. MSS. Com., *Salisbury*, XVI, 405.

5. Hist. MSS. Com., *12th Report*, VII, Le Fleming MSS., 12. See also S. P. 14/1/10; S. P. 14/9/87; Rymer, *Foedera*, XVI, 506; Robert Steele (ed.), *Tudor and Stuart Proclamations, 1485–1714* (2 vols, 1910), I, 108; John Strype, *Annals of the Reformation* (4 vols, 1824 edn), IV, 527; Hist. MSS. Com., *Salisbury*, XIV, 193.

6. S. P. 14/10B/38; S. P. 14/10B/39; S. P. 14/10B/40; *Statutes of the Realm*, IV, ii, 1134–7.

7. The Carey brothers were included in a commission of oyer and terminer for the northern counties issued 25 June 1603, but they were omitted from the 1604 Northumberland commission of the peace. Thereafter neither of them resided in the county: C 181/1 f.56; B. M. Add. MS. 38139; Wards 5/31; James Raine, *The History and Antiquities of North Durham* (1852), 30–2; Hist. MSS. Com., *Salisbury*, XV, 23, 135.

8. B. M. Add. MS. 38139; 'A General Catalogue of all the Bachelors, Knights, made by our sovereign lord King James and gathered into a perfect alphabet with the place of their knighthood and the day of the month and the year of our Lord until 1616', V. A. 258, Folger Library, Washington, D. C.

9. Vetera Indictamenta, f.46d and *passim*; S. P. 14/5/58; Hist. MSS. Com., *Salisbury*, XV, 133, 258–9; XVI, 376.

10. See above, p. 30.

11. S. P. 14/9A/88.

12. *Ibid.*; C. H. Hunter Blair, 'The Sheriffs of Northumberland, 1603–1942', *Arch. Aeliana*, 4th ser., xxi (1943), 2; John P. Collier (ed.), *The Egerton Papers* (Camden Society, XII, 1840), 389–90.

13. S. P. 14/9A/88; *Cal. S. P. Dom., 1603–10*, 74; Collier (ed.), *op. cit.*, 389–90.

14. E 401/2584; E 401/2585; S. P. 14/56/42; 3 James I, c. 26, *Statutes of the Realm*, IV, ii, 1124–5. In May 1609 Northumberland gentlemen contributed to a Privy Seal loan: S. P. 14/45/119; Delaval Papers, Box 17 K.

15. S. P. 14/10/43.

16. S. P. 14/5/58; S. P. 15/6/179; Hist. MSS. Com., *Salisbury*, XV, 46.

17. Vetera Indictamenta, f.18d.

18. C 181/1 fos.56, 88d; S. P. 14/2/5; S. P. 14/5/59; S. P. 14/10/43; Hist. MSS. Com., *Salisbury*, XV, 257, 260; Rymer, *Foedera*, XVI, 510; George Ridpath, *The Border History of England and Scotland* (1776), 483.

19. G. C. Williamson, *George, Third Earl of Cumberland, 1558–1605* (1920), *passim*; George Cokayne, *The Complete Peerage of England, Scotland and*

Ireland (13 vols, rev. edn, 1949), III, 568; Oliver Lawson (ed.), *Aubrey's Brief Lives* (Ann Arbor, Michigan, 1949), 65–6; Lawrence Stone, *The Crisis of the Aristocracy, 1558–1641* (1965), 163–4; *Acts of the Privy Council, 1601–4*, 495. See also R. T. Spence, 'The Cliffords, earls of Cumberland, 1579–1646: a study of their fortune based on their household and estate accounts', unpublished Ph. D. dissertation, University of London, 1960.

20. S. P. 14/10/43.
21. S. P. 14/5/58.
22. S. P. 14/6/43.
23. Vetera Indictamenta, f.57d and *passim*.
24. Hist. MSS. Com., *Salisbury*, XVI, 376, 457–60; *D. N. B.* See also Ralph Winwood, *Memorials of Affairs of State in the Reigns of Queen Elizabeth and King James I*, ed. Edmund Sawyer (1725), II, 44.
25. S. P. 14/3/87; S. P. 14/5/4; S. P. 14/5/5; S. P. 14/5/7; Hist. MSS. Com., *Salisbury*, XV, 345; XVI, 4, 13, 30, 171, 345, 376.
26. Joseph Tanner (ed.), *Constitutional Documents of the Reign of James I* (1930), 27; *Workes of James . . . King of Great Britaine, op. cit.*, 485–97.
27. 1 James I, c. 2, *Statutes of the Realm*, IV, ii, 1018–19; James Spedding (ed.), *Life of Francis Bacon* (2 vols, 1878), I, 456; Strype, *op. cit.*, IV, 540.
28. S. P. 14/9/87. See also Sta. Cha. 8 249/2.
29. S. P. 14/9/87; Rymer, *Foedera*, XVI, 603.
30. S. P. 14/9/87.
31. S. P. 14/6/42; S. P. 14/10B/38; S. P. 14/10B/39; S. P. 14/10B/40.
32. Hist. MSS. Com., *Salisbury*, XVI, 405.
33. *Cal. S. P. Dom., 1603–10*, 10, 13; *Statutes of the Realm*, IV, ii, 1016; Raine, *op. cit.*, 32–3; *D. N. B.*; John Nichols, *The Progresses, Processions and Magnificent Festivities of James I* (4 vols, 1828), II, 44n.
34. S. P. 14/3/85; S. P. 14/9/98; S. P. 14/61/4; E 112/112/169; B. M. Add. MS. 38139; Raine, *op. cit.*, 28–9; Hodgson, II, i, 77; Hist. MSS. Com., *Salisbury*, XVI, 78; *Cal. S. P. Dom., 1603–10*, 64, 76, 91, 148, 177; N. C. H., XIII, 472; John Scott, *Berwick-upon-Tweed: the history of the town and guild* (1888), 189; Sanderson, *passim*; Frederick Devon, *Issues of the Exchequer* (1836), 14; F. H. Mares (ed.), *The Memoirs of Robert Carey* (1972), 67.
35. Hist. MSS. Com., *Salisbury*, XVII, 168–9, 394; XVIII, 369.
36. *Ibid.*, XVII, 13–14.
37. Pennington-Ramsden MS. fos.1–3d; S. P. 14/12/57; Hist. MSS. Com., *Salisbury*, XVII, 81; *Cal. S. P. Dom., 1603–10*, 202.
38. S. P. 14/10B/38; S. P. 14/10B/39; S. P. 14/10B/40.
39. Pennington-Ramsden MS. fos.1–2.
40. *Ibid.*, fos.3d–4d.
41. S. P. 14/12/65; S. P. 15/36/7.
42. S. P. 59/30/125; N. C. H., II, 354; Talbot, 151. See also Sta. Cha. 8 261/20; Sta. Cha. 8 257/10; Sta. Cha. 8 152/18; C 2 S/8/13.
43. S. P. 13/F/11; C 181/1 fos.10, 55; N. C. H., IX, 91–2, 169sqq.; C. H. Hunter Blair, 'The Sheriffs of Northumberland to 1603', *Arch. Aeliana*, 4th ser., xx (1942), 88.

44. Deleval Papers, letter 26.
45. S. P. 14/17/16; *List of Sheriffs*, 28; *Visitations, 1615, 1666*, 23. See also Syon MSS. O I, 2 d; L. C. Duke of Nd's MSS. Aln. 4 9a/23/6 f.123; Pennington-Ramsden MS. f.47d; N. C. H., II, 95; Joseph Nicholson and Richard Burn, *The History and Antiquities of the Counties of Westmorland and Cumberland* (2 vols, 1777), II, 95; M. E. James (ed.), *Estate Accounts of the Earls of Northumberland, 1562–1637* (Surtees Society, CLXIII, 1948), 167, 173; C. B. Phillips, 'County Committees and Local Government in Cumberland and Westmorland, 1642–60', *Northern History*, v (1970), 47–48; James Wilson (ed.), *Victoria County History of Cumberland* (1905), II, 320.
46. There are two copies of Pennington's record of this correspondence. The one which we used, the Pennington-Ramsden MS., is in the Cumbria County Record Office in Carlisle. The other is on deposit in the John Rylands Library, Manchester. These MSS. have been calendared in Hist. MSS. Com., *10th Report*, Appendix 7, Muncaster MSS.
47. Pennington-Ramsden MS. fos.1, 3, 5, 15; S. P. 14/6/42; S. P. 14/12/58; Hist. MSS. Com., *Salisbury*, XVII, 132, 151; Thomas I. Rae, *The Administration of the Scottish Frontier, 1513–1603* (1966), 55.
48. Pennington-Ramsden MS. fos.33d, 30d–31, 34; S. P. 14/5/59; Hist. MSS. Com., *Salisbury*, XVII, 410.
49. Pennington-Ramsden MS. fos.30d, 31, 33d–34; Hist. MSS. Com., *Salisbury* XVII, 400, 410. See also Vetera Indictamenta, f.54; Pennington-Ramsden MS. fos.70d, 184; Hist. MSS. Com., *Salisbury*, XVIII, 212.
50. Pennington-Ramsden MS. f.25; Hist. MSS. Com., *Salisbury*, XVI, 393; Nicholson and Burn, *op. cit.*, I, cxii. See also T. H. B. Graham, 'The Border Grahams', *Trans. Cumberland and Westmorland Antiquarian and Archaeological Soc.*, new ser., XI (1912); John Graham, *The Condition of the Border at the Union; Destruction of the Graham Clan* (1907).
51. Pennington-Ramsden MS. fos.15, 18–19; Hist. MSS. Com., *Salisbury*, XVII, 132, 238, 289, 308, 310, 382.
52. Thomas Garden Barnes, *Somerset 1625–40, a County's Government during the 'Personal Rule'* (1961), 82sqq.; William S. Holdsworth, *A History of English Law* (15 vols, 1922–65), IV, 146; Alexander Hamilton, *Quarter Sessions from Queen Elizabeth to Queen Anne* (1878), 67–9.
53. Hist. MSS. Com., *Salisbury*, XVII, 382, 427–8.
54. Pennington-Ramsden MS. f.88.
55. David Harris Willson, *King James VI and I* (1956), 223.
56. James (ed.), *op. cit.*, xxiii–xxiv.
57. S. P. 14/216/79. According to Kentish legend Sir William's wife Dorothy, who had returned to Kent, knew of the plot well before 4 November. In a piece of "curious" needlework she "disclosed that plot which had it taken, Rome had triumphed and Britain's wall had shaken": J. Oldric Scott, 'Ightham Mote House and Church', *Arch. Cantiana*, XIV (1900), 193.
58. Folger Library, Cecil MSS. 113/7; S. P. 14/16/64; Hist. MSS. Com., *Salisbury*, XVII, 483, 495.
59. Pennington-Ramsden MS. fos.47d, 51–51d; S. P. 14/15/106; Delaval Papers,

Box 17 N; J. M. W. Bean, *The Estates of the Percy Family, 1416–1537* (1958), 164.

60. Pennington-Ramsden MS. f.45. But according to the records of the Northumberland clerk of the peace the crime rate was declining: Vetera Indictamenta, *passim*.

61. Pennington-Ramsden MS. f.1.

62. *Ibid.*, fos.6, 9d–11, 149d; S. P. 14/14/10; S. P. 14/14/11; Hist. MSS. Com., *Salisbury*, XVII, 191; *Cal. S. P. Dom.*, 1603–10, 217. See also Sta. Cha. 8 249/2.

63. Pennington-Ramsden MS. f.45; S. P. 14/16/72. Sessions 10 May 1605; Vetera Indictamenta, f.40d; Pennington-Ramsden MS. f.183d; Hist. MSS. Com., *Salisbury*, XVIII, 212. Session in June 1605: Vetera Indictamenta, f.38. Session in Nov. 1605: Pennington-Ramsden MS. fos.45, 183d; Vetera Indictamenta, f.50.

64. S. P. 14/20/48.

65. S. P. 14/216/79; Pennington-Ramsden MS f.47; S. P. 14/16/106; Martin, 212, 167; Hist. MSS. Com., *Salisbury*, XVII, 519.

66. Sanderson, 105, 116.

67. Vetera Indictamenta, f.46d; S. P. 14/20/48 I; Pennington-Ramsden MS. f.103d; Talbot, 153. Henry Guevera was the younger brother of John Guevera: Bruce Dickens, 'The Gueveras of Stenigot: Spanish Squires in Tudor Lincolnshire', *Bulletin of Hispanic Studies*, XXXVII (October 1960), 218sqq.

68. Pennington-Ramsden MS. fos.70–1, 78, 184–4d; S. P. 14/18/40; S. P. 14/19/10; Hist. MSS. Com., *Salisbury*, XVIII, 78–9, 212–13.

69. From internal evidence it would appear that Roger Widdrington wrote this letter between 21 January and 2 February 1606: Hist. MSS. Com., *Salisbury*, XVIII, 457–60.

70. *List of Sheriffs*, 99.

71. S. P. 14/21/10.

72. Pennington-Ramsden MS. fos.88–88d.

73. *Ibid.*, fos.88d–89.

74. *Ibid.*, f.91d.

75. *Ibid.*, fos.108, 185; S. P. 14/21/8.

76. S. P. 14/21/9. It appears that Widdrington and his three immediate predecessors did account to the exchequer at the ends of their terms of office. Accounts for all these sheriffs who served between 1594 and 1602 were rendered together: *List of Sheriffs*, 99.

77. S. P. 14/20/48; Pennington-Ramsden MS. fos.107d–8.

78. S. P. 14/21/10.

79. Pennington-Ramsden MS. f.103d; S. P. 14/21/8. See also Pennington-Ramsden MS. f.83d.

80. Hist. MSS. Com., *Salisbury*, XVIII, 186–7; 3 James I, c. 27, *Statutes of the Realm*, IV, ii, 1126sqq.

81. Pennington-Ramsden MS. f.124.

82. *Ibid.*, f.131.

83. *Ibid.*, f.156.

84. *Ibid.*, f.164. In 1600 Salkeld was said to be one of the leaders of Francis Dacre's anti-Howard party: S. P. 59/39/1242.
85. Cecil MSS. 119/143.
86. *Workes of James . . . King of Great Britaine, op. cit.*, 517.
87. Cecil MSS. 119/143.
88. *Ibid.*, 115/55; C 181/2 f.4; Pennington-Ramsden MS. fos.128, 136–7; Hist. MSS. Com., *Salisbury*, XIX, 6, 29, 31, 51. For a list of the 68 malefactors brought to justice by Lord William Howard see Ornsby, 463–5.
89. 3 & 4 James I, c. 5.
90. S. P. 14/24/18; Pennington-Ramsden MS. f.162d. Dunbar had held a commission of oyer and terminer for County Durham since 19 September 1606: C 181/2 f.50d.
91. Hist. MSS. Com., *Salisbury*, XIX, 11–12. See also Pennington-Ramsden MS. f.175d.
92. Pennington-Ramsden MS. fos.175d, 176.
93. Vetera Indictamenta, f.68d; Cecil MSS. 120/164.
94. Cecil MSS. 120/164.
95. *Ibid.*, 120/162.
96. Pennington-Ramsden MS. f.103; S. P. 14/27/23. In November King James had dismissed Widdrington from the captaincy of Tynemouth Castle and gave the post to Sir William Selby of Branxton: S. P. 15/38/86.
97. Cecil MSS. 124/168. See also S. P. 15/38/86.
98. Cecil MSS. 121/86. David H. Willson (ed.), *The Parliamentary Diary of Robert Bowyer, 1606–1607* (Minneapolis, 1931), 353.
99. S. P. 14/27/42; S. P. 15/36/93; Willson (ed.), *Bowyer*, 314–19; Samuel R. Gardiner, *History of England from the Accession of James I to the Outbreak of the Civil War, 1603–42* (10 vols, 1883), I, 338–9.
100. Cecil MSS. 121/86.
101. *Journals of the House of Commons*, I, 377.
102. *Ibid.*, I, 375; Willson (ed.), *Bowyer*, 296, 302.
103. *Journals of the House of Commons*, I, 385.
104. 4 James I, c. 1, *Statutes of the Realm*, IV, ii, 1134–7. For a general discussion of some of the parliamentary aspects of the proposed union see Wallace Notestein, *The House of Commons, 1604–1610* (1971), chapter III.
105. *Statutes of the Realm*, IV, ii, 1134–7; Holdsworth, *op. cit.*, I, 336.
106. *Ibid.*, I, 332; David Ogg, *England in the Reign of Charles II* (2 vols, 1956), II, 519. 16–17 Charles II, c. 5 required jurors to be £20 freeholders.
107. Cecil MSS. 124/168.
108. Norman McClure (ed.), *The Letters of John Chamberlain* (American Philosophical Society Memoirs, XII, pts 1–11; Philadelphia, 1939), I, 294. See also Cecil MSS. 121/129.
109. The letter which Roger wrote to his brother describing the gaol delivery of 20 January 1606 fell into government hands in October: Hist. MSS. Com., *Salisbury*, XVIII, 333, 457–60.
110. *Ibid.*, XIX, 507.
111. *Ibid.*, XIX, 239; S. P. 14/88/128; Cecil MSS. 122/55; L. R. 2/223 f.227.

112. S. P. 59/40/1434; C 181/2 f.12d; N. C. H., XI, 396.
113. Talbot, 152.
114. Hist. MSS. Com., *Salisbury*, XIX, 254.
115. Vetera Indictamenta, *passim*.
116. Hist. MSS. Com., *Salisbury*, XIX, 254. See also *ibid.*, XIX, 307, 425.
117. Vetera Indictamenta, *passim*.
118. C 181/2 fos.48, 50d; S. P. 38/8.
119. C 181/2 f.50d; N. C. H., IX, 171.
120. C 181/2 f.50d. Also included in this commission were five active members of the Council of the North and Bishop James of Durham, an *ex officio* member of the Council: *ibid.*; S. P. 14/27/24; Vetera Indictamenta, fos.75, 91d.
121. Pennington was still active in county affairs; he served as sheriff of Cumberland in 1610: *List of Sheriffs*, 28.
122. *Register of the Privy Council of Scotland, 1610–13*, 128–9.
123. Syon MSS. P II, 3 d.
124. Cecil MSS. 121/4; 123/1.
125. *Ibid.*, 123/1; 123/118; 124/129; 124/130; Vetera Indictamenta, f.75d.
126. Cecil MSS. 122/136.
127. *Ibid.*, 123/118.
128. Ornsby, 420.
129. Cecil MSS. 123/106; 123/107; 123/108; 123/109; S. P. 38/8. The names of some of the Northumberland men who later returned home without licence are found in S. P. 14/103/68 I (1618). For reactions at Court to the impressment see Cecil MSS. 123/25; 124/86. For shire levies 1585–1602 see C. G. Cruikshank, *Elizabeth's Army* (1966), 291.
130. Cecil MSS. 112/136.
131. *Cal. S. P. Dom., 1603–10*, 438, 440; Frederick Devon, *Issues of the Exchequer* (1836), 111.
132. Each deputy commissioner was granted an annual stipend of 100 marks: Devon, *op. cit.*, 127; *Cal. S. P. Dom., 1603–10*, 440. Pickering was sheriff of Cumberland in 1606, 1607 and 1611, knight of the shire in 1597–8: *List of Sheriffs*, 28; *V. C. H., Cumberland*, II, 320.
133. Syon MSS. Q II, 66; Mark Girouard, *Robert Smythson and the Architecture of the Elizabeth Era* (1966), 33–4.
134. Vetera Indictamenta, f.91.
135. Robert Chambers (ed.), *Domestic Annals of Scotland* (1859), I, 423.
136. S. P. 14/48/25; S. P. 14/33; Vetera Indictament, f.83; *D. N. B.*
137. In 1609 the Parliament of Scotland established the office of J. P.: Gordon Donaldson, *Scotland, James V to VII* (1965), 224–5.
138. *Statutes of the Realm*, IV, ii, 1156–7; Elizabeth Read Foster (ed.), *Proceedings in Parliament, 1610* (2 vols, New Haven, 1966), I, 109, 110, 140, 247; II, 251; Gardiner, *op. cit.*, I, 338.
139. 7 James I, c. 23, *Statutes of the Realm*, IV, ii, 1187–1201. Berwick alone was exempt: S. P. 14/56/42; E 179/158/88; Foster, *op. cit.*, II, 286.
140. Some malicious Scotsmen attributed Dunbar's death to poison given to him by the Earl of Salisbury: Raine, *op. cit.*, 33n.
141. S. P. 14/16/74.

142. S. P. 14/88/128. See also Delaval Papers, Box 17 K; S. P. 14/97/37.
143. Vetera Indictamenta, *passim*. See Appendix 1.
144. Vetera Indictamenta, *passim*.
145. *Workes of James . . . King of Great Britaine, op. cit.*, 517–18.

Chapter 8

1. Sanderson, 115.
2. L. R. 2/223 f.61; E 164/37 f.379.
3. S. P. 14/6/42; Hist. MSS. Com., *Salisbury*, XVI, 8.
4. Sanderson, *passim*; L. R. 2/223, *passim*. Cf. R. H. Tawney, *The Agrarian Problem in the Sixteenth Century* (new edn, New York, 1967), 25, 422, which gives figures based on a much smaller number of manors. The number of cottagers is probably greatly underestimated for such people were rarely recorded in official surveys.
5. David H. Willson (ed.), *The Parliamentary Diary of Robert Bowyer, 1606–7* (Minneapolis, 1931), 318.
6. S. P. 16/357/27. William was Sir Henry's son and heir.
7. Gordon R. Batho, 'The Finances of an Elizabethan Nobleman: Henry Percy, Ninth Earl of Northumberland', *Ec. H. R.*, 2nd ser., IX no. 3 (1957), 433–50; M. E. James (ed.), *Estate Accounts of the Earls of Northumberland, 1562–1637* (Surtees Society, CLXIII, 1948), xxiii–xxiv. See also the earl's own statements in his *Advice to his Son* (ed. G. B. Harrison, 1930), 82–3.
8. E 164/37 f.109. For a discussion of the development, theory and practice of the custom of Cockermouth *c.* 1570 see M. E. James, 'The Concept of Order and the Northern Rising 1569', *Past and Present*, LX (August 1973), 63–8.
9. S. P. 14/17/16.
10. James (ed.), *Estate Accounts*, xxxix and *passim*.
11. N. C. H., II, 385; Lawrence Stone, *The Crisis of the Aristocracy, 1558–1641* (1965), 316–17.
12. Stone, *op. cit.*, 314–16. For a discussion of the merits of leases with economic rents compared with leases and copies with high fines and low rents see *ibid.*, 313–22.
13. Syon MSS. Q VII, 1.
14. Syon MSS. Q II, 53.
15. Syon MSS. Q XI, 30, quoted in N.C.H., VIII, 238, where it has been the cause of considerable confusion; it is most unlikely that this document refers to Tynemouthshire.
16. N. C. H., II, 384.
17. Syon MSS. R II, 5 d.
18. Syon MSS. Q I, 46; C 2 1/6/28; E 164/37 f.128d. Some Rothbury copyholders had already taken leases; Syon MSS. R V, 1 b.
19. Syon MSS. Q I, 46.
20. Syon MSS. Q II, 97. Whitehead makes it clear that the Hunter case did not involve authentic tenant-right, a term used loosely by Fotherley and some modern historians, i.e. James (ed.), *Estate Accounts*, xliii. See S. J. Watts,

'Tenant-Right in Early Seventeenth Century Northumberland', *Northern History*, VI (1971), 84–5.

21. Syon MSS. Q I, 46.
22. Syon MSS. P X, 2 i.
23. Syon MSS. Q II, 97.
24. See chapter 9, pp. 184–5.
25. Syon MSS. Q II, 98.
26. *Ibid.*; Gordon R. Batho (ed.), *The Household Papers of Henry Percy Ninth Earl of Northumberland, 1554–1632* (Camden Society, 3rd ser., XCIII, 1962), XXV.
27. N. C. H., II, 427–8.
28. Syon MSS. P II, 1 1. These instructions were repeated in February 1619: Syon MSS. P II, 1 i.
29. Syon MSS. Q III, 10.
30. L. R. 2/223 fos.286, 295, 297, 299, 301, 306, 308–11. An accounting unit distinct and separate from the rest of Northumberland, Tynemouthshire contributed substantially to the earl's landed income. His receivers collected £698 17s. 5d. from Tynemouthshire in 1608, compared to £1,063 14s. 8d. from Northumberland proper: James (ed.), *Estate Accounts*, 221 and *passim*; Batho (ed.), *op. cit.*, 435.
31. L. R. 2/223 f.327. This area included Tynemouth Town, North Shields and the Seven Towns of Earsdon, Monkseaton, Whitley, Preston, Backworth, East Chirton and Murton.
32. *Ibid.*, fos.10, 136.
33. S. P. 14/49/14. See also Syon MSS. Q XI, 31.
34. S. P. 14/49/14; L. R. 2/223 fos.6–7, 130–2, 274sqq.; N. C. H., VIII, 238–9.
35. L. R. 2/223 f.326; N. C. H., VIII, 293–8.
36. L. R. 2/223 f.231. The survey of the regality, formerly belonging to the archbishop of York, included Hexham town, Hexhamshire, East Errington, Keepwick and Heselden and the grieveships of Allendale Town, East Allendale, West Allendale, Catton, Keenley, Wall and Acomb: *ibid.*, fos.138–232.
37. E 134, 9 James I, Mich. 22. Although some of the customary tenants in Wall and Acomb claimed tenant-right in 1608 this form of tenure was not at issue: *ibid.*; L. R. 2/223 fos.212, 218.
38. Spec. Coll. 2/195/114; N. C. H., IV, 137.
39. N. C. H., III, 59–60.
40. Joan Thirsk (ed.), *The Agrarian History of England and Wales*, vol. IV, *1500–1640* (1965), xxxiv–xxxv, 2, 109, 160.
41. Syon MSS. P II, 2 r; O II, 2 b. See also Hist. MSS. Com., *Salisbury*, XI, 393.
42. Sanderson, 94, 98. The same discrepancy was found in rents paid by customary tenants in the manor of Wark: *ibid.*, 61.
43. *Ibid.*, 104, 109.
44. S. P. 14/9A/98.
45. Syon MSS. P IX, 1 a.
46. Syon MSS. P IX, 1 b. See also Alnwick MSS. Q III, 1 p; Syon MSS. Q II, 105; P II, 2 r; James (ed.), *Estate Accounts*, 197.

47. Hodgson, II, iii, 414; James (ed.), *Estate Accounts*, 165, 172; Sanderson, 55.
48. Syon MSS. Q X, 2.
49. Syon MSS. Q X, 3.
50. Syon MSS. P II, 2 r.
51. Syon MSS. Q X, 5; Q II, 70.
52. Syon MSS. Q II, 75; Q II, 72.
53. L. C. Duke of Nd's MSS. Aln. 4 9a/23/6 f.139.
54. Syon MSS. P X, 2 i.
55. Syon MSS. Q II, 98. See also Q X, 3.
56. Syon MSS. R IX, 1 a.
57. H. G. Ramm, R. W. McDowall and Eric Mercer, *Shielings and Bastles* (1970), xii, 3; John Walton (ed.), *National Forest and Park Guides: the Border* (1962), chapter on the Border Forests by H. L. Edlin.
58. Syon MSS. Q II, 146. For a fuller discussion of the tenant-right controversy see Watts, *op. cit.*
59. S. P. 14/187/84.
60. Joseph Nicholson and Richard Burn, *The History and Antiquities of the Counties of Westmorland and Cumberland* (2 vols, 1777), I, 56.
61. Syon MSS. P I, 3 n; S. P. 14/154/11.
62. Nicholson and Burn, *op. cit.*, I, 56–9.
63. Hodgson, II, i, 78.
64. E 112/113/211. For Wark see E 124/16/52 d; E 124/16/98 d; E 112/112/ 195.
65. E 124/31/12; E 124/33/24 d.
66. E 124/31/135 d; E 124/33/25, in which the Ridleys and other tenants in Wark compounded with Roger Widdrington, Lord Walden's agent.
67. Syon MSS. P IX, 2 a.
68. R. W. Hodgson (ed.), 'A Rental of the Principality of Redesdale, copied from an Original Roll in the possession of William John Charlton', *Arch. Aeliana*, II (1832), 337.
69. Syon MSS. P IX, 2 a. In 1604 the surveyors had calculated that the whole of the manor ought to yield £766 11s. 9d. p. a.: Sanderson, 75.
70. Syon MSS. P IX, 3 a.
71. E 112/228/26.
72. N. C. H., XII, 191.
73. Thirsk (ed.), *op. cit.*, 27.
74. *Ibid.*, 210–11.
75. N. R. O., Thomas Delaval's Book, fos.3, 7, 12, 22, 23; N. C. H., IX, 125.
76. Syon MSS. R V, 1 g. See also Q VII, 3; C 2 1/6/28.
77. Syon MSS. Q II, 32.
78. Syon MSS. Q II, 44.
79. Syon MSS. Q VII, 1.
80. Syon MSS. Q II, 83.
81. Syon MSS. P X, 2 i.
82. L. R. 2/223 fos.114–16.
83. *Ibid.*, f.85; E 134, 17 James I, Mich. 24; E 179/158/88.

84. Syon MSS. P II, 2 u.
85. The fields of Tynemouth, Whitley, Preston, Monkseaton, Backworth and Earsdon were enclosed in the mid-seventeenth century: N. C. H., VIII, 265, 397, 345, 406, 244. Other enclosure dates are as follows: Thirston, 1657: *ibid.*, VIII, 314; Embleton, 1730: *ibid.*, II, 45; Acklington division into north and south sides, 1702; *ibid.*, V, 372; Shilbottle, 1758: *ibid.*, V, 430; Birling, by the end of the seventeenth century: *ibid.*, V, 202; Rennington, 1707: *ibid.*, II, 159; South Charlton divided into two, 1685: *ibid.*, II, 308; Hauxley, open until 1640: *ibid.*, V, 302–3; Bamburgh, 1896 still refers to "common fields": *ibid.*, I, 114; Budle, mention of "town fields" in 1659: *ibid.*, I, 197; Swinhoe, near Beadnell, enclosed 1731: *ibid.*, I, 339; Benwell, still unenclosed in 1637: *ibid.*, XIII, 231; Newton-by-the-Sea, near Embleton, divided 1725: *ibid.*, II, 98; Ellingham, divided into two parts *c.* 1685: *ibid.*, II, 308; Acomb, Hexhamshire, enclosed 1649: *ibid.*, IV, 140; Birtley, open until 1750: *ibid.*, IV, 357; Stamfordham, unenclosed in 1680: *ibid.*, XII, 319.
86. *Ibid.*, XII, 184.
87. Syon MSS. Q VIII, 7; N. C. H., XII, 157.
88. Syon MSS. Q VIII, 1.
89. N. C. H., XII, 141–2.
90. Syon MSS. P I, 1 a; R II, 18 b; N. C. H., II, 368–9.
91. Sta. Cha. 8 90/7.
92. Sta. Cha. 8 152/23.
93. Sta. Cha. 8 261/19; Sta. Cha. 8 261/20; C 2 F/1/14; C 2 F/8/60.
94. James Balfour (ed.), *Annals of Scotland* (4 vols, 1924), II, 16. But Stone puts Lord Gray of Wark down as having a gross rental in the £2,200–£4,399 range in 1641: *op. cit.*, 761.
95. N. C. H., XIV, 230.
96. Syon MSS. P X, 2 i.
97. Syon MSS. P II, 13 a; Alnwick MSS. Q III, 2 f.
98. James (ed.), *Estate Accounts*, xxxix.
99. Stone, *op. cit.*, 772.
100. C 3 327/50; Ornsby, 4, 69, 119, 186, 212, 224–5. Penry Williams has pointed out the inconsistencies in the printed household books: 'The Northern Borderlands under the Early Stuarts', in *Historical Essays 1600–1750 Presented to David Ogg*, ed. H. E. Bell and R. L. Ollard (1963), 6. For Howard's relations with the burgessess of Morpeth see Durham University, Department of Paleography and Diplomatic, Howard Family Documents . . . formerly at Naworth Castle', Cottingwood 22 a; Hodgson, II, ii, 517.
101. Quoted by Mark Girouard, *Robert Smythson and the Architecture of the Elizabethan Era* (1966), 33–4.
102. Nikolaus Pevsner, *The Buildings of England: Northumberland* (1957), 137.
103. N. C. H., IX, 178–9.
104. *Ibid.*, XIV, 334; Pevsner, *op. cit.*, 124–5.
105. *Ibid.*, 126. See also C. J. Bates, *The Border Holds of Northumberland* (Arch. Aeliana, N. S. XIV, 1891), 413.
106. N. C. H., X, 277, 286–91. See also B. W. Barley, 'Rural Housing in England', 707–8 in Thirsk (ed.), *op. cit.*

107. N. C. H., XV, 376sqq.
108. *Ibid.*, X, 329–30; XII, 211, 341; Pevsner, *op. cit.*, 319.
109. Ramm *et al.*, *op. cit.*, 66–8.
110. *Wills and Inventories*, IV, 114.
111. *Ibid.*, IV, 235.
112. *Ibid.*, IV, 287sqq.
113. Thomas Delaval's Book, f.208, quoted in N. C. H., IX, 158.
114. *Wills and Inventories*, IV, 287.
115. *Ibid.*, IV, 237.
116. Frontispiece in Ornsby.
117. Thomas Delaval's Book, f.208.

Chapter 9

1. Quoted by Gertrude Himmelfarb in *Victorian Minds* (New York, 1968), 184.
2. S. P. 14/65/10; Vetera Indictamenta, *passim*; Sta. Cha. 8 200/12. For an example of standards elsewhere see F. G. Emmison, *Elizabethan Life; Disorder* (1970).
3. S. P. 14/63/99 I; S. P. 14/63/99; S. P. 14/63/99 II; S. P. 14/64/2.
4. The other commissioners were Sir Wilfrid Lawson, Christopher Pickering, Bishop Robinson of Carlisle and Bishop James of Durham: C 181/2 f. 137d. The two bishops served without pay: Frederick Devon, *Issues of the Exchequer* (1836), 127.
5. S. P. 14/63/12.
6. S. P. 14/63/13.
7. S. P. 14/65/17. The Scottish members of this new commission were William Lord Cranston, Sir Gideon Murray, Sir William Seton and Sir David Murray.
8. S. P. 14/64/18; S. P. 14/64/55.
9. S. P. 14/65/17.
10. S.P. 14/71/21. For Lawson, Fenwick and Hutton's rebuttal see S. P. 14/71/27. As the Scots intimated, Selby was absent in Kent.
11. Vetera Indictamenta, *passim*; Appendix 1.
12. Samuel R. Gardiner, *History of England from the Accession of James I to the Outbreak of the Civil War, 1603-42* (10 vols, 1883), II, 168–86. For more recent accounts of this see Vernon Snow, *Essex the Rebel* (Lincoln, Nebraska, 1970), 49sqq.; G. P. V. Akrigg, *Jacobean Pageant; the Court of King James I* (Cambridge, Mass., 1962), 177sqq.
13. Hodgson, II, i, 78; see also Lawrence Stone, *Family and Fortune: studies in aristocratic finance in the sixteenth and seventeenth centuries* (1973) 285, 289.
14. S. P. 14/67/163; Martin, 87, 222.
15. John Nichols, *The Progresses, Processions and Magnificent Festivities of King James I* (4 vols, 1828), III, 391–2n.
16. *Ibid.*, II, 341n.
17. D. N. B., Clifford.
18. *Acts of the Privy Council, 1613–14,* 595–6.
19. C 181/2 f.215d.

20. For an account of the dispute between Sir Ralph Gray and Sir George Selby over one of the Northumberland seats, see William W. Bean, *The Parliamentary Representation of the Six Northern Counties of England* (1890), 470; *Journals of the House of Commons*, I, 457, 458, 494, 495; Hodgson, I, i, 377; Norman McClure (ed.), *The Letters of John Chamberlain* (American Philosophical Society Memoirs, XII, Philadelphia, 1939) I, 151; C. H. Hunter Blair, 'Members of Parliament for Northumberland and Newcastle upon Tyne', *Arch. Aeliana*, 4th ser., XXIII (1945), 110.
21. *Statutes of the Realm*, IV, ii, 1156–7.
22. Vetera Indictamenta, *passim*; Appendix 1 A, 1 B.
23. *Ibid.*; Bowden in Joan Thirsk (ed.), *The Agrarian History of England and Wales*, IV, *1500–1640* (1967), 826; *Wills and Inventories*, IV, 47, 94.
24. Syon MSS. R V, 1 d; Vetera Indictamenta, f.135d; C 4211/97; *Cal. S. P. Dom.*, *1611–18*, 292; Hist. MSS. Com., *Salisbury*, XVIII, 485. See also Syon MSS. Q II, 84; P II, 2 s; Sta. Cha. 8 295/20; C 2 0/1/30.
25. For Craddock see Vetera Indictamenta, f.139 and *passim*; Ornsby, 421n; John and J. A. Venn, *Alumni Cantabrigienses* (pt I, 4 vols, 1922–7), I, i, 411.
26. C 2 C/21/14.
27. S. P. 14/80/116. See also S. P. 14/21/10 I; Hist. MSS. Com., *Salisbury*, XVII, 568–9.
28. C 181/2 f.236d; S. P. 14/86/125.
29. There is an extensive literature about Somerset's fall. See for example Gardiner, *op. cit.*, II, 331sqq.; Akrigg, *op. cit.*, 190sqq.
30. For an example of evidence from the North see Henry Sanderson of Brancepeth's letter, S. P. 14/83/37.
31. Mary F. Keeler, *The Long Parliament, 1640–1, a Biographical Study of its Members* (Philadelphia, 1954), 86; Joseph Foster (ed.), *Alumni Oxonienses, 1500–1714* (1891), I, 23.
32. Venn, *op. cit.*, I, iii, 219. By 1616 Morton had undoubtedly lost his "wits and memory": see S. P. 14/87/15, S. P. 14/87/14, printed in Ornsby, 427–30. Cf. J. S. Cockburn, *A History of the English Assizes 1558–1714* (1972), 224–5.
33. Keeler, *op. cit.*, 86; Richard Welford, *Men of Mark 'Twixt Tyne and Tweed*, (3 vols, 1895), I, 74.
34. S. P. 14/86/125; *List of Sheriffs*, 99.
35. Ornsby, 417–18. During the last quarter of 1615 33 criminal incidents were reported in Northumberland; this was the highest quarterly total since 1603: Vetera Indictamenta, *passim*.
36. Ornsby, 417–18.
37. S. P. 14/86/45.
38. *Acts of the Privy Council, 1615–16*, 404–7.
39. C 181/2 f.246.
40. S. P. 14/86/113; S. P. 14/86/125. See also S. P. 14/80/116.
41. S. P. 14/86/113. See also S. P. 14/67/162; S. P. 14/67/163; S. P. 14/87/37.
42. S. P. 14/86/113.
43. S. P. 14/86/125.

44. S. P. 14/87/37; S. P. 14/86/136; S. P. 14/87/4. For earlier unsuccessful attempts by Sanderson, Sheffield and Salisbury to implicate Roger Widdrington in the Gunpowder Plot see Hist. MSS. Com., *Salisbury*, XVII, 112, 193, 219, 293.

45. S. P. 14/87/37. See Nikolaus Pevsner, *The Buildings of England: Northumberland* (1957), 137.

46. Two unsigned and undated letters alleging that Lord William entertained Thomas Percy at Naworth in 1605 and charging Howard and his officers in Cumberland with treasonable activity should probably be dated April 1616: S. P. 14/40/11; S. P. 14/86/34.

47. S. P. 14/86/136.

48. For Copeman, a retired thief and former recusant, see S. P. 14/87/3; Martin, 232; Vetera Indictamenta, f.45d; Delaval Papers, 'A book of examinations touching Mr William Delaval's death', extracts printed in N. C. H., VIII, 172; A. L. Rowse, *The Expansion of Elizabethan England* (1955), 13.

49. S. P. 14/87/3; S. P. 14/87/4; S. P. 14/87/5.

50. S. P. 14/87/14; S. P. 14/87/15; S. P. 14/87/37; S. P. 14/89/30; *Acts of the Privy Council, 1615–16*, 566, 631.

51. Vetera Indictamenta, f.158d. Crane served as a grand juror in October 1611 and October 1613: *ibid.*, fos.109d, 130d. He is mentioned in his father's will: *Wills and Inventories*, III, 97.

52. S. P. 14/87/4; *Acts of the Privy Council, 1615–16*, 629.

53. S. P. 14/87/5; S. P. 14/87/37; S. P. 14/89/30; Hist. MSS. Com., *Buccleuch MSS.*, 174–5.

54. S. P. 14/88/128; C. H. Hunter Blair, 'The Sheriffs of Northumberland, 1603–1942', *Arch. Aeliana*, 4th ser., XXI (1943), 6.

55. S. P. 14/90/157; S. P. 14/90/156; C 4211 (21 July, 1615).

56. Vetera Indictamenta, f.28d and *passim*.

57. *Acts of the Privy Council, 1616–17*, 220; *1617–19*, 16.

58. S. P. 14/92/17 printed in Ornsby, 434–6.

59. Sta. Cha. 8 183/51.

60. Vetera Indictamenta, *passim*.

61. Nichols, *op. cit.*, III, 297, 309.

62. S. P. 14/92/10; Delaval Papers, Box 29 A; *Acts of the Privy Council, 1616–1617*, 260; Ornsby, 219–20.

63. Delaval Papers, Box 17 K.

64. *Ibid.* See also map 3.

65. Delaval Papers, Box 17 K.

66. *Acts of the Privy Council, 1616–17*, 385.

67. S. P. 14/95/19.

68. Robert Steele (ed.), *Tudor and Stuart Proclamations, 1485–1714* (1910), I, 142; Delaval Papers, Box 17 K; *Statutes of the Realm*, II, 575–6; Ornsby, 419; *Acts of the Privy Council, 1616–17*, 381–3. In May 1619 Lord Walden reminded the Privy Council that North and South Tynedale and Redesdale were no longer liberties or privileged places: S. P. 14/109/6.

69. *Acts of the Privy Council, 1616–17*, 380–1.

70. C 4211/116.

71. C 4211/117. Clifford had been added to the Northumberland commission of the peace in December 1617: C 4211/107.
72. Delaval Papers, Box 17 K; S. P. 14/97/37.
73. C 4211/111; Rymer, *Foedera*, XVII, 58, 83. Had he been alive Edward Talbot would have been the 30th English member.
74. Probably William Selby of Branxton and Ightham Mote, sheriff in 1617, rather than William Selby of Shortflatt.
75. Delaval Papers, Box 17 K; *Acts of the Privy Council, 1616–17*, 381–3. The Scottish border garrison was not dissolved until 1621: *Register of the Privy Council of Scotland, 1619–22*, 255.
76. S. P. 14/124/134.
77. *Register of the Privy Council of Scotland, 1619–22*, lxxxiii, 345–6.
78. C 181/2 f.307; C 4211/109; C 4211/111; C 4211/117.
79. C 4211/109; *Acts of the Privy Council, 1616–17*, 381–3.
80. C 4211/110; Steele (ed.), *op. cit.*, I, 142; *Acts of the Privy Council, 1616–17*, 380–3; *1618–19*, 79.
81. S. P. 14/97/34; *Acts of the Privy Council, 1618–19*, 79.
82. *Acts of the Privy Council, 1618–19*, 111; Delaval Papers, Box 29 A. Sheffield had held a session of gaol delivery in Newcastle the day before this letter was written: Delaval Papers, Box 17 K; Sta. Cha. 8 217/29.
83. S. P. 14/97/65.
84. Delaval Papers, Box 17 K; Box 30 L, 12; Box 30 L, 13; Box 30 L, 15; Box 30 L, 46; 'A book of examinations touching Mr William Delaval's death'; S. P. 14/93/10; *Acts of the Privy Council, 1618–19*, 194.
85. Rachel R. Reid, *The King's Council in the North* (1921), 371sqq.
86. Delaval Papers, Box 17 K. The deputy lieutenants were Sir Henry Widdrington, Sir Ralph Delaval and Sir John Fenwick. For a discussion of the role of deputy lieutenants in local government see Thomas Garden Barnes, *Somerset, 1625–40, a County's Government during the 'Personal Rule'* (1961), 102sqq.
87. S. P. 14/97/44; C 4211/109; Rymer, *Foedera*, XVII, 53; *Acts of the Privy Council, 1616–17*, 381–3. Sir Ephraim was recorded as a recusant in 1625 and 1629: S. P. 16/10/64; Martin, 244.
88. See for example *Acts of the Privy Council, 1616–17*, 390, 411, 417; Ornsby, 437, 452–8.
89. Delaval Papers, Box 17 K; S. P. 14/97/17.
90. S. P. 14/97/60; S. P. 14/97/60 I.
91. S. P. 14/97/60; Delaval Papers, Box 17 K.
92. Original returns by Widdrington, 20 October 1618: Delaval Papers, Box 17 K. A similar list was presented at Morpeth on 21 October by Sir John Fenwick: *ibid.* Master list: S. P. 14/103/68.
93. S. P. 14/103/69.
94. Delaval Papers, Box 29 A.
95. *Acts of the Privy Council, 1616–17*, 381; Ornsby, 420.
96. Ornsby, 420.
97. C 4211/161; Delaval Papers, Box 29 A (May 1625); *Acts of the Privy Council, 1623–5*, 212, 372, 467. See also S. P. 16/65/107.

98. In 1623 when Walden, Lord William and the Earl of Northumberland petitioned the king about the tenant-right controversy, Percy noted that Arundel "must be our best help for our redress in this business": Syon MSS. P I, 3 n.

99. Gardiner, *op. cit.*, III, 185–9, 205.

100. *Ibid.*, 208–10; Akrigg, *op. cit.*, 213.

101. *D. N. B.*; Nichols, *op. cit.*, III, 588. See also *Cal. S. P. Venetian, 1628–9*, 213.

102. C 193/13/1; S. P. 16/1/75; Nichols, *op. cit.*, IV, 754.

103. C 181/3 f.83; S. P. 16/34/42; *Acts of the Privy Council, 1621–3*, 38.

104. *Acts of the Privy Council, 1621–3*, 18; *D. N. B.*

105. Delaval Papers, Box 29 A. Keeler suggests that Fenwick succeeded Middleton as sheriff in November 1619: Keeler, *op. cit.*, 174. Ogle received his B. A. from University College, Oxford, and attended Lincoln's Inn: H. A. C. Sturgess (ed.), *The Records of the Honourable Society of Lincoln's Inn, 1420–1799*, 126. For his vendettas with his neighbours see Sta. Cha. 8 34/9; Sta. Cha. 8 225/21; E 123/26/220; E 125/5/241d. Sir Francis Brandling (1595–1640), eldest son and heir of Sir Robert, was the king's host at Alnwick Abbey in May 1617, M. P. for Northumberland in 1624 and 1625, and sheriff in 1625: C 4211/116; Robert Surtees, *The History and Antiquities of the County Palatine of Durham* (4 vols, 1816–40), II, 90; N. C. H., I, 247; Nichols, *op. cit.*, III, 297; Hunter Blair, 'The Sheriffs of Northumberland, 1603–1942', 7; 'Members of Parliament for Northumberland and Newcastle upon Tyne' *op. cit.*, 111.

106. Martin, *passim*. See chapter 4 above, n.54.

107. Wilbur K. Jordan, *The Development of Religious Toleration in England from the Accession of James I to the Convention of the Long Parliament* (reprinted Gloucester, Mass., 1965), 91; *V. C. H., Durham*, II, 41; *D. N. B.*, Neile, Snowden.

108. S. P. 14/109/6.

109. S. P. 14/124/132; E 124/33/25. See also E 134, 18 James I, Easter 13.

110. S. P. 16/12/64.

111. Reid, *op. cit.*, 498.

112. Akrigg, *op. cit.*, 312.

113. Martin, *passim*.

114. Delaval Papers, 17 K.

115. C 4211/193.

116. Delaval Papers, Box 17 K.

117. S. P. 14/149/100.

118. S. P. 14/152/64.

119. S. P. 14/149/100.

120. S. P. 14/143/12 I.

121. S. P. 14/149/100; Delaval Papers, Box 17 K.

122. Rymer, *Foedera*, XVIII, 138.

123. S. P. 14/152/64; Delaval Papers, Box 17 K, letter 5; Wards 5/31; Wards 7/70/192; N. C. H., II, 351; IX, 170, 172.

124. The Crown did not re-establish a functioning Conjunct Commission for the Middle Shires until November 1635: S. P. 16/302/107; S. P. 16/343/75; C 4212/95; C 4212/186; C 4212/205.

125. Delaval Papers, Box 29 A.
126. Hunter MSS. 23, fos.83–108.
127. P. C. 2/48/330 (1637); Hunter MSS. 23, f.109; N. C. H., X, 274; VIII, 307; Barnes, *op. cit.*, 172sqq.; *Cal. S. P. Dom.*, *Charles I, 1635–6*, 135–40; *1636–7*, 41–4; *1637*, 266–75; *1637–8*, 546–8; *1638–9*, 282–5; E. M. Leonard, *The Early History of English Poor Relief* (1900), 184sqq.
128. S. P. 16/7/74 II.
129. *Acts of the Privy Council, 1625–6*, 235.
130. See for example S. P. 16/6/46a; S. P. 16/7/74 II.
131. S. P. 14/143/12 I.
132. S. P. 16/3/107.
133. S. P. 16/6/46.
134. Delaval Papers, Box 30 L, 36.
135. *Ibid.*, Box 17 K.
136. Hist. MSS. Com., *Salisbury*, XVI, 405.

Appendix

1 Incidence of crimes, 1601-17

(a) All crimes

	Livestock theft	Other theft	Crimes of violence	Murder	Misc.	Total
1601	19	1	—	5	1	26
1602	39	4	2	2	2	49
1603	50	2	3	2	2	59
1604	48	3	1	5	2	59
1605	30	4	2	1	2	39
1606	26	5	1	2	6	40
1607	20	5	1	—	6	32
1608	18	3	—	2	2	25
1609	13	3	2	—	7	25
1610	15	2	1	1	7	26
1611	21	5	—	4	7	37
1612	14	3	1	1	4	23
1613	12	—	4	—	3	19
1614	34	2	3	1	7	47
1615	41	3	6	—	9	59
1616	22	7	6	2	—	37
1617	13	—	8	—	8	29

Source: Vetera Indictamenta.

Appendix

(b) Livestock theft

	J	F	M	A	M	J	J	A	S	O	N	D	Total	Livestock theft as % of all crimes
1601	–	–	2	–	–	4	–	–	2	4	6	1	19	72%
1602	4	2	5	–	2	2	3	3	4	3	2	9	39	60
1603	1	3	5	8	2	1	1	2	10	9	7	1	50	84
1604	3	–	–	4	4	2	7	4	4	9	7	4	48	81
1605	–	–	1	1	–	1	1	2	8	4	5	7	30	74
1606	–	2	1	1	3	1	3	2	1	6	5	1	26	65
1607	–	–	–	3	1	2	1	1	5	1	4	2	20	62
1608	1	–	–	1	–	3	4	–	2	3	4	–	18	72
1609	3	–	1	1	1	1	1	3	–	–	2	–	13	52
1610	2	–	–	–	–	2	–	1	1	8	1	–	15	58
1611	–	–	1	1	1	3	3	1	2	3	2	4	21	56
1612	2	2	–	2	1	–	1	1	3	1	1	–	14	61
1613	1	–	2	–	–	–	3	–	2	–	2	2	12	63
1614	–	–	–	1	4	2	2	4	1	5	8	7	34	72
1615	2	–	–	–	2	2	2	3	5	3	13	9	41	70
1616	1	–	1	1	3	3	1	4	2	1	4	1	22	61
1617	–	3	–	–	2	2	1	–	–	1	2	2	13	44

Source: Vetera Indictamenta.

2 Heads of the 89 gentry families in Northumberland in 1615

The figures refer to the National Grid system and enable the gentry residences to be located on the 1″ and ¼″ to the mile Ordnance Survey maps.

1. Alder, Francis   of Alnwick. NU 1813.
2. Armorer, Thomas   of Belford. NU 1034.
3. Aynsley, Gawin   of Shaftoe. NZ 0582.
4. Bates, Thomas   of Holywell. NZ 3174.
5. Bednell, George   of Lemmington. NU 1211.
6. Bell, John   of Bellasis. NZ 1978.
7. Blenkinsopp, George   of Bellister. NY 7063.
8. Blenkinsopp, Thomas   of Blenkinsopp. NY 6664.
9. Bradford, Thomas   of Bradford. NU 1532.
10. Brandling, Robert   of Gosforth. NZ 2368.
11. Burrell, John   of Howtel. NT 8934.
12. Carnaby, John   of Langley. NY 8361.
13. Carnaby, Lancelot   of Halton. NY 9967.
14. Carr, Thomas   of Ford. NT 9437.
15. Carr, William   of Woodhall. NU 1114.
16. Charlton, William   of Hesleyside. NY 8183.
17. Clavering, John   of Callaly. NU 0509.
18. Clennell, Robert   of Clennell. NT 9207.
19. Collingwood, Henry   of Great Ryle. NU 0211.
20. Collingwood, Robert   of Eslington. NU 0412.
21. Collingwood, Thomas   of Little Ryle. NU 0112.
22. Cramlington, Thomas   of Newsham. NZ 3079.
23. Craster, John   of Craster. NU 2519.
24. Delaval, John   of Dissington. NZ 1171.
25. Delaval, Ralph   of Seaton Delaval. NZ 3276.
26. Errington, Anthony   of Denton. NZ 2065.
27. Errington, John   of Errington. NY 9671.
28. Errington, Mark   of Ponteland. NZ 7316.
29. Errington, Mark   of West Denton. NZ 1865.
30. Featherstonehaugh, Albany   of Featherstonehaugh. NY 6761.
31. Fenwick, George   of Brinkburn. NU 1198.
32. Fenwick, George   of East Heddon. NZ 1368.
33. Fenwick, George   of Longshaws. NZ 1288.
34. Fenwick, John   of Butterlaw. NZ 1869.
35. Fenwick, John   of Wallington. NZ 0284.
36. Fenwick, Richard   of Stanton. NZ 1389.
37. Fenwick, William   of Meldon. NZ 1184.
38. Forster, Claudius   of Bamburgh. NU 3518.

39. Forster, John   of Tughall. NU 2126.
40. Forster, Matthew   of Adderstone. NU 1430.
41. Forster, Matthew   of Fleetham. NU 1928.
42. Gray, Edward   of Morpeth. NZ 2086.
43. Gray, Ralph   of Chillingham. NU 0625.
44. Gray, Thomas   of Kyloe. NU 0539.
45. Haggarston, Thomas   of Haggarston. NU 0443.
46. Hebburn, Arthur   of Hepburn. NU 0624.
47. Heron, Cuthbert   of Chipchase. NY 8875.
48. Heron, Richard   of Bockenfield. NU 1797.
49. Hesilrige, Robert   of Swarland. NU 1601.
50. Horsley, Lancelot   of Horsley. NZ 0966.
51. Killingworth, Oliver   of Killingworth. NZ 2870.
52. Lawson, Thomas   of Cramlington. NZ 2677.
53. Lisle, Lancelot   of Newton-on-the-Moor. NU 1905.
54. Loraine, Robert   of Kirkharle. NZ 0182.
55. Middleton, Thomas   of Belsay. NZ 0878.
56. Mitford, Michael   of Seghill. NZ 2974.
57. Mitford, Robert   of Mitford. NZ 1785.
58. Muschamp, George   of Barmoor. NT 9939.
59. Ogle, John   of Cawsey Park. NZ 1794.
60. Ogle, Oliver   of Burradon. NZ 2672.
61. Ogle, Thomas   of Bebside. NZ 2881.
62. Ogle, Thomas   of Tritlington. NZ 2092.
63. Orde, Thomas   of Ord. NU 9851.
64. Proctor, Thomas   of Shawdon. NU 0914.
65. Radcliffe, Francis   of Dilston. NY 9763.
66. Read, Clement   of the Close. NZ 1265.
67. Reveley, George   of Ancroft. NU 0045.
68. Ridley, John   of Walltown. NY 6766.
69. Ridley, Nicholas   of Hardriding. NY 7563.
70. Ridley, William   of Westwood. NY 9165.
71. Ridley, William   of Willimontswick. NY 7763.
72. Roddam, Edmund   of Roddam. NU 0220.
73. Salkeld, John   of Hulne Park, Alnwick. NU 1615.
74. Selby, Alexander   of Biddlestone. NT 9508.
75. Selby, John   of Twizel. NT 8843.
76. Selby, Ralph   of Weetwood. NU 0129.
77. Selby, William   of Branxton, Nd (NT 8937) and Ightham Mote, Kent.
78. Selby, William   of Shortflatt (NZ 0881) and Bolam.
79. Shaftoe, William   of Bavington. NY 9978.
80. Strother, John   of Kirknewton. NT 9130.
81. Swinburn, John   of Edlingham. NU 1109.
82. Swinburn, Thomas   of Capheaton. NZ 0380.
83. Swinhoe, Thomas   of Goswick. NU 0545.
84. Thirlwall, Richard   of Thirlwall. NY 6666.
85. Thornton, Nicholas   of Netherwitton. NZ 1090.

86. Wetwang, Richard   of Dunstan. NU 2419.
87. Widdrington, Ephraim   of Trewitt. NU 0006.
88. Widdrington, Henry   of Widdrington. NU 2596.
89. Widdrington, Roger   of Cartington. NU 0304.

3 Some genealogies (pp. 254–65)

N.B. These abbreviated pedigrees are designed to enable the reader to identify persons mentioned in the text and the marriage alliances of important Northumberland gentry families. In addition to the principal sources mentioned after each pedigree see also Joseph Foster (ed.), *Pedigrees Recorded at the Heralds' Visitations of the County of Northumberland . . . in 1615 and 1666* (1891); C. H. Hunter Blair, *Visitations of Yorkshire and Northumberland in A.D. 1575* (Surtees Society, vol. CXLVI, 1932); *idem*, 'The Sheriffs of Northumberland to 1603', *Arch. Aeliana*, 4th ser., xx (1942), 11–90; *idem*, 'The Sheriffs of Northumberland, 1603–1942' *Arch. Aeliana*, 4th ser., xxi (1943), 1–92; *idem*, 'Members of Parliament for Northumberland and Newcastle upon Tyne, 1559–1831', *Arch. Aeliana*, 4th ser., xxiii (1945), 102–55; *idem*, 'Members of Parliament for Berwick and Morpeth', *Arch. Aeliana*, 4th ser., xxiv (1946), 71–112; *idem*, 'Wardens and Deputy Wardens of the Marches of England toward Scotland in Northumberland', *Arch. Aeliana*, 4th ser., xxviii (1950), 18–95.

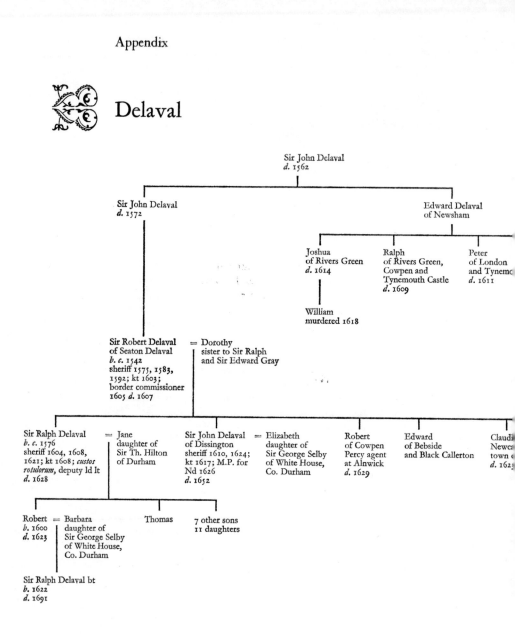

Delaval

Sir John Delaval
d. 1562

Sir John Delaval
d. 1572

Edward Delaval
of Newsham

Joshua
of Rivers Green
d. 1614

Ralph
of Rivers Green,
Cowpen and
Tynemouth Castle
d. 1609

Peter
of London
and Tynemo
d. 1611

William
murdered 1618

Sir Robert Delaval
of Seaton Delaval
b. c. 1542
sheriff 1575, 1583,
1592; kt 1603;
border commissioner
1605 *d.* 1607

= Dorothy
sister to Sir Ralph
and Sir Edward Gray

Sir Ralph Delaval
b. c. 1576
sheriff 1604, 1608,
1621; kt 1608; *custos
rotulorum*, deputy ld lt
d. 1628

= Jane
daughter of
Sir Th. Hilton
of Durham

Sir John Delaval
of Dissington
sheriff 1610, 1624;
kt 1617; M.P. for
Nd 1626
d. 1652

= Elizabeth
daughter of
Sir George Selby
of White House,
Co. Durham

Robert
of Cowpen
Percy agent
at Alnwick
d. 1629

Edward
of Bebside
and Black Callerton

Claudi
Newca
town o
d. 162

Robert
b. 1600
d. 1623

= Barbara
daughter of
Sir George Selby
of White House,
Co. Durham

Thomas

7 other sons
11 daughters

Sir Ralph Delaval bt
b. 1622
d. 1691

Source: N. C. H., VIII, 171; IX, 169–72.

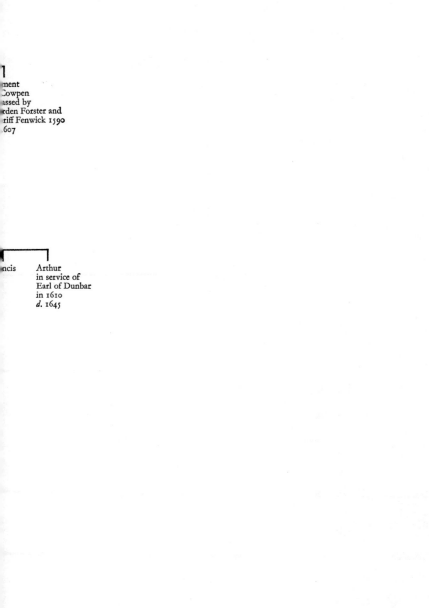

ment
Cowpen
assed by
rden Forster and
riff Fenwick 1590
607

ncis   Arthur
       in service of
       Earl of Dunbar
       in 1610
       d. 1645

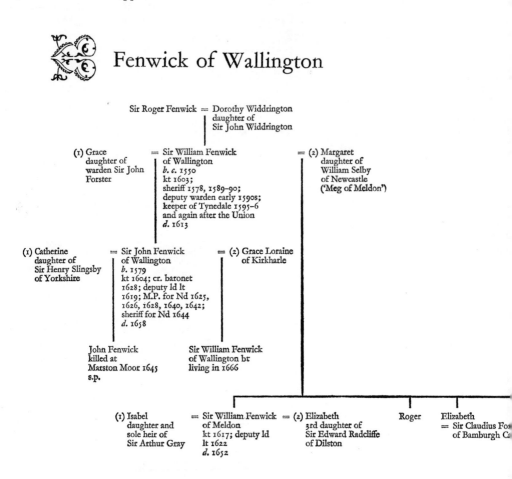

Fenwick of Wallington

Sir Roger Fenwick = Dorothy Widdrington
daughter of
Sir John Widdrington

(1) Grace = Sir William Fenwick = (2) Margaret
daughter of of Wallington daughter of
warden Sir John *b. c.* 1550 William Selby
Forster kt 1603; of Newcastle
sheriff 1578, 1589–90; ('Meg of Meldon')
deputy warden early 1590s;
keeper of Tynedale 1595–6
and again after the Union
d. 1613

(1) Catherine = Sir John Fenwick = (2) Grace Loraine
daughter of of Wallington of Kirkharle
Sir Henry Slingsby *b.* 1579
of Yorkshire kt 1604; cr. baronet
1628; deputy ld lt
1619; M.P. for Nd 1625,
1626, 1628, 1640, 1642;
sheriff for Nd 1644
d. 1658

John Fenwick Sir William Fenwick
killed at of Wallington bt
Marston Moor 1645 living in 1666
s.p.

(1) Isabel = Sir William Fenwick = (2) Elizabeth Roger Elizabeth
daughter and of Meldon 3rd daughter of = Sir Claudius For
sole heir of kt 1617; deputy ld Sir Edward Radcliffe of Bamburgh Ca
Sir Arthur Gray lt 1622 of Dilston
d. 1652

Sources: Hodgson, II, ii, 17; II, i, 256; N. C. H., XII, 352.

```
        ┌──────────────┬──────────────┬──────────────────┐
```
Dorothy   Anne   Margaret   Mary
= Cuthbert Heron   = Ralph Carnaby = Sir Ralph Blakeston = Thomas Forster
  of Chipchase   of Halton   of Adderstone

I

 Forster

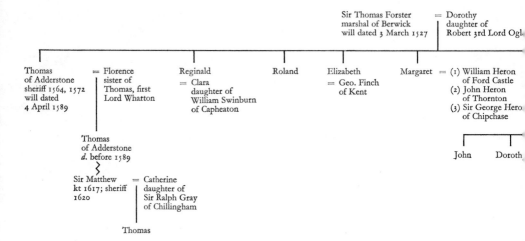

Sir Thomas Forster = Dorothy
marshal of Berwick | daughter of
will dated 3 March 1527 | Robert 3rd Lord Ogl|

Thomas | = Florence | Reginald | Roland | Elizabeth | Margaret = (1) William Heron
of Adderstone | sister of | = Clara | | = Geo. Finch | of Ford Castle
sheriff 1564, 1572 | Thomas, first | daughter of | | of Kent | (2) John Heron
will dated | Lord Wharton | William Swinburn | | | of Thornton
4 April 1589 | | of Capheaton | | | (3) Sir George Hero|
| | | | | of Chipchase

Thomas
of Adderstone
d. before 1589   John   Doroth|

Sir Matthew = Catherine
kt 1617; sheriff | daughter of
1620 | Sir Ralph Gray
| of Chillingham

Thomas

Sources: James Raine, *The History and Antiquities of North Durham* (1852), 306–7;
N. C. H., I, 156, 228.

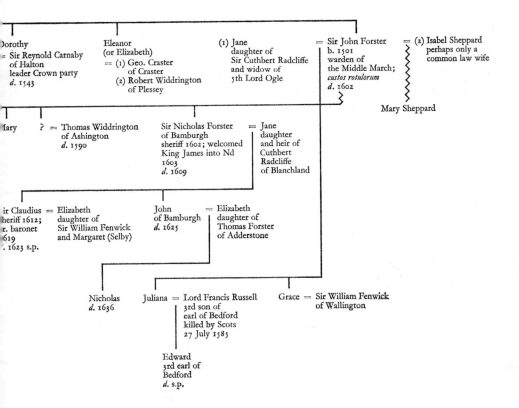

Dorothy
= Sir Reynold Carnaby
of Halton
leader Crown party
d. 1543

Eleanor
(or Elizabeth)
= (1) Geo. Craster
of Craster
(2) Robert Widdrington
of Plessey

(1) Jane
daughter of
Sir Cuthbert Radcliffe
and widow of
5th Lord Ogle

= Sir John Forster
b. 1501
warden of
the Middle March;
custos rotulorum
d. 1602

= (2) Isabel Sheppard
perhaps only a
common law wife

Mary Sheppard

Mary

? = Thomas Widdrington
of Ashington
d. 1590

Sir Nicholas Forster
of Bamburgh
sheriff 1602; welcomed
King James into Nd
1603
d. 1609

= Jane
daughter
and heir of
Cuthbert
Radcliffe
of Blanchland

Sir Claudius
sheriff 1612;
cr. baronet
1619
d. 1623 s.p.

= Elizabeth
daughter of
Sir William Fenwick
and Margaret (Selby)

John
of Bamburgh
d. 1625

= Elizabeth
daughter of
Thomas Forster
of Adderstone

Nicholas
d. 1636

Juliana = Lord Francis Russell
3rd son of
earl of Bedford
killed by Scots
27 July 1585

Grace = Sir William Fenwick
of Wallington

Edward
3rd earl of
Bedford
d. s.p.

Gray of Chillingham

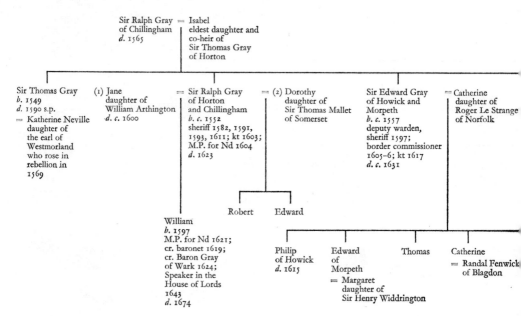

Sir Ralph Gray = Isabel
of Chillingham | eldest daughter and
d. 1565 | co-heir of
Sir Thomas Gray
of Horton

Sir Thomas Gray
b. 1549
d. 1590 s.p.
= Katherine Neville
daughter of
the earl of
Westmorland
who rose in
rebellion in
1569

(1) Jane
daughter of
William Arthington
d. c. 1600

= Sir Ralph Gray
of Horton
and Chillingham
b. c. 1552
sheriff 1582, 1591,
1593, 1611; kt 1603;
M.P. for Nd 1604
d. 1623

= (2) Dorothy
daughter of
Sir Thomas Mallet
of Somerset

Sir Edward Gray
of Howick and
Morpeth
b. c. 1557
deputy warden,
sheriff 1597;
border commissioner
1605–6; kt 1617
d. c. 1631

= Catherine
daughter of
Roger Le Strange
of Norfolk

Robert   Edward

William
b. 1597
M.P. for Nd 1621;
cr. baronet 1619;
cr. Baron Gray
of Wark 1624;
Speaker in the
House of Lords
1643
d. 1674

Philip
of Howick
d. 1615

Edward
of
Morpeth
= Margaret
daughter of
Sir Henry Widdrington

Thomas

Catherine
= Randal Fenwick
of Blagdon

Sources: N. C. H., XIV, facing 328, II, **351**.

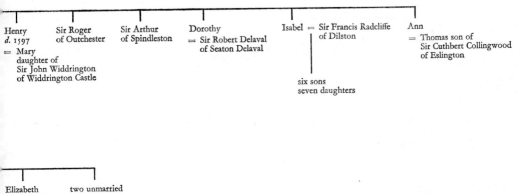

Henry
d. 1597
= Mary
daughter of
Sir John Widdrington
of Widdrington Castle

Sir Roger
of Outchester

Sir Arthur
of Spindleston

Dorothy
= Sir Robert Delaval
of Seaton Delaval

Isabel = Sir Francis Radcliffe
of Dilston

six sons
seven daughters

Ann
= Thomas son of
Sir Cuthbert Collingwood
of Eslington

Elizabeth
of Morpeth

two unmarried
sons

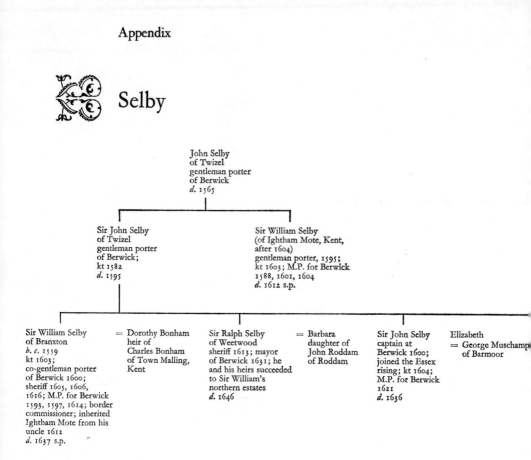

Selby

John Selby
of Twizel
gentleman porter
of Berwick
d. 1565

Sir John Selby
of Twizel
gentleman porter
of Berwick;
kt 1582
d. 1595

Sir William Selby
(of Ightham Mote, Kent,
after 1604)
gentleman porter, 1595;
kt 1603; M.P. for Berwick
1588, 1601, 1604
d. 1612 s.p.

Sir William Selby
of Branxton
b. c. 1559
kt 1603;
co-gentleman porter
of Berwick 1600;
sheriff 1603, 1606,
1616; M.P. for Berwick
1593, 1597, 1614; border
commissioner; inherited
Ightham Mote from his
uncle 1612
d. 1637 s.p.

= Dorothy Bonham
heir of
Charles Bonham
of Town Malling,
Kent

Sir Ralph Selby
of Weetwood
sheriff 1613; mayor
of Berwick 1631; he
and his heirs succeeded
to Sir William's
northern estates
d. 1646

= Barbara
daughter of
John Roddam
of Roddam

Sir John Selby
captain at
Berwick 1600;
joined the Essex
rising; kt 1604;
M.P. for Berwick
1621
d. 1636

Elizabeth
= George Muschamp
of Barmoor

Sources: James Raine, *The History and Antiquities of North Durham* (1852), 315;
Robert Surtees, *The History and Antiquities of the County Palatine of Durham*
(1816), II, 275.

William Selby
mayor of Newcastle
1589; grand leasee;
hostman

'sabel
= Thomas Carr
of Ford

Margaret = Sir George Selby
of Newcastle
sheriff Nd 1607;
sheriff Co. Durham
1614 when disqualified
to sit as M.P. for Nd;
entertained King James
1617
d. 1625

Margaret
('Meg of Meldon')
= Sir William Fenwick
of Wallington

Sir William Selby = Elizabeth
after 1611 of   daughter of
Shortflatt and   William Widdrington
Bolam
M.P. for
Nd 1601; kt 1613
d. 1649

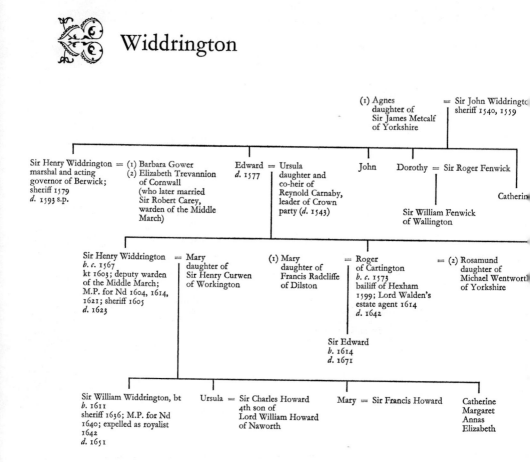

Widddrington

Sources: Hodgson, II, ii, 235–7; N. C. H., X, 408.

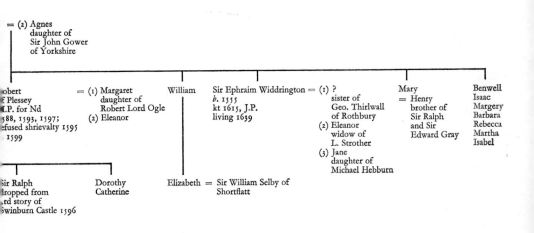

= (2) Agnes
      daughter of
      Sir John Gower
      of Yorkshire

obert   = (1) Margaret   William   Sir Ephraim Widdrington = (1) ?   Mary   Benwell
f Plessey   daughter of   b. 1555   sister of   = Henry   Isaac
.P. for Nd   Robert Lord Ogle   kt 1615, J.P.   Geo. Thirlwall   brother of   Margery
88, 1593, 1597; (2) Eleanor   living 1639   of Rothbury   Sir Ralph   Barbara
efused shrievalty 1595   (2) Eleanor   and Sir   Rebecca
  1599   widow of   Edward Gray   Martha
                                                                            L. Strother   Isabel
                                                                        (3) Jane
                                                                            daughter of
                                                                            Michael Hebburn

ir Ralph   Dorothy   Elizabeth = Sir William Selby of
lropped from   Catherine   Shortflatt
rd story of
winburn Castle 1596

Bibliography

Primary sources

1. Manuscript

Alnwick Castle
  Syon MSS.
  Alnwick MSS.
British Museum
  Additional MSS.
  Cotton MSS.
  Harleian MSS.
  Lansdowne MSS.
Cumbria County Record Office
  Corbridge MSS.
  Pennington-Ramsden MSS.
Durham Cathedral Library
  Hunter MSS.
Folger Library, Washington, D.C.
  Cecil MSS. (on microfilm)
Library of Congress
  Duke of Northumberland's MSS. (Syon and Alnwick MSS. on microfilm)
Newcastle Public Library
  Mary T. Martin, 'Index of the Northumberland Forfeitures in the Recusancy Rolls in the Public Record Office' (typescript)
  'Craster Transcript'
  Allendale MSS.
Northumberland Record Office
  Delaval MSS.
  Belsay MSS.
  'Vetera Indictamenta: Criminal Records of the General Gaol Delivery and

Bibliography

General Quarter Sessions of the Peace for Northumberland, 1594–1630' (type-script by H. A. Taylor)
Public Record Office
  Chancery Proceedings, series I and II
  Chancery, Patent Rolls
  Chancery, Inquisitions Post Mortem
  Chancery, Entry Books of Commissions (Crown Office)
  Chancery, Miscellaneous Books (Crown Office)
  Chancery, Crown Office Docquet Books
  Court of Requests, Proceedings
  Court of Wards and Liveries, Foedaries Surveys
  Court of Wards and Liveries, Inquisitions Post Mortem
  Exchequer K. R. Bills and Answers
  Exchequer K. R. Entry Books of Decrees and Orders, series I and II
  Exchequer K. R. Depositions taken by Commission
  Exchequer K. R. Miscellanea of the Exchequer
  Exchequer K. R. Miscellaneous Books, series I
  Exchequer K. R. Special Commissions of Enquiry
  Exchequer Pipe Office Series, Recusant Rolls
  Exchequer of Receipt Loans on Privy Seal
  Exchequer of Receipt Miscellaneous Books and Papers
  Privy Council Office, Register
  State Paper Office, Docquets
  State Papers, Borders
  State Papers, Domestic, Elizabeth I, James I, Addenda 1547–1625, Charles I
  State Papers, Supplementary
  Special Collections, Court Rolls
  Star Chamber Proceedings, Elizabeth I, James I
  Subsidy Rolls
Sheffield Public Library
  Strafford MSS.

2 Printed

Acts of the Privy Council.
Cadwallader John Bates, The Border Holds of Northumberland (Arch. Aeliana, new series, vol. XIV, 1891).
Gordon R. Batho (ed.), The Household Papers of Henry Percy, Ninth Earl of Northumberland, 1564–1632 (Camden Society, 3rd series, vol. XCIII, 1962).
J. M. W. Bean, The Estates of the Percy Family, 1416–1537 (1958).
Thomas Birch (ed.), Memoirs of the Reign of Queen Elizabeth from the year 1581 till her death (2 vols, 1754).
John Bruce (ed.), Correspondence of King James VI of Scotland with Sir Robert Cecil and others in England during the Reign of Queen Elizabeth (Camden Society, old series, vol. LXXVIII, 1861).

Calendar of Letters and Papers relating to the Affairs of the Borders of England and Scotland, ed. Joseph Bain.

Calendar of Letters and Papers, Henry VIII.

Calendar of Patent Rolls.

Calendar of State Papers, Domestic, Elizabeth I, James I, Addenda 1567–1625, Charles I.

Calendar of State Papers, Foreign.

William Camden, Britannia, trans. Philemon Holland (1610).

Arthur Clifford (ed.), The State Papers and Letters of Sir Ralph Sadler (2 vols, 1809).

William Cobbett (ed.), The Parliamentary History of England (1806–20).

John P. Collier (ed.), The Egerton Papers (Camden Society, old series, vol. XII, 1840).

Simon D'Ewes, The Journals of all the Parliaments during the Reign of Queen Elizabeth (rev. edn, 1682).

Elizabeth Read Foster (ed.), Proceedings in Parliament, 1610 (2 vols, 1966).

Joseph Foster (ed.), Alumni Oxonienses, 1500–1714 (1891).

Joseph Foster (ed.), Pedigrees Recorded at the Heralds' Visitations of the County of Northumberland . . . 1615 and 1666 (1891).

Joseph Foster (ed.), The Register of Admissions to Gray's Inn, 1521–1887 (1889).

General Register House, Edinburgh, Acts of the Parliament of Scotland.

General Register House, Edinburgh, Registers of the Privy Council of Scotland, 1545–1625.

Samuel Haynes and William Murdin (eds), Collection of State Papers . . . left by William Cecil, Lord Burghley (2 vols, 1740–59).

Historical Manuscripts Commission:
  Calendar of MSS. belonging to the Marquis of Salisbury at Hatfield House
  Third Report (MSS. of Duke of Northumberland at Alnwick Castle)
  Tenth Report (Muncaster MSS.)
  Eleventh Report (Waterford MSS. at Ford Castle)
  Twelfth Report (Le Fleming MSS., Rutland MSS.)

R. W. Hodgson, 'A Rental of the Principality of Redesdale', Arch. Aeliana, II (1832), 326–38.

C. H. Hunter Blair (ed.), Visitations of Yorkshire and Northumberland in A.D. 1575 (Surtees Society, vol. CXLVI, 1932).

M. E. James (ed.), Estate Accounts of the Earls of Northumberland, 1562–1637 (Surtees Society, vol. CLXIII, 1948).

Journals of the House of Commons, 1803.

Journals of the House of Lords, 1846.

Lists and Indexes: Sheriffs, escheators.

William Longstaffe, The Acts of the High Commission within the Diocese of Durham (Surtees Society, vol. XXXIV, 1858).

Norman McClure (ed.), The Letters of John Chamberlain (American Philosophical Society Memoirs, vol. XII, Philadelphia, 1939).

F. H. Mares (ed.), The Memoirs of Robert Carey (1972).

John Nichols, The Progresses, Processions, and Magnificent Festivities of King James I (4 vols, 1828).

William Nicholson (ed.), *Leges Marchiarum or Border Laws . . . from the Reign of Henry III to . . . James I* (1705).

Wallace Notestein *et al.* (eds), *Commons Debates, 1621* (7 vols, New Haven, 1935).

George Ornsby (ed.), *Selections from the Household Books of the Lord William Howard of Naworth Castle* (Surtees Society, vol. LXVIII, 1878).

James Raine (ed.), *The Inquisitions and other Ecclesiastical Proceedings of Richard Barnes, Bishop of Durham, from 1575 to 1587* (Surtees Society, vol. XXII, 1849).

Thomas Rymer (ed.), *Foedera . . .* (20 vols, 1727–35).

Roundell P. Sanderson (ed.), *Survey of the Debateable and Borderlands adjoining the Realm of Scotland and Belonging to the Crown of England 1604* (1891).

Cuthbert Sharp (ed.), *Memorials of the Rebellion* (1840).

James Spedding (ed.), *Life of Francis Bacon* (2 vols, 1878 edn).

Statutes of the Realm.

Robert Steele (ed.), *Tudor and Stuart Proclamations, 1485–1714* (1910).

John Strype, *Annals of the Reformation* (4 vols, 1824 edn).

James Stuart, *The Workes of the Most High and Mightie Prince, James . . . King of Great Britaine* (1st edn, 1616).

H. A. C. Sturgess (ed.), *Register of Admissions to the Honourable Society of the Middle Temple* (1949).

H. A. C. Sturgess (ed.), *The Records of the Honourable Society of Lincoln's Inn, 1420–1799.*

H. A. C. Sturgess (ed.), *Students Admitted to the Inner Temple, 1547–1660.*

Surtees Society, *Wills and Inventories from the Registry at Durham* (1835; 1900; 1906; 1929).

Clare Talbot (ed.), *Recusant Records* (Catholic Record Society, vol. LIII, 1960).

Joseph Tanner (ed.), *Constitutional Documents of the Reign of James I* (1930).

Hayward Townshend, *Historical Collections: or, An exact account of the last four Parliaments of Elizabeth* (1680).

John and J. A. Venn (eds), *Alumni Cantabrigienses* (Pt I, 4 vols, 1922–7).

David H. Willson (ed.), *The Parliamentary Diary of Robert Bowyer, 1606–7* (Minneapolis, 1931).

Secondary sources

1   Local history: the borders

G. R. Batho, 'The Finances of an Elizabethan Nobleman: Henry Percy, Ninth Earl of Northumberland', *Ec. H. R.*, 2nd ser., IX no. 3 (1957), 433–50.

R. A. Butlin, 'Enclosure and Improvement in Northumberland in the Sixteenth Century', *Arch. Aeliana*, 4th ser., XLV (1967), 149-60.

George Carleton, *The Life of Bernard Gilpin* (1629).

Charles A. Coulomb, *The Administration of the English Borders during the Reign of Elizabeth* (New York, 1911).

M. Claire Cross, 'Berwick on Tweed and the Neighbouring Parts of Northumberland on the Eve of the Armada', *Arch. Aeliana*, 4th ser., XLI (1963), 123-34.

George F. S. Elliot, *The Border Elliots and the Family of Minto* (1897).

George M. Fraser, *The Steel Bonnets: the story of the Anglo-Scottish border reivers* (1971).

William Gray, 'Chorographia: Or, a Survey of Newcastle-upon-Tine', *Harleian Miscellany*, XI (1810).

John Hodgson, *A History of Northumberland* (3 pts in 7 vols, 1820–58).

Roger Howell, *Newcastle upon Tyne and the Puritan Revolution; A Study of the Civil War in North England* (1967).

C. H. Hunter Blair, 'Members of Parliament for Northumberland and Newcastle upon Tyne, 1559–1831', *Arch. Aeliana*, 4th ser., XXIII (1945), 102–55.

C. H. Hunter Blair, 'Members of Parliament for Berwick and Morpeth', *Arch. Aeliana*, 4th ser., XXIV (1946), 71–112.

C. H. Hunter Blair, 'The Sheriffs of Northumberland to 1603', *Arch. Aeliana*, 4th ser., XX (1942), 11–90.

C. H. Hunter Blair, 'The Sheriffs of Northumberland, 1603–1942', *Arch. Aeliana*, 4th ser., XXI (1943), 1–92.

C. H. Hunter Blair, 'Wardens and Deputy Wardens of the Marches of England toward Scotland in Northumberland', *Arch. Aeliana*, 4th ser., XXVIII (1950), 18–95.

M. E. James, *Change and Continuity in the Tudor North: The Rise of Thomas, First Lord Wharton* (1965).

M. E. James, 'The First Earl of Cumberland, 1492–1542, and the Decline of Northern Feudalism', *Northern History*, I (1966), 43–69.

M. E. James, *A Tudor Magnate and the Tudor State: Henry Fifth Earl of Northumberland* (1966).

M. E. James, 'The Concept of Order and the Northern Rising 1569', *Past and Present*, LX (August 1973), 49–83.

Allen Mawer, *The Place Names of Northumberland and Durham* (Cambridge Archaeological and Ethnological Society, 1920).

Joseph Nicholson and Richard Burn, *The History and Antiquities of the Counties of Westmorland and Cumberland* (2 vols, 1777).

Northumberland County History Committee (eds.), *A History of Northumberland* (15 vols, 1905–40).

William Palmes, *The Life of Mrs Dorothy Lawson of St Anthony's near Newcastle-upon-Tyne in Northumberland* (1851).

Nikolaus Pevsner, *The Buildings of England: Northumberland* (1957).

Thomas I. Rae, *The Administration of the Scottish Frontier, 1513–1603* (1966).

James Raine, *The History and Antiquities of North Durham* (1852).

H. G. Ramm, R. W. McDowall and Eric Mercer, *Shielings and Bastles* (1970).

George Ridpath, *The Border History of England and Scotland* (1776).

John Scott, *Berwick-upon-Tweed* (1888).

R. L. Storey, 'The Wardens of the Marches of England towards Scotland, 1377–1489', *E. H. R.*, LXXII (1957), 593–616.

George Tate, *History of the Borough, Castle and Barony of Alnwick* (2 vols, 1866–9).

G. H. Thomson, 'Some Influences of the Geography of Northumberland upon its History' (Historical Association Leaflet 28, 1912).

William Weaver Tomlinson, *Life in Northumberland during the Sixteenth Century* (1897).

D. L. W. Tough, *The Last Years of a Frontier: a History of the Borders during the Reign of Elizabeth* (1928).

Helen Wallace, 'Berwick in the Reign of Queen Elizabeth', *E. H. R.*, XLVI (January 1931), 79–88.

S. J. Watts, 'Tenant Right in Early Seventeenth Century Northumberland', *Northern History*, VI (1971), 64–87.

Richard Welford, *History of Newcastle and Gateshead* (3 vols, 1884–7).

Richard Welford, *Men of Mark 'Twixt Tyne and Tweed* (3 vols, 1895).

Penry Williams, 'The Northern Borderlands under the Early Stuarts', in *Historical Essays 1600–1750 Presented to David Ogg*, ed. H. E. Bell and R. L. Ollard (1963).

James Wilson (ed.), *Victoria County History of Cumberland* (2 vols, 1905).

2   General

A. R. H. Baker and R. A. Butlin (eds), *Studies of Field Systems in the British Isles* (1973).

Thomas Garden Barnes, *Somerset, 1625–40, a County's Government during the 'Personal Rule'* (1961).

Thomas Garden Barnes and A. Hassell Smith, 'The Justices of the Peace from 1558–1688, a revised list of sources', *Bulletin of the Institute of Historical Research*, XXXII (1959).

William W. Bean, *The Parliamentary Representation of the Six Northern Counties of England* (1890).

B. W. Beckingsale, 'The Characteristics of the Tudor North', *Northern History*, IV (1969), 67–83.

Maurice W. Beresford, *The Lost Villages of England* (1954).

Georgina Bertie, *Five Generations of a Loyal House* (1845).

S. T. Bindoff (ed.), *Elizabethan Government and Society; essays presented to Sir John Neale* (1961).

C. M. L. Bouch and G. P. Jones, *A Short Economic and Social History of the Lake Counties, 1500–1830* (1961).

F. W. Brooks, *The Council of the North* (Historical Association, 1966).

E. J. Buckatzsch, 'The Geographical Distribution of Wealth in England, 1086–1843', *Ec. H. R.*, 2nd ser., III (December 1950), 180–202.

J. T. Cliffe, *The Yorkshire Gentry from the Reformation to the Civil War* (1969).

George Cokayne, *The Complete Peerage of England, Scotland and Ireland* (13 vols, rev. edn, 1949).

Claire Cross, *The Puritan Earl: the Life and Times of Henry Hastings, Third Earl of Huntingdon, 1536–1595* (1966).

Frederick Devon, *Issues of the Exchequer* (1836).

Bruce Dickens, 'The Gueveras of Stenigot: Spanish Squires in Tudor Lincolnshire', *Bulletin of Hispanic Studies*, XXXVII (October 1960), 215–21.

Madeleine H. and Ruth Dodds, *The Pilgrimage of Grace, 1536–37, and the Exeter Conspiracy, 1538* (2 vols, 1915).

Gordon Donaldson, *Scotland, James V to James VII* (1965).

Francis Edwards, *Guy Fawkes: the real story of the Gunpowder Plot?* (1969).

G. R. Elton, *The Tudor Constitution* (1965).

F. J. Fisher (ed.), *Essays in the Economic and Social History of Tudor and Stuart England* (1961).

Samuel R. Gardiner, *History of England from the Accession of James I to the Outbreak of the Civil War, 1603–42* (10 vols, 1883).

Mark Girouard, *Robert Smythson and the Architecture of the Elizabethan Era* (1966).

Charles Montgomery Gray, *Copyhold, Equity, and the Common Law* (Cambridge, Mass., 1963).

Phyllis M. Handover, *The Second Cecil; the Rise to Power, 1563–1604, of Sir Robert Cecil, later First Earl of Salisbury* (1959).

Christopher Hill, *Economic Problems of the Church, from Archbishop Whitgift to the Long Parliament* (1956).

Christopher Hill, 'Puritans and the "Dark Corners of the land" ', *Trans. R. H. S.*, 5th ser., XIII (1963), 79–102.

William S. Holdsworth, *A History of English Law* (15 vols, 1922–65).

G. C. Homans, 'The Explanation of English Regional Differences', *Past and Present*, XLII (February 1969), 18–34.

W. G. Hoskins, *The Midland Peasant: the Economic and Social History of a Leicestershire Village* (1965).

Wilbur K. Jordan, *The Development of Religious Toleration in England from the Accession of James I to the Convention of the Long Parliament* (reprinted, Gloucester, Mass., 1965).

Mary F. Keeler, *The Long Parliament, 1640–1, a Biographical Study of its Members* (Philadelphia, 1954).

Eric Kerridge, *Agrarian Problems in the Sixteenth Century and After* (1969).

Roger B. Manning, *Religion and Society in Elizabethan Sussex: a study in the enforcement of the religious settlement 1558–1603* (1969).

Patrick McGrath, *Papists and Puritans under Elizabeth I* (1967).

John Neale, *Elizabeth I and her Parliaments* (2 vols, 1953, 1957).

John Neale, *Essays in Elizabethan History* (1958).

John U. Nef, *The Rise of the British Coal Industry* (2 vols, 1932).

Conyers Read, *Mr Secretary Cecil and Queen Elizabeth* (1955).

Conyers Read, *Mr Secretary Walsingham and the Policy of Queen Elizabeth* (3 vols, 1925).

Rachel R. Reid, *The King's Council in the North* (1921).

Rachel R. Reid, 'The Rebellion of the Earls, 1569', *Trans. R. H. S.*, 2nd ser. XX (1906), 171–203.

E. E. Rich, 'The Population of Elizabethan England', *Ec. H. R.*, 2nd ser., II (1953), 247–65.

A. L. Rowse, *The Expansion of Elizabethan England* (1955).

Charles Sisson (ed.), *Thomas Lodge and other Elizabethans* (Cambridge, Mass., 1933).

Leslie Stephen and Sidney Lee (eds), *Dictionary of National Biography*.

Lawrence Stone, *The Crisis of the Aristocracy, 1558–1641* (1965).

R. H. Tawney, *The Agrarian Problem in the Sixteenth Century* (new edn, New York, 1967).

John Taylor, *The Pennyles Pilgrimage* (1618).

Joan Thirsk (ed.), *The Agrarian History of England and Wales*, vol. IV, *1500–1640* (1967).

Philip Tyler, *The Ecclesiastical Commission and Catholicism in the North, 1562–1577* (1960).

Sydney and Beatrice Webb, *English Local Government*, III, *The Manor and the Borough* (1908).

David Harris Willson, *King James VI and I* (1956).

Index

In indexing place-names, the county is given only in the case of places outside Northumberland.

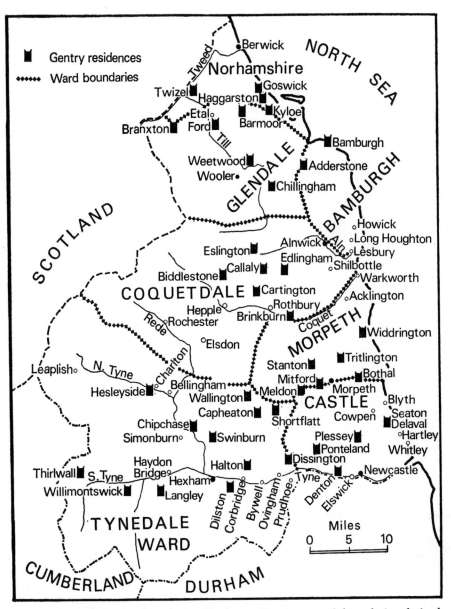

3. Wards and frequently mentioned places. (Sources: ward boundaries derived from hearth tax and subsidy lists: E 179/158/106; E 179/158/88; Durham Cathedral Library, Hunter MSS. 23).

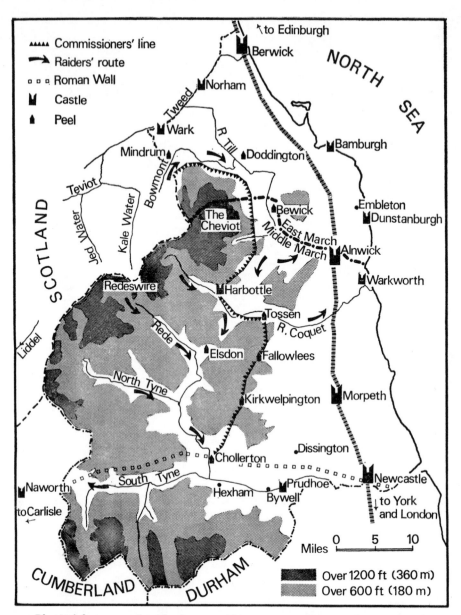

1. Physical features and raiders' routes. (Sources: commissioners' line derived from
Christopher Dacre's maps, 1584, in C. J. Bates, *The Border Holds of Northumberland* (Arch. Aeliana, n.s., XIV 1891); East March/Middle March boundary from
1580 muster reports: S. P. 59/20/47, S. P. 59/20/50.)